Places of Pain

Space and Place

Bodily, geographic, and architectural sites are embedded with cultural knowledge and social value. This series provides ethnographically rich analyses of the cultural organization and meanings of these sites of space, architecture, landscape, and places of the body. Contributions examine the symbolic meanings of space and place, the cultural and historical processes involved in their construction and contestation, and how they communicate with wider political, religious, social, and economic institutions.

Volume 1
Berlin, Alexanderplatz: Transforming Place in a Unified Germany
Gisa Weszkalnys

Volume 2
Cultural Diversity in Russian Cities: The Urban Landscape in the post-Soviet Era
Edited by Cordula Gdaniec

Volume 3
Settling for Less: The Planned Resettlement of Israel's Negev Bedouin
Steven C. Dinero

Volume 4
Contested Mediterranean Spaces: Ethnographic Essays in Honour of Charles Tilly
Edited by Maria Kousis, Tom Selwyn and David Clark

Volume 5
Ernst L. Freud, Architect: The Case of the Modern Bourgeois Home
Volker M. Welter

Volume 6
Extreme Heritage Management: The Practices and Policies of Densely Populated Islands
Edited by Godfrey Baldacchino

Volume 7
Images of Power and the Power of Images: Control, Ownership, and Public Space
Edited by Judith Kapferer

Volume 8
Performing Place, Practising Memories: Aboriginal Australians, Hippies and the State
Rosita Henry

Volume 9
Post-Cosmopolitan Cities: Explorations of Urban Coexistence
Edited by Caroline Humphrey and Vera Skvirskaja

Volume 10
Places of Pain: Forced Displacement, Popular Memory and Trans-local Identities in Bosnian War-torn Communities
Hariz Halilovich

Volume 11
Narrating Victimhood: Gender, Religion and the Making of Place in Post-War Croatia
Michaela Schäuble

Volume 12
Power and Architecture: The Construction of Capitals and the Politics of Space
Edited by Michael Minkenberg

Volume 13
Bloom and Bust: Urban Landscapes in the East since German Reunification
Edited by Gwyneth Cliver and Carrie Smith-Prei

Volume 14
Urban Violence in the Middle East: Changing Cityscapes in the Transition from Empire to Nation State
Edited by Ulrike Freitag, Nelida Fuccaro, Claudia Ghrawi, and Nora Lafi

Volume 15
Narrating the City: Histories, Space and the Everyday
Edited by Wladimir Fischer-Nebmaier, Matthew P. Berg, and Anastasia Christou

Places of Pain

Forced Displacement, Popular Memory and Trans-local Identities in Bosnian War-torn Communities

Hariz Halilovich

berghahn
NEW YORK · OXFORD
www.berghahnbooks.com

First published in 2013 by
Berghahn Books
www.berghahnbooks.com

© 2013, 2015 Hariz Halilovich
First paperback edition published in 2015

All rights reserved. Except for the quotation of short passages for the purposes of criticism and review, no part of this book may be reproduced in any form or by any means, electronic or mechanical, including photocopying, recording, or any information storage and retrieval system now known or to be invented, without written permission of the publisher.

Library of Congress Cataloging-in-Publication Data

Places of pain : forced displacement, popular memory and trans-local identities in Bosnian war-torn communities / Hariz Halilovich.
   p. cm. -- (Space and place ; v. 10)
   Includes bibliographical references and index.
   ISBN 978-0-85745-776-9 (hardback : alk. paper) -- ISBN 978-1-78238-762-6 (paperback : alk. paper) -- ISBN 978-0-85745-777-6 (ebook)
   1. Yugoslav War, 1991-1995--Refugees--Bosnia and Hercegovina. 2. Refugees--Bosnia and Hercegovina. 3. Forced migration--Bosnia and Hercegovina. 4. Group identity--Bosnia and Hercegovina. 5. Collective memory--Bosnia and Hercegovina. 6. Bosnia and Hercegovina--Ethnic relations. I. Title.
   DR1313.7.R43H35 2012
   305.800949742--dc23

2012033459

British Library Cataloguing in Publication Data

A catalogue record for this book is available from the British Library

Printed on acid-free paper.

ISBN: 978-0-85745-776-9 hardback
ISBN: 978-1-78238-762-6 paperback
ISBN: 978-0-85745-777-6 ebook

To Ron Adams, friend and colleague

CONTENTS

List of Illustrations	ix
Acknowledgements	x
A Note on the Pronunciation of Some Bosnian, Croatian and Serbian Characters	xii
Glossary of Non-English Words	xiii
List of Selected Abbreviations	xvii

INTRODUCTION: THE JOURNEY THROUGH BOSNIAN WAR-TORN COMMUNITIES ... 1
    Writing about the Displacement of Bosnians ... 5
    Practical Challenges ... 8
    Theoretical Challenges ... 9
    Methodological Challenges ... 11
    Ethics and Politics of the Research ... 15

CHAPTER 1: KLOTJEVAC: FORCED DISPLACEMENT AND ETHNIC CLEANSING IN AN EASTERN BOSNIAN VILLAGE ... 21
    Reunion ... 22
    Once There Was a Community ... 27
    Human Geography of the Place ... 33
    The '(UN)Safe Area' Srebrenica ... 37
    Mapping Displacement ... 45
    Conclusion ... 48

CHAPTER 2: BEYOND THE SADNESS: NARRATIVES OF DISPLACEMENT, REFUGE AND HOMECOMINGS AMONG BOSNIAN REFUGEES IN AUSTRIA ... 53
    Debating Displacement ... 54
    Narrating Displacement ... 55
    The Prijedor Region – Blueprint for Ethnic Cleansing ... 68
    Edita, Ibro and Sejo in Austria ... 74

CHAPTER 3: (DIS)PLACING MEMORIES: MONUMENTS, MEMORIALS AND COMMEMORATIONS IN POST-WAR BOSNIA AND HERZEGOVINA ... 79
   The Funeral at Hegići ... 81
   Omarska ... 84
   Keraterm and Trnopolje ... 90
   Srebrenica/Potočari Commemorations ... 93
   Mostar Carrying its Cross ... 98
   Sarajevo Remembers ... 103

INTERLUDE: REFRAMING IDENTITY IN PLACES OF PAIN: PHOTOGRAPHIC ESSAY OF DISPLACEMENT AND MEMORY ... 111

CHAPTER 4: TRANS-LOCAL DIASPORIC COMMUNITIES IN THE AGE OF TRANSNATIONALISM: BOSNIANS IN AUSTRALIA, EUROPE AND THE U.S.A. ... 118
   Debating Diaspora ... 119
   Emergence of the Bosnian Diaspora ... 124
   The Trans-local within the Transnational ... 132
   The Formation of Trans-local Diasporic Communities ... 149
   Conclusion ... 151

CHAPTER 5: MEASURING THE PAIN OF OTHERS: GENDERED DISPLACEMENT, MEMORY AND IDENTITY ... 155
   Re-counting the Displaced ... 161
   (Mis)using IDPs ... 179
   Refugee Women in Diaspora ... 182

CONCLUSION: CONCLUDING THE JOURNEY THROUGH BOSNIAN WAR-TORN COMMUNITIES ... 201
   Bosnian Vikings ... 206
   Bosnian Midwesterners ... 213
   Vienna Blues ... 221
   Unearthing the Missing in Bosnia ... 225
   From St. Louis to St. Albans: All Roads Lead to Hanna's Cafe ... 227

   Bibliography ... 233
   Index ... 261

LIST OF ILLUSTRATIONS

1. Geography of genocide in ethnically cleansed Podrinje	111
2. Returning 'home'	111
3. Klotjevac 2011	112
4. Trans-local emplacements	112
5. 'Ethnic engineering' in post-war BiH	112
6. Returnees to Hegići	113
7. Domicide in Hegići	113
8. New emplacement	113
9. Geography of genocide in Prijedor	114
10. Hijacked memories	114
11. Memorials as landmarks	114
12. Inscribing embodied memories	115
13. The 'Sarajevo Roses'	115
14. Lest we forget	115
15. United in remembrance	116
16. Reclaiming the place called home	116
17. Podrinje under the gum trees	116
18. Synchronising local dialects	117
19. Trans-Atlantic performance	117
20. Place of sensory memories	117

ACKNOWLEDGEMENTS

There are many people who made the completion of this book possible, by giving parts of themselves and their time, and by being a source of support and inspiration to me during, before and beyond the production of the book. I thank them all, starting with my mentor and friend, Ron Adams.

I thank Ron for teaching me the power of words, for helping me turn writing into composing, and for reminding me that 'nothing is written before it's read'. I thank Ron for repeated readings of and listening to my 'compositions', and for helping me to find – and encouraging me to keep – my voice in the book. I was also very fortunate to have Ron's company in the field, in 'ethnically cleansed' Bosnia, where his human and academic qualities shone to the full.

A special thanks goes to Jasna Čapo, whose scholarship on displacement and emplacement has been a major source of inspiration and an important compass in developing and articulating my own ideas for researching the forced displacement, memories and identities of Bosnians.

I thank Ann Przyzycki DeVita, Associate Editor at Berghahn Books, whose editorial guidance in turning my written ideas into the final product and delivering this book to the reader has been invaluable. And I thank Addis, Azra, Goran and Pavel for their artistic and technical input into the visual aspects of the book.

I would like to thank my former teachers Elsie Hill who, in 1998, taught me how to write my first sentence in English; and Rob Watts who, three years later, gave me my first academic job.

My colleagues Angela Carbone, Peter Phipps, Damian Grenfell, Robert Nelson, Adis Fejzić, Dubravko Lovrenović, Lejla Voloder, Anne Gilliland, Lara Nettelfield, Senka Božić-Vrbančić, Mario Vrbančić and Adnan and Nirha Efendić keep being a whirlpool of intellectual stimulation and never-ending conversations. Thank you.

I would need a long list to include all the names of my many dear friends and colleagues from around the world who deserve a big, special 'thank you'. They know who they are.

Now, I want to thank my family: Zerina, and our son Suad, for being supportive, tolerant and patient with my research and writing, which at stages seemed endless. I thank them for tolerating my prolonged absences from home, for letting me live my passions, and for believing in me when I was beginning to doubt myself.

I thank my big brother Halil, a Srebrenica survivor, for not giving up on himself and his family while being headhunted – wandering lost and exhausted for ten days – through the forests, landmined fields and Serb ambushes between Srebrenica and Tuzla, in July 1995. And I thank his school friend Mirsad, who found my brother lying unconscious, more dead than alive, and made the decision not to leave him to die – sharing his last atoms of energy, his last drops of water, and carrying my brother on his shoulders for the last seven kilometres to freedom, knowing that his own chances of survival were severely reduced with an almost lifeless body on his back. If my brother had not survived, my priorities would have been different: I would have had his family to provide for and could not even have thought of pursuing an academic career and writing this book.

I also thank my little brother Dado for finding his way to remain a part of our decimated family.

Last but not least, my deepest gratitude goes to the hundreds of Bosnian community members who, in various ways, supported or participated in my research project. Thank you for sharing your stories, your (be)longings and your hopes with me. This is not a book *about* you – this *is* your book.

A NOTE ON THE PRONUNCIATION OF SOME BOSNIAN, CROATIAN AND SERBIAN CHARACTERS

(Note: Serbian here refers to Latin script rendition.)

C, c: [**ts**] like the 'ts' in 'cats'.

Č, č: [**tʃ**] like the 'tch' in 'match'.

Ć, ć: [**tć**] a softer version of the above, like the thickened 't' in 'tune' or 'future'.

DŽ, dž: [**dʒ**] like the 'j' in 'jam'.

Đ, đ: [**dź**] a mixed sound between the 'j' of 'jam' and 'd', like in 'duke'.

J, j: [**j**] like the 'y' in 'Yugoslavia'.

LJ, lj: [**lj**] like the 'lli' in 'million'.

NJ, nj: [**nj**] like the 'ni' in 'onion'.

Š, š: [**ʃ**] like the 'sh' in 'ship'.

Ž, ž: [**ʒ**] like the 's' in 'measure' or the 'zh' in 'Zhivago'.

ᘐ GLOSSARY OF NON-ENGLISH WORDS ᘏ

(Unless stated otherwise all words are in Bosnian/Croatian/Serbian.)

Altbau (German): lit. 'old building', an architectural style characterised by large rooms, high ceilings and large windows and doors.

ašikovanje: romantic liaisons, dating.

Ausländer (German): foreigner, alien, 'the other', often used in derogatory way: 'Ausländer raus!' (Foreigners out!) was one of the most common neo-Nazi slogans and graffitis in Germany and Austria.

avlija: front yard or backyard, the private space designed to accommodate not only the social needs of the inhabitants of a house, but also those of their neighbours and local community.

Bajram: (Eid) Islamic religious holidays celebrated by Bosnian Muslims; the first *Bajram* (*Eid ul-Fitr* in Arabic) marks the end of Ramadan while the second (*Eid ul-Adha*) celebrates the pilgrims conducting *Hajj*.

bajramluci: *Bajram* gifts exchanged between family members and friends during *Bajram* festivities, similar to Christmas presents given by Christians.

bajramsko odijelo: festive garments worn during *Bajram*.

Bezirk (German): district, city quarters, area, suburb, local council, *Berzirke* being part of administrative organisation of Vienna.

Brčaci: residents of Brčko, or those from Brčko.

Četnici (Chetniks): the name of the Serb ultra-nationalist militia of the Second World War , subsequently used as the name for various Serb militias and the Serb military during the 1991–95 wars in Croatia and Bosnia, and, at the time, used by Bosniaks and Croats to refer to Serbs in general.

čaršija: downtown.

čevapčići: small BBQ minced-meat sausages popular across the former Yugoslavia, especially in Bosnia.

Cockta: a soft drink of brown colour, invented in 1950 in Slovenia, the Yugoslav answer to Coca-Cola. Once popular across Yugoslavia, Cockta has become the favourite non-alcoholic beverage among the members of the Bosnian and other former-Yugoslav diasporas.

došljaci or **došlje:** newcomers, internal migrants, IDPs; this term is often used in a pejorative context, suggesting non-belongingness of *došlje*.

Duldung (German): lit. 'to be tolerated'; name of the temporary refugee visa given to Bosnian refugees in Germany.

fatiha: Islamic prayer for the souls of the dead.

fildžan: small, round china coffee cup without handles, often regarded as an important part of Bosnian tradition.

Flüchlingsheim (German): refugee centre, colloquially also called *Heim* ('home' in German) by the Bosnian refugees in Germany.

Fräulein (German): girl, miss, young lady.

Gastarbeiter (German): lit. 'guest worker'; usually referring only to those 'temporary migrants' who work(ed) in Austria, Germany and Switzerland, this term has been widely used by people in Bosnia and across the former Yugoslavia, sometimes in a derogatory way.

grehota: sin, bad deed, a harmful act.

imam (or **hodža**): Muslim priest, Islamic scholar or religious leader.

izbjeglica (pl. *izbjeglice*): refugee.

izvorna muzika: traditional folk music in Bosnia, sometimes also referred to in a derogatory way as 'peasants' music' (*seljačka muzika*), with people in eastern and northern Bosnia (Podrinje and Posavina) particularly known for their rich tradition of *izvorna muzika*.

kafana: pub, cafe.

Klotivljani: residents of Klotjevac, or those from Klotjevac.

kolo: lit. 'circle' or 'wheel'; traditional Bosnian folk dance involving dancing in a circle while holding hands with other dancers, with many local variations in Bosnia, and also popular among people in Croatia and Serbia as well as across the Balkans.

kum (m), **kuma** (f), **kumovi** (pl.), **kumstvo** (n), **kumovati** (v): fictive kinship usually established through roles of bridesmaid and best man, but also through other rituals such as name-giving to children, with unreserved loyalty to *kumstvo* (kinship) expected and regarded as a very honourable trans-generational commitment.

manjinski povratak: minority return of refugees.

matica: motherland, also refers to a spiritual, national or ethnic centre of one's collective identity.

moba: helping out; joining a communal labour force to accomplish a larger project such as building a house, harvesting crops, etc., commonly used across rural Bosnia with some of its forms revived in the Bosnian diaspora.

most: bridge.

Mostarci: residents of Mostar, or those from Mostar.

narod: people, nation, ethnic group, folks.

narodni običaji: folk customs, often seen as pagan and superstitious, though many *narodni običaji* survived in Bosnia and have been revived in the Bosnian diaspora communities.

naš jezik: lit. 'our language', referring to Bosnian, Croatian, Serbian ('B-H-S') and what used to be called Serbo-Croatian or *SH-HS jezik*.

Podrinjci: people from the region of Podrinje (along the river Drina) in eastern Bosnia.

povratnici: returnees returning to their pre-war homes.

Prijedorčani: residents of Prijedor, or those from Prijedor.

prijatelji: friends.

prognanici: expellees/refugees.

rakija šljivovica: *slivovitz*, plum brandy, the most popular alcoholic beverage in Bosnia.

raseljena lica: displaced persons.

rodbina: family, relatives.

saz: musical stringed instrument similar to the Bouzouki and Oud.

Šehid: lit. 'Muslim martyr'; during the 1992–95 war in BiH this term was adopted to refer to all Muslim victims killed in the war, whether religious or not.

Šehidsko groblje or **Šehidsko mezarje**: Muslim Martyrs' cemetery.

sevdah: the traditional Bosnian songs about love and longing, sometimes extended to include the whole folk heritage of Bosnia and Herzegovina, a synonym for the lifestyle, mentality and collective consciousness of Bosnians.

sevdalinke: *sevdah* songs.

sijelo: evening gathering of relatives, friends and neighbours at someone's home, and before the introduction of television one of the common nightly occurrences in Bosnia, though nowadays used more in a symbolic way to refer to similar gatherings of Bosnians.

splavarenje: rafting.

starosjeditelji: the 'old dwellers'.

stećak (pl. stećci): the monumental medieval tombstones that lie scattered across the landscape of Bosnia-Herzegovina.

Stimmung (German): atmosphere, mood, setting (widely used in Bosnian as *štimung*).

tambura: smaller version of *saz*; main musical instrument used in Bosnian *izvorna muzika*.

udruženje: association.

Ustaše: Croatian fascists during the Second World War; some of the Croatian militias in Bosnia and Croatia used the name and symbols of *ustaše* during the wars in the 1990s, though the term was most widely used by Serbian nationalist propaganda as synonymous for Croatian state, Croatia's army and Croat people.

Vijećnica: the State Library in Sarajevo, built in 1896, during the Austro-Hungarian administration of Bosnia, as the City Hall, and almost completely destroyed and burned down by Serb artillery fire in August 1992.

vikendica: holiday house.

wienerisch: distinct local dialect of German spoken in Vienna.

zabava (pl. zabave): various cultural events, communal celebrations, parties, concerts; while rarely used in Bosnia, the term is commonly used in the Bosnian diaspora to refer to almost any communal gathering involving music and entertainment.

zadruga (pl. zadruge): traditional family union, which before modernisation took hold in the Balkans was a fundamental socio-economical organisation among the South Slav peasants, with many members of an extended family – brothers, uncles, cousins – working on common land and sharing the income.

zavičaj (pl. zavičaji): emotional and intimate home, local homeland, place where one grew up, place of belonging, one's native region, local community.

Zvorničani: residents of Zvornik, or those from Zvornik.

LIST OF SELECTED ABBREVIATIONS

ARBiH: Army of the Republic of Bosnia and Herzegovina (during the 1992–95 war).

BiH: Bosnia and Herzegovina.

DPA: Dayton Peace Accords or Dayton Peace Agreement (Peace agreement reached on Nov. 21, 1995, by the presidents of Bosnia, Croatia, and Serbia, ending the war in Bosnia and outlining a General Framework Agreement for Peace in Bosnia and Herzegovina.)

EUFOR: (Euro Force) the EU-led army contingent (7,000 troops) present in Bosnia, which replaced SFOR in December 2004.

Federation: Bosniak-Croat Federation (51 per cent of the country).

HDZ: Croatian Democratic Union; nationalist political party of Bosnian Croats.

HVO: Croatian Defence Council; armed forces of Bosnian Croats during the 1992–95 war.

ICMP: International Commission on Missing Persons.

ICTY: International Criminal Tribunal for the Former Yugoslavia.

ICRC: International Committee of Red Cross.

IDPs: Internally Displaced Persons.

IOM: International Organisation for Migration.

JNA: Yugoslav National Army which, between 1991 and 1992, transformed into a Serb Army supporting rebellious Serbs in Croatia and Bosnia.

KM: (Konvertibilna Marka): Convertible Mark, official Bosnian post-war currency (1KM = ca. €0.5).

SDA: Party of Democratic Action; nationalist political party of Bosnian Muslims (Bosniaks).

SDS: Serb Democratic Party, the nationalist political party of Bosnian Serbs.

SFOR: Stabilisation Forces, the NATO-led 70,000-strong contingent representing the military aspect of the Dayton Peace Accords in Bosnia and Herzegovina, responsible for: providing a safe and secure environment; establishing a unified, democratic Bosnia and Herzegovina; rebuilding the economy; and allowing the return of displaced persons and refugees to their pre-war homes.

RS: Republika Srpska (Serb Republic) (49 per cent of BiH).

UNHCR: United Nations High Commissioner for Refugees, the UN Refugee Agency.

UNPROFOR: United Nations Protection Force, initially established to ensure demilitarisation of designated areas in Croatia, its mandate was later extended to Bosnia and Herzegovina to support the delivery of humanitarian relief, and monitor 'no fly zones' and 'safe areas'.

VCE: The Victorian Certificate of Education, awarded on completion of Year 12 in Victorian high schools (Australia).

VRS: Army of Republika Spska, armed forces of Bosnian Serbs during the 1992–95 war.

YUTEL: (Yugoslav Television): television news program between 1990 and 1992 based in Sarajevo and run by popular non-nationalist Yugoslav journalists, the last true Yugoslav television station, which was destroyed in the 1992–95 war, as were all other common Yugoslav institutions.

Introduction

The Journey through Bosnian War-torn Communities

> The Universe sent darkness to our humble home
> which is gone now. The letter and every single book,
> and dear things: they all burned like Rome.
> Ferida Duraković, 'A War Letter',[1] *Heart of Darkness*, p. 92

It is a straightforward enough question: what is the relationship between forced displacement, popular memory and trans-local identities? In striving to answer it, we discover that it is anything but straightforward. Places – unless simply understood as geographically situated social networks – do not move, remember or create their identities. People do. Hence, displacement, memory and identity are embodied experiences of real people and the communities they belong to. These experiences are remembered, (re)constructed and enacted in diasporic spaces and in the original homeland as well as in cyber space, creating an in-between space, which is sometimes both *here* ('where I live') and *there* ('where I come from') and sometimes neither completely *here* nor *there* ('I am only here temporarily until I'm able to go back home'). However, the sheer magnitude of the forced displacement of 2.2 million men, women and children during the 1992–95 Bosnian war[2] and its aftermath renders any generalisation problematic. The spectre of genocide – or the more sanitised 'ethnic cleansing' as it was euphemistically described – cries out for a visceral as much as analytical response, especially as many people I knew and loved perished or were displaced as part of the violent campaigns. Popular memory – encompassing the private and local memories of the survivors, collective narratives and all performative actions such as memorialisation, commemoration and funerals – is reconceptualised on a daily basis and is often the only form of resistance survivors have at their disposal. Similarly, identity – or more accurately identities – is never fixed, but is constantly (re)imagined and (re)imaged, (re)constructed and (re)embodied, narrated and remembered, locally embedded and collectively enacted.[3] It is anything but a straightforward question.

But it is a question that needs to be asked. It is a question – notwithstanding all the objections and qualifiers and caveats implied above – that demands an answer. Not just because of the tragedy of the 1992–95 Bosnian war, the scope and the intensity of the destruction, the scale of the displacement and the long-lasting consequences of the conflict. There are other, more significant and morally informed reasons why is it a question that needs to be asked.

Before elaborating some of these reasons, let me first broadly define the common Bosnian labels and describe who my informants are. 'Bosnia', 'Bosnia-Herzegovina', 'Bosnia and Herzegovina' and 'BiH' are all the terms that are interchangeably used when referring to Bosnia and Herzegovina (in its full and official name) as a country with distinct geography, history, politics and culture(s). Unlike any other country in the region, the country's name does not directly relate to a single ethnic group but to the river Bosna, which rises from a spring (Vrelo Bosne) near Sarajevo and flows across a large part of the country, merging with the River Sava, Bosnia's border river to the north, at the city of Bosanski Šamac.

The terms 'Bosnian' and 'Bosnians' are generally used to describe all people who live(d) in Bosnia-Herzegovina regardless of their ethnic, religious or regional identities, and that's how I use these terms here. In terms of ethnic identities, Bosnians are made up of three 'constitutive peoples': Bosniaks (also known as Bosnian Muslims), Bosnian Croats and Bosnian Serbs. Each ethnic group has a separate religious identity: Bosniaks are Muslims, Croats are Catholics and Serbs are Orthodox Christians. However, there are many Bosnians who do not identify with any of the ethnic and religious identities, as well as those who regard 'their' religion as a lesser part of their ethnic identity. Thus, many people in/from BiH prefer to see themselves only as Bosnians, a more civic and inclusive identification without ethnic connotations. There are also members of Bosnian minority ethnic groups such as Albanians, Jews, Roma, Ukrainians and Yugoslavs, who do not have the status of constitutive peoples, but are nonetheless regarded as Bosnians. Those writing about Bosnian identities, however, often ignore the fact that beyond – or below – the broader ethnic identities there are also at least four distinct regional non-ethnic identities representing people from different parts of the country – like *Hercegovci* (those from Herzegovina), *Podrinjci* (those from the region of Podrinje along the river Drina in eastern Bosnia), *Posavci* (those from Posavina, along the river Sava in northern Bosnia), and *Krajišnici* (people from Bosanska Krajina in western Bosnia). In addition to these, there are numerous identities expressed through identifications with specific local places where people live(d) or claimed provenance (Halilovich 2011b).

In post-war BiH, many of these different identities – especially the ethnic identities of the constitutive peoples Bosniaks, Serbs and Croats – have become exclusive political identities. During the war and in the post-war period, the ethnic identities solidified, with each ethnic polity becoming monopolised by its own ethno-nationalist politics and politicians. As a consequence of this politics of ethnicisation, each of the three ethnic nationalisms has promoted their particular ethnic concept of homeland(s) in relation to Bosnia. Often in antagonistic relationship, these concepts, while competing for a shared homeland, often invoke the idea of 'external homelands' (Brubaker 1996). While many Bosnian Croats and Bosnian Serbs regard their external homelands to be Croatia and Serbia respectively – and have, over the last two decades, embraced the citizenship and political identities of their external homelands – Bosniaks do not have an external homeland to refer to (Filandra 2012). This has been one of the main qualitative differences between Bosniak and the other two ethnic nationalisms in BiH. Some Bosniak nationalists have used this to argue that, by turning to their external homelands, Bosnian Croats and Bosnian Serbs have betrayed their 'first homeland' and become 'lesser Bosnians', with Bosniaks remaining the most authentic (if not the only) Bosnian people loyal to Bosnia and Herzegovina (Ibrahimagić 2003). Of course, there is also an inclusive civic (i.e., non-ethnic) form of Bosnian nationalism appealing to many people – especially to many urban intellectuals – who continue to reject the idea that political subjects are inherently ethnic subjects.

While the ideas of external homelands continue to be contested and seen as incompatible with the idea of Bosnia as a multicultural homeland for all the Bosnian peoples and citizens (cf. Mahmutćehajić 2000), Barrington, Herron and Silver argue that 'an individual or group can have several possible homelands' (2003: 293). In addition to the external homeland, these include, as they outline, such forms as 'internal homeland', 'mixed homeland' and 'state of residence' (Barrington, Herron and Silver 2003). All these different understandings of and relationships with homeland(s) can be found among Bosnians in BiH and in diaspora.

After the war many Bosnian Serbs developed a strong sense of identification with Republika Srpska (RS), their internal national homeland within BiH. Similarly, but much less territorially defined, Bosniaks and Croats regard parts of the Federation of BiH (Federacija) as their internal homelands. The difference between Serbs, Bosniaks and Croats in relation to their internal homelands can be explained by the fact that RS – a direct product of ethnic cleansing – was created as an exclusive *Lebensraum* for Serbs during the 1992–95 war, while Federacija was a more or less imposed peace agreement accepted by Bosniak and Bosnian Croat political representatives in March 1994 (Hoare 2004). This means that Bosniaks and Bosnian Croats have not completely defined their separate internal homelands even though there is a high degree of such division between the two ethnic groups in western Herzegovina and calls by Bosnian Croat nationalists for the establishment of a third – i.e., Croat – entity in BiH (Barbir-Mladinović 2009). As Barrington, Herron and Silver (2003: 292) argue, 'an ethnic group becomes "national" when it recognises a particular territory as one that it has a right to control politically'. Nationalist politics in RS, which continues to exercise political control over the ethnically cleansed territories as described in the book, regard Bosnian Serbs in RS as a national group, while defining RS as an exclusive Serb (home)land. However, as RS, together with Federacija, is an *entitet* (entity, constitutive unit) of the post-Dayton[4] state of Bosnia and Herzegovina, attitudes of many Bosnians towards their first homeland could be best described as what Barrington, Herron and Silver (2003) call, a 'mixed (internal–external) homeland'.

There is also an additional type of homeland these authors refer to: 'state of residence'. State of residence – referring to a less affectionate and less political relationship citizens have towards the state in which they live – is often reserved for the category of 'national minorities' (Barrington, Herron and Silver 2003: 294). While, for different reasons, many Bosnians of different ethnic backgrounds may regard parts of BiH, or the state of BiH, only as their state of residence, this category may be even more applicable to many of the 1.6 million Bosnians living in diaspora.

While Bosnia and the Bosnian war have come to symbolise ethnic violence and ethnic cleansing, the war in their multicultural homeland was the last possibility that many Bosnians expected. In 1991, even after the armed conflict had erupted in Slovenia and spread to Croatia, many Bosnians still believed that their multicultural, multi-confessional and ethnically intermixed way of life would prevent a similar conflict in their immediate homeland and communities.[5] The policy of Yugoslav brotherhood and unity might have been seen as an outdated artificial creation and an integral part of the communist ideology – as the various nationalist parties claimed at the time – but most ordinary Bosnians wanted to believe that there was something more authentic and more organic about the shared culture, history and mentality of fellow Bosnians of different ethno-religious backgrounds (Mahmutćehajić 2000, 2003; Banac 2002; and Džaja 2002). Sadly, precisely because of the organic multicultural[6] fabric of Bosnian society – and the political objectives of the war to create zones of ethnic exclusion – the war in Bosnia was much more brutal and tragic than in other parts of the former Yugoslavia.[7] However, it would be wrong to suggest that Bosnian cultural diversity was the source of the conflict, as some have implied.[8] Cultural diversity was, rather, the target of carefully orchestrated ethnic violence aimed at the 'ethnic unmixing' of Bosnians. As Anthony

Oberschall (2000) points out, in most cases ethnic cleansing involved military and militias against civilians rather than neighbour against neighbour, as is sometimes believed. Thus, this book is both a homage to and celebration of that multicultural Bosnia – or the ideal of such a Bosnia – where neighbours do not kill each other but rather see themselves reflected in the differences of those around them. That Bosnia, the one I personally remember and continue to believe in, deserves a chance – even though the current socio-political realities in BiH are far from that ideal.

But Bosnia and the survival of its multicultural way of life matters not only to Bosnians of any or no ethno-religious background. Bosnia is also a test case for the ideals of the EU and our increasingly globalised world (Mahmutćehajić 2000). It is not just rhetoric anymore to say that local and global are interconnected, that local events have larger regional and global effects, and the other way around. Even here, Bosnia may be a case in point: in a tragic way, the last century started and ended in Bosnia. The assassination of Archduke Franz Ferdinand in Sarajevo in 1914 sparked the Great War that took the lives of millions of people and reshaped the political map of the world. At the end of the twentieth century, Bosnia's local conflict involved many regional and global players, often polarising diplomatic relationships between them (Cigar 1995: 139–65; Power 2002: 247–58). As Slavoj Žižek (1994) pointed out, the Bosnian conflict revealed many hypocrisies of the so-called international community and the West, hesitant to defend some of its core values and principles enshrined in conventions and constitutions of the UN member states, the principles of basic human rights, of sovereignty and the prevention of genocide.

Writing about the Displacement of Bosnians

In addition to the systematic destruction of cultural heritage, large-scale human rights abuses and the immense loss of human life, culminating in the 1995 Srebrenica genocide, the war in Bosnia also resulted in unprecedented displacement from and within the country. It created the largest refugee crisis in Europe since the Second World War (Hitchcock 2003: 380–409). While close to a million Bosnians were turned into internally displaced persons (IDPs), a further 1.3 million people became refugees, asylum seekers and migrants in many countries, predominantly in Europe, Northern America and Australia (Bosnia and Herzegovina Ministry for Human Rights and Refugees 2008). Most of those displaced never returned – at least not permanently – to their original homes, and most who did return were transformed into 'ethnic minorities' (Halilovich 2008, 2011a; Stefansson 2006; Toal and Dahlman 2006, 2011).

Researchers have investigated aspects of the Bosnian question. Anthropologists and some political geographers in particular have focused extensively on in-country studies.[9] There have been studies dealing with settlement issues and other aspects of (dis)placement of Bosnians in receiving countries. Marita Eastmond (1998, 2005, 2006), Maja Povrzanovic Frykman (2009, 2011) and Zoran Slavnić (2011) have written about the settlement issues, interethnic relations and transnational practices of Bosnians in Sweden, where close to 100,000 Bosnian refugees have settled since 1992.[10] Barbara Franz (2000, 2003, 2005, 2011), Urlike Davy (1995) and Hariz Halilovich (2011a) have written about the experiences of Bosnians in Austria. Germany – the country which, with some 350,000 Bosnian refugees, at one stage was host to the largest refugee group from Bosnia – has been the focus of half a dozen researchers: Bagshaw (1997), Davy (1995), Dimova (2006, 2007), Graf (1999), Koser (2001) and Luebben (2003). Laura Huttunen (2005) has written about the situation in Finland; Bosnians settling in Norway have been researched by Marko Valenta (2009) and Valenta and Strabac (2011). In Denmark research has been carried out by Hervik (2006), Dmitruk, Hadzic and Sherman (2005); in Switzerland by Behloul (2007); in the U.K. by Esterhuizen (2006), Kelly (2003) and V. Robinson (2000). The 350,000 displaced Bosnians who have settled in the U.S.A. over the last eighteen years have been researched by Coughlan (2005, 2011), Coughlan and Owens-Manley (2006), Hansen (2001), Oakes (2002), Ives (2005), Kent (2008), Matsuo (2005), McCarthy (2000) and Mišković (2011). For Bosnians in Canada there are George and Tsang (2000); for New Zealand, Madjar and Humpage (2000). Bosnians in Australia have been the focus of R. Adams (2006, 2008), Colic-Peisker (2003, 2005), Halilovich (2005a, 2006b, 2011b, 2012b), Haverić (2009), Kokanovic and Stone (2010), Markovic and Manderson (2002), Voloder (2008), Vujcich (2007) and Waxman (1999, 2001).

Some studies have compared the experiences of displaced Bosnians in two or more countries, such as the Netherlands and Italy (Korac 2003), the Netherlands and the U.K. (Al-Ali 2002, 2003; Al-Ali, Black and Koser 2001a, 2001b), Austria and the U.S.A. (Franz 2003, 2005, 2011), Germany and Austria (Davy 1995), Germany and Australia (Halilovich 2006b), the Netherlands, U.K. and Australia (Jansen 2008), the Scandinavian countries (Brochmann 1997) and Denmark and the U.S.A. (Ives 2005). Kalčić and Gombač (2011) have considered the situation of Bosnian refugees in Slovenia. Markowitz (1996) has described them in Israel. Hozic (2001) has dealt with Bosnians who moved beyond real space, constituting a 'digital diaspora'.

But none of these researchers has addressed the question that this book seeks to answer, which requires us to go beyond the established research trajectory and treatment of the Bosnian refugee diaspora and the IDPs in BiH as two completely separate(d) groups. The book explores the meaning and significance of forced displacement in relation to memory and identity (re)construction in war-torn communities from and within Bosnia and Herzegovina (BiH). The key themes – place, memory and identity, or places, memories and identities – understood as experiential and performative actions that are situational, relational and self-perpetuating, have been explored in a variety of socio-cultural settings both in the worldwide Bosnian diaspora – particularly in Austria, Australia, Sweden and the U.S.A. – and within BiH, as well as, to a lesser extent, in cyber space. In line with Tuan's analysis of place and space, these different spaces become places; for they are remembered, embodied, experienced and performed through social networks (Tuan 1977). And through these very processes, especially as they are carried out by displaced people, they transcend increasingly their very geographical roots. While displacement implies one-way movement, the book describes how that movement, physical and metaphorical, real and imagined, is in most cases multidirectional. The book itself can be seen as a multidirectional movement, a journey – not merely because of the extensive travel undertaken during the fieldwork – which starts with Chapter 1 and the reunion of survivors from Klotjevac, an ethnically cleansed village in eastern Bosnia near Srebrenica, and continues, back and forth, throughout the following chapters. Through ethnographically documented reunions of survivors – as well as through symbolic reunions with their perished relatives and friends, visits to their destroyed homes, and encounters with fellow Bosnians and non-Bosnians alike – the book describes how such contacts and events form the basis of what it means to be a survivor, a displaced person, a member of the Bosnian diaspora and a person belonging to a specific (trans-)local community or *zavičaj*.

By exploring forced displacement, migration and 'emplacement' of Bosnians both at home and abroad, I demonstrate that these different forms and experiences of displacement and emplacement are often impossible to disentangle and dichotomise. Rather, they can be seen as parts of the complex process of displacement and a (re)constructed web of vibrant trans-local social networks (Halilovich 2011b, 2012b). The present study is the largest to date of displaced Bosnians. But it is not a global survey of the Bosnian diaspora, a catalogue of Bosnian clubs, pubs and associations worldwide, a precise demographic breakdown of displaced Bosnians. By going beyond – and below – demographic and statistical categories, it provides deeper understanding of the reality of displacement and post-war Bosnian identity and memory, combining narratives with Geertzian thick description and ethnographic vignettes from the sites, places, networks and events that constitute the diaspora. It can also be seen as a collection of previously untold stories that deserve to be written down, passed on and explored. Including such stories brings them – and not just symbolically – from the margins to the centre, from the private into the public domain. Even if it is only partly answerable, the question 'What is the relationship between forced displacement, popular memory and trans-local identities in Bosnian war-torn communities?' draws attention to these interrelated issues.

Practical Challenges

Before embarking on any physical journey into the field, I had to confront the practical issue of how and where to look for answers to the research question. Eventually, I decided to include both groups of the displaced – the IDPs in BiH and the refugees in what came to be known as the Bosnian diaspora. Within BiH I focused on the eastern Bosnian region along the river Drina known as Podrinje, and the Prijedor region in western Bosnia. Both regions were emblematic of large-scale forced displacement and the systematic use of violence, ranging from concentration camps and torture to summary executions and genocide. However, Podrinje and Prijedor cannot be seen outside the broader context of Bosnia – and the Bosnian diaspora – so my research expanded to include other parts of BiH, such as Mostar and Sarajevo, and many places in the Bosnian diaspora. I soon realised that it would be almost impossible to include every single country and every place where displaced Bosnians have settled over the last eighteen years. In the end I chose the countries with the largest Bosnian diasporic communities: the U.S.A, Austria, Sweden and Australia. In the U.S. I conducted my fieldwork in St. Louis, the 'Little Sarajevo' as it is sometimes called, home to some 70,000 Bosnians. During my stay in Sweden I focused on Bosnians who had settled in and around Stockholm, Eskilstuna and Karlskrona. Most of my data in Austria comes from Vienna and Styer. In Australia, where I live, my primary research site was Melbourne. In addition to the actual physical sites, I also explored how social networks between these different sites are constructed and maintained. This took me on a different type of journey in the realm of cyber space and digital ethnography. However, I did not collect my data in cyber space – in terms of interviewing people, using blogs, Facebook or chat rooms. Rather, I was interested to learn how displaced Bosnians re-imagined and re-imaged their local identities and memories on the numerous websites dedicated to very specific places and social networks.

In some cases I traced and followed members of war-torn communities from Bosnia, like the village of Klotjevac (Chapter 1), to distant places like St. Louis, Stockholm, Vienna and Melbourne. In other instances I made multiple visits to their original villages and towns, such as the ethnically cleansed village of Hegići (Chapters 2 and 3), and the town of Brčko (Chapter 4), after discovering members of these communities in the Bosnian diaspora, in Vienna and Melbourne respectively. I also made repeated visits to the sites of suffering – Omarska, Keraterm, Trnopolje and Potočari, where large-scale war crimes and genocide were committed during the 1992–95 war in Bosnia – and visited mass grave sites. I attempted ethnography of mass events, such as the annual commemorations and collective funerals of genocide victims in Srebrenica and in Prijedor, as well as the replicas of these events in the Bosnian diaspora. When exploring different types of memory in post-war Bosnia, I also visited new 'sites of memory' – in Prijedor, Mostar, Sarajevo and Srebrenica – looking for patterns and the meanings of new public memories, how they have been constructed and interpreted. During this time I had many encounters and in-depth conversations with several prominent survivor-activists, like Kemal Pervanić, Rezak Hukanović, Muharem Murselović, Hasan Nuhanović, Munira Subašić and Fata Orlović, as well as with many ordinary survivors keeping a low profile – whose names have been changed or not mentioned.

Theoretical Challenges

When dealing with the major theoretical frameworks and debates around displacement and identity, I aimed to avoid being pulled into either the sedentarist or the anti-sedentarist camps – the first promoting the idea of rootedness, and suggesting almost a natural link between people's sense of belonging and territory, the latter arguing that, especially in the age of globalisation, place becomes somehow outdated and identities increasingly detached from territory. From a variety of different perspectives, these views continue to be debated and contested by a number of prominent, contemporary anthropologists.[11] In practice, however, the dichotomy seems to be more important and meaningful to academics than to (dis) placed people: as my research findings and personal experience suggest, regardless of the level of their (im)mobility, people can develop and maintain multiple attachments to different places as well as construct their identities in the absence of an actual place. While identity is a life-long work-in-progress, this book shows that people who experience forced displacement do not remain in a stage of permanent liminality. Their migration into new identities, even if these identities are only transitory – from refugees to IDPs, to migrants, to citizens of new countries, or returnees – is often founded on the remnants of their earlier place-based identities and locally embedded social networks.[12] Even when it is reduced down – or elevated – to the level of an idea(l), the *place called home* remains a 'symbolic anchor', a metaphor around which narratives of belonging and memories of home are constructed and performed (Gupta and Ferguson 1992: 11). The attachment to the idea of the old place as home, as Ghassan Hage (1997) argues, should not be seen as a hindering factor for migrants and refugees in their new places of settlement. Rather, it provides them with a 'sense of possibility' to (re)create their new home constructed around '[the] desire to promote the feeling of being there *here*' (Hage 1997: 102–08). In practical terms this means that displacement leads to a new placement, which is in line with Deleuze's and Guattari's claim that 'there is no deterritorialisation without an effort for reterritorialisation' and reterritorialisation inevitably 'produces a new territoriality' (Deleuze and Guattari 1980: 214).[13] For many people who experienced forced displacement, the original place is not located in space anymore, but in time which has passed – in memories, narratives and performative enactments of local identities (Ahmed et al. 2003). Thus, rootedness after forced displacement does not necessarily equal sedentarism; it is rather an emotional attachment that transcends geography, or, as Leslie Van Gelder (2008: 58) puts it, 'people in diasporas do not root in place, but in each other'.

Another popular approach that was of limited value to my research was transnational theory, which over the last two decades has been viewed in many quarters as the dominant theoretical framework in migration studies.[14] While some scholars of transnationalism, such as Luis E. Guarnizo and Michael P. Smith (1998), do write about 'transnationalism from below', recognising the importance of locally embedded identities and social networks within the transnational process, it is more often the case, as Vered Amit (2002: 21) argues, that transnational process and practices are understood 'to first and foremost involve the production of ethnic [and national] collectivities that straddle state borders'. What I found, and what this book describes, is that displaced groups from BiH primarily follow the patterns that are local – or *zavičaj*-based[15] – rather than national, transnational or even ethnic and religious.

The 1992–95 war in Bosnia-Herzegovina and its consequences have become synonymous with ethnic violence, ethnic cleansing and the 'ethnicisation' of political discourse. While killings and the expulsion of the 'ethnic other' from places and strategic territories, that were remade into exclusive ethnic homelands, were a key feature of the conflict in BiH, the emphasis on ethnicity as a natural and political group identity of Bosnians has come at the expense of shared place-based local identities – defined by local geography, cultural norms, dialect, kinship, neighbourliness, a common way of life and embodied relationship with the place and social networks – or *zavičaj*, a term encompassing the wholeness of person-in-place and place-in-person (R. Adams and Halilovich 2010). Sometimes translated as 'local homeland', *zavičaj* goes beyond both the strictly private domain and the public sphere of identification with group categories like family, kin, religion or ethnicity. With its use of toponyms and nicknames it unites landscape and people. With its emphasis on shared local dialect, cultural practices and social networks, it encourages the accommodation of difference that can attach to religion and ethnicity. In this way *zavičaj* both reflected and contributed to the multicultural and multi-ethnic pattern of life that was so characteristic of Bosnia right up to the 1990s. In countless villages and towns across the country it was for many the most powerful point of reference for their sense of belonging – more powerful by far than the exclusivist claims of religion and ethnicity.

The sociological concept of *Gemeinschaft*, as opposed to *Gesellschaft* (Tönnies 2001), comes close to *zavičaj*'s sense of community, social network and home. In this sense, *zavičaj* is a social reality, a lived experience for discrete groups, and also a metaphor for modalities that go beyond conventional state or party-based modes of social organisation.

While for many people in Bosnia and other Yugoslav successor states – especially those who were forcibly displaced – the term *zavičaj* evokes deep feelings of belonging to and nostalgia for a place that is or was the intimate and ultimate home, for ethno-nationalist political elites it was fashionable to regard *zavičaj* as an outdated pre-modern concept of home, incompatible with the ideas of greater ethnic homelands and exclusive nation states. The orchestrated violent campaigns of ethnic cleansing and ethnic unmixing that took place during the 1992–95 war, in which whole areas were depopulated and many local places erased from the map as human settlements, can be seen as part of a much longer campaign to unmake *zavičaj* in Bosnia. However, as I argue in this book, for those whose identity remains embedded and embodied in the idea of a distinct locale, the *zavičaj* continues to coexist as an experiential reality despite its physical destruction and forced displacement.

Methodological Challenges

While relying on and drawing from many different disciplines, such as history, political science, sociology, psychology and literature, my research – and this book – is theoretically and methodologically situated in social anthropology. In particular I have been influenced by George Marcus's writing on multi-sited ethnography, and his claim that 'multi-sited research is designed around chains, paths, threads, conjunctions, or juxtapositions of locations in which the ethnographer establishes some literal, physical presence, with an explicit, posited logic of association or connection among sites that in fact defines the argument of the ethnography' (Marcus 1995:

105). In line with Marcus's view of multi-sited ethnography – applying a variety of roles as a researcher, such as completely participant, completely observer, observer as participant and marginal native – I have followed the people, the metaphors, the plots, the stories, the biographies and the conflict. As such, my exploration goes beyond real and imagined fixities and certainties of place and cannot be seen in isolation or disentangled from the life stories and experiences of my informants.

This is not to say that the life stories somehow exist outside the concept of place. As Van Gelder (2008: 4) puts it, 'We are always somewhere, and it is through place that we are able to root our sense of story and our sense of self. Our stories make places important to us, and places become vessels for holding and keeping our stories'. However, the relationship between stories and place – especially after experiences of forced displacement – also works the other way round. Stories become vessels for holding and keeping places. We are able to root our sense of place and our sense of self through story, for 'it is through the activity of narration that we create meaning to our lives' (Andrews 2000: 77).

Using the narrative method proved to be highly appropriate and engaging – as well as personally difficult at times – as it enabled my informants to reconstruct, reinterpret and relive their memories and experiences of people, places and events by being active parties in the process of data collection rather than dismissing their reflections on the social world (Bryman 2001: 277). In line with a Foucauldian approach to narratives – based on the interrelationships between narrative, subjectivity and power (cf. Tamboukou 2008) – the stories of survivors of ethnic cleansing and genocide described in this book represent more than just personal stories and testimonials. They are part of a fragmented collective knowledge, or what Michel Foucault (1975, 1977) termed 'popular memory', the memory of those who do not have access to publishing houses, film studios or political and cultural institutions. Following Foucault's recognition of popular memory as a political force against official discourse – a form of resistance (Foucault 1975: 25) – the popular memory narrated and performed by my informants might be viewed as the only form of defiance and resistance possible against the dominant nationalist discourses that have been behind their forced displacement.

When selecting participants I started with my pre-existing social and research networks and let them unfold across my participants' families, friends, *zavičaj* associations, localities and continents – literally, across their personal human geographies, often defying the logics of space and time. The result was that many of the stories – and people who told them – became, in one way or another, connected with each other. Many of these stories are of horrific experiences of loss, forced displacement and survival.

Nonetheless, I avoid using the word 'trauma' when describing and referring to such experiences, memories and narratives. In my view – based not only on an extensive literature review and research experience with Bosnian refugees, but also on my professional role as a former counsellor and mental health worker working with a range of refugee and asylum seeker groups in Australia and Germany[16] – the overuse of the term 'trauma' has led to the medicalisation and pathologising of human suffering, and in particular of memories and experiences of refugees and survivors of violence (Lambert, Haasen and Halilovic 1998; Summerfield 2004; Kokanovic and Stone 2010).

I do not argue that people go unchanged through difficult, life-changing experiences. Clearly there were invisible injuries of soul in many of my informants, but I did not treat them as psychopathological and clinical conditions that needed to be or could be corrected. I saw them instead as normal, human responses – coping mechanisms – to the extraordinary situations and experiences these people had gone through. Therefore, I do not label and stigmatise my informants and their memories as PTSD and trauma, and do not see symptoms like 'obsessive reliving of the traumatic experience' in their need to (re)tell me their stories (J. Herman 1992; Kenny 1996). Inspired and encouraged by Claude Lanzmann's (1985) monumental work with survivors of the Holocaust, my role was more as a witness to their testimonials than someone who would look for symptoms of psychopathology in what they told me.

What the testimonies revealed is that, just as forced displacement is not something that happens in a linear, orderly way, so memories and narratives of displacement are not (re)collected in a coherent, (chrono)logical order. They are most often made up of fragments, where gaps, silences, sighs and body language tell as much as spoken words. When conveying these narratives in written text, I have used different writing styles, techniques, and different voices, connecting many different fragments and supplementing them with my own observations and participation.

Reflexive Ethnography

This brings me to me. As sociologists Peter Berger and Thomas Luckmann recognised forty years ago, 'Reality is socially defined. But the definitions are always *embodied*, that is, concrete individuals and groups of individuals serve as definers of reality' (Berger and Luckmann 1967: 134). In this context it is important to acknowledge my positioning and my subjectivities not only in relation to my informants but also in relation to the broader context of the question I am attempting to answer. In her book *Reflexive Ethnography*, Charlotte Aull Davies argues, 'all researchers are to some degree connected to, or part of, the object of their research' (2008: 3). Or, as

Friedrich Nietzsche put it more bluntly, '… however far man may extend himself with his knowledge, however objective he may appear to himself – ultimately he reaps nothing but his own biography' (1994: 238). There can be no denying my passion for researching forced displacement, memory and trans-local identities in Bosnian war-torn communities. Beyond an academic inquisitiveness and the epistemological relevance of the topic, my research has been driven by a search for answers to ontological questions that affect me at a deep personal level.

Even if I wanted to, I could not claim historical, personal or simply human distance from the issues of forced displacement, ethnic cleansing and genocide in Bosnia. My family is part of the displaced. In fact, we may well represent the quintessential 'made-in-transit' family, having been born in three different countries – in Bosnia, Slovenia and Germany – and now living in a fourth country, Australia.

In 1993 my girlfriend Zerina and I – in a dramatic turn of events – exchanged our student lives at the University of Sarajevo for the 'careers' of refugees, the displaced and immigrants, firstly in Europe and later in Australia. In 1997, in Hamburg, three years after we reunited, our son Suad was born. Born to refugee parents: the first official letter that baby Suad received stated that he would not be allowed to claim any residency rights based on the fact that he was born in Germany. He was de facto born in transit and classified as a refugee at birth. Being parents to our son, born as a displaced person in a 'united Europe' at the end of the twentieth century, we felt responsible for providing him with a future, a place where he would not be classified and discriminated against because of his and his parents' place of birth and refugee background. That is why we migrated to Australia in 1998.

While neither Zerina nor Suad have maintained or developed a strong sense of belonging to the place of their birth, in the last twenty years my place of birth has become an important identity mark – more a scar than a mark – that I am often identified by. Upon learning about my place of birth, I know what kind of questions to expect from people. Spread across the first page of my Australian passport, 'S r e b r e n i c a' almost reads like my name and like my name travels with me wherever I go. Although I left Srebrenica at the age of fourteen and was not there during the 1992–95 war, the Srebrenica genocide – which claimed more than a hundred of my extended family – has had a profound impact on my life.

This impact is reflected in my research. But this book should not be read as an autoethnography. I have dealt with my personal experiences of displacement through both works of fiction and academic, non-fiction genres elsewhere.[17] This book is about other people, places and memories, and neither I nor members of my family have been involved in it as informants. Having said this, I fully acknowledge my double role: as a cultural insider born and socialised in Bosnia (and Yugoslavia), and a professional outsider, an anthropological scholar living in Australia. My ethnographic approach is a mix of both *emic* and *etic* perspectives. It also comes close to 'ethnology of the proximate', where 'research is a continual blend of personal experience and the creation of anthropological knowledge' (Čapo Žmegač, Gulin Zrnić and Šantek 2006: 287). Sometimes, in the field and when describing the events, interactions and stories I engaged with during my research, I let the me fade from the picture, let my presence and autobiographical elements disappear between the lines, to focus on the exchange between the participants I observe (Chapters 1, 3 and 5). At other times (Chapters 2, 4 and the Conclusion) I acknowledge my presence by using first person voice or through reflexive vignettes of my own thoughts, feelings, assumptions and role as a researcher in a given situation.

Ethics and Politics of the Research

Being a cultural insider – a person speaking the relevant languages and having experienced displacement myself – has definitely been an advantage in understanding the issues, gaining access to prospective participants and establishing trusting relationships with them. Being seen and accepted as an insider has provided access to information that is off limits to outside researchers (T. Hermann 2001). Certainly, insider status at times complicated my role as a researcher and even became a source of potential risk – including physical danger and personal safety issues. There were times when my loyalties were questioned when identified as the 'ethnic other', and I was accused of taking sides. Bizarrely, I felt safer when suspected of being a spy – I was asked by a local official what Western intelligence service I was working for – as officials seemed to have more respect for spies than for pestering anthropologists visiting ethnically cleansed villages and talking to survivors.

Once in the field(s) there was no easy way out of the ethnographer-activist role, nor was I looking for an easy escape. Instead, I learned that doing multi-sited ethnography of forced displacement inevitably leads into researching and dealing with the harsh realities of causes and consequences. The forced displacement executed through the policy of ethnic cleansing in Bosnia and Herzegovina between 1992 and 1995 was carried out through the systematic violation of human rights, the complete disregard for the lives and dignity of others, and war crimes that culminated in the 1995 Srebrenica genocide.[18] Therefore any average Bosnian story of displacement has to include dispossession, personal loss, dramatic flights and homelessness. This book is full of 'average' stories, of persecution, ethnic cleansing and genocide. For me, these stories represent some of the most profound and cathartic experiences I have had – as a researcher and a person. The academic genre can demand (over)theorised and detached scholarly (scientific) accounts of stories of which I have become a part in the course of my research, and – if it was not for the feeling of indebtedness to my informants – I might have left out some powerful and moving narratives.

The stories described in this book have become my stories and I have become part of the stories of those who opened their hearts and their homes to me. I followed and carried their stories across the globe and, in some cases I went back with my storytellers to their destroyed homes and places that are no more. In this way I was able to visualise their stories by linking them to the material evidence of their past lives. I was invited to their wedding celebrations, the first birthdays of their children, and the mass graves and funerals of their loved ones who perished in the war.

A cluster of storytellers came from the ethnically cleansed village of Klotjevac near Srebrenica, my birth village, which naturally has special meaning for me. Confronted with the magnitude of the loss of human lives and the continuing institutional discrimination against the handful of survivors who returned to their decimated village ten years after they fled, the advocacy and activism, which I see as part of the researcher's ethical responsibility, has been more pronounced here than in other parts of Bosnia. In addition to public speaking, presenting papers at international conferences and seminars, speaking on radio and TV, participating in documentaries and publishing articles and interviews, in July 2007 I led a group of twenty-two Australian students to Klotjevac. The 'Bosnian Study Tour' (BST), was planned in advance with the locals of the village and was designed as a fully accredited university subject involving both theoretical and practical learning aspects. The study tour's objective was to explore and to learn firsthand about the effects of genocide and ethnic cleansing on local communities in BiH by directly engaging with members of such communities, as well as to identify ways in which these devastated communities could be supported (Halilovich 2008).

The students' visit had a profound impact on the villagers who, for the first time in a long time, felt that they were not completely abandoned and that someone does care about them. Their village was again the destination for friendly foreigners. After being destroyed, depopulated and written off by almost everyone apart from a handful of survivors, the students' visit made Klotjevac visible again (Halilovich and Adams 2011). Memories of genocide, invasion, destruction and continuing occupation were suspended. What was remembered (and reminisced about) were the summers of visitors, the occasions of celebration, the forging of new contacts on their own terms with outsiders. In addition to these sentimental and symbolic benefits, the local community also gained some modest economic benefit from hosting a group of twenty-five people for ten days. Facilitating a positive change in the village by BST members has included various other acts of advocacy and activism. Dissemination of information about the village and the living conditions of returnees resulted in the village being put back on the map (literally!) and its residents being provided with material aid in the form of livestock, a tractor and agricultural machinery by international NGOs assisting returnees. Inspired by the BST, other researchers, journalists and human rights activists from Bosnia, the region and faraway places flocked to the village to take up the issues of discrimination and the marginalisation of the villagers by the institutions and the government of Republika Srpska (RS).

Returning to Australia the students founded the association, Friends of Klotjevac, its mission being the advancement of the human rights cause of the villagers, advocacy and the provision of practical support for their sustainable return. One of the first major projects involved working together with the villagers – both returnees and those displaced, now living in Australia and fifteen other countries across the globe – to collect funds for building a monument to the 108 villagers who perished in the war. Less than two years later three of the students and more than 200 displaced Klotjevac villagers and their friends participated in the unveiling ceremony of the monument in the heart of the village still lying in ruins. The Klotjevac survivors insisted on the Australian students being acknowledged on the monument. The monument to the dead also represents a monument to the friendly foreigners from a distant country who injected new optimism in those who returned or are planning to return to their devastated village. The monument project not only acknowledged and commemorated the victims, but it also helped the locals to reclaim and transform their collective past. To the idyllic pre-war past and the tragic war past, was added a newer past – a new narrative told by Klotjevac returnees of 'that hot summer when Australian students visited us'. It is to these three parts of Klotjevac – the idyllic, the tragic and the optimistic – that we now turn.

Notes

1. Translated from Bosnian by Amela Simic and Zoran Mutic.
2. The 1992–95 war in Bosnia–Herzegovina (BiH) was the longest and the most brutal in a series of the Yugoslav wars of succession. The war started in March 1992 when the BiH government followed the examples of Slovenia and Croatia and – after holding a referendum (boycotted by the Serb Democratic Party [SDS], the main political party of Bosnian Serbs at the time) – declared independence from the Yugoslav Federation. In late March and early April 1992 the

Serbian government-controlled militias invaded the eastern Bosnian border towns of Bijeljina, Brčko and Zvornik, killing non-Serb civilians. By mid April 1992 there was all-out war in the country between the SDS militias (later Army of Republika Srpska or VRS) and the Yugoslav National Army (JNA) on the one side and on the other, the BiH government-controlled police and territorial defence (later Army of BiH) and Croatian Defence Council (HVO), the armed wing of the Croat Democratic Union (HDZ), the nationalist party of Bosnian Croats. However, within the main war (simplified as Serbs versus Bosniaks and Croats), at different times different armed groups fought together and against each other. Between 1992 and 1993 rival groups of Bosnian Croats, HVO and HOS (Croatian Armed Forces) fought a brief but bitter war for monopoly control in Croat-dominated parts of the country (western Herzegovina). By early 1993 war had broken out between HVO units and the Army of the Republic of Bosnia and Herzegovina (ARBiH) in central Bosnia and Mostar, followed by further fratricide between Bosniak troops in western Bosnia, when Fikret Abdić's troops (Autonomaši) fought against ARBiH. Four years of bloodshed in the country left 100,000 to 150,000 people killed, about 2 million forcibly displaced, between 20,000 and 50,000 women raped, 35,000 missing, tens of thousands of people imprisoned and tortured, more than 800,000 homes destroyed ... The war ended in December 1995, with the country divided in two semi-autonomous political entities: Republika Srpska (Serb Republic or RS) and the Federation of Bosnia and Herzegovina, with a special status given to District Brčko. For more information on wars in Bosnia and ex-Yugoslavia see Cigar (1995), Glenny (1996), Lampe (2000), Silber and Little (1996), Hoare (2004) and Halpern and Kideckel (2000).
3. Throughout the book I use the term 'identity' to include belonging, memory, identification, label, narrative and embodiment. Some of the main relational, situational, experiential and existential identity categories with(in) which my participants are described include: place, culture, ethnicity, nationality, community, diaspora, gender, survivor, war widow, refugee, IDP, old dweller, newcomer and guest worker. Thus, identity is understood and explored in its multiplicity of meanings as being always a work in progress that can never be completely fixed or encompassed by a single definition.
4. Dayton refers to the 1995 Dayton Peace Accords (DPA) that ended the war in BiH and defined the state of BiH as a federation made up of Republika Srpska (49 per cent of the territory) and the Bosniak-Croat Federation (51 per cent).
5. According to the 1991 Census of Population the ethnic composition of Bosnia and Herzegovina included 43.5 per cent Muslims (Bosniaks), 31.2 Serbs and 17.4 Croats. The fourth largest group was 'Yugoslavs' (5.6 per cent), those who did not identify themselves in ethnic terms. (See http://www.fzs.ba/Dem/Popis/NacStanB.htm)
6. By 'organic' multiculturalism I understand 'diversity from below' – a way of life made up of different cultural influences, and negotiation of differences on a daily basis, as it existed in Bosnia (four faiths, shared language, two scripts, no segregated ethnic quarters, etc.) – rather than 'multiculturalism from above', which is result of a deliberate state policy (like in Australia, for instance).

7. See, for instance, Cushman and Meštrović (1996), Denich (1993), Halpern and Kideckel (2000) and Ramet (2002, 2005).
8. Hayden (1996, 2000), Bakic-Hayden (1995) and Huntington (1996: 272).
9. Bax (1997a, 1997b, 2000a, 2000b, 2000c), Black (2001, 2002), Bougarel (2007), Campbell (1998, 1999), Cushman (2004), Dahlman (2004), Dahlman and Ó Tuathail (2005a, 2005b, 2006), Duijzings (2007), Helms (2007, 2008), Hunt (2005), Ito (2001), Jansen (1998, 2008), Maček (2001, 2007), Toal and Dahlman (2006, 2011) and Stefansson (2004a, 2004b, 2006, 2007).
10. I am using various estimates – those from BiH Ministry for Human Rights and Refugees, UNHCR, World Bank, official reports and published articles – about the actual number of Bosnians in different countries, as there are no completely reliable statistics on the exact numbers of Bosnians in most countries in which they have settled. There are many reasons for the lack of precise data of Bosnian refugees and migrants in these countries: many Bosnian refugees arrived in these countries without valid Bosnian documents, while others did so on former Yugoslav passports and many were classified 'stateless'. Many Bosnians were classified as economic migrants, guest workers and family reunion migrations rather than refugees. Over the years many Bosnian refugees and migrants have opted to obtain the citizenship of their adoptive countries – becoming Swedes, Austrians, Germans, Americans, Australians, Serbians, Croatians and so on – and their 'Bosnianess' regularly escapes the official statistics, as they are now officially regarded as nationals of these countries. The World Bank (2005) estimates that the number of Bosnians living outside the country is close to 1.5 million (1,471,594), or 37.7 per cent of the pre-war country's population.
11. Brun (2001), Escobar (2001), Feld and Basso (1996), Gupta and Ferguson (1992, 1997), Jansen and Löfving (2009), Kibreab (1999), Lovell (1998), Malkki (1992, 1995), Povrzanovic Frykman (2002, 2004, 2009, 2011), Rapport and Dawson (1998) and Rodman (1992).
12. See Božić-Vrbančić (2008), Čapo Žmegač (2003), Gow (2002), Nolin (2006) and Olwig (1998).
13. See also Boutang and Pamart (1995), cited in Fortier (2000: 13).
14. See Friedman (1998), Glick Schiller et al. (1992, 1995, 1999), Hannerz (1996), Kearney (1995), Koopmans and Statham (2001), Levitt and Glick Schiller (2007), Mahler (1998), Olwig (2003), Ong (1999), Portes et al. (1999), W. Robinson (1998) and Vertovec (1999, 2001, 2004, 2007).
15. The word zavičaj (plural: zavičaji) in Bosnian/Croatian/Serbian refers to a specific local or regional homeland.
16. Between 2001 and 2005 I worked as a counsellor advocate at the Melbourne-based Victorian Foundation for Survivors of Torture. Between 1995 and 1998 I was involved as a research assistant and mental health worker in the project Psychiatric Disorders in Migrants.
17. See, for instance, Halilovich (2005b, 2007, 2009, 2010a, 2010b, 2011c, 2011d and 2012a).
18. As R. Cohen (1995) commented in *The New York Times*, a CIA report on Bosnia blames Serbs for 90 per cent of the war crimes committed in the country between 1992 and 1995.

⊰ Chapter 1 ⊱

Klotjevac
Forced Displacement and Ethnic Cleansing in an Eastern Bosnian Village

I don't miss home, *mati*. I'm there all the time. In the past. In fiction.
Ismet Prcić, *Shards*, p. 41

Before 1992 hot summers would always attract visitors to Klotjevac and other towns along the river Drina, separating Bosnia from Serbia. Famed for its beauty, its clean water and the breathtaking canyon through which it flows, for centuries the river has boasted many notable bridges – including the bridge at Višegrad made famous by Ivo Andrić in his Nobel Prize winning novel *The Bridge over Drina*. In 1992, when war broke out in Bosnia, the eastern Bosnian border region along the Drina known as Podrinje assumed strategic importance for Serbia and their separatist Serb[1] compatriots in Bosnia, who planned to join the 'Serb' parts of Bosnia with Serbia and other 'Serb lands' such as Krajina (in Croatia), Posavina (in northern Bosnia) and eastern Herzegovina to create a Greater Serbia (Bećirević 2009). From a strategic point of view, it was practical to join the border region first. The problem was that Bosniaks (Bosnian Muslims) were the largest ethnic group in Podrinje, with no Serb majority in any of its twelve major cities. To make the region Serb, a policy of ethnic cleansing was executed by regular and irregular troops from Serbia and Montenegro with militias made up of radicalised local Bosnian Serbs mobilised through Radovan Karadžić's Serb Democratic Party (SDS) and the Yugoslav National Army (JNA).[2] At the beginning of the war, in the spring of 1992, the towns of Bijeljina, Zvornik, Bratunac, Srebrenica, Višegrad, Foča and Goražde were subjected to heavy attacks, and in the months and years that followed almost all non-Serbs were expelled from most of Podrinje's major towns and villages. Mass executions, including the Srebrenica genocide of July 1995, saw some 30,000 predominantly Bosniaks massacred along the river Drina (Research and Documentation Centre 2007a, 2007b). Included in the carnage were 108 men, women and children from the eastern Bosnian border village of Klotjevac.

Reunion

Halid was one of the survivors. When he touched down at Sarajevo airport on 10 July 2006 he had more than twenty hours' flying behind him. Waiting for him at the airport was a distant relative, Omer, an 'internally displaced person' and jobless chemical engineer. Ahead of them were four hours of driving in Omer's twenty-two–year-old Volkswagen Golf. They had not seen each other since Halid, now a father of three sons, had migrated to Australia under the special humanitarian programme almost ten years earlier. Omer had tried to join him in Australia but his application was rejected. When they recognised each other in the crowd at the airport, they hugged firmly and greeted each other, an almost universal image of reconnection at any airport in the world. After the usual questions about each other's health and the health of family members, the conversation turned more specific and included questions like, 'Have they found any more people from our village lately?' and 'Any news about Senad?' The questions related to the process of exhumation and identification of men and boys who had been gunned down eleven years earlier in the mass executions at Srebrenica. Senad was Omer's only brother and Halid's school mate – one of the tens of thousands of the missing who are yet to be positively identified,[3] including many other of Halid's and Omer's relatives and friends who had perished at Srebrenica in July 1995.

But Omer and Halid shared more than this tragedy. They shared childhood memories and similar sentimental attachments to the eastern Bosnian village of Klotjevac, which had perished during the 1992–95 war. They both treasured memories of long summer school holidays spent on the Drina, where their village was located. They remembered the same customs and rituals, the same people with their distinctive nicknames, the same communal narratives and anecdotes passed down among the villagers over many generations. They knew the places and bays along the lake where a particular fish would bite, what bait to use and when. They knew the smells of each other's mother's kitchens and all the familiar landmarks, such as houses, trees, rocks and water wells that constituted the sense of place, that delineated the community to which they had once belonged – a community made up of people, places, stories and rituals (Rodman 1992). In such a community the subtle and sometimes not so subtle changes ushered in by the passage of time would usually be experienced as variations on a theme rather than a radical break with the known past and the anticipated future. But very little of this existed anymore, outside the memories of the few hundred survivors now dispersed across the globe in fifteen different countries.

Halid asked if their childhood village friends Sakib and Fadil had arrived yet from Germany and Sweden, to join up with them and Almir, now living in Austria, and Halćo, now in the U.S. For more than three years they had been planning the July reunion at Srebrenica, the first time since the war that they would all be on Bosnian soil.

When You Forget July[4]

July was traditionally a month reserved for holidays in Bosnia and Herzegovina. Before the war it was the month when all the schools and universities would start their three-month vacation. Two major public holidays, 4 July and 27 July, both marking anti-fascist uprisings during the Second World War, were publicly acknowledged and celebrated. The cities would lose more than half of their population during the summer: almost everyone went to spend some time somewhere else. Many people flocked down to the Adriatic Sea. Many university students and urban dwellers would temporarily move to one of more than a thousand villages across the country to visit parents, relatives and friends, spending at least a part of their holidays helping with picking fruit and harvesting crops, mowing and collecting grass and doing other fieldwork that required many hands to be completed in time.

Times have changed, but hundreds of thousands of displaced Bosnians have reinvented July and the holiday season and, on a more or less regular basis, have started to revisit the old homeland during the European summer. They come from places as distant and diverse as Melbourne, Atlanta, Stockholm and Kuala Lumpur. Many visit the place of their birth. Some build holiday houses on the ruins of their burned-out family homes, perhaps even occupying them for a week or two once every couple of years. Others include in their four-week visits to Bosnia a week or two holidaying on the Adriatic coast, feeding the nostalgia for times past.

But for Halid, Omer and the thousands of displaced people from Podrinje and the Srebrenica region, July has forever lost its old connotations and attractiveness as a month of relaxation and holidaying. For them July is overwhelmingly associated with July 1995, when the UN safe haven at Srebrenica was overrun by the Serb military and more than 8,000 Bosniak men and boys were systematically executed. Since 2003, on every 11 July, the commemoration and burial of identified bodies recovered from the mass graves has been taking place at the memorial centre in Potočari, at the spot where the victims were separated from loved ones and taken to killing fields by the Serb military (Stover and Peress 1998). Each 11 July survivors from Srebrenica and supporters from all over the country, the region and the world attend the burial ceremonies; as Katherine Verdery (1999: 108) points out, 'burials and reburials serve to order and reorder community'. While most of the people attending the ceremony have in one way or another been directly affected by the Srebrenica massacres or genuinely moved by the great human tragedy, the occasion has also become political opportunism, a photo opportunity for local, regional and international politicians. The presence of former U.S. President Bill Clinton at the first Potočari commemoration in 2003 – like his decision to finally send in planes against the Serbs in September 1995 – was seen by many as a political act which came far too late to change anything for the victims of Srebrenica.

On 11 July 2006 more than 500 identified bodies of victims killed eleven years earlier were to be put to rest and Halid and Omer wanted to pay their last respects to the victims, many of whom were their relatives and friends. At Potočari they met with Halćo, Almir, Sakib, Fadil and many others among the crowd of 50,000 people who had come for the same reason. Many had once lived in the area, and survived Srebrenica. On their faces one could read that they were conscious of the fact that this could have been *their* burial and that by some random act of fortune they had survived – unlike the five hundred and five in the seemingly endless row of green coffins. One could read the deep sadness in their eyes, the omnipresent silence only serving to amplify their survivors' guilt. Many of the names read out belonged to members of the same family: the remains of sons and fathers, brothers and cousins carried in coffins to a long row of freshly dug graves and finally laid to rest next to each other.

Thoughts turned to the victims' last hours in that tragic July in 1995, when, with no escape from the 'UN safe haven' of Srebrenica, most families decided not to separate from each other. In the mass of thousands of desperate men, women and children, people were frantically calling the names of relatives trapped in the crowd. And then came probably the most dramatic and most shameful moment in the history of the UN when UN Dutch troops stood by while the Serb military selected men and boys and ordered them to leave all their belongings behind and get onto the convoy of buses and trucks. Mothers desperately tried to cling to their underage teenage sons being dragged away by the feared and despised Chetniks.[5] Herded to the dozens of buses and trucks waiting to take them to their fate, hundreds of fathers, sons and brothers held each other's hands as the only comfort, the only thing they could do for each other. The buses took them to warehouses and the killing fields at Bratunac, Kravica, Zvornik, Pilica … One can only hope that they could not have believed that this was happening to them. A couple of survivors have given detailed testimonies about their last moments[6] and the executioners themselves, the Serb military, have provided graphic evidence in the form of triumphant amateur videos they took of the killings. Serb soldier Dražen Erdemović[7] has told the story from the perspective of a member of a death squad that participated in the killings of twenty busloads of people from Srebrenica at a farm in Pilica, confessing how many of his victims were elderly and teenage underage boys, none of whom had tried to escape (Drakulić 2004). The thousands of bodies recovered by forensic anthropologists working on the mass graves around Srebrenica – their hands tied by a wire to each other – tell their own story (cf. Koff 2004 and Samarah 2005).

In 2006, courtesy of Bosnian satellite NTV Hayat, displaced Bosnians across the globe could watch the burial ceremony at Potočari live in their new homes and, in this way, vicariously participate in a transnational mourning. This year, with no list of names available before the ceremony, many waited anxiously to hear if the names of their relatives were called. Watching the satellite broadcast from the sitting room of his outer-suburban home in Melbourne Australia, Suad texted his old school friend Omer:

> Suad: Is there anyone I know being buried today?
>
> Omer: They just read the name of our friend from primary school, Fajko. Do you remember, he always used to sit in second row on the left in the classroom? And his name was the second on the class list – Avdić Fahrudin – just after his relative Alija?
>
> Suad: Yes, he was the best mathematician – I didn't know he was killed.

A number of names from their village followed. But not the name of Omer's brother, Senad. Nor of his brother-in-law, Sadik. Nor any of Halid's uncles and cousins. But the names of Ahmet, Džemal, Dževad, Džemir and Islam, members of three generations of the same family and Halid's, Fadil's and Sakib's distant relatives were called. Together with Omer, Almir and Halćo they pushed themselves forward to help carry the five coffins to the graves. At that moment they felt closer to their dead fellow villagers and to each other than ever before.

Journey to a Village

Later that afternoon, after the funeral and the commemoration ceremony, Omer and his overseas guests travelled together to their village of Klotjevac – that is to say, to the place where it once stood – some 25 kilometres from Srebrenica. They took a road now rarely used, which used to connect a number of villages along the Drina. With villages reduced to rubble and with no people in sight, they hardy recognised the area. Only the river looked the same.

The Drina, Bosnia's fastest flowing and second largest river, was once a demarcation line between the eastern and the western portions of the Roman Empire (Ibrahimagić 2003: 9). Historically it mirrored other parts of the world where human settlements were first established on riverbanks and fertile valleys with access to drinking water and the other natural resources essential for survival (Hamidović 2000). The Drina valley has never lacked any of these. The hinterland to the east, known as Podrinje, covers the largest part of eastern Bosnia, with some of the country's oldest towns: Zvornik, Srebrenica, Višegrad, Foča and Goražde. Smaller prehistoric settlements like Klotjevac, Žepa, Đurđevac and Divić had played an important role as the first populated areas in Podrinje (Bojanovski 1964; Wilkes 1992, 2003). Initially the region's strategic, economic and communication centres, during Roman times, they were overtaken in size and importance by newer and bigger towns. They either regressed and stagnated, or maintained the size of their population at a more or less constant number for hundreds of years as they continued to play an important role as trading centres and defence outposts against invaders from regions to the east of the Drina. The glorious past of such towns, in the modern era reduced to isolated villages and hamlets, is still evident through the presence of the ruins of medieval castles, Roman fortresses and numerous *stećci*,[8] the medieval stone tombs found mainly in Bosnia and Herzegovina and the regions bordering the country – in Serbia, Montenegro and Croatia (cf. Bešlagić 2004; Fine 1994; D. Lovrenović 2010; Miletić 1982).

Many of the ruins date back to Roman times, as does a still functional road stretching along the Drina valley, connecting this part of Bosnia with the rest of the world (Bibanović 2012). The river itself was also used as an important communication line for most of its 360-kilometre length. After the Second World War, during the period when Bosnia and Herzegovina was the central republic of the Socialist Federal Republic of Yugoslavia, three dams for hydroelectric plants were built across the river, at Zvornik, Perućac and Višegrad. This resulted in the creation of three artificial lakes that partially tamed the wild Drina and put an end to the region's long history of *splavarenje*[9] (raft navigating).

Although relatively geographically isolated from the outside world, the Podrinje region was never completely immune to outside influences, good and bad. However, such influences tended to adjust to the social norms and a way of life in Podrinje, albeit often masked by outward conformity to the new forces. Flexibility and pragmatism had ensured not only physical survival but also survival of many aspects of the local culture and social order in the form of *narodni običaji* (folk customs) (cf. Mulahalilović 1989;

F. Friedman 1996; Malcolm 1994). Of course, the succession of empires that ostensibly ruled this area believed and behaved as if their ideas would last forever. But after hundreds of years of administering its vast territories and peoples, the Roman Empire vanished, as did the Ottoman and then the Austro-Hungarian, followed by the 'first' Yugoslavia (1918–1941), the Independent State of Croatia (1941–1945), and the 'second' Yugoslavia (1945–1991).

Once There Was a Community

Klotjevac,[10] the destination of Omer and his former neighbours and fellow displaced IDPs and refugees, is located in a fertile valley some 50 kilometres down the Drina from Višegrad and 30 kilometres from Srebrenica. It faces Mount Tara and Mount Zvezda across the river in Serbia and is backed by the Sušica gorges on the Bosnian side. Just under 280 metres above sea level, its geographical location is fixed at 43.9864 latitude and 19.3442 longitude.

Like other Podrinje villages, Klotjevac was one of the places that had successfully managed throughout its long history to accommodate different conquests, administrations and all manner of social and cultural incursions. According to Ivo Bojanovski (1964) and John Wilkes (2003), its origins date back to at least the second century BC when it was already a well-developed Illyrian settlement (Wilkes 2003). Archaeological sites have revealed a rich and vibrant history, which, in addition to Slavic, also included Illyrian, Celtic and Roman cultures. The presence of some hundred *stećci* scattered in and around the village points also to the significant Gnostic Christian *Bogumil*[11] heritage of Klotjevac (Bešlagić 2004).

Klotjevac was part of all three of the largest empires that controlled vast swathes of Europe over many centuries – the Roman, Ottoman and Austro-Hungarian. These influences resulted in a very specific, and in many ways unique, mix of religious beliefs and cultural practices that continued to evolve among the local population for hundreds and thousands of years before Klotjevac was finally erased as a human settlement in the Serbian aggression of 1992–95.

The legend of Klotjevac's origin, passed down through the generations by word of mouth, recounts how a brave and furious woman warrior called Jerina Kloja fought against invaders from the other side of the Drina and built the Klotjevac fortress, which resisted all outside attempts to militarily conquer this part of the Drina valley. She had a mighty army of men and horses and was feared and respected by followers and enemies alike. Klotjevac was established by her and the name retained in her honour. She had six sisters or Jerinas, among them Srebra, Đurđa and Diva, who built similar fortress towns along the Drina, which are recalled right up to the present in the names of Srebrenica, Đurđevac and Divić. The legend of Jerina, as 'remembered' by the Klotjevac residents, was finally written down in 1952 and saved for future generations by Vlajko Palavestra, one of the best-known Bosnian ethnologists (Palavestra 2004: 189–93, 238–40). The ruins of Klotjevac fortress, built on a rocky plateau 309 metres over the Drina and called by the locals *Stari Grad* (the Old City), is one more indication of the former size and importance of what had become by the twentieth century a relatively small and marginal village.[12]

When the last census was conducted, in 1991, Klotjevac and the attached hamlets of Prohići, Urisići and Sejdinovići had a total population of 1,047 people, the vast majority of whom were Bosniaks (Bosnian Muslims), with only 14 Serbs (Government of Bosnia-Herzegovina 1991). The Serbs were not natives of Klotjevac and were either professionals, such as teachers, or regular tourists who had decided to settle in the village and convert their holiday houses into more permanent homes.

In Klotjevac, as in other villages and rural communities across the country, interethnic and interreligious marriages were not as common as in urban areas (Bringa 1995; Sivric 1982). While the older generation of *Klotivljani* (people of Klotjevac) married exclusively within their own ethnic and religious group, the post Second World War generation often intermarried with other groups. Although the majority of marriages still remained predominantly Bosniak-to-Bosniak, there were Croats, Serbs, Albanians and Germans married to the locals of Klotjevac. Most of those living in ethnically mixed marriages were professionals and intellectuals who kept Klotjevac as their second place of residency while spending most of the year where they worked. As Klotjevac did not offer many employment opportunities, jobs were found in nearby industrial towns on both sides of the Drina – in Srebrenica, Bratunac, Višegrad, Bajina Bašta and Užice – as well as in more distant places like Belgrade and Sarajevo. Further afield jobs were to be found as 'guest workers' in Austria and Germany, where dozens of locals went to work. Many people from the village, men and women, completed tertiary studies and filled influential positions as doctors, company directors, teachers and politicians in the Srebrenica municipality and in different parts of Bosnia.[13]

Beliefs and Rituals

The easy integration of outsiders should come as no surprise. Religious syncretism involving retention of pre-Christian pagan as well as Christian beliefs and practices were characteristic of the inclusive tradition of Podrinje's Muslims, with many examples of hybrid cultural practices involving a combination of Islamic prayers and pre-Islamic customs (Halilovich 2008). One communal ritual performed by locals from Klotjevac during long periods of drought when rain was needed to save the crops and prevent famine included chanting Islamic *dovas* (prayers) and watering the pre-Islamic stone tombs (*stećci*) of the ancestors *Dobri Bošnjani* (Good Bosniaks), with mothers encouraged to bring their babies and let them cry during the ritual.[14] Another Klotjevac tradition combining pre-Islamic ancestral and Christian beliefs with Islamic practices was the making of special bread with walnuts to honour the earth before planting wheat. The inclusion of both pre-Christian beliefs and Christianity in the local rituals and practices of Muslims in Klotjevac was evident in the many folk and saint days named *godovi*, where particularised forms of local interpretation and meaning were acknowledged and celebrated within an overarching regional epistemological framework, or what Geertz (1973) called 'internal conversion'. Thus, religious syncretism, as practised in Klotjevac, was 'not to determine ... a fixed meaning, but one which [had] been historically constituted and reconstituted' (Shaw and Stewart 1994: 6). For instance, on certain days of the year no works, including digging soil or dirtying water, were performed. Holidays like *Vodena Marija* (The Holy Mary of Water) and *Vatrena Marija* (The Holy Mary of Fire) were observed literally as holy days by the predominantly Muslim population. On the second day of August the villagers of Klotjevac would pay particular respect to St. Elijah. St. Elijah's day, called *Ilin-dan*, or *Ali-džun* in the Turkish version adopted by the Muslims, was also an important pre-Christian and pre-Islamic seasonal marker traditionally celebrated as midsummer. Thus St. Elijah's day was observed with fear and respect as St. Elijah was believed to be the master of summer storms, hail, rain and thunder. No fieldwork was carried out on the day, children were kept from the river, and particular care was paid to taking shelter from lightning if there was summer rain on the day. In case of hail or thunder a man would call *ezan* (the Islamic call for prayers), praying for divine intervention.

In disparate diaspora communities around the world today many former villagers still recall that on at least two occasions people were killed by lightning strikes, once in 1975 and again in 1989. Such accidents only reinforced half-dormant traditional beliefs about the importance of the strict observance of St. Elijah's day. Orthodox Serbs in the area may have regarded *Sveti Ilija* (St. Elijah) as exclusively theirs, but St. Elijah as celebrated by the Muslims of Klotjevac was a hybrid of Christian and pagan mythology adapted to the local interpretation of the Islamic faith.[15]

So it was with other seasonal holidays. On the sixth day of May villagers celebrated *Đurđevdan* or *Jurievo* (St. George's Day) to announce the coming of warmer days after a long winter. Đurđevdan was also celebrated by Serbs and Gypsies in the region, though as their own separate holiday. Muslims of Klotjevac would venture out early on Đurđevdan to collect fresh water from a water mill, with which, using branches and leaves of a young willow tree, parents would bless their sleeping children by spraying them with the water. Later in the day a collective celebration in the form of a folk festival would be organised with other villages in the area.

Muslims of Klotjevac also acknowledged Christmas (*bozuk*) and Good Friday (*veliki petak*). On Good Friday Easter eggs would be coloured and exchanged between the children. On Christmas Day children would go from house to house greeting the hosts with '*Rodila ti pšenica bjelica*' ('May your fields yield a lot of wheat'), after which they would receive presents – usually cakes, biscuits, smoked beef and (if the child were the first visitor to call) money – from every house they visited. They would put the collected presents in their bags and continue going from house to house until each child had visited every house in the village – a powerful means of reinforcing a child's developing identification as *Klotivljani*.

While such folk customs (*narodni običaji*) were taken seriously and marked accordingly by the Muslims of Klotjevac and surrounding villages, they were not necessarily interpreted as strictly religious events nor acknowledged at the local mosque – which had its own repertoire of religious festivities. Throughout the year religious celebrations known as mevluds would be organised at the mosque, when all villagers – men, women and children – would gather on the locally handmade woollen carpets covering the wooden floor. In the first rows the men would be seated, then the women and then the children, usually on the balcony overlooking the main prayer room. After reciting and singing religious hymns, sweet lemonade called *šerbe* was served and members of the community would engage in chatting and socialising.

More important Islamic religious holidays, the two *Bajrams*, were celebrated very much in the fashion that Christmas was celebrated in traditionally Christian countries. Each *Bajram*, one at the end of the month of Ramadan and the other two months later, lasted for three days. An unwritten rule, not always rigidly observed, reserved the first day of *Bajram* for men, the second for women and the third for children. During the three days friends and relatives exchanged visits, after which the visiting of neighbours for coffee drinking and sweets continued for many weeks. Women prepared *Bajram* cakes, mainly baklava, children received presents (*bajramluci*), and both adults and children wore their most festive garments (*bajramsko odijelo*). A public celebration – with music, food, drinks and sporting competitions, such as a soccer tournament, running and, in former days, horse racing – was organised at a central location, close to as many other villages as possible. A couple of thousand people of all ages would engage in dancing the traditional *kolo*. This tradition, even though it was changed and modernised, was kept until the war, the last being held in 1992 at Karačića Brdo, some seven kilometres from Klotjevac.

For villagers, *Bajram*, *Đurđevdan* and similar festivities sustained their sense of village and regional identity. For young people they provided an opportunity to meet with potential girlfriends and boyfriends. Occasionally, a young bride would 'run away' with her lover and start living with him at his home. Through a number of cultural rituals and intermediaries involved in negotiations between the two affected families, this act would be recognised as a marriage and the two families would become *prijatelji* (friends/affined).[16] In this way ostensibly religious occasions like *Bajram* continued to serve an important social function in places like Klotjevac, even while other aspects of society became increasingly secularised.

In line with its long history of cultural inclusion, modern secular holidays like New Year's Eve, May Day (1 May) and other commemorations promoted by the state and the ruling Communist League were embraced by Klotjevac and other Podrinje villagers and incorporated into their ever expanding cultural mosaic. There were always enough days in the year to accommodate all the different holidays, and no one in the village saw any problem in celebrating traditional, religious, secular and the state-promoted occasions, even though they might have not believed or understood what each holiday signified.

In response to this situation, from the mid 1980s the central Islamic authority *Rijaset* in Sarajevo started sending young students studying *medresa* (Islamic school for *imams*[17]) to Klotjevac during the month of Ramadan. They led prayers and gave regular sermons at the local mosque, attempting to convince the locals that many of their cultural practices were un-Islamic and as such should be abandoned. However, the success of the enthusiastic imams in influencing the cultural rituals observed in Klotjevac was questionable – the villagers simply added a couple of new holidays, such as Islamic New Year and the birthday of Prophet Mohammed, into their calendars.

Taboos

The same cultural and religious mix extended to the taboos relating to nature that were observed and interpreted as sin, bad deed, or *grehota*. The unnecessary harming of any animal or plant was seen to be a very bad deed that God would punish. On the other hand, God would bless those who planted fruit trees, built wells and roads and were kind to both humans and animals. The most dangerous creatures like snakes and bears had a special place in local myths and taboos: snakes were believed to have magical powers, while the bear was feared and respected as an animal close to humans. There were special rituals against snake bites, bad spirits, psychological trauma and the evil eye, which only a limited number of women trained in folk magic and traditional healing methods could perform.

Taboos reflected centuries of local knowledge and played an important role not only in maintaining social order but even in ensuring, it might be argued, a healthy genetic pool through the generations. Klotjevac villagers were very strict in observing 'the nine generation taboo' (*princip devetog koljena*) by which blood relations from both maternal and paternal sides who could be traced as in some way related to each other within nine generations were treated as *rodbina* (family), with any intermarriage between members of *rodbina* strictly prohibited. If the taboo were broken it was believed that this would bring misfortune for the next nine generations of the family.

Similar to other places, such beliefs formed a large part of the traditional stories and fairy tales passed from generation to generation in Podrinje. They included motifs and supernatural beings of both Slavic and Oriental tradition: *vile* (nymphs), *džini* (genies) and *aždahe* (dragons). Although acknowledged as fairy tales, people would nonetheless talk respectfully about them and give them credit for good or bad happenings. For some *Klotivljani* there was no denying their existence: it was believed that nymphs lived in forests and clouds, genies were masters of the dark, while dragons were monsters living in the river Drina.

In Šljivovica Veritas

Grafted onto the rootstock of traditional beliefs and ancient rituals, Islam blossomed as a vibrant component of Klotjevac's collective cultural identity. The village was famed for its mosque, which was visited every Friday by most men from the village itself and many from the nearby hamlets of Prohići, Urisići, Sejdinovići and Ljeskovik. Attending the prayers once a week was an important community event for the local men, who would exchange news, negotiate a business deal or just socialise with fellow villagers and visitors from surrounding settlements. It was not unusual for men from Klotjevac to invite their friends home after the Friday prayer and offer them their best homemade *rakija šljivovica* (*slivovitz*, plum brandy). Although it was known that Islam does not officially allow alcohol consumption, many Muslims from Podrinje (as in other parts of Bosnia and Herzegovina) never abandoned the tradition of making good *šljivovica* and drinking socially. A good practical reason for maintaining this tradition was the fact that Klotjevac had always been known for its orchards, with plums being the most common fruit tree in the village. Plums were used to make a variety of jams, but there was always a surplus for *šljivovica*. Other sweet fruits like pears and mulberries were also used for making the alcoholic beverages *kruška* and *dudovača*. Each house in the village boasted its own homemade liquor, which traditionally had been used not just for imbibing but also as a disinfectant and universal medicine for a range of health problems from colds to rheumatism and arthritis. The remedy was applied internally or externally, depending on the patient and his/her condition. However, most of the supply was used for socialising with friends and for festivities such as weddings, the birth of a child, farewells – or for any other good reason! The importance of such activities is suggested in a number of special words in Bosnian describing social occasions involving alcohol: *šamlučenje, šenlučenje, merakluk, akšamluk* and *bekrijanje*. Such social activities were not just for getting drunk, but were as important to Bosnians culturally as the fiesta is to Italians. *Šljivovica* was always accompanied by a good *meza*, a tasty food, usually a meat dish such as *čevapčići* (small barbecued minced meat sausages), *sudžuk* (smoked beef sausage), *janjetina* (roast lamb) or smoked beef. A commonly heard excuse by nominal Muslims consuming alcohol was: 'Sin is not what goes into your mouth, but what comes out of it'. There was an exception to this, which most Muslims in Podrinje strictly observed: they stopped drinking alcohol during the month of Ramadan – which is not to say that they necessarily fasted as well. But at the end of Ramadan, most locals from Klotjevac would return to their usual way of celebrating and socialising, which invariably featured the distilled essence of local plums.

Human Geography of the Place

Before it was eradicated from the map as a populated settlement, Klotjevac was well known for its natural beauty and its wind – the *Sopur*, a fresh breeze from the Drina canyon. In summer hundreds of tourists flocked to Klotjevac and its surrounding areas to enjoy swimming and fishing in the clear, deep waters of the lake, created in the mid 1960s after the dam was built for the hydroelectric power plant seven kilometres downstream at Perućac-Studenac. At the time of its construction the dam was one of the largest projects in the rapidly industrialising post Second World War Socialist Yugoslavia. Ninety metres tall and 460 metres wide, the dam symbolised the 'brotherhood and unity between peoples of Bosnia and Serbia' – at least this is what comrade Tito had said at the official opening ceremony of the power plant 'HE Bajina Bašta' on 27 November 1966 (Milivojević 1966, cited in Salimović 2002).[18] While the dam was seen by many young people in Klotjevac as a sign of progress and better times to come, older villagers were upset about their ancestral land being flooded by the newly constructed lake. Some of the most fertile agricultural land along the river Drina was lost forever, the green fields replaced by an emerald-green lake, which gradually turned Klotjevac into an attractive tourist destination.

The lake is 56 kilometres long, with a width ranging from about a kilometre near the dam to less than 40 metres in its upper part, closer to Višegrad. Reaching 90 metres in depth, the lake forms part of the Drina canyon, which is the third deepest in the world after the Colorado in the U.S.A. and the Tara in Montenegro. As acknowledged on the official tourist website of neighbouring Serbia, its most beautiful part is *Klotjevačka klisura*, the 24-kilometre section between Klotjevac and Žepa.[19] The lake transformed Klotjevac into a flourishing beach resort during the warm months of the year. Speed boats, water skiing, sailing and tourist ships were frequent features of Klotjevac in the summer. Across from Klotjevac on the Serbian side, students from the University of Belgrade regularly camped on the lake's shore. Attracting hundreds of students, at the end of the summer season they would organise an event for the locals from Klotjevac and other villages on the Bosnian side, forging enduring friendships between visiting students and resident locals. It was a local man from Klotjevac, Atif, who looked after the camp facilities during the dormant winter months.

Many tourists used the two commercial ships and smaller boats to enjoy the breathtaking Drina canyon and to visit the famous bridge over the Drina in Višegrad, famously described by Nobel Prize winning writer Ivo Andrić. The wide variety of fish in the lake attracted anglers from all over Yugoslavia, who, together with the tourists from Austria, Germany and further afield were welcomed as friendly (and income-generating) visitors. Regional, ethnic or religious background was irrelevant. Some regular better-off visitors from Bosnian cities like Srebrenica, Bratunac and Sarajevo as well as Serbs from inner Serbia, including Belgrade, bought land from the locals and built holiday houses, *vikendica,* around Klotjevac. New friendships were made and new connections established as typically Orthodox Serbian names like Dragan, Zoran and Žiko were added to the register of local residents – albeit if only for a few weeks each summer.

Annihilation of a Community

Neither the recent integration of Serbian holiday-makers as local landowners nor Klotjevac's long history of cultural inclusion and secularism spared it from being branded a 'dangerous Muslim fundamentalist stronghold' by Serbian propaganda in the early 1990s. On the other hand, the emerging Bosnian (or more precisely Bosniak) nationalism at the time saw the border region of Podrinje and the local communities along the river Drina (like Klotjevac) as the heartland of Bosnia and Bosnian statehood (cf. Imamović 1997; Ibrahimagić 2003). Similar nationalist appropriation of local, apparently marginal communities has been described by Michael Herzfeld (1985) in his ethnographic study of the Cretan mountain village of Glendi. Referring to such communities, Herzfeld (1985: 8) notes that 'often, their location at the territorial edges of the country is sufficient reason to insist on their typicality in defiance of counterclaims from across the border'. In Podrinje and Klotjevac, the counterclaims from across the border – from the other side of the Drina, from Serbia – came, in the form of propaganda and calls for the 'liberation' of Klotjevac, as early as 1990 (Mašić 1999). Then – as the survivors from Klotjevac recall – without any official announcement of hostilities, one day in May 1992 heavy artillery located on Mount Tara in Serbia started shelling their village and the surrounding hamlets. Apart from the holiday houses owned by absent Serbians, not a single house was spared. As in the Second World War the local population of Klotjevac sought safety in and around the ruins of the old Klotjevac fortress *Stari Grad* and its surrounding caves. As in the past war[20] they hoped that the trouble would pass in a couple of weeks and they would somehow reach a truce with their neighbours from the other side of the river. But this time, with no armed force to bargain for peace, the old common-sense argument, 'Don't attack us and we won't attack you', did not count. The couple of hunting rifles in the hands of Klotjevac residents were no match for the heavy guns aimed at them from distant Tara, and the Serbian side did not even try to negotiate.

The first victim of the artillery pounding was 12-year-old Sabera, who was mortally wounded by shrapnel from a shell that destroyed her family's house – where she died after two hours in the cellar cum makeshift bomb shelter. The next victim, father of four Nasko, was cut to pieces by a shell that scored a direct hit on his recently completed family home. After this the residents of Klotjevac started leaving their damaged houses early in the morning, before the shelling commenced, and sought refuge deep in the forest, using natural barriers as protection. After long-distance artillery had partially or completely destroyed most of the houses, the invisible enemy on the Serbian side advanced right to the lake's edge, where, hidden in the thick forest of Tara, they started using sniper fire to kill anything moving on the Bosnian side. Sniper fire took the lives of five more people of Klotjevac: Esed, Husein, Eso, Ramiz and Fićo. By the end of 1992 twelve Klotjevac residents, a significant proportion of the village's population, had been killed by shells and sniper fire from Serbia. The loss of life was just as devastating in the nearby hamlets of Prohići, Urisići and Sejdinovići.

Late May and early June 1992 were marked by refugees fleeing into Klotjevac from cities and villages that were under attack from the Serb military and paramilitary forces, commonly referred to as 'Chetniks', the most radical Serb militants. The largest number of refugees was from the town of Višegrad and the Skelani region. They brought with them horrific stories of atrocities committed by Chetniks. They had witnessed the slaughter of family, neighbours and friends on the famous bridge over the Drina and their unceremonious dumping into the river, like rubbish (Bećirević 2009; Sudetic 1998). Within days the first bodies from the mass killings in Višegrad were being fished out from the lake in Klotjevac. Most were young women and men. Some had body parts missing: a number of men had two fingers chopped off, as a grotesque reminder of the three-finger Chetnik salute resurrected by Serb nationalists in the early 1990s. During the coming weeks and months many more violated bodies were washed ashore in Klotjevac, Prohići and Sejdinovići. By the end of 1992 more than eighty bodies had been retrieved from the lake and buried in single and mass graves in the villages. Many more were collected upstream at Žepa, where some 300 bodies of the victims from Višegrad were buried (Kurtić 2006). An unknown number of bodies floated closer to the Serbian side of the lake, where no one dared to collect them. Many were destroyed by the turbines of the hydroelectric plant in Perućac and disappeared in the lake's deep waters (Šaponjić 2001). The exact number will never be known.[21] According to those investigating the mass graves and counting the bodies in Bosnia after the war, the Drina and its three lakes may be the largest mass grave of Bosniak victims of the 1992–95 reign of murder in eastern Bosnia.

The Chetnik atrocities in Podrinje were a re-enactment of the depraved methods of Draža Mihailović's Chetniks in the same region during the Second World War, when hundreds of Bosniaks had been ritually slaughtered on the bridge over the Drina (Dedijer and Miletić 1990: 591–2). Older Klotjevac villagers could remember how the Drina then had carried the bodies of victims from Foča, Goražde, Rogatica and Višegrad. At the local cemetery were many graves of these unknown victims, rendered invisible by the communist regime's suppression of the truth about Chetnik wartime atrocities in eastern Bosnia (Imamović 1997: 549–50; Redžić 1998: 115–286), and only officially remembered for the first time after the disintegration of the Communist League and the reintroduction of a multi-party system in the former Yugoslav states.[22]

By the summer of 1992 Klotjevac and most of the Srebrenica region, representing the largest area of territory under Bosnian government control, was completely cut off from the rest of the country and the outside world. As the year progressed, the free Bosnian territory in the east of the country started to shrink rapidly in the face of a massive offensive by the Serbian army involving three military corps based in Čačak, Užice and Novi Sad, in Serbia (Čekić 2005).

The offensive's modus operandi was as simple as it was brutal. As Edina Bećirević (2009) describes in her book *Genocide over Drina*, after each Bosniak house in the villages on the Bosnian side of the Drina had suffered multiple shellings, Serb tanks and infantry would cross the Bajina Bašta-Skelani bridge to complete the final phase of the ethnic cleansing by killing and expelling the remaining inhabitants, plundering and carting away on trucks anything of value – in the end physically occupying the Bosnian territory and declaring it part of Republika Srpska (Serb Republic). Halid and Omer remember how many people from the villages that first came under attack (Dobrak, Peći, Poljak, Studenac, Paljevine, Đurđevac …) escaped to Klotjevac, where the couple of hunting rifles incredibly delayed the Serb militants entering the village. But the Serbs occupied the hamlet of Prohići just one kilometre from Klotjevac, whence they continued shelling the village, forcing the inhabitants and refugees of Klotjevac to flee the village by the end of the year and seek safer refuge in the city of Srebrenica.

Once Klotjevac was emptied of its inhabitants, the Chetniks finally entered the village, burning houses and destroying everything they came across. The pillage already seen elsewhere in Podrinje was repeated in Klotjevac. Before leaving the village they mined the whole area and put booby traps next to the ruins of houses, and thereafter regularly sent heavily armed patrols to the area to ambush and kill the desperate, hungry people coming from distant Srebrenica to look for food in this once prosperous village. Many returnees and starving refugees were thus killed or maimed by Chetnik landmines. Halid – throughout the war a frequent returnee to his burned down village – survived all the booby traps, landmines and ambushes, but many of his neighbours and relatives did not. The victims were buried where they died or where they were found by those coming to search for them. In the end all that was left of Klotjevac were the ruins of houses, the old fortress, and countless old and new graves, many containing the remains of unnamed victims fished out of the lake. Every day more bodies would float by, but increasingly there was no one to retrieve them and improvise a burial. The turbines of the hydroelectric plant at Perućac completed the destruction, ensuring that the victims would forever remain uncounted and unaccounted for.

The '(UN)Safe Area' Srebrenica

In the following two and a half years survivors from Klotjevac were one of many refugee groups who sought shelter in Srebrenica. The ancient Bosnian town was swollen with refugees from villages and towns across Podrinje under attack or occupied by the Serb military. With its pre-war population of 6,000 swollen to more than 40,000, it had neither the resources nor the infrastructure to cope with the population influx (Sudetic 1998). Besieged and subject to constant artillery attacks by the Serb military, and with an acute shortage of food and medicine, the plight of the people of Srebrenica prompted the UN to declare it one of its first safe havens under UN protection. The town was demilitarised, which in reality meant that the defenders had to hand in the few weapons they had to the Canadian UN battalion, with no such condition applying to the Serbs besieging Srebrenica.[23] On the contrary, encouraged by the UN's lack of commitment to confront them, the Serb troops consolidated their positions and moved deeper into the demilitarised enclave of Srebrenica (Nuhanović 2005, 2007; Suljagić 2005).

The humanitarian and security situation in Srebrenica only worsened day by day. In early July 1995, by which time the Canadian soldiers had been replaced by Dutch, the Serb military under the direct command of the notorious General Mladić[24] launched a sudden all-out offensive against the enclave, which was quickly overrun by his soldiers (Honig and Both 1997). The poorly armed defenders, disorganised and expecting the promised protection from the UN and NATO, left their positions and either went to the UN military base at Potočari or set out on foot for Tuzla, 100 kilometres west of Srebrenica and still under Bosnian Army control (Honig and Both 1997). Under constant attack from the Serb military and subject to ambush every few hundred metres, only a few hundred of the thousands who attempted the epic journey ever reached their destination. Many were massacred en route (Rieff 1995). Thousands more were surrounded and captured, only to be systematically killed in the mass killings that took place in the days between 11 and 20 July 1995 (see United Nations 1999).

Encouraged by the total lack of resistance from the Dutch battalion, the Serb military had by 11 July encircled the UN base at Potočari, where tens of thousands of people from Srebrenica had taken refuge. In the following three days the Serb military and police committed hideous atrocities, brutalising, killing and raping refugees selected from the crowd (Nuhanović 2005). Rabija Džanić remembers how her husband Atif – the janitor who even during the war was looking after the students' camping site in Serbia across the lake from Klotjevac – showed his captors a phone book with names and addresses of influential Serb friends and university professors in Belgrade, hoping that this would help. But Atif was taken away with thousands of others, never to be seen again. Klotjevac and the surrounding hamlets of Prohići, Urisići, Karačići, Sejdinovići and Ljeskovik lost some 300 men, or a third of their population, in these massacres. Those killed ranged in age from boys as young as thirteen to the elderly in their seventies.

Recognising Genocide

From the beginning of the war and the first cases of ethnic cleansing in BiH, many informed commentators recognised and named the systematic killings, expulsion, torture and rape of the non-Serb civilians by Serb militias as 'genocide' or 'genocide-like'.[25] When he defined the ultimate crime against humanity, Raphaël Lemkin (2002) observed that:

> genocide does not necessarily mean the immediate destruction of a nation, except when accomplished by mass killings of all members of a nation. It is intended rather to signify a coordinated plan of different actions aiming at the destruction of essential foundations of the life of national groups, with the aim of annihilating the groups themselves. The objective of such a plan would be disintegration of the political and social institutions, of culture, language, national feelings, religion, and the economic existence of national groups, and the destruction of the personal security, liberty, health, dignity, and even the lives of the individuals belonging to such groups.

During the war in Bosnia and in its aftermath a number of cases against those involved in war crimes in BiH were brought before the International Criminal Tribunal for the former Yugoslavia (ICTY). Many perpetrators were convicted of various degrees of war crimes, while those who cooperated with the ICTY had their initial charges and sentences reduced.[26] In 2001 Serb General Radislav Krstić was convicted of the crime of genocide against the Bosniak population of Srebrenica. It was this conviction which proved – or perhaps it is better to say confirmed – that not only were the mass killings in and around Srebrenica in July 1995 an act of genocide as defined by Lemkin, but they were also the greatest act of genocide committed on European soil since the Holocaust (Nettelfield 2010; Rohde 1997, 1998; Power 2002). The evidence before the ICTY[27] revealed that this was a systematically planned operation which implicated not only the Serb military, but also the political leadership and the bureaucracy of Republika Srpska (Bećirević 2009; Nettelfield 2010; Wagner 2008).

Serb ultra-nationalists and a number of so-called 'Leftist revisionists' continue to dispute and deny that the genocide occurred, seeing instead a Western imperialist conspiracy against the erstwhile Serbian leader Milošević, 'the last true Communist leader in eastern Europe'.[28] To support their denial they point to the existence of survivors and the 'fact' that *only* men and boys were killed at Srebrenica. In fact, of the 8,372 killed at Srebrenica in July 1995 close to 500 were women and 1,040 were teenage boys.[29]

The deaths were the logical extension of the policy of ethnic cleansing, which included the physical extermination of a critical number of people in order to bring a lasting effect on the population of a targeted area. When it comes to Klotjevac, Srebrenica and the Podrinje region, the policy was very successful. Before the war Podrinje was populated mainly by Bosniaks, who formed the majority of the population in all fifteen major towns along the river Drina.[30] During the war the whole region was ethnically cleansed of non-Serbs, an essential precondition of being incorporated into the Serb Republic. All but one town (Goražde) was ethnically cleansed of non-Serb inhabitants.

Many of the region's Bosniak families have lost all their male relatives. There are extended families without a single surviving male. As further discussed in the final part of the book, the genocide has had a lasting effect on gender imbalance among the survivors: an average family from Srebrenica today has been reduced to a widowed mother with children born before or during the war. Almost every family has lost someone close. Taking into consideration the region's patriarchal tradition and the fact that most men were the family breadwinner, one can begin to grasp the social, psychological and economic enormity of the killings at Srebrenica. The population of the Podrinje region was not only decimated – its demographic structure was completely changed and its survivors permanently displaced (Kulenović and Suljić 2006).

Although many still remain in Bosnia as internally displaced persons (IDPs) or have settled in the part of the country called the Bosniak-Croat Federation, mainly in and around Sarajevo and Tuzla, thousands of the displaced survivors have been dispersed across the globe. Omer's father was one of the few lucky ones who owned a second house in what is now the Serb stronghold of Bratunac, near Srebrenica. Eight years after the war he managed to get the house back and exchange it with a Serb who had abandoned his house in Hadžići, near Sarajevo. The Serb family from Hadžići became the new residents of Bratunac and Omer and his parents became the new Hadžići residents. This kind of 'population exchange' has become something of a demographic trend – with Bosniaks and Croats ethnically cleansed from their home towns during the war exchanging their houses (if they still existed) with Serbs who felt obliged or more comfortable to live in Serb-dominated Republika Srpska. The result has been an ethnic homogenisation, with most of the towns across Bosnia now having less than 10 per cent of members of another ethnic group (Helsinki Committee for Human Rights 2005). In fact, only two municipalities in post-war BiH (Tuzla and Sarajevo Centar) have more than 10 per cent belonging to other ethnic groups, compared with the pre-war multi-ethnic composition of the country when 80 per cent of the municipalities did not have an absolute ethnic minority (Helsinki Committee for Human Rights 2006).

Many displaced people have abandoned any dream of ever returning to their destroyed homes. The first generation, which suffered the greatest losses, has neither the time nor the emotional strength to return to devastated homes and re-establish communities. The second generation, those who were too young or unborn at the time of the atrocities, have found new, safer places under the sun – ranging from places within BiH where they make an ethnic majority to the polar region of Scandinavia to the faraway suburbs of Melbourne or St. Louis. But regardless of the physical distance from the place that once was home, many survivors remain connected to their individual and collective tragedies on a daily basis. Visiting homes of displaced Klotjevac villagers in Sarajevo or Tuzla, Berlin or Malmo, Melbourne or St. Louis, reveals a common picture. Surrounded by photos of missing fathers, husbands, sons and brothers, the conversation invariably turns to the problem of the missing, to the mass graves and identification of recently recovered human remains. In her rented suburban home in Melbourne, Ramiza, a mother of three young children, feels closer to something approximating 'closure' – a hopelessly inadequate word in the circumstances – since her father and a younger brother were identified and their remains put to rest at Potočari in 2005. Her older brother and both her husband's brothers and a nephew remain missing. Together with all the others yet to be accounted for and finally laid to rest, they continue to haunt the survivors, for whom genocide is not a matter of definition or court conviction, but part of the continuing experience and reality lived.

Back to the Present

Twelve years after being forced to abandon it, the survivors of only eight families have returned to Klotjevac. Of the eight, members of just four families remain living in the village on a more or less permanent basis. Others went to places in the Federation around Tuzla and Sarajevo; some tried to join their neighbours and relatives overseas. The village has lost forever not only the vast majority of its inhabitants, but also the central role it had maintained throughout its long history in the everyday lives of ordinary people. Without such people the story of Klotjevac risks becoming a forgotten history.

The recent displacement has not been the result of physical coercion so much as the absence of social contacts, infrastructure, schools and other institutional supports to overcome the profound sense of alienation in a Serbianised system where everything has been done to remind Bosniaks of their non-belonging to the Republika Srpska (cf. Pettigrew and Pettigrew 2009; Dahlman 2004; Dahlman and Ó Tuathail 2005a, 2005b). As Klotjevac was forcibly incorporated into what is now Republika Srpska (RS), its long existence and importance have been purposely ignored by the official administration of RS. Klotjevac is mentioned in only a couple of official RS documents. One states that Klotjevac is a part of the Serb Forests of the Serb Republic (*Srpske Šume Republike Srpske*).[31] There is no mention of the people who lived there for centuries. The few returnees to Klotjevac were bitterly reminded of their non-existence in the summer of 2004 when an official sign was erected at the entrance of the village, just a couple of metres from the few rebuilt houses, proclaiming 'Klotjevac Hunting Zone' (*Lovište Klotjevac*). The crude landmark signified the official transformation of Klotjevac from a human settlement to an area inhabited by wild animals that could be shot. It delivered an implicit but unambiguous message to the eight families who had returned to Klotjevac: that they were not recognised as human beings and would remain the unwanted, and (even worse) the hunted – calling to mind the manhunts carried out by Serb troops ten years before. It took six weeks before the SFOR (Stabilisation Forces) troops that occasionally patrol the Drina valley removed the sign.

The intimidation has not deterred Dule Mešanović, a fifty-year-old man who was the first to return to Klotjevac. He is there to stay. Other families have joined him over the last five years, and more than ten houses have been rebuilt. Dule lost both his brothers and his father at Srebrenica. Between 1995 and 2001 he lived as an IDP in a village near Tuzla and while others decided to look for a safer place to make a new start Dule opted to return to the village of his birth and his history. His wife and his younger son and daughter-in-law followed. 'It was very hard at the beginning and it still is,' he says, 'but this is the only place where I feel at home. I was born here and my forefathers were born, lived and are buried here. There is no way I could ever abandon this place.' In June 2006 the first baby since 1992 was born in Klotjevac, and Dule became a grandfather to a baby girl. None of those who returned – mainly widows and the elderly who did not have another place to stay – have school-age children, which is just as well as there is neither public transport nor a school available in the area. Before the war Klotjevac had its own primary school up to Grade 5, after which children continued their primary education in Osat, a village six kilometres from Klotjevac. A school bus was provided and there were dozens of children from Klotjevac attending various grades at both schools. While delighted that his granddaughter is the first child of the post-war generation in Klotjevac, Dule is worried about her future.

For Dule, homecoming was 'not merely the physical journey to the familiar sociocultural habitat' – as Anders Stefansson (2004c: 69) puts it – especially as that socio-cultural habitat had largely vanished with the people who perished or were displaced. The 'aspects of rupture and alienation' Dule experienced upon his return have been 'paralleled by the comforts of homecoming and continuous attachment' to his local, intimate homeland or *zavičaj* (Stefansson 2004a: 69). With the return of Dule's family and their few fellow villagers, life in Klotjevac was to continue, albeit under radically changed social conditions, and in the permanent shadow of the memories – and ruins – of the past life.

Dule's decision to be the first to return and revive the village has earned him great respect and admiration among Klotjevac's displaced population. Every summer Dule welcomes many of them coming from distant places Dule himself had never heard of before. His older son, Halil, who lives in St. Louis, visited him last year for the first time. Dule has not seen one of his sisters-in-law – his younger brother's widow who settled with her three children in Adelaide – since they left the village in 1992. Two years after he permanently returned to Klotjevac, his other sister-in-law, also a widow, who lived as an IDP near Tuzla, joined him with her teenage son. Encouraged by Dule's extended family's return, more IDPs from Klotjevac – mostly widows with children and the elderly – have made the decision to return to the village.

Thanks to donations from the European Union the returnees have been able to rebuild their houses. Omer's seventy-year-old father Salih, who spends up to six months a year in Klotjevac, was one of the beneficiaries, receiving donated building material to erect a small dwelling on the ruins of his obliterated home. The newly built structure in the centre of the village is surrounded by the ruins of houses destroyed more than a decade ago. Omer, who rarely visits the village on his own, describes the feeling of being in the new house, surrounded by the rubble of houses of relatives, neighbours and friends, as like being in the company of ghosts. For this reason most other new houses have been built on the outskirts of the village, out of eyesight of Klotjevac's 'ground zero'. Three of the ten houses have been built close to the forest, some two kilometres from the lake, 'at a safe distance from Serbia' according to returnees. All the houses built with the help of donations look exactly the same, with two bedrooms and basic amenities, in sharp contrast to the architectural diversity for which the village was once famous. In contrast, Meho, Alija and Mirso have built three magnificent mansions overlooking the lake, on the ruins of their former homes. By rebuilding their houses they attempt to reverse the outcome of the 'house war', the concept described by Anders Stefansson (2004b: 2, 2006: 118), referring to a conflict in which the politics of house and home played a central role, instrumentally as well as ideologically, in causing mass flight and making irreversible the effects of ethnic cleansing.

Nonetheless, the rebuilt houses represent a symbolic more than a real homecoming for their owners – as Alija, Meho and Mirso and their families have turned their temporary refuge in Germany and Netherlands into a more permanent settlement and come only to visit the village about once a year for up to six weeks. Even then, some of their children who grew up in Hamburg, Berlin and Utrecht are reluctant to accompany them.

For Alija, who lost one of his sons and a son-in-law, the luxurious three storey mansion is designed to make a statement: 'I want to show them [the Chetniks] that we are back on our land and that we always can build bigger and more beautiful houses than those they burned down'. The Chetniks have long gone and, except for the student camp during summer, the area in Serbia across the river from Klotjevac remains unpopulated. However, the Chetniks continue as a powerful metaphor and image in the consciousness of many displaced villagers, many of whom generalise and use the term to refer to any Serb, including former friends and property owners with whom they lost all contact during the war. Some of them, the owners of the vikendicas, have returned and rebuilt their holiday houses. Dragan, a university professor from Belgrade, continues to spend at least three months a year at his rebuilt *vikendica* in Klotjevac, on the land he had bought from Alija before the war.

Today there is peaceful coexistence between the Bosniaks who returned and the Serb *vikendica* owners, who during the summer months with their numerous guests outnumber the locals. However, it would be an overstatement to say that the old friendships and the mutual trust have been, or ever will be, completely restored. Dragan's best friends from the village have been either killed or displaced: the family Salihović, with whom he had particularly good relations, lost all their male members at Srebrenica. Another friend of his, the student camp janitor Atif, had hoped that their association would help him survive Srebrenica. It did not. The ruins of Salihović's burned-down houses, the absence of Atif's house – which had been an important landmark in the part of the village called Babajići – and the ruins of many other houses, act as more than mere monuments to those who once inhabited them. The ruins keep the absence of their owners present in the everyday life of the returnees: each ruin is still referred to by its known, original name – Mujo's house, Hasib's house, Rešid's house, or the road junction at Šaban Lekić's house, ensuring that Mujo, Hasib, Rešid and Šaban continue to exist in the memories of the Klotjevac survivors who once shared with them life in the village.

While they lost trust in their old Serb friends, the returnees to Klotjevac have come to admire and be grateful to the many unknown benefactors from more distant countries such as Australia, Germany, Sweden, the U.S.A. and Malaysia, whom they might never meet but who have nonetheless sent them practical aid on more than one occasion. For instance, the German NGO 'Bauer helfen Bauern' (Farmers Helping Farmers) has donated cows and sheep to the families in Klotjevac. Other international

NGOs have provided them with seeds and agricultural tools. Having the largest family, Dule has been the biggest beneficiary. Over the years he has assembled a flock of more than 100 sheep, a couple of milk cows and a horse. In the first year he lost a number of sheep due to landmines left in the village by Serbian troops, even though the area had been 'cleaned' by SFOR. Because of displacement and depopulation, Dule's livestock has unprecedented access to vast grazing areas in the village. Before the war Dule was a truck driver; now he sees himself more as a farmer and he likes this 'professional re-orientation'. However, access to the nearby markets for Dule's sheep is very limited: he cannot export his sheep to neighbouring Serbia, across the Drina, nor do his 'Muslim sheep' have many buyers in Republika Srpska. In order to sell his sheep in the Bosniak-Croat Federation, he needs certified documents about the health status of each of the sheep. Even though he paid for the veterinary tests, it took up to two years for the RS authorities to issue the required papers. During the summer holidays the trustiest buyers of Dule's sheep have been his fellow *Klotivljani*, now coming from many places in diaspora, or other parts of BiH, to visit the village and spend their holidays there. Each summer dozens of Dule's sheep are turned into roast lamb consumed as a part of the festive reunions of the displaced *Klotivljani*.

Mapping Displacement

Geographically the displacement of the people from Klotjevac – like those from many other places in Bosnia – has been global, politically transnational and experientially trans-local in character. Displacement and disconnectedness with the place where one was born and raised, where one's family had been born and raised stretching back over centuries, undoubtedly impacts on one's sense of identity. But place is a cultural as well as geographical category, and as such is never fixed or static. Even for those who stay at home, who never venture beyond their village boundaries, the sense of place – and hence identity – is neither fixed nor static. Every individual draws from their particular experience of the tradition and history of the place with which they identify to make sense of who they are. In the village of Klotjevac identity had always been variegated, deepened and enfolded by the diversity of the experiences of the people who make up the community – including the more recently integrated Serb *vikendica* owners. This largely fits the conceptualisation of community that has established a degree of anthropological orthodoxy (Amit and Rapport 2002); community as a multi-vocal symbol (A.P. Cohen 1985) whose members commonly hold a sense that they share understanding of their group belonging, but who, in fact, attribute multiple meanings to the concept, often to the point of 'talking past one another' about what it is (Rapport 1993). This does not, however, adequately represent the reality of community in Klotjevac. While not a single monolithic entity that is fixed but rather 'envisaged as a project' – in the words of Homi Bhabha (1994: 4) – in the tablet of tradition, it can be properly conceived as multiple articulations and intensities bound together by common threads of experience rising above, on the one hand, any constitutive individual perspective and, on the other, other larger and salient forms of community in the Bosnian context such as ethnic or religious groups.

Only in this way is it possible for a collective Klotjevac identity to be both sufficiently specific to distinguish it from other, competing, identities (such as Podrinje, Bosnian or Yugoslav) and at the same time flexible enough to accommodate the adaptation and change that life necessarily entails. Adopting the ideas of Stuart Hall (1996, 2006), we might think of Klotjevac identity as always positioned in time and place, and permanently in pursuit of completion in a constantly changing set of circumstances. Not only *in* but also *against* changing circumstances, because, within the pursuit of the collective interests we call a shared identity, individuals will still aspire for their personal sense of wholeness, belonging and even emancipation from the constraints of the shared social setting.

The relationship between the local and the global in this process of identity negotiation has been explored by a number of writers, like Anthony Giddens (1991) who argues that modernity is inherently globalising and that globalisation is a consequence of the enlargement of modernity. For the first time in history, he suggests, 'self' and 'society' are interrelated by the disembedding mechanisms of modernity, which have displaced social structures from their traditional settings. The result for the individual is ontological insecurity and reflexive self-monitoring of identity as a continuing condition that applies throughout life. While the genocidal fragmentation and displacement in Klotjevac and surrounding areas was of an altogether different order of motivation, intensity and outcome from what Giddens was writing about, in the stoic perseverance of Dule Mešanović and the grandiose architectural statements of Meho, Alija and Mirso, one could claim that the reflexivity and self-conscious identity formation to which Giddens refers is now an integral part how the returnees determine who they are – and that, contrary to Giddens' suggestion, their ontological security has been maintained through reclaiming their local homeland (*zavičaj*).

In contrast to other forms of collective identities such as ethnicity or nation that are more 'imagined' than real, the village community of a place such as Klotjevac had an existential basis for group identity based on all members of the social group personally knowing each other and being interlinked in a complex web of meaningful social relations where principles of kinship, solidarity and reciprocity have been crucial for sustaining life over many hundreds of years (Halilovich and Adams 2011). More recently the 'real' community of Klotjevac village has become increasingly an imagined one as the one on the ground was literally destroyed. 'I'm from Klotjevac and that's where I feel I belong even if the place does not exist anymore', declared Omer, affirming his attachment to the place where he was born and had lived before the war. Other displaced survivors from the village have expressed similar sentiments.

Many, like Omer, who have found durable solutions by settling in other parts of Bosnia dominated by their ethnic group still refer to themselves as *Klotivljani*, and continue to feel displaced, uprooted and dispossessed within their official homeland. Such a feeling is shared, perhaps to a greater extent, by those displaced outside of Bosnia.

Wherever their location, identification as *Klotivljani* is more than a matter of subjective feeling. Identification is through public performance, such as the revival of traditional *moba* – a sharing of labour and communal solidarity – among the returnees to Klotjevac, as well as the almost ritualised pilgrimages of displaced *Klotivljani* each summer, which is increasingly turning into a sort of a festival similar to the *teferići* and *pilavi* (traditional folk celebrations) once celebrated in the village.

Due to the forced displacement Klotjevac has been deterritorialised and become a trans-local community, a concept that is further discussed in Chapter 4. In Sweden Fadil performatively enacts his trans-local identity through special chat rooms on the internet where he 'meets' and exchanges news with former neighbours now living in sixteen different countries, across three continents, using a distinct local dialect to 'perform' their identity as *Klotivljani*.[32] Through such means being *Klotivljani* is given social substance and expression, and traditions associated with a village that in physical terms has largely ceased to exist are kept alive. Through such practices *Klotivljani* signal to each other, to the wider world and, most importantly, to themselves, who they are, and what they have become and are in the process of becoming. Of course, like members of any other community, *Klotivljani* will employ essentialist arguments in support of their construction of identity and traditions – but in reality even the most essentialist claims and reified concepts exist only to the extent that they are brought to consciousness and expressed and constructed through performative enactment. Debates over whether this or that particular performance – this or that ritual, this or that use of a phrase, this or that social interaction – are true to tradition tend to invest tradition with a life of its own, and mask the fact that tradition (any tradition) represents and expresses human choices and actions. And if tradition ultimately represents and expresses human choices and actions, so too does the village of Klotjevac.

While the Drina and the physical landmarks of Klotjevac remain powerful images and themes in narrating home, it would be wrong to suggest that the only point of reference for identity of displaced residents of Klotjevac is to be found in the geographical location of the river and the village (or where it used to be). As Margaret Rodman (1992) argues, it is individuals, not just physical environment, that create place. Thus Klotjevac is being created, is being consciously and reflexively embraced, by individuals through cultural practices, embodied memory and social networks to be found not only at the intersection of 43.9864 latitude and 19.3442 longitude, but equally in the suburb of St. Albans in Melbourne, or Hadžići near Sarajevo, or Zagreb, or the provincial town of Styer in Upper Austria, or St. Louis, Hamburg, Utrecht ...

Conclusion

In July 2009 the displaced Klotjevac survivors, supported by the Friends of Klotjevac, unveiled the monument we were introduced to at the end of the introductory chapter. Carved from greenish granite, in the shape of Bosnia and Herzegovina, it is inscribed with the names of 108 relatives, friends and neighbours killed between 1992 and 1995. In the local context of Klotjevac the use of a symbol of Bosnia was not so much to express a statement of belonging to an imagined national community as it was to symbolically represent the borderlines (Podrinje) of which Klotjevac is a part. Of course, this symbol – the BiH geographic map – can also be read as incorporation of localism into nationalism. The monument was erected atop the village fountain, the heart of Klotjevac, where *Klotivljani* traditionally gathered and socialised. To attend the ceremony many survivors travelled long distances: from the U.S., Australia, Sweden, Denmark, Austria, Germany, Croatia, the U.K., and the Netherlands. With them were family members and children, many born far away from Klotjevac. With them also were new friends, including some of the students who had come all the way from Australia to participate in the event. There are still only a few new red roofs of rebuilt houses, only a handful of permanent returnees in the village. But as this chapter has shown, Klotjevac is more than buildings, and the gathering in July 2009 was the largest reunion of survivors and their friends since 1992. It was more than a return of the survivors. Through the act of inscribing the names of the dead in a memorial stone, the reunion of the survivors and the unveiling of the monument served also as a symbolic return to their village of the 108 *Klotivljani*, who continue to belong to the place even in death.

Postscript

In July 2010 the summer holiday-making of returning *Klotivljani* was cut abruptly short when some of the lake was drained to enable routine maintenance on the hydroelectric plant at Perućac – exposing the remains of 260 of the estimated 2,000 victims who had been murdered and thrown from the bridge at Višegrad in 1992, many of which were to end up lodged in the rocks downstream. Most will never be found – a bitter reminder in Klotjevac and neighbouring lakeside villages of the recent tragic past.

Notes

1. When referring to Serbs I would like to point to an important distinction I make between Serbs as ethno-national identity and Serb nationalists, who, like other nationalists, misappropriated the collective name of their ethnic compatriots as means for political and military ends. While many ordinary Serbs were manipulated and often forced to join the Serb nationalist project in BiH, many others actively opposed the politics of war crimes and genocide in their name. Some of them, like the Serb poet Vladimir Srebrov, were jailed and tortured by Karadžić's henchmen, others – among them many prominent personalities like General Jovan Divjak, Professor Mirko Pejanović and writer Marko Vešović – remained loyal to the Bosnian government in Sarajevo throughout the war. Thousands more fled the country refusing to fight on any side.
2. Radovan Karadžić, the war-time leader of SDS, was indicted at the Hague Tribunal (ICTY) for genocide, crimes against humanity, violations of the laws or customs of war and grave breaches of the Geneva Conventions. See ICTY Case Information Sheet (IT-95-5/18), Karadžić and Mladić, available at http://www.un.org/icty/glance/karadzic.htm.
3. Between 100,000 and 150,000 people died during the war in Bosnia-Herzegovina. In addition, at the end of the war there were between 30,000 and 35,000 missing – presumably killed – people, according to the International Commission on Missing Persons (2007). The Sarajevo-based Research and Documentation Centre has come up with close to 100,000 names and confirmed identities of those killed and missing. However, even this figure has been disputed by some (as being too low). While my book is not about the numbers and the body count, all the figures referenced in the book come from the documents of the Research and Documentation Centre, the International Commission on Missing Persons and the Missing Persons Institute as well as my interviews with the directors of these organisations, Mr Mirsad Tokača, Ms Kathryne Bomberger and Mr Amor Mašović.
4. This subtitle, 'When you forget July', is borrowed from a popular love song 'Kad zaboraviš juli' of the once cult Bosnian rock band Bijelo Dugme.
5. Chetniks (Četnici) was the name of the notorious Second World War Serb ultra-nationalist militia, subsequently used as the name for various Serb militias and the Serb military during the 1991–95 war in Croatia and Bosnia. For the role of Chetniks in Bosnia during the Second World War see Redžić (1998: 211–96).

6. In a detailed report 'Srebrenica: Ten Years On', Ed Vulliamy (2005) wrote down the story of Mevludin Orić, a survivor from Srebrenica: 'I was on the sixth truck with my nephew Haris. We huddled up, so that if we were going to a camp we could be together. They took us to a field, and when they stopped the trucks and said "Line up!" I knew what was coming. I could see bodies in the field. They were cocking their guns. I took Haris by the hand; he asked '"are they going to kill us?"; I said no, then they started shooting. Haris was hit; I was holding him, he took the bullet and we both fell. Nothing hit me; I just threw myself on the ground; my nephew shook, and died on top of me.'
7. See also ICTY Case Information Sheet – Drazen Erdemovic www.un.org/icty/glance/erdemovic.
8. The *stećci* (singular: *stećak*), the monumental medieval tombstones that lie scattered across the landscape of Bosnia and Herzegovina are the country's most legendary symbol. Appearing in the twelfth century, the *stećci* reached their peak in the late fourteenth and fifteenth centuries, before dying away during the Ottoman occupation. Their most remarkable feature is their decorative motifs, many of which remain enigmatic to this day (Bosnian Institute 2008).
9. *Splavarenje* refers to taking *splavi* – rafts made out of big logs – down the river. People from Klotjevac were famed for their skills and bravery in doing this dangerous work. In the past they would often cover hundreds of kilometres navigating rafts from the upper part of the Drina to the industrial towns in its lower parts where the logs were used for building and other industrial purposes. *Splavarenje* as a traditional trade died out after the Second World War when rapid industrialisation demanded the faster means of transportation by trucks, railway and ships.
10. Klotjevac is sometimes also written and pronounced as Klotijevac and Klotivac.
11. The Bosnian *Bogumils* or *Paterenes* (*Bogumili, Bogomili* or *Krstjani*) were members of the Bosnian Church, a version of early Christianity which was outside of both Orthodox and Catholic dogma. *Bogumils* were Gnostics and dualists, and opposed to the existence of an institutionalised church. Because of their beliefs, the Bosnian *Bogumils* were branded as heretics and were subject to persecution by the Catholic Church, which, between the twelfth and fifteenth centuries, sent many crusades and inquisitions to Bosnia. The *Bogumils* are sometimes even called 'the first European Protestants' (Brockett 1879). See also Jukić (1953), Hadžijahić (1975), Malcolm (1994) and I. Lovrenović (2001).
12. In an ethnography of Podrinje, Deroko (1939) provides a detailed description of the Klotjevac fortress and his observation of the village in the 1930s.
13. For instance, Daut Sulejmanović, born in Klotjevac, was one of the first engineers in Bosnia and Herzegovina, having graduated from the University of Belgrade in the 1930s.
14. An almost identical local custom was described by Zehrudin Isaković (2008) in the village of Jezero, in Herzegovina.
15. In other parts of Bosnia and the wide Balkan region St. Elijah was honoured not only by the Muslims and the Christian Orthodox, but also by the Catholics and the Jews, which is not surprising given that St. Elijah, also known as

St. Elias, is a prophet of the Old Testament on which Jewish, Christian and Islamic faiths are based ('a fiery chariot, and fiery horses parted them both asunder, and Elias went up by a whirlwind into heaven', Kings 2:11). However, according to official church calendars, St. Elijah's day is 20 July, not 2 August as celebrated by the villagers of Klotjevac.

16. The term *prijatelji*, which literally means friends, is used for families (in-laws) that become connected through marriage.
17. *Imam* is a term for a priest, an Islamic scholar and a religious leader.
18. Milivojević (1966) described how there were many people from Klotjevac working on the construction site of the dam between 1961 and 1966. One of them, Nazif Halilović, was awarded the Worker's Medal, a prestigious award in socialist Yugoslavia, for his enthusiasm and hard work. Special awards were also presented to two other workers from Klotjevac: Kadrija Halilović and Idriz Idrizović.
19. Žepa was another Bosnian enclave, a UN safe heaven, which was overrun by Serb military in July 1995. For more about the Drina canyon see Bajina Bašta Portal (2007).
20. In addition to the Četnik massacres of Muslim civilians, in Višegrad and Foča, which became emblematic of the Second World War in Podrinje, some of the fiercest battles between the Tito-led Partisans and the Četniks took place in the region on both sides of the river Drina – on Mount Zelengora in Bosnia, and around the town of Užice in Serbia. In these and many other skirmishes between the Partisans and the Četniks, the Partisans often prevailed, but due to the mountainous region and thick forests in the area the Četniks were able to regroup and launch counterattacks against both the Partisans and the civilian Muslim population. As a response many Bosnian Muslims in Podrinje joined the Partisans, while several Muslim paramilitary units joined the Axis powers to counter their own persecution by Četniks. Četniks continued to be active in Podrinje until 1946 when General Draža Mihailović, the Četnik leader, was finally captured near Višegrad (some 50 kilometres from Klotjevac) and sentenced to death by the Yugoslav court for war crimes. For more detailed historical accounts of the Second World War in BiH and Podrinje see Hoare (2007), Dedijer and Miletić (1990), Đilas (1996), Malcolm (1994) and Redžić (1998).
21. Although the Serbian media has avoided reporting on the floating bodies in the lake or used them to misrepresent their identity, 'Hydroelectric plant Perućac still without Investigators', a report on a refrigerated truck containing an unknown number of bodies being dumped into the lake near Klotjevac was published in the Serbian newspaper *Glas Javnosti*. The report quotes a number of eyewitnesses who saw massacred bodies floating in the lake and mentions those collected and buried by Klotjevac residents. See Šaponjić (2001).
22. See Dedijer and Miletić (1990). The first public commemoration of and the funeral ceremony for the Muslim (Bosniak) victims of the Chetniks' slaughter in eastern Bosnia during the Second World War was held in 1991.
23. Between 1993 and 1995 Hasan Nuhanović and Emir Suljagić, at the time university and secondary students respectively, were UNPROFOR's (the United

Nations Protection Force's) official interpreters in Srebrenica. They worked closely with the UN commanders, shared the hardship of their families and fellow refugees trapped in Srebrenica, and on a number of occasions acted as interpreters in meetings between the UN staff and Serbs in charge of besieging Srebrenica. When Srebrenica was finally taken over by the Serb military in July 1995 both Hasan and Emir survived thanks to their interpreter positions with UNPROFOR. However, their employers, the UN Dutch battalion, refused to offer any protection to their families. In fact, they handed them over directly to the Serb military. Since then all Hasan's family – mother, father and a younger brother – has disappeared. Emir's grandfather was to share the same fate as Hasan's family. Their books, *Under the UN Flag*, written by Hasan, and *Postcards from the Grave*, written by Emir, provide a unique insight into the life under siege in the UN safe area and the role of the UN in the Srebrenica tragedy.

24. After sixteen years on the run General Mladić, indicted by the ICTY for genocide, war crimes and crimes against humanity, was arrested in Serbia on 26 May 2011, and extradited to the Hague Tribunal where, at the time of finishing this book (January 2012) he has been tried for the crimes committed at Srebrenica and other places in BiH. See Halilovich (2011c, 2011d and 2012a).
25. Gutman (1993), Vulliamy (1994, 2005), Žižek (1994), Cigar (1995), Rieff (1995), Maass (1996), Sells (1996), Rohde (1997, 1998), Honig and Both (1997), G. Robertson (1999), Sudetic (1998), Neuffer (2001) and Power (2002).
26. ICTY website http://www.un.org/icty/cases-e/index-e.htm
27. ICTY: Krstic (IT-98-33) http://www.icty.org/x/cases/krstic/tjug/en/krs-tj010802e.pdf. See also Karon (2001).
28. Such views have been promoted by E. Herman (2005) and Johnstone (2003). A comprehensive response to those on the Left denying the Srebrenica genocide has been provided by Hoare (2003, 2005) and Lippman (2006). See also Žižek (1999).
29. Federal Commission for Missing Persons (2005) and Research and Documentation Centre (2007a, 2007b). See also Srebrenica Commission of Republika Srpska (2004).
30. Based on statistics from the 1991 Census of Population in Bosnia and Herzegovina, all the major towns in Podrinje had a Bosniak majority.
31. See *Službeni glasnik Republike Srpske*, volumes: 13/94, 10/97, 23/98 43/02.
32. There are some fifty to a hundred unique words used only by the people of Klotjevac – words like: *hripa* (rock), *rahtilo* (tools), *ćivtelija* (unlucky person), *vižo* (devil, bad spirit), *čestita* (wedding celebration), *omačić* (sour cream), *točilo* (creek), *kaja* (cow), *patoka* (weak *slivovitz*) and so on – while many other words used elsewhere in Bosnia and former Yugoslavia have completely different meanings, such as *kotar* (garden), *košara* (stable) and *kêva* (girl).

Chapter 2

Beyond the Sadness
Narratives of Displacement, Refuge and Homecomings among Bosnian Refugees in Austria

> Someone is always in the heart of something. In the heart of Europe, of Bosnia, of Prijedor. Someone is always in the heart of a concentration camp.
> Amir Kamber, *Constructing Kamber*, p. 81

We now move outside the borders of Bosnia-Herzegovina, to explore three individual stories of displacement of Bosnians in Austria: Sejo, Edita and Ibro – separate individuals with separate life stories, which intersect. The stories do not necessarily represent three typical Bosnian stories of flight, refuge and homecoming; nor is it possible to label any such story as typical, as each story of displacement is based on a unique individual experience, so that different individuals are differently affected. Nonetheless, these three narratives – presented in this chapter as one story, involving different actors – are very much emblematic of the memories of violence and ethnic cleansing of many other Bosnian survivors from different parts of the country. We will see how factors like age, gender, level of education, family roles, social networks, level of exposure to violence and degree of loss significantly contribute to memory and identity construction in forcibly displaced people or refugees. After dealing with the theoretical aspects of displacement and memory in the first part of the chapter, I limit my analytical interventions in order to preserve the authenticity and flow of the narratives as much as this is possible when reconstructing such life stories. As Paul Ricoeur (1990: 152) puts it, 'every story ... in principle explains itself. In other words, narrative answers the question "Why?" at the same time that it answers the question "What?" To tell what has happened is to tell why it happened'.

Debating Displacement

Forced displacement has profoundly influenced – and sometimes radically reshaped – the identities of those who fled the 1992–95 campaign of violence known as 'ethnic cleansing' in Bosnia-Herzegovina. As Val Colic-Peisker (2003: 3) observes, '[this] goes beyond the experience of spatial displacement of refugees or internally displaced people: it was, and has been, a displacement of identity as well'. In some instances, identities of the displaced have been partially or completely replaced, adapted, hybridised and entangled with new identities, roles and places, while in other instances there is a prevalent feeling of permanent 'misplacement', with an inability to reconstruct a sense of belonging in a new social environment. As described in this chapter, how identities and memories get changed, adapted and (re)constructed depends on a range of different social and psychological factors. It is important, however, to clarify that when referring to displacement I do not suggest that fixity of place, *emplacement*, is a natural human condition and that identities 'placed' or rooted in a particular place are static and unchangeable (Halilovich 2011a). As we have seen in the case of Klotjevac, even local identities at a village level are very much in a state of constant flux. Regardless of the level of (im)mobility, identities are never fixed or stable as fluidity of identities comes from different socio-cultural factors both from within and from outside a particular place. Or as Sara Ahmed et al. (2003: 1) put it, 'being grounded is not necessarily about being fixed; being mobile is not necessarily about being detached'. However, when people are subject to a forced displacement involving dramatic separation from specific practices and familiar social environment – as well as involving loss of close family members – their sense of belonging, displacement and alienation may be quite profound.

At the outbreak of the war, Bosnian cultural diversity became a matter of ethno-nationalistic politics; students, workers, housewives, farmers, mothers, teachers and children were all primarily defined by 'their' ethno-religious identity, which for many became the only basis for persecution – physical extermination and the forced expulsion of whole communities from towns and villages across the country. Almost half of Bosnia's population of 4.5 million people were forced to leave their homes, with about 1.6 million finding temporary refuge outside the country (Bosnia and Herzegovina Ministry for Human Rights and Refugees 2008). The temporary refuge – as discussed in Chapters 4 and 5, and in the Conclusion – has, for most of those who fled, turned into permanent exile in many different places across the globe. Back home, in BiH, the forced displacement has resulted in huge demographic changes creating 'ethnically clean' territories in large parts of BiH, with previously majority populations – like Bosniaks in eastern Bosnia – either completely disappearing from the demographic map or being reduced to a tiny minority (Halilovich 2004, 2008; Toal and Dahlman 2006).

Displacement as an embodied experience of those who were expelled from their homes has been described and felt by many Bosnian refugees I interviewed as homelessness, sometimes as 'misplacement' or 'living at the wrong place that will never become home', as a fragmented sense of belonging ('a part of me will always be there') or compromise ('I can't go back now; I've got work here, my children go to school ...'). This temporality – or feeling of living in a state of permanent transition – has made many places feel more like 'non-places', as defined by Marc Augé (1995), than places of dwelling (Čapo 2011). In contrast to 'anthropological place', as place 'formed by individual identities, through complicities of language, local references [and] the unformulated rules of living know-how', 'non-place', according to Augé (2005: 101), refers to 'places of transience that do not hold enough significance to be regarded as places'. Not only are many new destinations – places of refuge and resettlement – experienced as 'non-place' by many displaced Bosnians, but so too are their original home towns and villages turned into places associated with temporary visits, transits and departures. Throughout Bosnia – like in the village of Klotjevac described in the previous chapter – many old, burned-out houses have been reconstructed and turned into new holiday houses (*vikendice*), places of seasonal visits, while the 'real' life for many returnees continues to be lived somewhere else. As Stef Jansen and Staffan Löfving (2009: 11) point out, 'violence lives on, beyond memory, affecting moving people and their home-making efforts in ways that cannot be explained with recourse to the mere history of war itself'.

Narrating Displacement

Because of its cataclysmic proportions – from the perspective of many families and local communities – forced displacement and its aftermath continue to be told, retold and remembered, in many different ways. In fact, I would suggest, displacement has played the central role in (post)war memory construction in displaced Bosnians. Many of my respondents described displacement as a memory of the previous life; but also, when they talked about 'who they are now', they did so in relation to their memories of places, past experiences and social histories. This is in line with Martha Nussbaum's (2001: 177) thesis that memory is '... a highly important element in the account of what it is to be a person, as it is the central medium through which identities are constituted: A really successful dissociation of the self from memory would be a total loss of the self – and thus of all the activities to which a sense of one's identity is important'. Hence, loss of place, as an important anchor of social identity, gets substituted – or kept alive – with memory of and narrative about the place.

While the 1992–95 Bosnian war can be defined as an event in the past, displacement is much more stretched out in time and includes both the past and the present – the war and its aftermath – as for many people the life they once had and knew has gone forever and displacement has become a continuing social condition and a matter of new group identities. In BiH this new collective identity formation has been reinforced through bureaucracy and labels such as *raseljena lica* (displaced persons), *prognaninci* (expellees), *povratnici* (returnees), *manjinski povratak* (minority returns), and *izbjeglice* (refugees), while in the countries that accepted Bosnian refugees this is reflected through legal status, visa regimes, humanitarian immigration programmes and settlement policies. Those subjected to such categorisations – refugees/migrants outside of Bosnia and their compatriots and IDPs, who settled in other parts of Bosnia – have often been reduced exclusively to such prescribed group typologies. In the absence of a former home, homeland and old social networks, memory – of not only who I once was, but also who I now am – very often becomes the quintessential aspect of identity in displaced individuals and groups they belong to.

As such, memories as expression of identities, embodied in concrete individuals and groups of individuals, are actively performed. Performance of memory and its construction is a deeply meaningful cultural practice and, like all psychological phenomena, is an action – essentially the action of telling a story (Dening 1996; Leys 1996). Hannah Arendt observed that 'the world is full of stories just waiting to be told' (cited in Cavarero 2000: 143). The stories that get told have multiple audiences and multiple purposes. Laurence Kirmayer (1996) writes about culturally constructed 'landscapes of memory'. By 'landscapes of memory' he understands 'the metaphoric terrain that shapes the distance and effort required to remember affectively charged and socially defined events' (Kirmayer 1996: 175). As such, memories are shaped in part by the narratives and conventions of time, place and position – and thus depend on the social environment (Halbwachs 1992). Similarly, Agnes Heller (2001) argues that identity creation works on old cultural memories, selecting from among them, reinterpreting them, extending them, enlarging them, fusing into them new contents and experiences. Without shared cultural memory there is no identity, she argues. As such, memories are never simply records of the past, but rather 'interpretative reconstructions that bear the imprint of local narrative conventions, cultural assumptions, discursive formations and practices, and social context of recall and commemoration' (Antze and Lambek 1996: vii).

Anastasia Christou (2003: 1456) argues, 'personal narratives are valuable tools for investigating the depths of personal meaning as they illustrate socio-cultural and historical meaning'. Indeed, as Catherine Riessman (2008: 10) points out, 'telling stories about difficult times in our lives creates order and contains emotions, allowing a search for meaning and enabling connection with others'. This is particularly true for the survivors of injustices who experienced grave crimes being committed against them and their family and community members. Narrating memories enables them to connect with their own past lives, mourn their losses and get closures, as well as connect with other survivors and sympathetic audiences. Such personal stories, as fragments of local knowledge and memories, often get lost in or purposely excluded from the 'bigger' narratives, recognised as historical knowledge (Huyssen 2003). Sometimes these personal stories tell a different story from what has become the official nationalist discourse and as such act as alternative truths and 'countermemories', or forms of resistance from below to memory (un)making projects from above.

To reiterate, Michel Foucault (1975, 1977) has termed such forms of fragmented collective knowledge 'popular memory'. The performance of popular memory among displaced Bosnians and their fragmented communities takes many different forms; from personal remembering and narration to maintaining and constructing memory through social networks of other displaced individuals – family, friends, former neighbours, fellow survivors – to public acts of collective remembrance such as commemorations, funerals and anniversaries. Many of these different forms of memory making are present in the following three life stories, (re)constructed through a combination of 'event-centred' and 'experience-centred' narratives (Squire, Andrews and Tamboukou 2008: 4–6).

Sejo in Vienna

After returning home from his two-week visit to Bosnia – where he worked on building a house for his mother in the town of Živinice, visited the ruins of his completely destroyed and depopulated village near Zvornik, and met with some of his surviving friends and relatives – Sejo Nuhanović was making his way through the busy streets of Vienna on the way to the place where his *kuma* Edita worked. Some seven years before, Edita and her husband Mevlo were *kum* and *kuma* (bridesmaid and best man) at Sejo's and his ex-wife Sanela's wedding. Since then this fictive kinship, very common among Bosnians, had grown into a family-like relationship between Sejo and Edita, even after his marriage with Sanela came to an end in early 2007. Like any good *kumovi*,[1] Sejo and Edita have treasured their friendship and have been there for each other in good times and bad. They knew each other's past and present and their life stories – which were quite different but in some ways very much alike. A decade and a half before, they had both lost close family members in the war in Bosnia, while their family homes still remain burned-down ruins in ethnically cleansed areas of their original homeland. Sejo's sense of belonging and memory of home and homeland reflected his lived experience in eastern Bosnia; Edita was born and grew up in western Bosnia. They never visited each other's regional homelands and spoke quite different dialects, and could easily pick up the many cultural differences between people from these two distant parts of Bosnia. Sejo and Edita came to Austria as refugees, dispossessed and uprooted, and met in Vienna through mutual acquaintances in 1996. Edita told Sejo how she once had a home, a family and many friends. Sejo told her about his lost home, lost family and lost friends.

One of the many hopes (and worries) they have shared for years has been to learn about the fate of their missing fathers. In April 1992 Džemo, Sejo's father, a *Gastarbeiter* (guest worker) in Austria, fearing for the safety of his family left in Bosnia, drove to his native village of Kaludrani near Zvornik, in eastern Bosnia, to collect them and to bring them to Salzburg where he worked. The day after his arrival the village was attacked by Serb militiamen and all the male villagers, including Sejo's father, were rounded up and taken away never to be seen again. Close to a thousand men and boys from the area were brutally murdered and their bodies 'disappeared' (Hadžić 2003; Karup-Druško 2009b). With other women and children from the village, Sejo's mother and two younger sisters were expelled from their home and joined the wave of refugees looking for safety in the Bosnian-government-controlled town of Živinice. Sejo's grandma, Naila Nuhanović, refused to leave her home and years later her bones were discovered in the ruins of the burned-down house. Forensic experts confirmed that she was killed by a bullet in the head.

At the time when his village was raided and ethnically cleansed by Serb militia, Sejo was a student at the University of Belgrade, where he remained until 1995. He left Serbia, travelling illegally on a false passport, to Austria, where he has been living and working since. His Serb friends helped him not only to survive as a Bosnian (Muslim) student in Belgrade during the war, but also to obtain a false passport for him to leave Serbia; travelling with a Bosnian document in his real name would have exposed him to serious risks. As Svetlana Broz (2005) writes, there are many untold stories like Sejo's, as, even in the midst of the madness of war, there were still 'good people in an evil time'.

In Austria Sejo initially went through a series of refugee centres and, after having learned German and managing to get recognition for his nursing qualifications, Sejo started his professional career in a nursing home, where he worked as a low-skilled worker, mostly on night shifts. Although he had not initially planned to stay permanently in Austria, his life and his legal status gradually changed from refugee to *Gastarbeiter*. In some five years, having worked and studied hard, Sejo obtained a job as a specialised nurse at the nephrology department of the AKH Vienna hospital (Algemeines Krankenhaus Wien), the most prestigious hospital and a learning centre for health professionals in Austria. His continuous employment secured him permanent residency and a working visa in Austria. Although he became eligible to apply for Austrian citizenship – a status that would improve his opportunities in the country – he has been hesitant to do so due to a number of 'unresolved issues' including the possibility of being called to do a year of national service, compulsory for all Austrian male citizens up to forty years of age.

Since 1992 Sejo has not stopped searching for information about his father's fate, a search that has turned into waiting for his father's remains to be exhumed and identified in a mass grave in the region. Mass graves – like forced expulsion of civilian population, concentration camps, deliberate destruction of homes, or 'domicide',[2] summary executions of men and boys and systematic rape of women and girls – have been an integral part of the ethnic cleansing campaigns in Bosnia (Cigar 1995; Suljagić 2010). Mass graves, 'as a sophisticated instrument of terror' (Ferrándiz 2006: 7), are 'intended to bury the social memory of violence and thus to strengthen the fear-based regimes of the perpetrators, which can survive for decades'. Indeed, it has been almost two decades since the disappearance of Sejo's father, but he still has not come any closer to finding out the truth about the details of a death that can only conclusively be established once the body is found. Those behind the killings of Sejo's father and tens of thousands of other victims, not only the actual killers but also their political and military leaders, have been silent about the *corpus delicti* – in fact, *corpora delicti* – of their crimes, hidden in the mass graves. Sejo gave blood samples to the International Commission on Missing Persons (ICMP) for DNA identification and has followed the news about discoveries of new mass graves and the exhumation of bodies in Bosnia. Literally, Sejo's own identity, his DNA, is used to identify the remains of his father, the scientific identification process reminding the survivors of the embodied link they continue to have with their relatives who perished. The survivors' bodies effectively become a crucial piece of evidence in establishing the crimes committed against their families (cf. Wagner 2008). While the remains of some of Sejo's neighbours, who were taken away together with his father, were positively identified, his father's remains are missing up to this day.[3] The waiting for the remains of family members continues to hold the past very present in the everyday lives of survivors like Sejo. While for many local and international actors exhumations – or, as Iosif Kovras (2008) puts it, 'unearthing the truth' – have been a political issue, for the survivors this is a deeply personal issue that touches the core of their identity. But exhumations and 'unearthing the truth' are also important at the broader community and society levels. As Francisco Ferrándiz (2006: 7) puts it, 'the emotions, narratives and commemorations triggered by exhumations are crucial to a necessary reassessment of an uncomfortable past'.

Like Sejo, Edita had been preoccupied with searching for her father. However, her search and waiting for the remains of her missing father and other male relatives seemed to be nearing its end in summer 2007. One of the reasons for visiting his *kuma* Edita on the day I accompanied Sejo in Vienna was to talk about the news about her father. He knew that it would not be an easy topic to talk about, although they had both told and retold their stories to each other many times over the previous ten years. They were both looking for the day when they could bring closure to their long waiting.

Edita's 'Wonderland' in Vienna

I followed Sejo through the streets of the historical part of Vienna – which could apply to most of the former centre of the Habsburg Empire – in the Second *Bezirk* (district), to Bachinger's, a hairdressing salon, which has kept much of Austria's history and its glorious past within its walls. Located on the corner of two prominent streets, it is hard to miss.[4] The salon's furniture and interior itself could be classified as cultural heritage and would fit well into any museum collection of the late 1800s/early 1900s. A framed picture of the once much-beloved Kaiserin Sisi[5] overlooking the room might have been hanging on the same wall for most of the previous century. The salon was built in an open-plan style, connecting three rooms into one large functional unit. There was no surplus of mirrors and flashy lighting in any of the rooms. High ceilings, typical of the Viennese *Altbau*,[6] have retained the same ornamental design, with antique, ice-like crystal chandeliers hanging in mid air high above clients' heads. The display of hairdressing tools, lotions and pumps – as well as the dimmed lights and pleasant smell of freshly washed hair – evoked a tranquil, decadent atmosphere of times long gone. The whole setting suggested continuity, stability and harmony, with everything and everyone in the right place. It did not look a likely place to accommodate a Bosnian refugee, a survivor of a massacre.

Established in 1902, the hairdressing salon Bachinger's has been in business for more than a century. The current owner, the sixty-five-year-old Herr Bachinger, is the third generation in his family to inherit the salon, keeping the family tradition of cutting and beautifying the hair of Viennese ladies and gentlemen. For most of his life he has been enjoying his trade and only in the last decade has he needed to reduce his work from hairdressing to mainly managing the place. The two reliable and hardworking employees, Edita and Rosa, both in their late twenties, ensure that Bachinger's hairdressing salon continues to maintain its good reputation. They make a good team: Edita, an energetic and talkative brunette; the blonde Rosa giving the impression of being a shy girl who knows how to listen empathetically to any story her clients might tell. Having worked for some ten years in the profession and gained the highest qualifications as a hairdresser, Edita is a senior in the trade and does more demanding hairstyling and managerial tasks when needed. Rosa, who had started as Edita's apprentice a couple of years prior to my visit, has been a fast learner on the way to becoming a *Meisterin* like Edita.

In Bachinger's salon everything is Viennese: the interior, the clients, the local stories and the town gossip being told and retold again and again. Even the language spoken is a distinct local dialect of German, the so-called *wienerisch* or Viennese. Edita is popular with the regular clientele for her conversational skills and good sense of humour. Her *wienerisch* is as fine as that of any Viennese woman who grew up in the vicinity of the Stephans Platz, going to the Marien Kirche or Prater on Sundays and enjoying the *Neujahrskonzert* on the first day of January.[7]

The boss, the ailing Herr Bachinger, who increasingly has been spending less and less time in the salon due to deteriorating health, has great admiration and respect for Edita. He had no reservations when entrusting most of the responsibilities of running the business on a daily basis to her. And Edita has proved to be a talented business woman, just as she is a master of the hairdressing trade. Rosa, on the other hand, could not ask for a better senior colleague, knowing that she has Edita to thank for almost everything she has learned about hairdressing. She is also well aware how much effort and time Edita invests in the salon as the paperwork and logistics demand overtime hours and sometimes even work on Sundays. Although loyal to Bachinger's, Rosa would not be ready to make such sacrifices for someone else's business. There is a much more exciting life for Rosa outside the hairdressing salon, especially at weekends, when the Viennese clubs and pubs are packed with young fun-seeking people.

For Edita, however, Bachinger's salon has been more than a job. It has become a part of who she is, a place where she belongs and is respected for what she does. Those who come regularly to the salon have learned that Edita is the backbone of Bachinger's. But not many know or have ever asked who Edita really is and where she comes from – mainly for the reason that there is no suggestion that Edita might not be Viennese by birth. She could have been related to Herr Bachinger. Her first name is not uncommon in Vienna, nor does her appearance make her look distinctive in any particular way. She just looks like any ordinary young Viennese woman, maybe slightly too enthusiastic about her job, which is another 'Germanic' virtue, some might say. And this is who Edita has been for many years now: an excellent hairdresser at Bachinger's, a jolly Viennese *Fräulein*, an Austrian citizen. But her acculturated belonging that goes with her work also conceals her ever-present sadness and her immense personal loss. Only a few in Vienna know that some sixteen years ago, when she was still a child, Edita lived a completely different life, in a different country, in a small village with many relatives. And then she became a refugee, and 'grew up' in a matter of days and months.

Mapping Edita's Lost Home

Until the summer of 1992 Edita Hegić, who was fourteen years old at the time, lived with her family – her seventeen-year-old brother Fikret, her mother Enisa, her father Alija and her grandfather Smajo – in the hamlet of Hegići, which belonged to a cluster of smaller villages attached to the larger village of Bišćani, seven kilometres from the city of Prijedor, in north-western Bosnia. Most of the forty-five houses in the hamlet belonged to other members of the extended Hegić family, nominal Muslims who had inhabited the area for generations. In fact, the hamlet, as its name reveals, was founded by a Hegić ancestor many years ago. Apart from the Hegićs, there were a few families to which the Hegićs were not directly related as well as four Orthodox Christian (Serb) families living in the hamlet.

The closeness of the village to Prijedor made the village more of a suburb of the city than a village in a traditional sense. The village was connected with the town and other villages by modern roads, with regular bus services throughout the day. Most villagers worked or studied in the city and commuted daily. Edita and her brother Fikret were attending the secondary trade school in Prijedor. Their mother Enisa was a housewife and their widowed grandfather Smajo helped in the garden.

Edita's father Alija was a postman, delivering mail in the local area. Like most other government jobs in the former Yugoslavia, especially those that involved an official uniform, a postman held a well-respected position in the community. Alija Hegić proudly wore his blue postman's uniform, which very much resembled that of a pilot or an air force officer. The post office also provided a reliable motorbike, which Alija was free to use and look after as his own. Postmen, with policemen and rangers, were among the rare professionals who were allowed, and sometimes obliged, to carry arms, usually an official *Tetejac* pistol visibly displayed on their belts. The pistols served more to symbolically represent the state authority than to uphold the law, as violent crimes against public officials were almost unheard of in the region. Alija Hegić never carried his gun around while on duty. He was not fond of arms and resented the whole idea of armed postmen. Postmen were supposed to deliver mail, pensions and the news to people, not represent state power, he believed. Ever since he had received it many years before, his weapon had been sitting in a box, hidden from the children in a safe spot in the house. He loved his job, riding on his motorbike between villages and from house to house, exchanging the news and making many friends. He was popular and respected for his reliability, honesty and good sense of humour. He was always ready to crack a joke without insulting anyone. It seemed that everyone loved 'Postman Ale', as they fondly called him. Edita and her brother Fikret especially loved him and were very proud of their dad. He would put them on his motorbike and they would hold onto him tightly while riding around, feeling excited and safe behind his back. By any standards they could be considered a happy family, living their ordinary lives. This is how Edita likes to remember her childhood.

Fewer than 'Six Degrees of Separation' between Edita and Ibro

In the village of Brdo, some eight kilometres from Hegići and fifteen kilometres from Prijedor, Postman Ale would very often stop at the house of Ibro Sušić, a prosperous farmer and respected member of the village community. They would usually talk over a cup of strong Turkish coffee (which in Bosnia is called 'Bosnian coffee' as in Greece it is called 'Greek coffee'). In the early 1990s, since the communist one-party system had been replaced by 'democracy' – which in turn brought ethno-nationalist right-wing parties to power – their conversations increasingly turned to politics and the socio-economic and political crisis through which the country was going. Ibro believed that, due to the nature of his job, Postman Ale knew more about the politics than an average villager. Ibro loved Ale's optimism. 'Everything will be fine', he would tell him, 'all this will turn into something good'. Ibro wanted to believe him.

When, in 1990/91, Yugoslavia started falling apart, Ibro was in his late fifties and was still seen as the unofficial head of his extended family. He and his three younger brothers had built houses next to each other and worked as farmers on their fertile land, producing everything they needed and selling the surplus at the local market in Prijedor. They were known in the village as the 'Sušićs' football team' – for their large extended family which included eleven adult male members as well as for their family name, which happened to be the same as the Bosnian football legend, Safet Sušić.[8] Ibro and his brothers never contemplated leaving their village to look for a factory job and possibly a more luxurious lifestyle in a major town in Bosnia or elsewhere, as some from the area had done. They were quite happy with their simple lives and were known as hardworking farmers who had acquired most of the machines needed for cultivating the land and harvesting the crops. They exchanged or leased their labour and machinery with other villagers, which in turn gained them respect and relative prosperity in their community, a rural community comprising people with common cultural practices and a similar way of life. On most Fridays Ibro would attend the weekly prayer at the local mosque, which was built solely from the donations of the village community. Ibro's family was also known for generosity when it came to any communal project, such as building the mosque, roads and other communal infrastructure. His brothers were not so regular at the Friday prayers, but, like other villagers, saw important Muslim holidays like the *Bajrams*[9] as an integral part of their culture and tradition (Mulahalilović 1989).

In late 1991, at regular nightly gatherings (or *sijelo*), Ibro's family would discuss politics and the war, which less than a hundred kilometres away was engulfing neighbouring Croatia. Ibro was worried. He could well remember the Second World War and all the sufferings that a war would bring. He was, however, still hopeful that this was a small-scale conflict between extremists and not a war that would reach his small village of Brdo. He stopped watching the regular news broadcasts on television, as increasingly they were spreading nationalist propaganda, and would only turn on his television to see the YUTEL news bulletin broadcasted from Sarajevo. YUTEL included some of the finest journalists from different ethnic groups, many of whom had been expelled from Belgrade by the Milošević regime (Kurspahić 2003). YUTEL, 'a voice of tolerance and liberalism', was the last media institution still sincerely – albeit naively – promoting 'brotherhood and unity' between the Yugoslav peoples, ethnicities and religions (Ramet 2002: 41). They were independent from, and the most vocal opponents of, nationalistic leaders like Milošević, who at that time had already turned most of the media in Serbia, Vojvodina, Kosovo and Montenegro into a propaganda machine appealing to Serb pride, unity, heroism and Orthodox Christianity, interpreting history as an ongoing struggle for Serb survival (Anzulović 1999; Cigar 1995; Čolović 1999; Ramet 2002; Žanić 2007). The media portrayed Serbs as both glorious victors and innocent victims (Macdonald 2003). The propaganda about 'endangered Serbs' (*ugroženost Srba*) went to such extremes that it seemed ridiculous even listening to such paranoid ideas, much less taking them seriously (Kurspahić 2003). Ibro knew that the Serbs were in charge in all the federal institutions and were disproportionately represented in local government and state-owned enterprises. 'How could they have been endangered?!' he asked himself.

However, Serb nationalism – which was launched by the Serb Academy of Arts and Sciences (SANU)[10] and Slobodan Milošević in the mid 1980s and swiftly spread outside Serbia to be embraced by an increasing number of Serbs in Bosnia and Croatia – triggered a chain reaction resulting in the ethnic nationalism of Bosniaks and Croats in Bosnia and Herzegovina, as well as other national and ethnic groups across Yugoslavia (Ramet 2002). The nationalist euphoria culminated when the Yugoslav Communist League finally relinquished their monopoly on power in 1989/90 and allowed other political parties to be established as a precondition for the first democratic elections in Yugoslavia since 1945. Democracy became a prominent and popular word, with almost every major political party incorporating it in its name. In addition to a small number of civic Yugoslav parties, such as the Party for Democratic Change led by the charismatic Yugoslav premier Ante Marković, the majority of the parties formed at the time were almost exclusively appealing to their ethnic constituencies. In BiH these were the nationalist parties of Bosnian Serbs (SDS: Serb Democratic Party), Bosnian Croats (HDZ: Croat Democratic Union) and Bosniaks (SDA: Party for Democratic Action). SDS, led by Radovan Karadžić, was closely linked to the politics of Serbia's president Slobodan Milošević, while HDZ was an offshoot of the Croatian HDZ based in Zagreb and led by Franjo Tudjman. The SDA was the only one of the three ethnic parties that did not have an ethnic adjective in its name; however, the political programme of the party stated that SDA was 'a political alliance of Yugoslav citizens who belong to the Muslim cultural-historical sphere' i.e., Bosniaks (Hoare 2007: 342). Each nationalist party – the SDA, the SDS and the HDZ – focused on the 'national' interest of their ethnic compatriots, giving themselves exclusive rights to represent their peoples. Voting for one's ethnic party was seen as a 'national' duty and necessity, a kind of political census of the population where one was asked to declare oneself in ethnic terms. Nationalist parties also promoted themselves as responsible for national emancipation and renewal of their people's cultures. They all were strongly anti-communist even though many of their leaders and members were themselves former Communists. While the nationalist parties were inherently antagonistic with the parties of the 'ethnic other', they also regularly hosted nationalist politicians from these parties at mass rallies throughout 1990 and 1991 to demonstrate a joint front against 'Communists', who by now had become symbols of everything that was bad in the previous system. However, across Bosnia, the SDS, the SDA and the HDZ became more than acronyms for political parties: increasingly they were viewed as symbols of the three Bosnian ethnic groups. Graffiti and posters representing one or other of the three parties appeared on every place imaginable, from walls of houses to traffic signs to electric power poles and trees. In many places these symbols also came to serve and represent the ethnic borders between villages, towns and neighbourhoods (Glenny 1996: 147–8).

All the nationalist parties relied on support from their respective religious authorities and incorporated religious symbols into their political iconography (Žanić 2007). SDA, the Bosniak nationalist party at the time when the Bosniak ethnic name was still 'Muslims', used Islamic symbols like the colour green and the crescent to appeal to Bosniaks as Muslims (in a religious sense). The Islamic image of the SDA was further strengthened by the SDA's leader being Alija Izetbegović, who, in the early 1980s had been imprisoned by the Communists for publishing his book, *Islamic Declaration*. Together with other Muslim dissidents, Izetbegović was advocating not only the political rights of Bosniaks but also their religious renewal. He was accused by the SDS of wanting to create an Islamic republic in BiH, an accusation that could not be substantiated but nonetheless had an effect on rallying Serbs under the SDS political umbrella (Silber and Little 1995: 207–8).

The nationalist mobilisation from above worked, with many people embracing the nationalist rhetoric as liberating, protective and hope-giving, and, between November and December 1990, overwhelmingly voting for the nationalist parties (SDA, SDS and HDZ) that soon after formed a coalition government. The new Bosnian Parliament was dominated by the three parties, with 41 per cent of the seats held by Bosniaks, 35 per cent by Bosnian Serbs and 20 per cent by Bosnian Croats, 'figures that broadly corresponded to the national make-up of the Bosnian population' (Hoare 2007: 346). However, the Parliament was often dysfunctional due to a lack of cooperation between the parties. When, in 1991, the debate on BiH independence was initiated in the BiH Parliament, SDS leader Radovan Karadžić threatened Bosniaks with annihilation. At the time not many knew or believed that he was already making preparations to fulfil his threat (Ramet 2002: 206).

In his first and the only free and democratic elections with the ability to choose between the three parties – the SDA, the SDS and the HDZ – Ibro Sušić voted for 'his' party, the SDA, as he correctly anticipated that Serbs and Croats would vote for their respective national parties. To him, this was just a statement of who he was, not a sign of intolerance towards members of the other two peoples living in his proximity, but he was also worried by the increasing aggressiveness of the Serb nationalists in what was still regarded as Yugoslavia. Alija Izetbegović, the president of the collective presidency of the Republic of Bosnia-Herzegovina and the leader of the largest Bosniak nationalist party, was sending somewhat mixed and contradictory messages via the state television (TVSA), stating, for instance, that unlike Croatia, BiH was safe from a war because 'for a war to be waged two warring parties are needed', implying that Serbs could not fight a war on their own if they did not have an enemy in BiH. At the same time he also publicly stated that he would 'sacrifice peace for the sovereignty of Bosnia'. At the peak of the crisis, in March 1992, he even sent televised messages to the citizens of BiH reassuring them to 'sleep peacefully as there would not be a war in the country' (Hoare 2007).

Ibro told me he would sigh after every YUTEL news broadcast, which would end with the words, 'Good night Yugoslavia, wherever you are'. To him it sounded rather like 'Goodbye Yugoslavia'; he feared that Yugoslavia as he knew it was already in the past and he was worried about what would come next. Even his worst nightmares were not as bad as what was to come. There were more and more rumours about imminent war in Bosnia. Some people sent their children to relatives abroad; others were preparing to defend their homes; while most people went on with their daily routines. All the Sušićs stayed in the village. Ibro did not allow anyone in his family to get involved in politics or to buy a gun. It was a public secret that anyone with a thousand Deutschmarks could buy an AK-47 automatic rifle from smugglers. The smugglers were generally Serbs and members of the Yugoslav People's Army (JNA) who had their middlemen from other ethnic groups.

The spring of 1992 was in many ways like many previous seasons, and Ibro was planting the usual crops on his land. But distant gunfire and explosions of heavy artillery shells in the neighbouring Republic of Croatia were disturbing the traditional natural cycle of a farmer cultivating his fields. He knew about long convoys of military vehicles from JNA barracks in Serbia crossing Bosnia on the way to Croatia. The fact that Bosnia was used for transit and logistics for such attacks was very disturbing to him. JNA, with all its military might, was the only armed force in the country. The Bosnian President Alija Izetbegović asked Bosnians of all ethnicities and religions not to continue with their compulsory conscription into the JNA, but this was open to interpretation as Bosnia and Herzegovina was not yet a sovereign state (Silber and Little 1995: 215–18). On the other hand, JNA fighters did not even attempt to hide their direct involvement in advancing the interests of an imaginary Greater Serbia. They had long stopped being the 'Yugoslav People's Army' and had become the most powerful instrument in the hands of Serb nationalists (Ramet 2002: 58–72, 203–4).

That spring, Ibro voted in the referendum on Bosnia's independence, believing that the best way for Bosnia to keep its peace was to become an independent and neutral country. Yugoslavia did not exist anymore as a country of 'brotherhood and unity from Vardar to Triglav' and Greater Serbia was not a desirable option even for moderate and open-minded Serbs, not to mention people from non-Serb backgrounds. He believed that the majority of the Bosnian Orthodox Christians, also known as Serbs, would see it this way. This was their homeland as much as it was the homeland of his Catholic neighbours and fellow Muslims. The numerical size of each group did not matter to him as he never felt that he was in any way 'more in charge' because he belonged to the largest ethnic group. They were all *Bosanci* (Bosnians) and both outsiders and they themselves saw it that way. Or that was what he wanted to believe.

The Prijedor Region – Blueprint for Ethnic Cleansing

For Ibro's family, Edita's family and thousands of other families in and around Prijedor, mundane lives were to take a radical turn on 30 April 1992 when the multi-ethnic municipality of Prijedor was taken over by the armed militiamen of the radical Serb Democratic Party along with their allies, the regulars and reservists of the JNA and various gangs of armed local Serbs and volunteers from Serbia and Montenegro. As Isabelle Wesselingh and Arnaud Vaulerin (2005: 37) have described, this was a meticulous operation that took more than six months of careful planning, so that 'the massacres committed there were the result of a specific deliberate strategy'. On 30 April 1992 the town was renamed Serb Prijedor in the Serb Republic of Bosnia Herzegovina (which later became Republika Srpska or the Serb Republic); and thereafter, the adjective 'Serb' was added to the names of all the public institutions. This practically excluded more than half of Prijedor's 112,543 population. At the time of the occupation the ethnically mixed town of Prijedor with its surrounding area had 49,351 or 43.9 per cent Bosniaks (Bosnian Muslims); 47,581 or 42.3 per cent Serbs; 6,316 or 5.6 per cent Croats; and a sizeable number of 'others' – 9,295 or 8.2 per cent (Yugoslavs, Roma, Ukrainians, Jews and members of other ethnic minorities).[11]

The demographic structure of Prijedor was to change radically in Serb favour as, by the end of 1992, most of the non-Serbs were expelled – ethnically cleansed from the area. Some 5,000 unarmed civilians (Bosniaks and Croats), were killed and thousands were detained and tortured in the notorious concentration camps of Omarska, Keraterm and Trnopolje (cf. Wesselingh and Vaulerin 2005; Tochman 2008; Halilovich 2011a). The policy of physical extermination, torture, illegal detention and forced expulsion of tens of thousands of non-Serbs from the Prijedor region was recognised very early and named for what it was, a war crime and genocide, by those who gained access to the notorious concentration camp of Omarska – journalists and authors like Ed Vulliamy (1994), Roy Gutman (1993) and Peter Maass (1996), and Tadeusz Mazowiecki (1994), the Special Rapporteur of the UN Commission on Human Rights.

The day Prijedor was renamed *Serb* Prijedor, the lives of non-Serb residents of Prijedor and the surrounding villages became worthless. Any armed Serb had by default a licence to rob, humiliate, kill, rape or detain anyone who was not a Serb. As soon as the town of Prijedor was occupied

– or 'liberated from Muslim extremists and Croat Ustaše without a single bullet being fired' as the 'Serb radio Prijedor' was claiming – an ultimatum was given by the 'Serb government of Prijedor' to all Muslims and Croats to surrender any weapons they might have and to put 'white flags' (bed sheets) on the balconies and roofs of their houses as an expression of their loyalty to the new order in town. In the ethnically mixed town of Prijedor this proved the most effective way to distinguish the non-Serb houses from those inhabited by Serbs. In exchange for loyalty, many of the houses with white flags were then sprayed with bullet fire from one of the many posts on high-rise buildings and other key buildings in the city manned by armed Serb militiamen. This was followed by arrests, humiliation and the expropriation of properties of the non-Serbs (Human Rights Watch 1996, 1997; Halilovich 2009). In heavily armed raids, demonstrating all the military strength of the Serb militias whose armaments ranged from armoured personnel carriers to tanks and helicopters, the suburbs of Puharska, Skela and Stari Grad, predominantly inhabited by Muslims, were emptied of their non-Serb male inhabitants.[12] In most instances it was only a name that could identify someone to be Muslim or Croat. The men were then taken for 'interrogation' to one of the three concentration camps established in and around the city, at Keraterm, Omarska and Trnopolje.

While the city was quickly occupied from the inside, surrounded from the outside and cut off from the rest of the world, the larger Muslim villages around Prijedor – Kozarac, Hambarine, Bišćani and Brdo – were still not under the control of the occupiers of Prijedor. It took the Serbs some six to eight weeks to complete the process. In Kozarac and Hambarine, as in some other places across BiH, sporadic resistance was organised by the local men, made up of small disorganised groups armed with hunting rifles and small military arms obtained illegally on the black market before the outbreak of the conflict. These men refused to surrender and the villages came under heavy artillery attacks by Serb military forces. First, the village of Hambarine was pulverised, followed by Kozarac. After the artillery levelled the houses in both villages, the ground forces of various Serb military and militia groups started 'cleansing the terrain' (čišćenje terena) – which later became known as 'ethnic cleansing' – which meant hunting down the population of whole villages. Many summary executions took place on the spot. Many captured men and boys were detained in concentration camps. As in other parts of Bosnia, sexual violence and the rape of women and girls was an integral part of ethnic cleansing in the region of Prijedor (Wesselingh and Vaulerin 2005; Halilovich 2005b). After the initial orgies of violence and humiliation – which sometimes took days and sometimes several weeks – those who survived were put on trucks and buses and taken to central Bosnia 'for exchange'.[13] This referred to an exchange of population, but in reality no exchange took place at all and the expulsion of civilians was only in one direction: from Serb-occupied territories to parts of Bosnia still controlled by the BiH government. This was exactly what happened in Hegići and Brdo, Edita's and Ibro's respective villages, as well as in distant eastern Bosnia in Sejo's village of Kaludrani.

Massacre in Hegići

Even when most of the Bosniak and Croat villages around Prijedor were destroyed and ethnically cleansed, Bosniaks of Hegići hoped that they still would be spared as they did not have any armed groups in the village to provoke a conflict with the Serbs. Their relations with their Serb neighbours became progressively less cordial and in most cases limited to essential greetings when they crossed each other's paths. Edita remembers that only Ljubica, a Serb woman living in the village, remained friendly with other Bosniaks. Discontent and tensions between the two groups were palpable but no one did anything to provoke the other side. While Bosniaks limited their movements to essential work in the fields and tending animals, Serb neighbours would frequently leave the village and on many nights would not return to their homes. This particularly worried the Bosniaks in Hegići as they suspected their neighbours of plotting against them with other Serbs outside the village.

On the night of 19 July 1992 none of the Serb villagers stayed in Hegići. The next morning two trucks and four armed transport personnel carriers packed with armed, uniformed men hastily entered the village. They quickly blocked all the exits from the small village, which numbered only 48 houses. The armed men identified themselves as Serb military police searching for 'Muslim extremists', members of the Muslim SDA political party and weapons. The police commander, barking orders over a megaphone, gave an ultimatum to the villagers to hand over all the weapons and all the men from sixteen to sixty years of age to come out. They would start burning the houses if the villagers did not comply within ten minutes. Within minutes Hegići men came out of their homes and gathered in the centre of the village. A few hunting rifles and pistols, including Ale's, were handed over to the militiamen. Most of the militiamen were not known to the villages and some spoke the distinct Serbian dialect of Serbs from Serbia, but villagers recognised one 'soldier' in the group. It was J.M., a local thug who lived just a few kilometres from Hegići, in the Serb village of Jugovci. He was armed Rambo-style and was yelling at the villagers, all of whom he knew so well, not to hide anyone or any weapons as he would personally kill each of them. No one dared to speak out.

Edita's parents panicked and did not know what to do with the seventeen-year-old Fikret. Edita's mother insisted on keeping him in the house, while her father thought it was too dangerous to hide him. In the end, Fikret joined his father. The grandfather, who was seventy years of age, stayed inside hoping that his son and grandson would be back soon. The morning started its bloody course in the following minutes. While most women were keeping away from the windows of their houses, hiding behind the blinds of her kitchen window, Edita's mother Enisa was trying to see what was happening outside. What she saw was the beginning of a nightmare which was to become a part of her life. First, J.M. started swearing at Bego Alagić, one of the villagers, asking him for weapons and accusing him of being an SDA supporter. Bego, a local farmer and a simple village man, tried to explain that he neither had a weapon nor knew anything about politics. J.M. hit Bego across his face. Bego was trying to say something, but before he was able to do that, J.M. aimed his gun at Bego's chest and pressed the trigger. Almost instantly Bego fell to the ground. Some twenty metres away, Enisa was witnessing a cold-blooded murder and she could not believe that what she saw was real. Was it so easy to kill a human being? Minutes later all the Hegići men were marched outside the village. Shortly after they disappeared from Enisa's view, salvos of gunfire started. The shooting went on for half an hour and then stopped. Enisa feared that the worst had happened.

The soldiers returned to the village and started searching the houses, looking for valuables, asking for money and harassing the women, children and the few elderly men. By noon most of the militiamen had left the village. Some dozen soldiers stayed in the village, preventing anyone from leaving. The person in charge seemed to be J.M. Later that evening J.M. and his gang were drinking and singing nationalistic Serb songs. No one slept that night in Hegići. Edita cried with her mother. Her grandfather Smajo silently smoked cigarette after cigarette.

In the morning Enisa could not wait any longer. With her grandfather, she went out and, taking a short cut behind the houses, walked to the paddock where the Hegići men were taken the previous day. On the paddock behind the houses, in groups of up to eight, eighty-four bodies were lying in the green grass. They were all dead. Enisa frantically started looking for Ale and Fikret. She turned each body to see the face of the victim. Her grandpa Smajo helped her. After a while they felt physically and mentally exhausted and started looking selectively for the light blue shirt Ale was wearing the previous morning. They spotted him among the other dead men. It took them a few minutes longer to find Fikret's body. He was lying some twenty metres from the others. He might have tried to run away before he was killed.

The bodies were left lying for the next two hot days. The soldiers refused Smajo's pleadings to bury the victims. This was an additional humiliation of the survivors as Muslim custom observed by the villages required the dead to be buried on the same day or within twenty-four hours of their death. On the third day two trucks arrived in the village and four elderly men – Smajo Hegić, Hasan Hegić, Hajrudin Pelak and Husnija Hadžić – were ordered to go with the soldiers to load the bodies onto the trucks. The fragile old men spent hours carrying the bodies of their closest relatives and loading them onto the trucks. More than half of those killed were from the Hegić family. When the collection of the bodies was complete, the four men were ordered to step onto the truck themselves. When the truck passed next to Edita's house, she saw her grandpa Smajo for the last time. He was standing on the uncovered truck among all the dead bodies. He waved at her while the tears were running down his old cheeks. Next to him was their neighbour, Hasan. Hajrudin and Husnija were on the second truck. All four disappeared with the trucks that were driving the eighty-four bodies away. Years later most of the bodies and body parts were found in a mass grave in Jakina Kosa near the distant town of Ljubija.

The surviving villagers of Hegići, the women and children, endured a month of pillage, humiliation and violence before they were ordered to march to the football stadium in Prijedor from where they were deported in trucks and buses to central Bosnia, near Travnik, on 21 August 1992. It took two days to empty the stadium of the thousands of desperate people expelled from their homes. During the trip the convoy was stopped many times by more armed Serb militias, each robbing and humiliating the expellees as they passed through. Some two hundred people were taken from the buses and trucks and disappeared before they reached safety on the other side of the demarcation line[14] on Mount Vlašić (Hećimović 2009; Obradović 2009).

Once in the Bosnian government-controlled town of Travnik –overpopulated with refugees from western Bosnia and thousands of other destitute people with no shelter and limited food rations from the humanitarian aid – Edita and her mother continued their one-way journey initially to Croatia and then further to Austria. They reached Vienna on 18 October 1992.

Shortly after their arrival in Vienna, for the first time in months, they were touched by the kindness of strangers. A friendly Viennese family invited Edita and her mother to stay with them and separated them from the other refugees at the overcrowded refugee reception centre. From that day Edita and Enisa have felt more like guests than refugees in Austria. They were accommodated in a small apartment owned by their host family, and shortly thereafter Edita's mother was employed by the hosts in their family-owned business, while Edita was enrolled in school. Both Edita and her mother still feel deeply indebted to their hosts, who, over the years, have become a second family to Edita and her mother.

Massacre in Brdo

In late June 1992, a few weeks before the massacre in Hegići took place, Ibro Sušić's village of Brdo was living its last days as an ordinary rural settlement of simple farming families. Ibro Sušić, who witnessed the killing of ten of his male family members, survived to tell his story.

One early afternoon in June 1992 the village was raided by some fifty Serb soldiers and paramilitaries, some wearing masks and balaclavas. They gave an ultimatum to the local Muslim villagers to give themselves up, to come out with their hands up and nothing would happen to them. The villagers had no other option as they were neither armed nor felt that they were guilty of anything. Some two hundred villagers were then rounded up and the men were ordered to separate from the women.

Shortly afterwards sixty-four men were taken to a paddock near the village, lined up and gunned down by machine guns. Those who tried to run away were killed before they were able to reach the safety of a forest nearby. Ibro was close to his two sons, his brothers and nephews when the gunfire started. He felt many hot bullets hitting his body and fell to the ground next to his relatives. He was bleeding profusely, but he was still alive and conscious. A number of men were not instantly killed and were screaming in pain. They were all shot again at closer range by their executioners until everything went silent. Squeezed between the bodies of his brothers and one of his sons, Ibro waited to die and finally lost consciousness. Many hours later he began to feel very cold, opened his eyes and realised where he was and what had happened. It was dark and some fifty metres from the place where he was lying two uniformed men were sitting on a pick-up truck, smoking and chatting. Ibro waited and some time later they drove away. Ibro then checked to see if anyone else was alive and discovered that he was the only survivor. He had been hit by six bullets in his legs, the lower part of his body and on both sides of his chest. He dragged himself into the woods where he hid all night and all the next day. That night it rained heavily and washed away his tracks in the ground. The next afternoon, when two elderly men were ordered by armed Serb soldiers to pick up the bodies and load them onto a truck, no one suspected that one body was missing. After that Ibro was found by his niece and hidden in the basement of a house. He was nursed by his female relatives and although the six bullets still in his body caused him a lot of pain, none of his vital organs had been hit. About a month later the village was raided again and all the surviving villagers were ordered to march to the camp in Trnopolje, one of the three concentration camps established for non-Serbs of the Prijedor region. Ibro pretended to be a paraplegic who had suffered a stroke and was transported to Trnopolje in a wheelbarrow pushed by his elderly wife. In September 1992, thanks to the effort of the International Committee of the Red Cross, Ibro and most other detained Muslims and Croats in Trnopolje were freed and evacuated to Croatia. He spent three months in a former military barracks in the Croatian town of Karlovac before he and his wife received a formal invitation letter sent by a relative from Austria which enabled them to obtain a visa to enter Austria.

Edita, Ibro and Sejo in Austria

Unlike Edita and Sejo, Ibro never adapted to the new place, Styer in Austria. He felt both physically and mentally drained and too old to even think of starting a new life in a foreign country. He spent his years in exile waiting for news of his dead relatives, whose remains have not been found up to this day. His identity was that of a survivor who lost ten of his close male relatives. Other Bosnian refugees in Styer felt sorry for the old man and would compare his loss to their own or that of others. Some survivors lost everyone in their family but none had experienced the horror of having ten relatives gunned down and being the sole survivor. Ibro's story was told and retold by many of those whom he might not have ever met. Although his physical wounds had healed long ago, the marks where his body was once pierced by hot bullets remained a permanent reminder of the most tragic episode in his life. The new cultural setting in a picturesque Austrian town did not help him forget it. Ibro's longing for a life he once had and his inability to forget and to move on was given an official, clinical name by the Austrian doctors: he suffered from depression and post-traumatic stress disorder (PTSD), the term used to describe 'invisible injuries inflicted on the mind, self or soul' (Young 1996: 89). Ibro's memory and remembering – in psychopathological terms described as 'obsessive reliving of the traumatic experience' – were treated as clinical conditions, but there was no cure for him. A few Bosnians from Prijedor whom he met in the town would occasionally pay him a visit. If he was talking, Ibro would talk about his lost family, the village of Brdo, the river Sana and his beloved Prijedor – all of which was taken from him. He could not find strength to return – even though he considered this option every single day – nor did he ever accept that he would spend his last days in a foreign country. 'Tuđa zemlja tuga je golema' ['Living in a foreign country means a life longing for the homeland'] and 'Moje kosti će u moju zemlju' ['My bones belong to my land'], he would say. And so his longing never ceased.

Shortly after I recorded his story, in late 2007, Ibro Sušić passed away in his exile. Thanks to the members of the Prijedor community living in Austria, who paid the costs, Ibro's remains were returned to his birthplace. His last wish was to be buried in his native village of Brdo. After fifteen years he finally returned to the place he had never stopped calling his home. His funeral was attended by a dozen returnees to the village. With Ibro's death died a memory of the Sušićs' football team, a family once famed for its eleven hardworking men who perished only because their names were Ibro, Osman, Mustafa, Nezir …

Edita's Homecoming

Some ten months after Ibro's final 'repatriation', Edita made her own homecoming to the place that was no longer home. There were almost no Hegićs left in Hegići, apart from a few ageing returnees, mostly widowed women. Edita did not return to stay or to rebuild her house burned down fifteen years earlier. As the only surviving child and grandchild, she was back to attend the burial of her father and her grandfather, whose remains were found in a mass grave. Edita's DNA had been used in the process of identifying their remains. She told me how, before the funeral, she went to the forensic morgue lab in Sanski Most where the bodies had been stored, and wept touching her father's and her grandfather's bones. Though the skeletons were incomplete as some bones could not be located, she 'felt' that they belonged to her relatives. But her brother Fikret was not to be buried that day: his remains had not been found and he continued to be counted as missing.

After a low-key religious ceremony for a hundred victims of the 1992 ethnic cleansing of Prijedor's Muslims to be laid to rest, the day ended at the rebuilt mosque in downtown Prijedor. Caskets with the remains were distributed according to the victims' place of origin. Most Bosniak villages around Prijedor received some of their lost residents. At the cemetery in Hegići, eleven fresh graves were dug. Surviving relatives came from Austria, Sweden and the U.S. to participate at the funeral. Edita knew all of them, but it was a sad reunion in the place that was once home but was now a place filled with sad memories. She was here to say her final goodbye to her dad Ale and her grandpa Smajo. At times her sadness was mixed with anger and something that could only be described as pride or defiance. 'We brought them home' – she declared – 'They returned to stay'.

On Edita's invitation I travelled to her former village to attend the funeral of her long-lost relatives. It was the second time Edita had visited her home village, now only the ruins of what used be her home. Edita's memories, which I had been 'in charge of recording', were for the first time graphically presented to me. I saw the ruins of her home; I saw the field behind the village where the Hegići men had been killed in a summary execution a decade and half earlier. I saw the coffins and fresh graves where her relatives were put to their final rest.

I even saw the 'banality of evil' embodied in one of the executioners, the neighbour, J.M. Without thousands of such ordinary people like J.M. – driven by a logic, albeit perverse, that they were following their conscience and doing good for their people – genocide in Bosnia would not have happened (Anzulović 1999: 4). While the visitors – former residents of Hegići – were leaving their dead relatives and their former village behind, some of the former Serb neighbours and their new Serb compatriots who had settled in Hegići were sitting in front of a shop which also serves as the only village pub. Among them was J.M., who had participated in the killings of the Hegići men and boys that fatal morning in July 1992. He was calmly drinking his beer and looking at the passing cars and the passengers in them as if all this had nothing to do with him. To me he did not look like someone who showed any remorse for his deeds, or like someone who was worried because he had committed a war crime fifteen years earlier. To him the crimes might have paid off as his pre-war status of a local thug was elevated to that of Serb war veteran. I could only think of Hannah Arendt and the banality of evil (Arendt 1963), even of the banality of my research – as here I was supposedly researching, but in reality overwhelmed by the grief of my research participants and their immense loss, and there he was, one of the executioners, having another of his dull days, drinking yet another beer. I was unable to do anything but take notes about those who survived, those who died and those who killed them.

Torn Between Home and Exile, Past and Present

Back in Vienna, sitting in a comfortable barber's chair at Bachinger's, Sejo listened to Edita's recollections of her relatives' funeral, imagining how it would feel to bury one's own father, killed in a summary execution many years ago. After a period of silence a customer entering the salon returned Sejo and Edita to their everyday realities. They both needed to move on.

That coming weekend, after another series of night shifts in the hospital where he worked, Sejo was planning to spend a few days in Bosnia, working on the house he had started to build some five years before in the town where his mother and sister initially found a temporary refuge after fleeing from their village in 1992 – his life more and more resembling that of his late father,[15] who worked as a *Gastarbeiter* in Austria and would use every opportunity to spend a few days with his family in Bosnia. In order to accumulate a few days leave he would often work overtime, sometimes going for weeks without a single day off.

Sejo was devoting most of his time, energy and thinking to Bosnia and the house. He even transported most of the home appliances and some building material from Austria down to Bosnia. He chose only the best quality for his home. Sejo's ailing mother lived in the house. Every school holiday Sejo would take his daughter Alisa down to Bosnia. In Vienna Sejo shared custody of Alisa with his estranged wife Sanela. Going to Bosnia for Sejo meant being a part of a family: Sejo looked after his mother, his mother looked after Alisa and one of Sejo's sisters lived next door with her family; everyone felt close to someone they loved and belonged to. For Sejo, building a house and reconstructing his home back in Bosnia, not only in a metaphorical but also a practical sense, meant (re)constructing a place for him and his family, or what was left of it.

Unlike Sejo, Edita's prevailing feelings in relation to Bosnia are those of 'non-place', displacement and personal loss. She could not wait to leave Bosnia and 'return home in Austria'. A few weeks after the funeral of her family members in Hegići, Edita's mother Enisa, now in her fifties, suffered a heart attack in Vienna. After initial hospitalisation she was continuing her recovery at home, while looking after her Austrian-born grandson Armin, Edita's and Mevlo's newborn son. Like Sejo in Bosnia, Edita has not only been constructing her home in Austria in a metaphorical sense: in a small village, some thirty kilometres from Vienna, she and her husband Mevlo have been building a double-storey house. Naming their son Armin – a typical Austrian name – was a conscious decision, as Edita, Mevlo and Enisa didn't want their son and grandson ever to stand out because of his name. They have learned the hard way that names matter and can decide one's destiny.

As Ibro did not have an opportunity to meet Edita and to tell her his stories about his memory of her father, I felt obliged to pass on my recollections of Ibro's narratives to Edita. For many survivors like Edita, memory is not only about remembering but also about forgetting. There are far too many episodes that Edita has been trying to forget. However, the story of friendly Postman Ale has been adopted into Edita's memory of her father – as has the story of Ibro, who might have been the last survivor who remembered Postman Ale delivering mail to villages around Prijedor in better times when these villages and their inhabitants existed. Now these narratives, like those lost villages and people – and all the unwritten, unsent and undelivered letters – live in Edita's memory and make connections with her sense of who she once was.

Notes

1. In many cases (as with Sejo and Edita) the fictive kinship called *kumstvo* or *kumovi* (plural of *kum*) is maintained as a life-long friendship which often

lasts even if the actual marriage between spouses ends in a divorce. Loyalty to *kumstvo* (kinship) is seen as a very honourable deed. The ethnic conflict in Bosnia destroyed many such relationships, which in many cases crossed ethnic lines.

2. In the context of the 1992–95 war in Bosnia and Herzegovina, 'domicide' refers to the systematic obliteration of homes and destruction of places, especially villages. See, for instance, Dahlman and Ó Tuathail (2005b) and Stefansson (2004b).
3. At the time of finishing this book in early 2012.
4. I included a part of Edita's story in the article 'Beyond the Sadness: Memories and Homecomings Among Survivors of "Ethnic Cleansing" in a Bosnian village'; see Halilovich (2011a).
5. Kaiserin Sisi was the popular name of the Queen Elisabeth of Austria. In 1854, as a young girl of sixteen years of age, she married the Austrian King (Kaiser) Franz Joseph and had been in the spotlight until she was tragically killed in Geneva in 1898. Her popularity at the time (which continues to fascinate many people today) could be compared to that of the late Diana Princess of Wales.
6. *Altbau* (lit. 'old building') refers to an architectural style characterised by large rooms, high ceilings and large windows and doors in which most of the historical buildings in Vienna and other central European cities have been built.
7. These represent some of the icons of the Viennese city culture.
8. Safet Sušić (born in 1955) was one of the best European and world football players of his generation.
9. Two *Bajrams* (Eids) are the main religious holidays celebrated by Bosnian Muslims. The first *Bajram* (*Eid ul-Fitr* in Arabic) marks the end of Ramadan while the second (*Eid ul-Adha*) celebrates the pilgrims conducting *Hajj*.
10. In 1986 SANU (the Serb Academy of Arts and Sciences) spearheaded Serb nationalism by issuing the infamous *Memorandum*, which is regarded as the blueprint for the Serb nationalist project and the wars that followed.
11. BiH Census of Population 1991 (Government of Bosnia-Herzegovina 1991).
12. See the final report of the United Nations Commission of Experts (1994) established pursuant to Security Council Resolution 780 (1992), 'Annex V: The Prijedor Report'.
13. Ibid.
14. Some 'stable' front lines between armed Serbs and BiH-government-controlled areas were established in the early summer of 1992. They were often treated as demarcation lines between two different territories rather than active front lines between two (or more) armies. Mount Vlašić separated Serb-controlled areas in western Bosnia from territories in central Bosnia controlled by Bosniaks and Croats. In many instances these demarcation lines became (un)official borders between Republika Srpska and the Bosniak-Croat Federation at the end of the war in 1995.
15. See Chapter 5. Džemal Nuhanović's body has never been found. Years after his disappearance, Sejo and his mother were required to declare him officially dead in order to be issued a death certificate needed for Sejo's mother to claim her husband's pension from Austria.

◈ Chapter 3 ◈

(Dis)Placing Memories
Monuments, Memorials and Commemorations in Post-war Bosnia and Herzegovina

The dead
Are here simply to set our sufferings
In perspective.
Abdulah Sidran, *Partisan Cemetery*,[1] p. 62

Edita's adoption of elements of others' narratives into her sense of who she once was might be viewed as a personal battle over memory. Many scholars have argued that the Bosnian war itself was a war over memory which involved the manipulation of 'traumatic memories' of real and perceived past sufferings and injustices done to one's own people.[2] The war over memory, which was so emblematic of the conflict in Bosnia, included systematic destruction of the institutions of cultural memory which symbolised the 'other'. Some authors, like the Bosnian historian Ivan Lovrenović (1994), have called such acts destruction of memory or 'memoricide'.

There has been significant scholarly work done in the area of collective memory[3] relating to both pre- and post-war Bosnia, as well as on 'individual memory'[4] – focused on traumatic, emotion-laden memories of individuals. While separation of collective and individual memories may be methodologically justified, these two types of memory do not exist independently from each other (cf. Heller 2001; Humphrey 2000). As Herbert Hirsch (1995: 13) points out, 'personal memory is the cornerstone supporting collective or social memory', and, in line with that, I argue in this chapter that there is a constant and active interplay between personal and collective memories, enmeshed in a two-way process in which individual memories coalesce into collective memories while collective memories get adopted and adjusted as individual or personal memories.

A plethora of empirical evidence in the form of narratives, memorials, monuments and commemorations from across BiH and the Bosnian diaspora provides valuable insights into the constant bottom-up and top-down interplay – change and exchange – between individual and collective memories. These memories do not only tell what happened but also how it was experienced and how a particular event has been remembered and contextualised at both individual and group levels. Knowing this, it should not come as a surprise that the memories of an individual and his/her social group are contested and contrasted with the memories of the 'other', as well as with the 'real events' as documented or officially interpreted. In such a contest, memory as a disputed subject becomes a source of ongoing antagonism between those articulating the conflicting memories. For instance, there is not even a common agreement in post-war BiH about the date the war started and the main reasons behind it (Maček 2001, 2007). This situation does not ease the tensions between different social and ethnic groups and individuals who were involved and/or affected by the war, as '[for] as long as the painful asymmetry of memory persists' – as Assmann (2006: 71) argues – 'the war continues to be present'[5] in both people's reality and imagination.

Prior to the war local ethno-nationalists from all the ethnic groups used memory very selectively, pointing to real and mythological episodes in the past when 'their people' were victimised by others, while purposely ignoring the long history of peaceful cohabitation of different ethnic groups in the region (Ramet 2002; Žanić 2007). Instead of interpreting violence and armed conflicts as aberrations of normalcy, peaceful times were seen as periods of suspended hostilities in a never-ending series of wars. This hypothesis was further developed by some Western scholars (e.g., Kaplan 1996) and uncritically accepted by many Western policy makers in order to justify their non-involvement in the conflict – as, for instance, Banac (2002), Baudrillard (1996), Bose (2002) Kumar (1997) and Power (2002) have argued.

The brutal war in Bosnia – which followed the prelude of orchestrated collective 'remembering' – showed that nationalist endeavours to stir up the ethno-nationalist sentiments and to spread the politics of fear and hate among ordinary people were very successful; ordinary people were ready to kill (and did kill) in the name of their people, to avenge lost mythological battles[6] and (re)create mythical homelands for their nations.

While the armed conflict in Bosnia did eventually stop in late 1995, the war over memory has only intensified and continues to be fought by 'other means' (Campbell 1998). This chapter explores these other means: monuments, memorials and commemorations and their relation to both personal and collective memories. My exploration begins where the previous chapter finished: the funeral at Hegići as an example of a contested memory-making process through monument, memorial and commemoration. I will then move to three other sites within the Prijedor municipality, taking the Prijedor cases as exemplars for a Bosnia-wide process of making/unmaking memory with different regional, municipal, ethnic and local variations. Other case studies discussed in the chapter include Srebrenica, Mostar and Sarajevo.

In all these places – as in other parts of the country – memory has not only been used to interpret the past but also to reaffirm and justify the present socio-political realities in the country. But memory has not only been about remembering; the memory making and unmaking process is as much about forgetting as it is about remembering (Ricoeur 2006). The control over both these aspects of memory is most directly related to power as, quite literally, 'those who control the past control the present'. This can be observed in the way official memory continues to be used as a means for political ends across the country. The control over the landscapes of memory extends to control over the real territories – to paraphrase Stephan Feuchtwang (2000: 72), territorial mapping is always drawn according to memories of home and grave sites as key points of reference. However, as discussed in the previous chapter, parallel to the official memory – expressed through official discourse, history books, monuments, commemorations, public holidays and similar forms of collective remembrance – there are also counternarratives based on countermemory, or popular memory, of those who do not have access to political institutions, the media and state-sponsored commemorations and monuments. Edita's village of Hegići provides an example of such unofficial, popular memory.

The Funeral at Hegići

While revisiting the Prijedor region and Edita's village in mid 2008, I was directly confronted with conflicting memories of the events that took place in the area during the 1992–95 war. The official history of the now dominant group, the Serbs, and the Republika Srpska (RS) government has been diametrically opposed to the popular memory of those who were ethnically cleansed from the area. In fact, the official RS history has been purposely used to deny and ignore the popular memory of the victims as well as influence judicial rulings about crimes committed in Prijedor during the war.[7] This is completely in line with Pierre Nora's (1989) claim that 'history is perpetually suspicious of memory, and its true mission is to suppress and destroy it' (cited in Sturken 1997: 5). These different interpretations of the past and conflicting memories intersect in the present time and on the same landscapes. The public memory of Serbs is publicly memorialised in public space and includes street and square names, such as Zoran Karlica Square, Jovan Rašković Street or Nikola Pašić Street,[8] grandiose monuments, usually in the form of exclusive religious symbols, and the official public holidays and commemorations sponsored by the RS government. The town's official holiday, 30 April, celebrated as Prijedor's Liberation Day, is the same day the Serb militias started the campaign of ethnic cleansing of non-Serbs from the area in 1992.

Public expression of the popular memory of ethnically cleansed Bosniaks and Croats has been reduced to private, low-key commemorations and burials of identified victims recovered from mass graves in the region (Tochman 2008; Halilovich 2011a). The majority – but not all – of the surviving relatives choose to bury Prijedor's victims of ethnic cleansing in the cemeteries in their native villages, even if these villages are in many cases still in ruins. But there are also those who decide to bury their relatives in the Bosniak and Croat dominated part of the country, the Federation, in towns close to Prijedor like Sanski Most, Ključ or Bihać. They explain that their decisions have been based on the fear that their relatives' graves could be desecrated by those who killed them or by the Serb nationalists who still deny or, even worse, justify the crimes committed in the region. However, most survivors still choose to bury the remains of their relatives in the villages where they lived and where they were killed – or from where they were taken, as happened in Hegići. For many of the displaced survivors, returning to their destroyed villages to bury their dead is seen as an act of reaffirming continuity of their local identities as well as an act of resistance and defiance – perceived by the survivors as two crucial steps in regaining control over their memories and their local identities, even if they often continue living thousands of kilometres from their 'reclaimed' local places. The return of the dead becomes a symbolic return of those who were expelled or killed. As Edita said, her dead relatives 'returned to stay'. In villages like Hegići, instead of rebuilding houses, in many cases only monuments to the dead are built. The monuments, the simple headstones in the local cemetery, become an important landmark, a symbol of family and communal identity. These ordinary monuments and simple religious funeral ceremonies might have been quite ordinary before 1992, but they have become quite extraordinary in post-1995 Bosnia and Herzegovina. For ethnically cleansed communities – decimated by the systematic killings just because of who they were – these monuments and rituals represent an assertion of being Bosniak/Muslim/local and as such are a form of resistance given the RS context. Indeed, the headstones are the quintessential symbol of each of these identities.

The eleven new marble headstones erected at the small village cemetery in the outskirts of Hegići in late July 2008 outnumbered the number of people who had returned to live in the village. On the day that the eleven victims were added to the graveyard, there was no public acknowledgement or mourning, or official recognition of any sort that something very bad had happened to the Hegići people sixteen years earlier. Only the dates of death engraved on the white headstones revealed that most of the people buried that day died together i.e., were killed on the same day in July 1992. The small congregation of some fifty people, made up of surviving relatives and neighbours, mourned in dignity and prayed for the souls of the victims of the massacre. The religious ceremony itself was transformed by the massacres in which mostly men had perished. In Islam only men are allowed to participate in funeral practices. However, on that day at the Muslim cemetery in Hegići women were burying their men, performing the roles traditionally reserved for men. The strict religious rules needed to be adjusted to reflect the new realities; mostly men perished and mostly women survived. Edita and her mother Enisa performed their roles stoically and with dignity.

From the cemetery the Hegići survivors could see the remains of what was once their village: the ruins and burned-out empty shells of their homes, with only a few new red roofs of those who had returned and rebuilt their houses. They could also see the old untouched houses of their Serb neighbours. Former neighbours. The sight of their destroyed village, the funeral of their dead fellow villagers who had been gunned down in the field clearly visible from the cemetery, the untouched Serb houses, and the same hot day in July must have reminded the Hegići survivors of the hot July fifteen years earlier. It seemed that time had stopped and everything that had happened was still happening to them and their village. On this hot July day, seven kilometres from Prijedor, in the green field marked by dozens of white headstones, again they felt as alone, abandoned and forgotten as they were in July 1992. There was no one asking for forgiveness that day; Serb neighbours and RS officials stayed away or watched from a distance yet another belated mass funeral of Muslims. There was no reconciliation or closure that day; it was just another return of those who once lived in the village bringing home their dead and leaving again until the next funeral brings them back.

For Edita and her mother, as for most other Hegići survivors who were expelled from their homes more than a decade and a half before, 'coming home' had increasingly come to mean coming to bury their relatives or occasional visits to the village to ensure that the headstones are still visible and the graves are well looked after by the few returnees to the village. In Hegići, as in other ethnically cleansed villages across Bosnia, the returnees agree to maintain the local graveyards for those who have resettled elsewhere – who in pre-war times would have tended the graves of their relatives. The returnees, rather than themselves being a symbol of life returned to the village, in a way become the keepers of communal memory and the human connection between the surviving and the dead villagers. The returnees, usually the older ones who did not have or look for options apart from returning to their original home village where they wanted to spend what remained of their lives, agree that the life of their place continues to be lived in faraway places, where their fellow villagers and relatives have resettled, much more than in the original location. 'There have not been any marriages or births in Hegići [since 1992]', sighs Hata, the elderly returnee to the village who lost her husband and her older son in the 1992 massacre. Her younger son survived only because he was hiding in the forest on the day the massacre took place. Since 1994 he has been living in Sweden where he met and married a girl from the neighbouring village of Hambarine. They have had two daughters and have made Malmö their new home. Once a year when they travel all the way from Malmö to Hegići to visit Hata, they often meet other survivors from Hegići now living in Austria and the U.S. While the displaced survivors from Hegići regularly keep in touch and exchange information about their new lives, they also talk about their past lives, recalling shared memories of living in Hegići as well as how now to commemorate their lost relatives. Effectively – like the deterritorialised villagers from Klotjevac, described in Chapter 1 – the Hegići survivors keep alive their reimagined Hegići identities thousands of kilometres from the actual place and from each other. For the maintenance of these trans-local connections and the performance of local identities, the original place – however destroyed and non-existent it may be – remains the most powerful anchor for communal identity and solidarity in displaced villagers.

Omarska

While the displaced Hegići villagers have been able to exercise some autonomy over their communal cemetery and the annual commemorations in the village, many other sites of massacres in Prijedor municipality continue to be controlled by RS authorities that actively obstruct memory-making initiatives by the survivors. Here in Prijedor, memory making and unmaking is not only about remembering, but also about forgetting. As in other societies after collective violence and genocide, there have been attempts 'to use history in the service of forgetting' (Lorey and Beezley 2002: xiv), and historical memory has been readjusted in order to provide perpetrators and those responsible with immunity from retribution for their earlier actions.

Apart from the still-potent ethno-nationalism in different variations in post-war Bosnia, the process of memory making and unmaking is coupled with many other parallel processes, like privatisation, globalisation, 'Europeanisation' and various projects – run by the UN, the EU and NGOs

– aimed at the socio-economic recovery of the divided society. In 2005 the transnational company Mittal Steel,[9] the world's largest steel company, bought the industrial complex and iron ore mine Omarska, near Prijedor. Once the pride of the local municipality, the industrial complex Omarska has become a symbol of the brutality of ethnic cleansing in the region. Although it only operated for some four months during the summer of 1992, the site was regarded as the most notorious Serb-run concentration camp during the war in Bosnia. Several thousand Bosniak and Croat men and forty women from the area were detained and tortured there in the summer of 1992. Hundreds of them were brutally killed.[10]

The first outsiders to gain access to the Omarska camp were a group of foreign journalists on 5 August 1992. What they saw there – and later presented to the rest of the world – was reminiscent of Nazi concentration camps half a century before. This is how Ed Vulliamy, a war reporter for *The Guardian*, described men detained at Omarska whom he was briefly allowed to see that day:

> The men are at various stages of human decay and affliction; the bones of their elbows and wrists protrude like pieces of jagged stone from the pencil-thin stalks to which their arms have been reduced. Their skin is putrefied, the complexion of their faces has been corroded. These humans are alive but decomposed, debased, degraded, and utterly subservient, and yet they fix their huge hollow eyes on us with what looks like knife blades of knives. (Vulliamy 1994: 102)

Vulliamy's colleague, Roy Gutman, a foreign correspondent for *Newsday*, provided very similar accounts of what he saw and what survivors told him about their ordeal at Omarska. They represented Omarska as a death camp and this recalled memories of the Second World War and the Holocaust in the West – at precisely the time that the United States Holocaust Memorial Museum in New York was to open and when memories of the Holocaust were once again entering public discourse and public consciences in the West. Western media showed pictures from Bosnia titled 'Never again?' (Brzezinski 1993). Thanks to Vulliamy's, Gutman's and other Western journalists' reports, Western politicians and policy makers increased their pressure on Karadžić and Milošević, which finally resulted in the closure of Omarska and a number of other concentration camps and the release of thousands of physically and psychologically scarred prisoners. With the assistance of the UNHCR, ICRC and IOM, most of the former camp inmates were then resettled in Western European countries, the U.S., Canada and Australia.

In the period after the war a number of war criminals arrested and handed over to The Hague Tribunal (ICTY) received long sentences for their participation in crimes at Omarska. The ICTY indictment against several Omarska guards and torturers describes crimes at Omarska in the following way:

> 2.6. Severe beatings were commonplace. The camp guards, and others who came to the camp and physically abused the prisoners, used all manner of weapons during these beatings, including wooden batons, metal rods and tools, lengths of thick industrial cable that had metal balls affixed to the end, rifle butts, and knives. Both female and male prisoners were beaten, tortured, raped, sexually assaulted, and humiliated. In addition to regular beatings and abuse, there were incidents of multiple killings and special terror. Many, whose identities are known and unknown, did not survive the camp.[11]

For many years the survivors and witnesses of Omarska have been campaigning for their right to commemorate and to construct a memorial at Omarska. As Rezak Hukanović, one of the Omarska survivors, stated:

> After initial reluctance by Mittal Steel to support such an idea the company's management has changed its mind and agreed to cooperate on the project. However, the authorities of RS oppose the project and would regard any monument construction as illegal, which they threaten to prevent building using all means available.

While the stalemate situation regarding the memorial continues, in 2006, after more than a decade of inactivity, Omarska resumed production.

Ironically, a year later, the industrial complex was used in another memory-making project, as a site for filming a grandiose film about the 'greatest Serbian battle during the First World War', the battle at Cer, which neither geographically nor historically had much to do with Omarska and the Prijedor region. The battle between Serbian and Austrian forces had taken place in western Serbia, on Mount Cer, between 15 and 20 August 1914, and was one of the first combat engagements of the First World War (Glenny 1999: 315–17). Almost a century later the film about the battle, financed by the governments of Serbia and Republika Srpska, turned Omarska into a fictitious battleground.[12] Many members of the local Serb community had the role of extras in the film, playing wounded and killed Serb soldiers and civilians (Pijetlović 2007). The real survivors, those who were detained and tortured at Omarska in 1992, understandably condemned the use of a former concentration camp site for making such a nationalistic film.

Ignoring the historical facts, survivors' testimonies, forensic evidence and the ICTY rulings,[13] and denying what really happened at Omarska, has involved various actors whose interest is not to have Omarska acknowledged and officially remembered as a concentration camp site. RS authorities, as both a legacy and a direct product of 'Omarska policies', have political reasons to oppose such an idea –it may undermine the legitimacy of RS if Omarska were to become known as a 'genocidal entity' – while many ordinary Serbs from Prijedor who were in the Serb army and police during the war prefer to close that chapter of their lives and not confront their contribution to ethnic cleansing in the area. For Rade, a local Serb, it was 'an unfortunate turn of events', 'part of a Western conspiracy', and he 'wasn't really sure' if camps like Omarska existed or were invented as part of the conspiracy to demonise the Serbs. 'We need to forget bad things that happened in order to move on', he explained. Although he might have not been one of the hard-core nationalists – or one of those who have benefited from ethnic cleansing by occupying flats and houses of those who were ethnically cleansed or by taking over their businesses and their jobs – Rade, an ordinary Serb in his fifties, was still denying and ignoring the facts about Omarska and other camps in the area. This is still the view – at least publicly – of the majority of the Serb population in Prijedor (Wesselingh and Vaulerin 2005; Pelz and Reeves 2008).

Mittal Steel's primary objective has been not to adversely affect its economic interests. Therefore it has been playing safe by giving the RS authorities the upper hand in the decision-making process about commemorations and the plan to turn a part of Omarska complex into a memorial. As was reported in the political weekly magazine *BH Dani*, making a profit at the site of a former concentration camp, without acknowledging what had happened there, would be bad for the Mittal Steel business (Hadžović 2007; Šehić 2011).

While the RS authorities do not recognise the memory of those who survived Omarska and continue to use public space to make claims about their version of history, the survivors have started an annual pilgrimage to the site of the former concentration camp. The first time was on 6 August 2004, twelve years after the camp's closure. Ed Vulliamy (2004) returned to the camp site with them. This time he noted:

> They walk in slow procession across a field of summer flowers, through the scent of mint into the nightmare of their memories. They arrive this time as survivors, not prisoners. Or else they come to pay homage to dead relatives at this accursed place: the now disused iron ore mine at Omarska, in northwest Bosnia. In 1992 it was a concentration camp, the location of an orgy of killing, mutilation, beating and rape, prior to enforced

deportation for those lucky enough to survive. The victims were Bosnian Muslims and some Croats, the perpetrators their Serbian neighbours.

In the last four years, the survivors and their supporters have marched to the camp and read the names of those who were killed at the site. Against the silence, ignorance and denial of Omarska, survivors Kemal Pervanić and Rezak Hukanović – who have written their memoirs of Omarska – continue to campaign for an official acknowledgement of what happened at Omarska in summer 1992. Kemal Pervanić, living in the U.K. since 1992, was one of the creators of the web-based petition to build a memorial at Omarska.[14] The petition includes five demands:

1) Survivors and families of the dead and missing must lead the design and management of the Memorial Project. For obvious reasons, survivors and families of the missing should not lose their right of participation by virtue of living in exile.

2) All stakeholders should acknowledge the psychological and historical significance of those buildings formerly used for purposes of incarceration, torture and extermination. For survivors to witness these buildings used for purposes outside of commemoration, encourages retraumatisation.

3) Mittal Steel should offer a lease over the main camp buildings to a Foundation (along the lines of the Foundation of the Srebrenica-Potočari Memorial and Cemetery) led by survivors and families of the dead and missing, for the purpose of establishing a memorial to the Omarska camp. It makes no sense for a commercial company to own and manage its own memorial to the camp.

4) Where such crimes are concerned, commemoration comes first and is a precondition for reconciliation; the victims have a fundamental right to tell the truth about what they suffered. This truth is in the best interests of all concerned, and should not be diluted for commercial or political reasons.

5) Mittal Steel urgently needs to make a public commitment to support investigations by internationally recognised bodies such as ICMP into mass graves on the Mine's land. This commitment should also include sharing information about the existence of any graves with local organisations representing survivors and families of the missing.

Between the launching the website in 2005 and April 2008, more than 2,500 people signed the petition. So far RS authorities and Mittal Steel management have ignored it.

While Kemal Pervanić has been mobilising public opinion using the internet, fellow Omarska survivor Rezak Hukanović – who, after the war ended, returned to his native Prijedor from Norway – has preferred face-to-face campaigning whenever and wherever he can. In April 2008, while I was conducting my research on deterritorialised Bosnian communities, I met Rezak far from his home town, in St. Louis, U.S.A, the adopted home of the largest Bosnian diaspora community. There he was, sharing his personal memory of Omarska with members of the Bosnian diaspora, many of whom like Rezak himself were survivors of ethnic cleansing. As in his widely read and quoted memoir *The Tenth Circle of Hell* (1996), he spoke in the third person when referring to what he survived at Omarska. 'There, at Omarska', he recalled, 'was a sixteen-year-old boy detained together with his father. They suffered together and the father, as much as he tried, was unable to protect his son from abuse by the guards. One day, the guards tortured the father while the son was forced to watch. They broke the father's arms, nose, kicked out his teeth and beat him long after he lost consciousness. For seventeen days after that, the father fought for his life, his son nursing him with a lot of loving care, a bit of water saved from drinking and shirts made into bandages. Ultimately, he saved his father's life. That brave sixteen-year-old boy was my son'. The room first went silent, then broke into a long applause with tears running down the faces of many people in the audience.

Rezak then told about difficulties and all the obstructions the local Serb authorities in Prijedor have been creating in order to silence the voice of survivors and prevent the construction of a memorial at Omarska. The planned memorial was nothing grandiose in terms of architecture, unlike the official government-built monuments. The survivors only wanted to turn a part of the Omarska complex into an open-air museum where visitors would walk in silence while a lone voice would come from the most notorious building at Omarska, the so-called 'white house' where the tortures and killings happened (Pelz and Reeves 2008). The voice would read the names of those who perished at Omarska.

A month before, in Rezak's home city of Prijedor, I interviewed Muharem Murselović, another prominent Omarska survivor and former businessman from Prijedor who, in 2000, was one of the first returnees to the city. Meanwhile, he has become a Bosniak political representative (MP) from Prijedor in the Serb-dominated government of RS. He said that Mittal Steel has not been indifferent to the construction of a memorial at Omarska but, on the contrary, has been collaborating with the RS authorities in keeping Omarska survivors away from the site. For instance, as he stated, out of 800 workers Mittal Steel employed at Omarska, only three were Bosniaks. Some of the Serbs employed were guards and torturers at the camp and knew about gross crimes committed there. Although Muharem has been gradually regaining his pre-war business prestige in the town, he continues to suffer from psychological and physical scars inflicted on him at Omarska. However, he said that he was not interested in his own sufferings being acknowledged and remembered, but felt obliged to make sure that those who perished at Omarska – his friends, neighbours and fellow citizens – would not be forgotten.

The only tool the survivors have had so far in fighting for their right to remember has been their own living memory – or countermemory in Foucauldian terms – which they have been sharing with others. Their main worry is who will remember and tell their stories once they have gone.

Keraterm and Trnopolje

Keraterm, a ceramic factory, used like Omarska as a concentration camp, has recently resumed production without any sign that in the summer of 1992 some 300 innocent civilians from Prijedor were killed there in the most brutal way. The ICTY verdict has found Duško Sikirica, the camp commander at Keraterm, guilty of various crimes, including 'violations of the laws or customs of war and crimes against humanity'.[15] Besides survivors' testimonies and the ICTY judgements Keraterm does not feature prominently in the memory debate in post-war Bosnia.

While Keraterm has been ignored and forgotten, Omarska actively denied and obstructed, the memory of Trnopolje, the site of the third concentration camp in the Prijedor region during 1992, has been 'hijacked', completely unmade and rewritten by the RS authorities. The Trnopolje camp has resumed its function as a local primary school, with the difference that it's mostly Serb children now who attend the school as the Bosniak children and their parents from Trnopolje and surrounding hamlets – previously the ethnic majority in the area – were ethnically cleansed in 1992. In this and other schools across RS, the school curriculum is used as an instrument in (un)making recent local history (Toal and Dahlman 2006), with no mention of ethnic cleansing of non-Serbs from the Prijedor region. Instead, a monument to Serb soldiers at the former concentration camp – now primary school – has turned Trnopolje into a memory site of Republika Srpska.

As in the case of other camps, large industrial and public buildings were used to house detainees during the 1992–95 ethnic cleansing in Bosnia. The local primary school in Trnopolje – called, by some bitter irony of fate, Bratstvo-Jedinstvo (Brotherhood and Unity) – was turned into a concentration camp in May 1992.

Trnopolje had generally a better reputation and was 'less bad' than Omarska as fewer people died at Trnopolje and the torture, rape and physical abuse were less systematic. In many cases it was the last destination for detainees before they were 'exchanged' or deported from the Republika Srpska territory. For those who survived Keraterm and Omarska, like Josip Dizdarević, a survivor who spent three months in the other two camps, Trnopolje was 'almost a summer camp'. 'Nothing, not even hell, could be compared to Omarska', he said. After having been severely tortured at Omarska, once transferred to Trnopolje Josip was only sporadically punched and kicked by the camp guards and their Serb volunteers.

Many detained people suffered more from a prolonged lack of food, shelter, psychological and verbal abuse than from direct physical maltreatment (Campbell 2002). While torture and killings in the other two camps occurred 'around the clock', the abuse in Trnopolje was less structured and depended on the guards' mood and the frequency of visits from local warlords and criminals – the same ones who went to the other two camps – who had free access to the camps and could do whatever they pleased with the detainees. In such random raids and orgies of violence, dozens of people were killed in Trnopolje and many more were tortured. The unseen crimes of Trnopolje included an unknown number of women and girls who were selected for rape and sexually abused by the Serb policemen, guards and soldiers in one of the houses next to the camp (Wesselingh and Vaulerin 2005: 56–9). The disappearances and killings of Trnopolje detainees took place mainly outside the camp during the 'prisoners' exchange', at the notorious Korićanske Stijene, on Mount Vlašić in central Bosnia (Hećimović 2009; G. Obradović 2009). By late summer the inmate population of Trnopolje comprised not only Bosniak and Croat men but also many women and children, in many cases surviving members of whole families and villages. At the time, the Serb military had carried out one last 'cleansing of the terrain' (*čišćenje terena*) in the burned villages around Prijedor, as well as in those parts of the city known to be populated by a large proportion of Bosniaks and Croats. In August 1992 the camp held some 3,500 people in the local primary school and the surrounding ground, which was filled with improvised shelters.[16]

Like Josip Dizdarević, a Bosnian Croat who today lives in Croatia, Ibro Sušić, who died in exile in Austria, and thousands of other Bosniaks and Croats from the Prijedor region, Mujo Jakupović went through the Trnopolje concentration camp before he was expelled to Croatia in late 1992. His story is similar to the stories of many other survivors: he was collected from his home in Prijedor, was severely beaten and physically abused by Serb soldiers and, but for a Serb soldier who recognised him as his father's friend, would have been killed by those who 'identified' him as a 'likely Muslim leader'. Thanks to that lucky coincidence, together with his wife Mejra and their two young daughters, Mujo was sent to the Trnopolje camp. They were not even allowed to put their shoes on. Their house was pillaged and all their belongings appropriated by the Serb soldiers. In Trnopolje, they suffered from lack of food and were randomly abused by the camp guards and Serb militiamen. The only survival strategy they had was to keep a low profile and wait. Like most other detainees, they survived but were expelled from their home city and their homeland.

After living as refugees in Croatia until 1996, Mujo and his family returned to Bihać, a Bosniak-dominated city in western Bosnia, some sixty kilometres west of Prijedor. He managed to exchange his house in Prijedor with a Serb from Bihać. In 2005 when Mujo, for the first time since the war, was driving to his native village of Kamićani, he passed through Trnopolje. He was impressed by the number of rebuilt houses, remembering that in 1992 all Bosniak houses in and around Kozarac and Trnopolje were in ruins. The modern asphalt road, made with a donation from USAID, as the sign said, connecting Trnopolje with the city of Prijedor, was further adding to his feeling that some kind of normalcy was returning to the area. However, he noticed that there were almost no people in sight, the balconies and front yards deserted. Those who had rebuilt their houses did not live in them. They were living in their new 'temporary homelands' – in Sweden, the U.S.A., Germany and elsewhere – and would use their newly rebuilt homes as holiday houses during their annual visits to their old home villages.

Approaching the site of the former concentration camp triggered Mujo's memories and the fear he had felt there many years ago. This time the school building, the sports ground and the local cultural centre – overcrowded with scared, broken and destitute people in 1992 – were empty of people, and the buildings looked freshly renovated. The whole site looked like an ordinary local school, only without children. Or that was his impression before he saw a big monument close to the main gate where once the guards' post stood. A large concrete two-headed eagle, a symbol of Serb nationalism, had been erected as a memorial 'to the fallen Serb heroes who gave their lives for the foundation of the Serb Republic'. Mujo felt bitter: 'no Serb had fallen here, not even by friendly fire – only Bosniak and Croat detainees were killed here, our lives were built into the foundations of the Serb Republic'. Mujo felt a mixture of feelings: strong anger, physical discomfort and great disappointment. This time he was convinced that he would never return to live in his old home town again. It was not *his* old town anymore. He did not want to be confronted on a daily basis with the denial of his memories. He did not ever want to forget. He was not ready to forgive.

Not only was the tragic past of Trnopolje not acknowledged and commemorated – as the survivors like Mujo, Josip and Safet would have liked it – the memory of Trnopolje was, in fact, unmade, expropriated and rewritten by those who control its physical site. Trnopolje has been used to commemorate the official memory of Republika Srpska; it has been effectively turned into *lieux de mémoire* of Republika Srpska. The real and true living memory has been replaced by constructed memory, which in turn has become the official history. On Serb national holidays schoolchildren bring flowers and recite patriotic poetry at the site, while local politicians give speeches about the heroism of Serb soldiers who gave their lives for Republika Srpska. No one talks about the real legacy of Republika Srpska: more than half of the Prijedor population, Bosniaks and Croats, who were ethnically cleansed from their homes between 1992 and 1995. And while this may be quite frustrating to survivors and their supporters, in Pierre Nora's view, most sites of nationalistic memories are artificial and deliberately fabricate the historical facts (cited in Carrier 2000).

Srebrenica/Potočari Commemorations

Regardless of their relation to the official histories, acts of collective remembrance, such as commemorations, funerals and memorials, act as performances of group identity and as such are inevitably political (Hoepken 1999; Žanić 2007). By giving identities to their lost relatives and by taking part in a traditional religious ceremony – in a silent grassroots act of defiance – the Hegići survivors made a clear statement to themselves and to others of who they were and are. Like in Hegići, collective funerals and commemorations in other parts of Bosnia bring together survivors, relatives, former neighbours and friends from many different places to participate in and contribute to the memory-making process. For many of them this is the only time when they meet, or hope to meet, members of their pre-war communities and say farewell those who perished. At the funerals personal relationships with the dead confirm the status of the remaining relatives as (genocide) survivors. In most instances this is an important moral category for survivors as the only recognition of their loss.

Apart from the performance of such grassroots identity politics, there has also been a strong tendency to appropriate these events for broader political, ethno-religious and nationalist agendas. The experience from Bosnia has shown that the larger the funeral, the greater the opportunity to politicise the event. This has especially been the case with the largest annual commemoration and burial – of Srebrenica genocide victims every 11 July, described in more detail in Chapter 1. While the massacres at Srebrenica constitute the largest, the most systematic and the most efficiently executed mass killings of civilians that have been legally defined by the ICTY as genocide,[17] Srebrenica has also been the most widely known and publicly acknowledged war crime committed in the region. Other 'smaller' crimes in which, in some cases, complete communities perished have been overshadowed by the great crime committed at Srebrenica in July 1995 (Halilovich 2007).

In recent years Bosniak religious and political establishments, as well as international and regional political actors, have increasingly been using the Srebrenica commemoration to affirm their political power. Turning the Srebrenica commemoration into a 'genocide festival' or a 'religious pilgrimage' has not been appreciated by Asim, a survivor and one of many IDPs who turned their internal displacement into a dual residency, spending time between his old home town of Srebrenica and his 'temporary' displacement in Tuzla. Asim felt that Srebrenica people had been used 'once again' for higher politics beyond their interests and their influence. He told how in the previous three years, due to traffic congestion and the many VIP cars carrying politicians, many survivors did not manage to get to Potočari on time to participate in the funeral procession of their relatives. To him – who had lost six close relatives at Srebrenica – all the VIP guests, religious and political leaders with their security escorts gave the impression of being more important than those burying their loved ones or even more important than the genocide victims being buried on the day. 'Then there were people – I think they even were the local Serbs – setting up stalls along the road and selling food and drinks like it was a festival here', tells Asim in anger.

The 'genocide festival' of which Asim was complaining and the accompanying aspect of 'genocide spectatorship' were felt by some of my colleagues and myself when we visited the Potočari commemoration as part of the International Association of Genocide Scholars Conference,[18] held in Sarajevo in July 2007. On that rainy day, on 11 July 2007, on the way to Potočari our buses were diverted to a mass grave site nearby. The site had been exhumed by local and international experts and prepared for our visit. Standing at the edge of the pit, Amor Mašović, the chairman of the Bosnian Federal Commission for Missing Persons, gave an overview of the mass grave and explained what it contained.

We could see some dozen skulls and many human bones scattered in the mud at the bottom of the pit. There were also pieces of clothing and shoes mixed with the body parts. Against the backdrop of visitors more befitting a school excursion, I was suddenly overcome with discomfort and a sense of shame for being where I was. It was not the direct confrontation with the magnitude of the tragedy called Srebrenica, or the realisation of what human beings were able to do to each other that overwhelmed me. Rather, I felt ashamed for being a spectator, for looking at the exposed victims' skulls and femurs still covered in mud. I and others felt our massive presence at the site was posthumously robbing the victims of their dignity. There they were, lying, still nameless, dismembered, their bones crushed, each piece of the remains holding clues to the secret of the way these people had died in July 1995.

I could understand the need for the professional detachment of those involved in exhuming the bodies on a daily basis, although this – as Clea Koff (2004), Kenneth Cain et al. (2004) and Sarah Wagner (2008) have written – was not always an easy task. However, I was not sure about how much the genocide scholars should feel detached from or attached to what they were observing and witnessing on that rainy day on a sodden hill near Potočari. Those bodily remains were someone's brothers, sons, husbands, fathers – but they were also forensic evidence about the genocide committed. The pit was a gruesome crime scene by all legal standards. And yet a number of the international 'scholars' entered the mass grave as they jostled to get better close-up shots with their digital cameras. Far from being detached, their actions were both completely disrespectful and inappropriate. Apart from any ethical issues, they did not even consider that they were contaminating a crime scene. They wanted a bit of Srebrenica memory captured with their cameras in order to be able to say 'I was here'. They behaved like tourists at an archaeological site, but instead of some interesting objects from antiquity, the grave contained 'ordinary', contemporary stuff like Adidas shoes and, Levi's jeans and T-shirts very similar to those some of the 'scholars' in the crowd were themselves wearing that day. The cameras kept zooming and the shoes of the mass grave visitors made fresh impressions in the mud very close to the objects of our attention, the human remains of the victims of genocide. There was something truly voyeuristic in the behaviour of those busy with their cameras. It was hard not to think of them as genocide spectators. I felt very uncomfortable being a part of the group and contributing to the spectacle. I could understand what Asim was talking about.

The memory of Srebrenica belongs first and foremost to the surviving relatives and friends of those who perished. Only they can personally remember the victims, who continue to occupy their memories and provide them with a sense of (lost) identity. Even ordinary objects such as the clothing of the victims were related to the survivors. Many relatives recognised some of the objects as a part of the victims' identification process. 'I recognised my son's trousers and the jacket ... I recognised all the patches I stitched many years ago' – recalled Rahima, who lost her only son and her husband at Srebrenica. As in Rahima's case, the survivors' memory and their ability to remember and recognise have also been used to provide the victims with their identities. Hence their memory has been of forensic significance. 'We won't forget' is a promise or a reminder to themselves of how important the process of memory making is. Understandably, Srebrenica commemorations have a completely different meaning for them than they do for outsiders, and many feel that outsiders have been taking over the control of their memory and their identity. They are worried that their memory of Srebrenica is being dispersed and appropriated, 'taken to a higher level', while their identity is being stereotyped and perceived as lacking agency. In the words of Asim:

> Our politicians from Sarajevo expect us – and I think it's a general perception of us [Srebrenica] survivors – to be more nationalistic, more religious, more patriotic, but all they really do for us is to come here once a year to talk about our tragedy like it was their own. They say 'our Muslim brothers were killed here', but they were not really their brothers, they were our brothers. Most of my relatives weren't religious at all ... When it comes to helping people to return to Srebrenica, to live here again, they've done a bare minimum ... It seems that for them we are of more value dead than alive.

Asim's frustration is shared by many other survivors. Hasan Nuhanović, a prominent Srebrenica survivor and author of the book *Under the UN Flag* (2007), observes:

> For most of these politicians, Srebrenica has been the only political capital they have. No one was interested in Srebrenica before we, the survivors, achieved our great victory, the right to bury our relatives at Potočari. At the time Bosniak politicians didn't have any idea – or didn't care – about the place where more than 8000 genocide victims were to be buried.

In an article addressing the ongoing denial of the Srebrenica genocide by the Serb nationalist ideologues, published in the renowned Bosnian political magazine *BH Dani*, Nuhanović (2008) also reminded his readers that 'Bosniak politicians shouldn't be using Srebrenica as their only excuse every time they were under attack, or they were asked about crimes committed against other ethnic groups in Bosnia'. Similarly, in an emotionally charged open letter published in *Start*, a Sarajevo-based magazine, another prominent Srebrenica survivor, Emir Suljagić, accused the Muslims' representative body in Bosnia, the Islamic Community of Bosnia-Herzegovina, of using the Srebrenica genocide for its own purposes by 'Islamising' this great tragedy (Suljagić 2008).

Many other Srebrenica survivors have felt that their memory has been under double attack: from public denial, moral relativism and triumphalism by the Serb nationalists on the one side, and from the Bosniak nationalists, on the other, who use Srebrenica to generalise about the 'victimised Bosniak nation', attempting to turn Srebrenica into the main pillar – a memory site – of the new Bosniak nationalism. As Asim pointed out, the survivors are also against banalising of the memory through turning the annual Srebrenica commemoration at Potočari into a 'tourist' attraction for politicians and spectators. They appreciate solidarity with foreigners and fellow Bosnians, but they also insist on being the sole keepers of the memory of their tragedy. Only they can remember those they lost. For the Islamic Community of Bosnia-Herzegovina and their leader, Mufti Cerić, the Srebrenica victims may be *šehids* (Muslims martyrs), and for the Bosniak political leadership, victims who died in the aggression against the Bosniak nation and the state of BiH, but for the Srebrenica survivors they were simply their fathers, brothers, sons, husbands, neighbours, school friends and members of their local community. For them, the Srebrenica genocide has been primarily devastating to their families, their neighbourhoods and their community – all of which were changed forever.

***

Popular memory of the survivors from Prijedor and Podrinje acts as countermemory, an alternative version of history, against both the Serb and Bosniak nationalist discourses in post-war BiH. While the official Serb nationalist history in places like Hegići, Prijedor, Omarska, Trnopolje and Srebrenica ignores, denies and silences memories of the survivors and expellees, the Bosniak nationalist memory, by claiming to represent them, selectively appropriates these memories, turning them into 'fixed memories and generic, blanket interpretations' of the history of suffering of the Bosniak people (Sorabji 2006: 13). As described in this chapter, both versions of nationalist memories, while being qualitatively different and exclusive of each other, misappropriate the memories of the survivors and expellees.

By sticking to their versions of memories through local narratives, embodied connections with funerals, and grassroots forms of de-centralised commemorations, the memories of the survivors act as a form of defiance and resistance against the 'generic' nationalist histories that either exclude them or selectively include only fragments of memories that fit with the broader versions of nationalist narratives. However, this does not imply that survivors' countermemories are somehow fixed, objective accounts of the actual events that took place in their communities. As Lisa Malkki, writing about Hutu refugees in Tanzania, argues, 'refugees' narratives are mythico-historical accounts of the past', emphasising that 'mythico-historical is not meant to imply that they were mythical in the sense of being false or made up' (1995: 55). 'What made the refugees' narratives mythical, in the anthropological sense', she argues, 'was not truth or falsity, but the fact that it was concerned with order in a fundamental, cosmological sense ... ordering and reordering of social and political categories, with defining of self in distinction to other, with good and evil'. At the funeral ceremonies at the cemeteries in Hegići and Potočari, survivors' 'ordering and reordering of social and political categories' and their distinction to 'other' is manifested through reclaiming the personal relationships with the bodies of their perished relatives and confirming their own status as (genocide) survivors. By doing this, the survivors position themselves vis-à-vis others, not only to the perpetrators and the ethnic other, but also their ethnic compatriots and 'outsiders' who are, like in Potočari, perceived by the local survivors as turning their local tragedy into a 'genocide festival'.

While the local memories described here often work against the dominant forms of nationalist histories, as Stef Jansen's study of five Serb and Croat villages in Croatia demonstrates, 'mythico-historical' aspects of local memories can also work as a form of bottom-up nationalism. He argues that 'through vagueness, amnesia and selective remembering, they [the local villagers] (re)constructed largely nationally exclusive memories in relation to several sets of events' (Jansen 2002: 78).

Local memories and narratives in BiH are not immune to similar constructions of local histories. For instance, the siege of Sarajevo and daily survival of those trapped in the city between 1992 and 1995 has been used to promote the 'barbarian thesis' of conflict, according to which rural, 'uncivilised' Serb besiegers were juxtaposed against urban, cosmopolitan Sarajevans, despite the fact that many 'on the hills' around Sarajevo were urbanites from Sarajevo (and Belgrade), while thousands of the Sarajevo defenders were recruited from the rural refugees and Sarajevans from less urban suburbs at the edges of Sarajevo. While many of the local memories of Sarajevans, as Cornelia Sorabji (2006) argues, are accurate autobiographical narratives, the interpretative frameworks of nationalists seek to constrain and channel these memories into a common narrative of collective suffering.

Mostar Carrying its Cross

The war in the country seems to have left its imprints on each person and each town, city and village in the country. Mostar has been one of the places where these imprints have turned into deep scars on the cultural landscape of a once multicultural city.[19] Once renowned as 'the jewel of Herzegovina' and its political, financial and cultural centre, famed for its Old Bridge (*Stari Most*), Mediterranean climate, river Neretva and surrounding mountains of Velež and Hum, more recently Mostar has become a symbol of communities divided along ethnic lines.[20] During the 1992–95 war, Mostar was the site of a three-way conflict, initially between Serb militias and the 'Serbianised' Yugoslav National Army (JNA) on the one hand and the Bosniak and Croat defenders on the other. In late 1992, once the frontlines with Serbs were established outside the city of Mostar, the conflict entered its second, much bloodier phase, between allies turned enemies: the Croat militia, Croatian Defence Council (HVO), and the Bosniak-dominated Army of the Republic of Bosnia and Herzegovina (ARBiH). Parts of the multicultural city, like most of the region of Herzegovina, were ethnically cleansed of the 'other', resulting in massive displacement within and from the city. At the same time there was a huge influx of refugees from the surrounding villages and towns looking for refuge in Mostar. Each of the refugee groups joined their respective ethnic communities.

As in most other parts of the country, symbols of the 'other' as well as symbols of togetherness were deliberately targeted and destroyed during the conflict in Mostar (Sells 1996). Before withdrawing from Mostar the JNA damaged or destroyed a number of cultural monuments such as a Franciscan monastery, the Catholic cathedral, the Karadžoz-bey and Roznamed-ij-Ibrahim-efendija mosques and twelve other mosques, as well as many secular buildings and crucial infrastructure. In a subsequent reprisal the HVO demolished the sixteenth-century Orthodox monastery Žitomislić and the 220-year-old Saborna Crkva (Orthodox Cathedral Church) in Mostar (Riedlmayer 2002a).

The culmination of hostilities and destruction of symbols of cultural memory came with the deliberate shelling and destruction of the Old Bridge by the HVO, in late 1993 (Coward 2002, 2009). The stone bridge, constructed by the Ottomans in 1566, was considered to be more a part of the cultural heritage of the Muslim Bosniak than Catholic Croat only at the time of its destruction (N. Adams 1993); as Colin Kaiser (2000), a cultural heritage expert and the former director of the UNESCO office in Sarajevo, points out, 'before the war, nobody in Mostar would have said that the Old Bridge was a "Muslim" monument. Its destruction by Croat tanks turned it into one'.

Two years of intense fighting left the city in ruins and the two traditionally friendly communities divided more than ever before. The communities even became divided geographically, with Croats claiming the western part of the city and Bosniaks its eastern side. Thousands of those who fled Mostar and did not accept the division of their city along ethnic lines turned their refuge into permanent resettlement in many different countries, as will be discussed in the following chapter.

As the nationalists on both sides continue to dominate the city politics in the post-war period, reintegration of the city and the process of communal reconciliation has been a serious challenge for both the local activists and the international community keen to reconstruct Mostar, not only physically but also socially and culturally. Against their endeavours to unite the divided city, the nationalists have been very eager to preserve and widen the divide between the communities. Instead of looking for commonalities, the ethno-religious – or rather simply religious – differences have been emphasised.

In post-war Mostar, symbols as divisive instruments in the identity- and memory-building process have been taken to the extreme. As Zdzislaw Mach (1993: 38) points out, 'social order, the way society is organised in a structure, is expressed and above all justified symbolically by reference to supreme values, like acts of God, the will of the people, the vote of the majority, an objective historical law, and so forth'. Mostar has had it all: new, higher domes of Catholic cathedrals have been competing with the new, higher minarets of Muslim mosques. The purpose of such competition has not been to get closer to God or to meet the increasing demands of the expended religious communities. Religion, as used in post-war Mostar, has been intrinsically linked to exclusive claims of cultural space, a process in which collective memory as an imagined anchor of historical continuity of each particular group has played a pivotal role. The booming of the symbols in post-war Mostar did not start as a series of spontaneous acts by disorganised masses, but was rather a carefully planned and tightly controlled process involving different local, regional and international actors who have had their interests at stake in Mostar (Robinson and Pobrić 2006).

Most historians agree that Mostar traces its name from the Old Bridge (*Stari Most* in Bosnian/Croatian/Serbian languages) – Mostar literally means 'Bridge keeper' – and that the medieval town was established as a trading centre in the fifteenth century by the Ottomans, who also built the bridge.[21] During the revival of ethnic identity politics in BiH in the early 1990s, the common cultural heritage was 'ethnicised': the cultural legacy of the four-centuries-long Ottoman presence in the country was exclusively linked to the collective identity and cultural heritage of Bosnian Muslims (Bosniaks) while the other two ethno-religious groups, Croats and Serbs, appropriated the pre-Islamic and Christian heritage of the country and linked their collective identities to those of their 'ethnic brothers and sisters' in neighbouring states, in Croatia and Serbia respectively. As Riedlmayer (2002b) concludes, such division of the common Bosnian cultural heritage was devastating to the institutions of cultural memory perceived as symbolising the 'other' (mosques, churches, bridges, libraries, archives ...). In the post-war period the ethno-religious communities in Mostar, as in the rest of Bosnia and Herzegovina, have been very keen to reconstruct their destroyed cultural monuments – mainly mosques, cathedrals and churches – and to reclaim their historical continuity in the area. However, this reconstruction has turned into an ethnocentric race, a competing symbolism over which community will erect more of what are 'their' exclusive monuments. Apart from religious sites, there has almost been no public space left untouched by the memorialising: streets, city squares, universities, schools, cultural centres, even the soccer stadiums were renamed and re-remembered.

While the competing symbolism has been mainly between the two largest ethno-religious groups – the Catholic Croats and the Muslim Bosniaks – the Serb institutions of collective memory, embodied in landmarks of historical continuity, Žitomislić Monastery and Saborna Crkva, destroyed in 1992, have also been rebuilt or are in the process of rebuilding.[22] Non-Serb Mostar residents have been divided about Serbs reclaiming their sites. Many Mostar residents I interviewed in Mostar and in diaspora welcome the return of Serbs and see this as a reconstruction of pre-war multiculturalism in their city. 'Mostar has always been proud of its Serbs, like the poet Aleksa Šantić [...] people like him would never have had anything to do with Serb nationalists and war criminals' – claimed Vahdet, a Bosniak man from Mostar who fled the 1990s' violence in his city and resettled with his ethnically mixed family in Melbourne. However, many others resent the idea as they link 'the treacherous Serbs' and their churches to the outbreak of the war in Mostar. 'They started it all and it's their fault that Mostar's way of life was destroyed' says Admir, whose family members were killed and wounded by the Serb military. Similarly, Marko, a Croat from the western part of the city, is against the reconstruction of Serb cultural sites: 'They have their Republika Srpska only for themselves and now they want to get parts of our territory'.

Marking the territory has been at the core of the politics of memory and competing symbolism in Mostar. When, in 2001, it became clear that UNESCO, the World Bank and the City of Mostar were committed to completely reconstructing the Old Bridge,[23] some political leaders of the Croats in the western part of Mostar perceived this as yet another act of triumphalism of their enemies of yesterday, the Bosniaks in the eastern part. As a response to this initiative, the Croats erected a huge cross on the highest spot of Mount Hum overlooking Mostar. The Jubilee Cross, as it was named, was to represent two thousand years of Christianity and continuity of this faith in the region as well as to 'commemorate the recent sufferings the city went through and, at the start of the new millennium, to give a new stamp to the city'.²⁴

The wording of this statement and use of metaphors such as 'stamp' and 'new millennium' reveals that the nationalist projects in Mostar attempt to change the city's culture in its totality and for eternity. 'Stamp' suggests authority and legitimacy; once a document gets its stamp it becomes official and is often regarded as representing the law. The cross on the Mount Hum can then be understood as a stamp with the ultimate authority of God. 'The new millennium' as a new start suggests a forward-looking orientation, implying at least a thousand years of projected future continuity of the collective identity in question.

The 'new stamp' is undoubtedly exclusive as it does not relate to Mostar's Muslims who perceive it as offensive and humiliating: 'Those who put that cross over there wanted to provoke us ... to create a new conflict and to announce that Muslim extremists are the problem and not them ... That cross should be removed by moderate Croats, but they don't dare to confront their extremists. As long as there is that cross above our heads there won't be reconciliation,' said Admir, who considers himself an 'atheist Muslim'.

In the western part of Mostar, Jadranka, a Croat woman, had a different view of the cross: 'It's our faith and if they [the Bosniaks] don't like it, they shouldn't look at it. Do they ask me when they build their mosques?' Marko – who 'identified' me as 'one of them' – was even more eloquent: 'If *your* bridge represents 500 years of Muslim [presence] than *our* cross represents 2,000 years of Christianity' – was the message he wanted me to pass across the Boulevard, once the frontline and now an unofficial border between the eastern and western parts of the city.

While those erecting the monuments keep making exclusivist claims on the past in order to reaffirm their positions in the present – and to project the future – a popular multi-ethnic movement of Mostar residents has been resisting and ridiculing – if not banalising – the politics of memory in Mostar. For instance, the whole controversy and tensions about the Jubilee Cross has inspired some to create a popular joke about the issue. The joke goes like this: Haso, (a fictitious character from many Bosnian jokes, representing an ordinary guy) was asked by a journalist (or a researcher like me) what he thought about the cross over Mostar. 'In my opinion', replied Haso, 'it is a big plus for Bosnia and Herzegovina'.

The joke, which may or may not be funny, exemplifies popular resistance to ethno-nationalist use of exclusive symbolism. In what some see as a religious symbol, or a provocation, many ordinary people are still able to distance themselves from it and see it only as a benign – or banal – plus sign overlooking their city. This view is shared by a group of reconciliation activists organised around the youth group Urban Movement Mostar, who claim to represent the Bruce Lee and rock 'n' roll ethos. When everyone was reconstructing and memorialising their own past, commemorating their heroes and remembering their victories and defeats, this group decided to build a monument to their own hero, the kung fu legend Bruce Lee. In November 2005, on the day that would have been his sixty-fifth birthday, they officially unveiled the life-size bronze statue depicting the Chinese-American actor in a typical defensive fighting position, facing neither east nor west but north so that no side could appropriate or alienate him. The activists behind the project commented that Bruce Lee represented 'loyalty, skill, friendship and universal justice' (Zaitchik 2006). However, it seems that these values and Bruce Lee's neutrality were not appreciated by some who, on many occasions, vandalised the statute so that it had to be removed for major repair. In early 2007, when I visited the site, Bruce Lee's statue was absent from its platform. When it was restored and reinstalled some time later a security guard was employed to watch it. For some, non-ethnic specific symbols are more offensive than those even of the ethnic other.

Sarajevo Remembers

Between 1992 and 1995 Sarajevo was at the epicentre of the Bosnian 'memoricide'. The deliberate targeting and setting ablaze of the *Vijećnica* – which housed the National and University Library – and the Oriental Museum, destroyed the largest collections of books and written documents in Bosnia-Herzegovina. In these two attacks more than two million books and more than two hundred thousand rare historical documents and unique manuscripts were destroyed (Donia 2006: 314; Riedlmayer 2002b: 105–6). Kemal Bakaršić (1994), a librarian of Bosnia's National Museum who risked his life attempting to save books from the burning *Vijećnica*, captured the moment in the following two sentences:

> The sun was obscured by the smoke of books, all over the city sheets of burned paper, fragile pages of grey ashes, floated down like a dirty black snow. Catching a page you could feel its heat, and for a moment read a fragment of text in a strange kind of black and grey negative, until, as the heat dissipated, the page melted to dust in your hand. (Bakaršić 1994: 14)

These written words might have immortalised the destruction of *Vijećnica* much more than any camera that filmed the event which took place from 25 to 27 August 1992. What Kemal Bakaršić personally experienced, and described in these sentences, has become Sarajevo's collective memory of the burning *Vijećnica*. In the memories of many Sarajevans, Bosnians and sympathetic outsiders, Kemal Bakaršić has posthumously become something of an urban hero, a hero who defended Sarajevo's cultural memory and in turn became a part of the memory of many of his fellow citizens and hence the collective memory of his city.[25]

No one – except those who ordered and executed the destruction of *Vijećnica* – remained indifferent to such unnecessary and unjustified destruction of cultural heritage. In the end, while there could be no justification for the destruction of any religious sites, the *Vijećnica*, a symbol of Sarajevo's civic identity, was not even a religious or exclusive ethnic symbol (Riedlmayer 2007). The *Vijećnica* was destroyed, as András J. Riedlmayer – a Harvard scholar and an expert on Bosnia's cultural heritage – stated in an interview, because it represented exactly that: the civic identity of the city and the material evidence that people of different ethnicities and religions could live together sharing common cultural heritage as part of their collective cultural memory (Čečo 2008). Those who destroyed *Vijećnica* wanted to erase that material evidence as it did not fit into the exclusive ideology of ethno-nationalism, just as Bruce Lee does not fit into ethnically divided Mostar (Šehić 2009).

The wide international condemnation of the acts of destruction of cultural heritage such as *Vijećnica* has influenced the way many Bosnians remember the war. They have absorbed the destruction of cultural icons into their individual and collective memories, though many of them were actually not present at the places where some of those events took place. Stana Zahović, a Sarajevan who was a refugee in Germany throughout the war recalls the destruction of the *Vijećnica* in Sarajevo as vividly as if she had actually been there on the day. She describes a 'countless number of burning books' and the 'flames and smoke reaching close to her house'. In reality, she watched the burning library far away from her house in Bistrik, a hill overlooking the *Vijećnica*, on television in a *Flüchlingsheim* (refugee centre) in Germany. However, the sense of personal loss and media coverage of the event made her adopt the image of the burning *Vijećnica* as it would have been seen from her own house at the time. It became Stana's lived memory – something that happened to her personally – regardless of where she was physically at the time. The fact that, since her return home in 1996, she has been watching the ruins of the burned-down library on a daily basis might have contributed to how she embedded this collective Sarajevan memory into her persona. Stana has not been alone in such an experience. Other tragedies, like those at Srebrenica and Prijedor, have also been internalised by many Bosnians who might never have even visited the places, but who 'remember' the events. Similarly, the pre-war memories of the 'good old days' are very much shared and complemented from both individual and collective sources.

Whilst Sarajevo has sought to incorporate many of its old, pre-war memories, the capital city of BiH has also had its own share of controversial memory making and unmaking. Immediately after the war a number of streets and public places in the city were renamed, in some cases returning to the old pre-Second World War names,[26] while others received new, more patriotic names,[27] or were sometimes named after their 'patrons', the donor countries.[28]

After the war a religious, Muslim, stamp was added to the memory of the siege of Sarajevo, when the old Muslim cemetery Kovači was reserved exclusively for Muslim heroes of resistance and renamed *Šehidsko groblje* (the Martyrs' Cemetery). President Alija Izetbegović was buried there, but so were some controversial figures such as the notorious warlord Mušan Topalović Caco.[29]

The memory of the secular resistance movement, made up of many Sarajevans for whom religion was of no or secondary importance, has been reinterpreted and 'Islamised'. Dino, who considers himself an atheist and who was on the first line of defence for most of the war, has been bitterly disappointed by such a trend:

> We fought together for a multicultural Sarajevo and later those of us who were killed got separated into *šehids* (Muslim martyrs) and *pali borci* (fallen defenders), but much more importance has been given to those regarded as *šehids* as if we fought for different causes ... I know my comrades would be turning in their graves if they knew how they've been separating us.

When it comes to religious architecture the most obvious and the most criticised of projects in Sarajevo have been the numerous mosques – not those that were restored and were a part of collective memory of most Sarajevans, but those that were built with the money of countries like Saudi Arabia, Kuwait and Malaysia. Many local Sarajevans – Muslims and non-Muslims alike – perceive these new mosques as alien not only because of their distinct architectural design but also because of their inconvenient locations (like the Saudi mosque King Fahd built in the midst of Sarajevo skyscrapers). But the most trenchant criticism has been for the influence they have been spreading among their congregations, promoting fundamentalist versions of Islam including Wahhabism. A number of Sarajevo intellectuals, including Islamic scholars, have openly criticised such trends and the official Bosniak Islamic bodies who are actively and passively supporting or tolerating the Islamisation of the Bosnian Muslims and their shared cultural heritage (Hafizović 2006; Duraković 2006). In their view these buildings and teachings have been displacing the original culture, tradition and memory of Bosnia and its Muslims.

Seven years after the Croat cross in Mostar was erected, a similar initiative was considered by Serb nationalists who planned to build their cross on Zlatište, one of the most prominent hills overlooking Sarajevo, the same hill from which the city was shelled during the war and from where the *Vijećnica* books were targeted. The 'Serb cross' – as presented by those advocating its creation – was to commemorate the 'Serb civilians killed in Sarajevo during the war' (SRNA 2008). This plan – which has not yet been completely abandoned – continues to seriously undermine the fragile peace and fuel the ever-growing divide between the Serbs and Bosniaks in the country. In March 2008, at the peak of the 'cross over Sarajevo' crisis, a number of Sarajevans I interviewed said that they were ready even to take up arms to stop the controversial project.[30] They saw it as a deliberate act of humiliation and triumphalism defaming their memory of what really happened in and around Sarajevo during the war. The common opinion held by most Sarajevo residents was that the Serb nationalists who were besieging the city and indiscriminately killing those in the town now wanted to commemorate some of those they killed. They were embittered by such a prospect.

While this monument was put on hold after considerable pressure was applied on the Serb political leadership, walking on the streets of Sarajevo it is hard not to remember all the pictures of shells landing in the queues waiting for bread or water, killing and maiming innocent civilians. The 'Sarajevo Roses', the simplest and possibly the most unique of monuments in BiH, remain the clearest reminder that people were massacred on the streets of the city (Tumarkin 2005). Spread throughout the city, these grenade craters filled with red plastic memorialise locations where nine or more people were killed in one single attack. Many 'Sarajevo Roses' have been filled with proper cement, leaving only the smaller shrapnel scars in red. For many, the sight of the 'roses' – that so closely resemble blood – functions as a prompt to remember, bringing back the memories of war. On many occasions I have observed how people avoid stepping on the red plastic at any cost, as if they felt that stepping on the spot where their fellow citizens lost their lives was disrespectful. Most Sarajevans, however, insist on the importance of keeping the 'roses' as a city-wide people's memorial for the thousands of civilians killed indiscriminately on the streets of their city.

In addition to the 'Sarajevo Roses', Sarajevo, unlike other cities in the region, has also preserved many of its pre-1992 monuments and commemorations, which rise above the post-1992 divisions. For instance, monuments to the Second World War, anti-fascism and commemoration of different dates from the period have remained significant to many Sarajevans. While most other cities across former Yugoslavia have renamed their Tito Streets, Sarajevo is one of the few that has not changed the name of its Marshal Tito Street. In the heart of Sarajevo, the 'Eternal Fire' (*Vječna vatra*) is still burning in Titova Street and an anti-fascist monument still stands, remembering those who liberated Sarajevo from fascist occupation in the Second World War. The old Marshal Tito (former Yugoslav army) Barracks – with Tito's statue still intact – have been privatised and partly converted into the new campus of the University of Sarajevo. Unlike most other cities in the country, in which all reminders of the communist past have been destroyed, it seems that Sarajevo has been able to integrate non-nationalistic history into the functional present.

Sarajevo has many other examples of inclusive monuments to the recent past. Just as Bruce Lee is remembered in Mostar, so too have Sarajevans chosen to memorialise some of their local popular culture heroes. They include many iconic personalities from sport, music, science and literature. The city's sports hall was named after the greatest Bosnian basketball player Mirza Delibašić, while the Koševo Stadium was named after the soccer legend Asim Ferhatović; a monument in glass to Davorin Popović, the pop singer and leader of the Sarajevo cult pop band Indeksi, was erected in the small park near the Presidential Palace. Such monuments have been widely accepted, especially by those who still resist the ethnicisation of memory and the cultural heritage of their city, as they do not represent heroes of any particular ethnicity or religion but, rather, are seen as the symbols of happier times when, instead of ethnicity and religion, loyalty to a particular sporting club or a band were much more important identity categories. These monuments keep memories alive, and have become part of the landscape of post-war Sarajevo. So too, in places far away from Sarajevo – in Europe, the U.S. and Australia – local and generational memories have been kept, maintained and performed wherever the individuals embodying such memories live.

Notes

1. Translated from Bosnian by Ted Hughes and John H. Williams.
2. Anzulović (1999), Bevan (2004), Denich (1993), Duijzings (2007), Hoepken (1999), I. Lovrenović (1994), Praštalo (1997), Tumarkin (2005) and Schwartz (2005).
3. Boose (2002), Bougarel (2007), Donia (2006), Duijzings (2007), Hirsch (1995), Sorabji (2006), Weinstein and Stover (2004) and Wesselingh and Vaulerin (2005).

4. Ajduković (2004), Brennen et al. (2007), Koso and Hansen (2006), L. Jones (2005) and Weine (1999).
5. Translated from German by Hariz Halilovich.
6. For instance, the battle at Kosovo in 1389 and reinterpretations of the event in academic and popular nationalist discourse in Serbia during the 1980s was the most powerful mobilising tool of the Serbian masses. Hatred for imagined ancient enemies from Kosovo, the Ottoman Turks, was applied to contemporary enemies: Albanians, Bosnian Muslims, Croats, Slovenes ... See Anzulović (1999).
7. See ICTY case information sheets (IT-94-1) Tadić, (IT-97-24) Kovačević and (IT-97-24) Stakić, available at http://www.un.org/icty/cases-e/index-e.htm.
8. All the names of streets and squares that did not reflect Serb history as defined by the RS authorities were changed during and after the war. While non-Serb street names were excluded, the new street names were inclusive of different Serb nationalisms and histories. The names in the text above include a local Serb militiaman who was killed during the war in Prijedor (Zoran Karlica); the first Serb political leader of rebellious Serbs in Croatia in the early 1990s (Jovan Rašković) and the forefather of the Serb Radical Party from the beginning of the twentieth century (Nikola Pašić). Other new street and square names in Prijedor include names from Serb history, such as King Aleksandar, Miloš Obrenović, Petar Petrović Njegoš, Vuk Karadžić, Solunska, etc.
9. In 2006 Mittal Steel merged with Arcelor creating a new company called Arcelor Mittal.
10. Hukanović (1996), Pervanić (1999), Wesselingh and Vaulerin (2005) and Pelz and Reeves (2008).
11. See ICTY Case Information Sheet IT-94-1-I available at http://www.un.org/icty/cases-e/index-e.htm.
12. The film was called *Sveti Georgije ubiva aždahu* (Director Srđan Dragojevića, Producer Dušan Kovačević); See Pijetlović (2007) and *Glas Srpske* (2007).
13. See ICTY case information sheets (IT-95-4) Mejakić et al. and (IT-98-30/1) Kvočka et al. available at http://www.un.org/icty/cases-e/index-e.htm.
14. See http://headgroups.com/hg/display/om/Online+Petition and http://bosniangenocide.wordpress.com/2012/05/06/petition-arcelor-mittal-purchased-omarska-concentration-camp-blocked-access-to-survivors-to-erect-memorial/.
15. See ICTY Case Information Sheet (IT-95-8) Sikirica et al. See also ICTY case information sheets (IT-95-8/1) Fuštar et al. and (IT-98-30/1) Kvočka et al. available at http://www.un.org/icty/cases-e/index-e.htm.
16. Human Rights Watch, 'Trnopolje Detention Camp: Helsinki Watch Report', October 1992–February 1993.
17. See ICTY case information sheets: (IT-95-5/18) Karadžić/Mladić, (IT-98-33) Krstić, (IT-98-33/1) Blagojević, (IT-01-43) Obrenović, (IT-02-53) Blagojević et al., (IT-02-56) Nikolić; (IT-02-57) Popović, (IT-02-58) Beara, (IT-02-60) Blagojević and Jokić, (IT-02-61) Deronjić, (IT-05-86) Pandurević and Trbić, (IT-96-22) Erdemović, and (IT-05-88/1).

18. See http://genocidescholars.org/conference/2007.html.
19. The 1991 census showed the city's population of 126,628 as 35 per cent Bosniak, 34 per cent Croat, 19 per cent Serb, and 12 per cent Yugoslavs and others.
20. See Campbell (1999), Cushman (1999), Grodach (2002), Gunzburger Makaš (2005, 2007), Hromadžić (2008) and Vetters (2007).
21. Donia and Fine (1994), Hoare (2004, 2007), Imamović (1997), Jezernik (2004: 23–5), Malcolm (1994), and I. Lovrenović (2001).
22. At the time of finalising the book, in January 2012.
23. The reconstruction of the Old Bridge was finished and the bridge was reopened on 23 July 2004. The resurrection of the Old Bridge was to symbolise the materialised memory of the 'good old times' and was heralded as a major step towards reconciliation in Mostar and post-war BiH. However, five years later, Mostar is far from a united city, with each community clinging to its own monuments, memorials and commemorations.
24. See http://www.zrinjski.info/modules.php?name=Newsandfile=articleandsid=73
25. For instance, Geraldine Brooks, the award-winning Australian-American author, acknowledges Kemal Bakaršić for being a source of inspiration for her book *The People of the Book* (2008).
26. For example, ulica Vase Miskina (the Vase Miskina Street) – named after a Communist partisan in the Second World War – was renamed ulica Ferhadija (Ferhadija Street); or *Principov most* (Princip's Bridge) – named after the (Serb) assassin who killed the Archduke Franz Ferdinand in 1914 – is now called *Latinska* ćuprija (the Latin Bridge).
27. The street Obala Vojvode Stepe (named after the First World War Serb general) was renamed Obala Kulina Bana (a Bosnian ruler in twelfth century, a symbol of Bosnian statehood).
28. E.g., Military Hospital which became the French Hospital (Francuska bolnica) and then more recently renamed into *Gradska bolnica* (City Hospital).
29. Mušan Topalović Caco's name has been linked to acts of violence and killings of Sarajevo civilians, mainly Serbs during 1992 and 1993. In 1993 he was killed by troops under the control of the BiH government. In 1996 his body was exhumed and honoured with a place at Kovači. See Selimbegović (2006).
30. Many of the interviewees were defenders of the city during the war, but not all of them were Bosniak or Muslim.

◅ Interlude ▻

Reframing Identity in Places of Pain
A Photographic Essay of Displacement and Memory

Figure 1: Geography of genocide in ethnically cleansed Podrinje. Once surrounded by the houses of the villages of Klotjevac, Prohići, Sejdinovići, Sjedaće, Studenac ... the Drina Lake is now a deserted area.

Figure 2: Returning 'home'.
10 July 2010, genocide survivors on the eve of the yet another collective funeral, this year for 538 identified victims of the 1995 Srebrenica genocide.

112 *Places of Pain*

Figure 3: Klotjevac 2011.
Ruined villages of Podrinje: a plum tree in the backyard of what used to be Mujo Salihović's house.

Figure 4: Trans-local emplacements.
Members of three Klotjevac families in Bevo, St. Louis.

Figure 5: 'Ethnic engineering' in post-war BiH.
Omer Sulejmanović with his parents in their 'exchanged' house in Hadžići. Many Bosniaks, Serbs and Croats exchanged their houses after the war.

Interlude: A Photographic Essay of Displacement and Memory   113

Figure 6: Returnees to Hegići. Graves of three generations of Hegići men and boys exhumed from a mass grave and buried at the Hegići cemetery in 2007. The panoramic view from the cemetery shows the green paddock where, in July 1992, 84 Hegići men were summoned and executed.

Figure 7: Domicide in Hegići. Decaying ruins of Edita Hegić's burned-down house – a monument to the lives lost.

Figure 8: New emplacement. Edita Hegić with her son Armin in front of her newly built house in Austria.

Figure 9: Geography of genocide in Prijedor.
Symbols of exclusion – the RS government-built monument to Serb heroes in the shape of an Orthodox cross in a city ethnically cleansed of 55 per cent of its population (Bosniaks and Croats). Almost every town in RS has a similar monument.

Figure 10: Hijacked memories. Trnopolje, the site of a Serb-run concentration camp during 1992. The official RS monument reads: 'To the Serb fighters who built their lives into the foundations of Republika Srpska'. There is no mention of Bosniak and Croat civilians killed, tortured and raped here in the summer of 1992.

Figure 11: Memorials as landmarks. Serb monument to the notorious Second World War Chetnik Leader, General Draža Mihailović, in the ethnically cleansed town of Brčko (2006).

Interlude: A Photographic Essay of Displacement and Memory 115

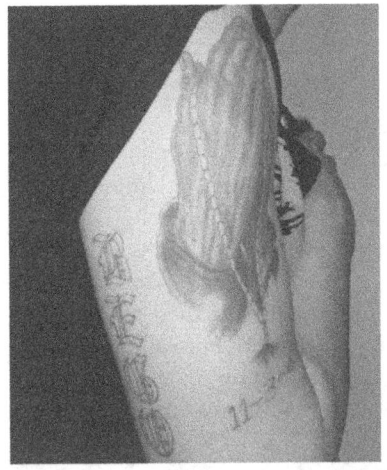

Figure 12: Inscribing embodied memories.
'Memorial to my father Bego born on 11.3.1967 – killed on 11.7.1995' – a tattoo on a Srebrenica survivor's arm.

Figure 13: The 'Sarajevo Roses'. The grenade craters memorialise locations where nine or more people were killed in one single attack during the 1992–95 siege of Sarajevo.

Figure 14: Lest we forget. Inscribing the names of the 108 genocide victims on the granite monument in Klotjevac.

Figure 15: United in remembrance. The first reunion in 17 years – *Klotivljani* visiting their village for the unveiling of the monument to their fellow villagers on 12 July 2009.

Figure 16: Reclaiming the place called home. Fata Orlović, a survivor and returnee to the ethnically cleansed village of Konjević Polje, with the author. Her insistence on reclaiming her home has brought her wide respect beyond Bosnia.

Figure 17: Podrinje under the gum trees. A twice-a-year gathering of Podrinje *zavičaj* communities – the picnic in Brimbank Park, in Melbourne.

Interlude: *A Photographic Essay of Displacement and Memory* 117

Figure 18: Synchronising local dialects. Learning 'Bosnian as a second language' (BSL) in Sweden.

Figure 19: Trans-Atlantic performance. Dancing the Bosnian kolo in St. Louis.

Figure 20: Place of sensory memories. Bosnians in front of the Hanna Café in St. Albans, Melbourne.

⌁ Chapter 4 ⌂

Trans-local Diasporic Communities in the Age of Transnationalism
Bosnians in Australia, Europe and the U.S.A.

> Home is where somebody notices when you are no longer there.
> Aleksandar Hemon, *The Lazarus Project*, p. 3

In previous chapters we have seen how, years after they were ethnically cleansed, many displaced Bosnians – like Edita, Sejo and Halid – have made a number of 'homecomings', in some cases turning their permanent displacement into regular seasonal movements between their new places of residence and their former home towns and villages. We have seen how physical and psychological displacement has created new forms of (non)belonging, with the feeling of permanent homelessness and exile contrasted with the dual or multiple senses of belonging. These conflicting feelings have been felt and described by the same individuals, with many displaced Bosnians developing complex relationships with places and their own identities as a result of their diasporic experience of 'living here but dreaming there'. During my fieldwork in many diasporic Bosnian communities in Austria, Sweden, the U.S.A and Australia, I came across many little Srebrenicas, little Prijedors, little Mostars, little Zvorniks and little Brčkos – reconstructed and reimagined communities with a clear local stamp of 'back home'.

Against this background, this chapter explores the extent to which recent scholarly literature is able to capture the uniqueness and complexity of these communities, and argues that its predominantly transnational conceptual framework needs to be expanded to include trans-local diasporic identity formation among displaced Bosnians around the globe.[1] This is explored in this chapter in terms of displaced residents of Brčko, Mostar, Prijedor and Srebrenica reclaiming their lost local homelands (*zavičaji*).

Debating Diaspora

As I pointed out in the introduction of this book, place – or lack of it – is the central issue of any displacement. However, places – unless understood as geographically situated social networks – do not move, remember or create their identities. People do. And, as Robert Sack (1997) argues, we are all inherently geographical beings (*homo geographicus*), able to negotiate multiple locations and positions. However, when people are subjected to forced displacement, they are often required to radically renegotiate their place-based identities and position themselves in relation to multiple locations. The process of negotiation and positioning refers to embodied experiences, memories and identities of real people and the communities they belong to. As I describe here, forced displacement of more than two million Bosnians has in many ways challenged and reshaped their identities and their relationships to places.

For many Bosnians the traditional Bosnian collective identities based on ethnicity, (Bosniaks, Croats and Serbs), and religion (Muslims, Catholics, Orthodox Christians and Jews) were just nominal categories before the Bosnian war. Since then a new identity formation based on displacement has become evident (Halilovich 2011b). Displacement has not only revived and (re)territorialised the traditional local and ethnic identities within the country, but it has also produced new categories and identities, such as 'stayers' and 'leavers', 'newcomers' and 'old settlers', 'defenders' and 'deserters', 'peasants' and 'city dwellers', IDPs and refugees, and so on (Maček 2001; Stefansson 2006). Of the 2.2 million displaced during the war, only some 400,000 have returned to their original places of residence. Today an estimated 1.3 to 1.6 million people are living outside Bosnia-Herzegovina, while approximately 500,000 are scattered as IDPs within the country.[2]

There are large communities of Bosnians living in almost every European country as well as throughout North America and Australia. In contrast with, and in response to, enforced displacement, many members of the Bosnian diaspora have retained strong family and other informal social ties both with Bosnians in other countries and with those still living in BiH. Even though they are context dependent, such ties – focused on the preservation of cultural memory and the performance of distinct local identities – form the basis of the global network of the Bosnian diaspora and its link with the original home(land) (Halilovich 2012b). The nature and significance of these networks will be described in this chapter.

While displaced Bosnians who settled in different countries and formed their distinct deterritorialised communities are seen and see themselves as part of a diaspora, on more than one occasion the diasporic character of displaced Bosnians has been questioned or even denied. For many

Bosnian academics, politicians and ordinary people, accepting that more than a third of the BiH population lives permanently overseas – in diaspora – is to accept the results of ethnic cleansing. Thus, any attempt to define or fix displacement of Bosnians inherently becomes a hotly debated political issue in Bosnia – and goes directly to the heart of the BiH Dayton Agreement, guaranteeing all displaced people the right to return.[3] Without the return of refugees, the results of ethnic cleansing will be de facto legitimised in the form of ethnically cleansed territories and the division of the once multicultural country along the ethnic lines. Angered by those not returning 'back home', Professor Muhamed Filipović, seen by many as the leading Bosnian academic, clashed with representatives of the Bosnian diaspora at the Sarajevo roundtable 'Days of Bosnian diaspora', in July 2007. He referred to displaced Bosnians as emigrants and not diaspora ('not like ancient Jewish or Greek diaspora'), suggesting the temporality of their displacement rather than displacement as a permanent condition. He pointedly withdrew from the roundtable to demonstrate his disagreement with those using the term diaspora for exiled Bosnians. In an article subsequently published in *Nezavisne Novine*, he displayed some of the common stereotypes held by 'homeland' Bosnians about Bosnians living in other countries, labelling them 'unpatriotic, snobbish cousins and materialistic *dijasporci*' (Filipović 2007).

In contrast to Muhamed Filipović, for whom the acceptance of the existence of the Bosnian diaspora is foremost a political question, a number of anthropologists have debated to what extent Bosnian refugee communities in countries of settlement could be regarded as diaspora. In one of his papers, Stef Jansen, for instance, calls them 'non-transnational Bosnian refugees', suggesting that 'specific remembered localised life-trajectories' – and not merely country-to-country connections – need to be taken into consideration when exploring the social realities of displaced Bosnians (2008: 181). Similarly, Nadje Al-Ali (2002: 101–2) argues that 'the political, social, religious and personal friction among Bosnians altogether challenges the concept of a community', i.e., diaspora. Similar questions about Bosnian refugees as a diasporic community in the U.K. have been posed by Lynnette Kelly (2003), who argues that the settlement polices in the U.K. have been instrumental in creating a 'Bosnian diaspora' there. Instead of an 'informal community', she argues, 'there is a contingent community: a group of people who will, to some extent, conform to the expectations of the host society in order to gain the advantages of a formal community association, whilst the private face of the group remains unconstituted as a community' (Kelly 2003: 35). Writing about Bosnian refugees in Finland, Laura Huttunen is also cautious when it comes to how to qualify Bosnians who settled there throughout the 1990s, calling them a 'hesitant diaspora

... because of the refugees' hesitation between their country of origin and their new country of settlement as their "homes" in a changing situation' (2005: 177).

Contrary to the Filipović school of thought that denies displaced Bosnians are diaspora, my investigations clearly indicate that the Bosnians displaced across the globe have been establishing themselves as diaspora of their own. In fact, they represent one of the most widely dispersed communities from the Balkans, meeting the criteria of most of the commonly accepted definitions of the term diaspora. The point, however, is not to compare displaced Bosnians with 'ancient Jewish or Greek diaspora', as Filipović does. As Stephen Castles (2002) and Stephen Castles and Mark Miller (2003) argue, the diasporic realities in the 'age of migration' are intertwined with many other processes, usually referred to as 'globalisation', that profoundly impact upon processes of identity formation. Filipović overlooks the new global realities in terms of which diaspora status must be assessed. While not directly caused by globalisation, the process of forced displacement of Bosnians coincided with and was influenced by globalisation. But before describing the nature and extent of this intersection it is important to consider the extent to which globally displaced Bosnian communities can be said to constitute a diaspora.

Most diaspora scholars agree that mobility and migration do not necessarily result in the formation of a diaspora as a distinct form of collective identity of a deterritorialised group of people.[4] Throughout history there have been many examples of temporary displacement and migration as well as complete assimilation of migrants into the mainstream culture of the host country. Many theorists of migration – like Brah (1996), R. Cohen (1997), Clifford (1994, 1997), Hall (1990), Safran (1991) and Barkan and Shelton (1998) – have attempted to define what exactly constitutes a diaspora. Safran's taxonomy, for instance, defines diaspora as a community with some of the following characteristics:

> 1) The original community has spread from a homeland to two or more countries; they are bound from their disparate geographical locations by a common vision, memory or myth about their homelands; 2) they have a belief that they will never be accepted by their host societies and therefore develop their autonomous cultural and social needs; 3) they or their descendants will return to the homeland should the conditions prove favourable; 4) they should continue to maintain support for the homeland and therefore the communal consciousness and solidarity enables them to continue these activities. (Safran 1991: 83–4)

Safran's second and third characteristics of diaspora may be irrelevant to many contemporary diasporic communities: even if there is a firm acceptance of migrants in the host country, many migrant communities opt to maintain stronger or weaker ties with their original culture, language and homeland. In most cases this does not, however, mean that 'they or their descendants will return to the homeland should the conditions prove favourable'. The majority choose to stay in their adopted homelands and successfully negotiate their new identities and differences created as a result of their diasporic experience.

R. Cohen (1997) broadens the definition of diaspora to include both voluntary migration and migration as a result of fleeing aggression, persecution or extreme hardship. He also defines different types of diaspora in relation to the main reasons behind migration as 'victim' (e.g., Jewish, African and Armenian), 'labour' (e.g., Indian), 'trade' (e.g., Chinese and the Lebanese), 'imperial' (e.g., British) and 'cultural' (e.g., Caribbean) diasporas. However, as Tsagarousianou (2004: 56) points out, there may be many limitations to such prescribed typologies, as they 'do not take into account the diversity of diasporic experience and do not really take on board late modern transnational mobility that takes significantly novel forms'. As Skrbiš (1999: 5) argues, 'late modern transnational mobility' – in combination with economic, cultural and political factors coupled with globalisation processes – is directly linked to rapid diaspora formation, challenging the traditional notions of diaspora. The new global context of living – including new technologies of communication such as the internet, satellite television and mobile phones as well as the availability and affordability of international travel – has redefined the notion of 'homeland', which can no longer be apprehended as only a physical, territorial category.

What emerges from these recent additions to the debate on diaspora is that diasporic identities are not static but, rather, a constant work in progress; over time many diasporic groups change, adapting to new contexts. As Hall (1990: 235) puts it, 'diaspora identities are those which are constantly producing and reproducing themselves anew, through transformation and difference'. So, for instance, a diasporic group may shift from 'victim' to 'trade' or 'cultural' diaspora. Indeed, as discussed in this chapter, many 'former Bosnian' refugees have become new guest workers, businessmen and transmigrants, while many Bosnian humanitarian and refugee relief organisations in diaspora have, more recently, turned into cultural associations. Moreover, both forced and voluntary migrations are very often present in the one diaspora; and an initial wave of forced migration might be followed by voluntary migration or vice versa. All these variations can be identified within the global Bosnian diaspora (cf. Ramet and Valenta 2011).

While it would be hard to find any displaced group that meets all the criteria for the different definitions of diaspora, displaced Bosnians display many of the elements of diaspora as defined by Safran and Cohen. They have 'spread from their homeland to two or more countries', in fact to some hundred countries across the globe (UNHCR 2005). As this chapter describes, members of the Bosnian diaspora are 'bound from their disparate geographical locations by a common vision, memory or myth about their homeland'. However, as argued here, the concept of homeland does not necessarily refer to a nation state and its structure, but more often refers to a quite specific place and local community, a place of departure and imagined return. Probably the most cohesive factor in displaced groups of Bosnians is their communal consciousness and solidarity that foster a sense of collective identity and shared responsibility to maintain support in the new countries for their original communities. Many displaced Bosnians I interviewed in the U.S.A., Australia and Europe believe that they will never be completely accepted by their host societies and therefore seek to meet their cultural and social needs within their diasporic community. They also express the desire that one day they or their descendants will 'return to the homeland should the conditions prove favourable'. Articulation of such desires, and in most cases an imagined future return, is very often contrasted with setting a footprint in the new soil: building or buying houses in the countries of settlement, participating in the labour force, sometimes setting up their own businesses, and to varying degrees actively engaging or showing interest in political processes in the adopted countries.

The social mobility of the 'former' Bosnian refugees, who form the bulk of the worldwide Bosnian diaspora, has in most cases been seen as a measurable indicator of successful integration into their host countries. Those who have 'made it' have been regularly recognised, and their success celebrated, by their diasporic community as well as by the mainstream in both their adopted and home countries.[5] The process of integration has also included the adjustment of political identities of 'former Bosnians' who have acquired citizenship of their adopted countries, even if this, in many cases, has meant that they needed to choose between their old citizenship and the new one. In the process of successful integration, 'former Bosnians' have become 'new' Swedes, Americans, Australians, Austrians, Dutch and Germans, to name just a few of the most common new collective political identities in Bosnian diasporas.

The trend of changing and adjusting identities clearly suggests that over the last seventeen years the Bosnian diaspora has moved on from a 'victim' identity, increasingly showing many aspects of 'labour', 'trade' and 'cultural' diasporas as outlined by R. Cohen (1997). For many former refugees from BiH, the main reason for continuing to live outside their country of origin has moved beyond the 'well founded fear of political persecution' to economic necessity, as post-war BiH does not provide sufficient employment opportunities or match the living standards that most Bosnian refugees have been enjoying in their host countries. From disorganised groups of refugees dispersed across many different countries, in less than two decades displaced Bosnians have evolved into a global web of well organised, interconnected deterritorialised communities in which a rich variety of social, cultural and economic exchanges takes place (Halilovich 2006a, 2011b). Demonstratively this is, in part, an aim of this book.[6] These developments are in line with Tsagarousianou's (2004) 'novel forms of late modern transnational mobility' and Skrbiš's (1999) 'rapidity' of (post)modern diaspora formation. Thus, when debating the Bosnian diaspora, its history and its present, in chronological or contextual terms, it is critical to recognise and unveil the multiplicity of different social, political, cultural and psychological factors that played – and continue to play – a role in its social morphology.

Emergence of the Bosnian Diaspora

It would be wrong to suggest that the history of the Bosnian diaspora starts with the most recent, and so far the largest, emigration from the country. Bosnians (and even more so, Herzegovinians) have a long history of migration.[7] Yet, a well organised and distinct Bosnian diaspora is a relatively recent phenomenon (Halilovich 2006a, 2011b). Before 1992 Bosnians – who were mainly labour migrants or guest workers living in Western Europe, North America and Australia – saw themselves either as a part of the Yugoslav diaspora or grouped around anti-Yugoslav religious and cultural societies (Imamović 1996). Those who were political émigrés resented in principle the Yugoslav identity as they tended to perceive the state of Yugoslavia as an oppressive communist imposition and the main reason for their exile. Many such dissidents, depending on their ethnic and political background, joined a more politically oriented diaspora dominated by either pro-Croat or pro-Serb nationalist politics. There were, however, influential Bosnian dissidents, such as the Swiss businessman Adil Zulfikarpašić and the Austrian academic Smail Balić, who were part of neither 'club' and worked on promoting Bosnian (and later Bosniak) nationalism (cf. Galić 1990; Zulfikarpašić 2005; Đilas 1996).

It was the 1992–95 Bosnian war and its aftermath that brought an organised Bosnian diaspora into existence. Those who fled the country were in most cases victims of ethnic cleansing, refugees and deserters fleeing forced conscription, as well as members of the privileged elites who, thanks to connections and money, could buy a safe passage out of the war-torn country. This diverse group of people – ranging from many semi-literate individuals from rural areas to highly skilled professionals, academics, former apparatchiks, economists, artists, politicians, urban city dwellers and university students – made the existing Bosnian expatriate communities in Europe, Australia and Northern America significantly larger and enriched them with fresh human and social capital. Not only did the groups become more organised, but a distinct national (as well as ethno-nationalist) consciousness of many Bosnians living abroad was awakened by the newly gained independence of their homeland, and the impetus of the million or so refugees who joined them. No longer 'Yugoslavs from Bosnia working overseas', now they could rightfully call themselves 'Bosnian expatriate nationals'. The refugees brought with them their emotional luggage of personal and collective sufferings that inspired solidarity and patriotism in Bosnian labour migrants in Germany, Austria and elsewhere. Refugees also brought knowledge and practical skills enabling them to organise politically and promote the Bosnian cause. Many of them were directly involved in setting up Bosnian clubs, societies, organisations and media outlets in the Bosnian language. There were also partisan associations promoting particular political parties or the exclusiveness of an ethnic group, and collecting of funds for a single political agenda. Many displaced Bosnians saw such activities as an extension of the Bosnian government – a government that had failed to warn its citizens of and protect them from the war – and chose not to join in the activities of formal diaspora organisations involved in such forms of 'long-distance nationalism'.[8] At the same time, most provided continuous moral and material support to families and local communities back home, as well as to members of their local communities in exile.

Over the last twenty years the Bosnians who took refuge abroad or migrated immediately after the war have (re)created their homes in different corners of the globe, from the polar circle of Sweden to the suburbs of Chicago and St. Louis, to metropolitan Vienna and Melbourne. A recent UNHCR report (2005), as well as my personal observations and research, suggest that the dispersal of Bosnians has been much broader than generally acknowledged, and includes over a hundred countries where Bosnians have found temporary or permanent refuge.[9] Host countries include some less expected destinations such as Israel, Malaysia, Iceland and Colombia. Like any other migrant community, Bosnians are a heterogeneous group of people with all the attendant social variables very often reflecting the local culture and the dominant values of the countries they have settled in. What is commonly shared between most of its members, however, is the experience of forced displacement, feelings of betrayal by 'their' politicians and, even worse, former neighbours and friends, as well as feelings of nostalgia for a homeland that can never be restored (Esterhuizen 2006). Many of these feelings, memories and nostalgia are nourished and disseminated in social clubs, associations, cafes, restaurants and at various cultural events (*zabave*) organised by one of those associations and clubs.

Apart from many country-specific associations and clubs addressing common needs and representing Bosnians in different countries, many 'former' Bosnians choose to meet their social needs outside the Bosnian diaspora associations through informal networks of like-minded fellow Bosnians, as well as within the mainstream culture of their new homelands. In this context, identification with the Bosnian diaspora is not so much identification with a monolithic global community as with Swedish Bosnians, American Bosnians or Australian Bosnians.

One Family, Two Languages, Many Cultures

While it may be seen as a betrayal of the old homeland not to talk about and imagine returning home, or to maintain an interest in 'affairs back home', the reality is that many diasporic communities – and the individuals who comprise such groups – inevitably grow apart from their original homeland and compatriots left behind. That 'growing apart' is a gradual process and it is sometimes directly related to the level of integration (and acceptance) by the host country. While 'assimilation' has more recently become a dirty word, migrants' integration – as they see it – is still being measured by how successful they are at replacing their original culture with the one of the country they settle in. The desired outcome of the process of acculturation, according to this understanding, is a change in migrants' identity according to which they become 'new locals' or 'new us'. Such perceptions of migrants' identities, as Rapport and Dawson (1998: 4–5) argue, are based on assumptions that identities, as 'fixities of social relations and cultural routines', are localised in time and space. However, the realities lived by migrants are much more complex, with much more fluidity than fixity when it comes to identity construction.

This is especially true for the younger generation – those who were small children when they fled Bosnia-Herzegovina and are now in their late teens and early twenties. Their primary language and culture are of the country to which they have migrated and in which they have been growing up, educated and socialised. Many of them have been contributing to the mainstream culture even in such privileged areas as music, arts, sports, innovation and senior management. For many of them, Bosnia might be their nominal first homeland, but in reality it is more the culture, identity and place performed and remembered by their parents.

What is clearly noticeable is that young people in diaspora are forgetting their mother tongue. In fact, many of them have had no or very limited education in the language of their parents. Many were born 'in transition', in countries like Germany, Austria and Croatia, or in the countries of resettlement where they live today. As 'language abstracts the world of experience into words', as Joseph (2004: 11) argues, the lived experiences and memories of the experiences of younger Bosnians in diaspora are 'inscribed' and abstracted not necessarily in the mother tongue, but more often in the language belonging to a cultural cluster of time and events in which the experiences took place. This means not only that the everyday reality of younger diaspora Bosnians has been articulated in adopted first languages (English, Swedish, German, etc.) but so are most of their memories. While each generation develops its own language, particularly popular jargon and linguistic codes, in diaspora there is a de facto linguistic difference between different generations. In a typical Bosnian family in diaspora, it is almost a rule that children and younger family members speak the language of the host country while parents speak their mother tongue. In many such 'Bosnian' homes children and parents speak different languages in all the combinations possible. Children speak the mainstream language with their siblings as well as with both their Bosnian and non-Bosnian friends. In most cases they speak the mainstream language with their parents while parents may use Bosnian (Croatian or Serbian) when speaking to them. Thus, in a Bosnian family in diaspora, a conversation between children and parents is usually conducted in two languages: parents speaking their 'old' language and children responding in 'their' language. The problems with miscommunication or limited understanding between the two generations in a family start when neither group has sufficient skills in both languages used, which is often the case in Bosnian homes in diaspora. Parents, being refugees and new migrants in the country, are usually preoccupied with working hard to secure a livelihood for the family and provide a better future for their children. To many this has turned into a busy lifestyle that only allows 'pyjamas to be exchanged for working uniforms', as I was told by my respondents in the U.S.A., suggesting that there is not much time left outside of work and preparing for work. This busy working lifestyle, including long working hours and working at weekends, leaves many parents very little time to spend with their children. At the same time, the mainstream culture in which the younger Bosnians are growing up and taking on as their own, alienates them from their parents' culture, of which they are sometimes ashamed as 'it is not cool to be an ethnic'. Even when living under the same roof, parents and children in diaspora are often growing apart culturally: while parents are desperately hanging onto their homeland culture, their children are eagerly assimilating into the host land culture. Having noticed this assimilation and growing-apart trend, most first-generation migrants, the parents, have been active in trying to prevent it. In a coordinated series of actions, Bosnian diasporic communities in many countries have been quite successful in introducing Bosnian language[10] into younger generations' education at primary, secondary and high school levels.

Unlike many other countries where this has been institutionalised at the level of community-run 'ethnic Saturday schools', in Austria, Sweden and Australia Bosnian diaspora communities have, to different degrees, been able to integrate the learning of the 'parents' language' into mainstream education. In most provinces in Austria this has been only partly achieved, at the level of primary education, within the 'Intercultural Learning' programme (*Interkulturelles Lernen*), in which the language lessons in the mother tongue are in the group of optional, non-assessable subjects together with religion and ethics.[11] The mother tongue for students of Bosnian background is taught under the name 'Bosnian/Croatian/Serbian' and includes students of the respective ethnicities not only from Bosnia but also from Croatia and Serbia. Language teachers have reported that attendance at such classes is quite low and therefore many schools in Austria do not offer the Bosnian/Croatian/Serbian classes.

In Sweden, learning Bosnian (as well as Croatian and Serbian) is part of a comprehensive 'mother tongue' programme granted by the Swedish government to each language group with a sufficient number of students at all levels of compulsory education. In Australia, teaching languages has been regulated at a state level, with each state accrediting the teaching of foreign languages in its schools. In the states of Victoria and New South Wales, 'Bosnian as a second language' has been recognised as a Year 12 elective subject equal to other mainstream subjects such as English or mathematics. Learning other official languages used in Bosnia and Herzegovina – Croatian and Serbian – mirrors the ethnic pattern in BiH, with most Bosnian-Croat children attending Croatian classes and Bosnian-Serb children the Serbian language classes. While the largest number of students in the Bosnian language classes could be identified as coming from a Bosniak background, there have been a number of students whose background is Bosnian Croat, Bosnian Serb or 'mixed'. Regardless of how the language is named – usually referred to as *naš jezik* ('our language', used to refer to Bosnian, Croatian, Serbian and what used to be called Serbo-Croatian) – it still remains one of the most practical cohesive factors in diaspora. Many businesses serving the diaspora – ranging from specialist medical clinics to cafes and grocery shops – have been flourishing because of the use of language, with the vast majority of diaspora Bosnians preferring to do business with those who speak 'our language' regardless of their names[12] and ethnic background.

Hence, 'our language' is seen not only as a necessity but also as an opportunity. For instance, 'Bosnian as a second language' has become a popular subject among many Bosnian high school students and their parents in Australia, whereby, in the final two years at high schools in Australia, students are required to select a group of subjects, usually a combination of science and arts subjects, for their final exams, the results of which are decisive for gaining entry into competitive university courses. As many Bosnian parents are able and willing to assist their children with language lessons and the essential writing, reading and speaking skills, they encourage their children to select 'Bosnian as a second language' as one of the Year 12 exam subjects. Over the last five years, since Bosnian has been recognised as a subject equal to any other VCE subject,[13] more than a thousand Bosnian children and young people have been enrolled in Bosnian classes throughout primary and secondary schools in the state of Victoria.[14] Many students have been able to increase their tertiary entry score (TES) thanks to high results in 'Bosnian as a second language'.

During my fieldwork in Australia and Sweden I attended, observed and participated in a number of 'mother tongue' or 'our language' classes. I compared how the language has been taught and mastered by Australian and Swedish students of Bosnian origin in these two countries as well as policy differences in relation to Bosnian as mother tongue or second language. The 'Swedish Bosnians' I observed tended on average to have better language skills than their 'Australian Bosnian' counterparts. One of the reasons could be more regular visits to Bosnia during the school holidays by the Swedish Bosnians as well more frequent visits by relatives from Bosnia. While most Swedish Bosnian students reported at least one visit to Bosnia per year, Australian Bosnians on average visited Bosnia once every five to seven years. In Australia 'Bosnian as a second language' is an optional subject throughout primary and secondary education, while in Sweden Bosnian is taught as a compulsory subject called 'mother tongue' if there are at least five students from a language group in any particular school. However, in both cases, the students regarded 'our language' as their second or even third language – their first languages being English and Swedish respectively. The mainstream languages, English and Swedish, are the languages the students feel most comfortable using with classmates and teachers.

Motivation – or lack of it – for learning 'our language' seems to differ between the groups. For many students in Australia, learning Bosnian has created a win-win situation for both the Bosnian students and their parents; for the high school students good marks from 'second language' have been beneficial in terms of enhancing their chances to get into the university course of their choice, while at the same time it has been a positive response to their parents' concerns about their alienation from 'their' language and culture. In Sweden, 'mother tongue', being a compulsory subject, is not universally popular among Bosnian students. Many students feel that their segregation from the rest of the class for separate language lessons makes them stand out from their Swedish peers. They are seen – or are worried about being seen – as 'ethnics', 'foreigners' and 'migrants', even though there has been wide acceptance of migrants and refugees in Swedish society. However, they agree that when visiting Bosnia they feel more at ease when speaking with their relatives because of the language lessons in Sweden.

'German Bosnians' in Sweden and 'Aussie Bosnians from Germany'

Language – with all its colloquial, generational variations – has almost the same role as a primary mechanism of inclusion and exclusion among young people as it has for members of an ethnic group: those who speak the language and know the right codes are automatically 'in' and those who do not are 'out'. Swedish colleagues, the 'Bosnian as mother tongue' teachers, told me anecdotes about 'their German Bosnians', children and young people who, in the late 1990s and early 2000s, arrived in Sweden from Germany. Before migrating to Sweden they and their families had lived as refugees in Germany, sometimes for more than a decade, and some of these 'German Bosnians' were in fact born in Germany. In 1995 the German government started the involuntary repatriation of some 400,000 Bosnian and other ex-Yugoslav refugees.[15] Their refugee visas were cancelled and many opted to migrate to third countries rather than return to their war-torn homeland. Pre-existing social networks with other fellow Bosnians, mostly their former neighbours, relatives and friends from back home, who had migrated to Sweden – as well as Sweden's relative proximity to Bosnia (and Germany!) compared to Northern America and Australia – made Sweden an attractive destination for many German Bosnians. However, despite the geographical proximity and anticipated cultural similarity to Germany, a culture shock was awaiting them once they arrived in Scandinavia. It was only then they realised how much of the German culture and way of life they had adopted while living 'in transition' in Germany. Compared to Germany, Sweden seemed to be a completely different world: people lived differently, the climate was different, as was the food. In contrast to their *Duldung* status in Germany,[16] which excluded them from many areas of social life, the Swedish policy of active integration of migrants and refugees also involved compulsory Swedish language lessons for adults and children. Language proved to be one of the main barriers for the newcomers.

When the young German Bosnians enrolled in primary and secondary schools in Sweden they did not speak any Swedish, nor much Bosnian, and were perceived as exotic by both their peers and their teachers, Bosnian and non-Bosnian alike. As a teacher reported, they would speak German with each other, filling in the gaps in Bosnian, and later in Swedish, with German words and phrases. The 'Swedish Bosnian' kids made jokes about their German fellow Bosnians.

The situation was similar in Australia. Around the same time, in the late 1990s/early 2000s, several hundred German Bosnians arrived in Melbourne. They displayed a very similar 'German' identity based on their German language, adopted cultural norms and attachment to their lived experiences in Germany. Many of these young people have attempted to retain their uniqueness through their social networks with other 'Aussie Bosnians from Germany', as I called them (Halilovich 2005a, 2006b). Over the last ten years, many Aussie Bosnians from Germany, especially those who were in their teenage years when they arrived in Melbourne, have continued to hang onto their 'Germanness', while others have 'given in' and partially or completely replaced German with English. Those who cling on to German tend to speak it with their siblings and friends who have had a similar journey through different cultures and languages. A number of them turned their German language and cultural knowledge to competitive advantage when applying for university courses (such as European studies with a major in German); some have been on student exchanges to universities in Germany, while a few, once they received Australian passports, have returned to Germany permanently.

What has been clearly noticeable in Bosnian classrooms in both Sweden and Australia is the variety of local Bosnian dialects spoken by the students. Their dialects reveal their distinct Bosnian regional and local origins, with parents, relatives and fellow community members being the main agents in transmitting the local dialect to the younger generation. Swedish and English serve to bridge the different dialects, as often the students coming from different regions have difficulty speaking and understanding each other's common mother tongue.

The famous and much quoted saying, credited to Max Weinreich, 'a language is a dialect with an army and navy', implying the critical importance of languages in nationalist projects – as 'language boundaries appear to coincide with boundaries of peoples' (Joseph 2004: 43) – could well apply to the Bosnian linguistic context. Even though it was not the first time that languages developed alongside historical events and conflicts, the separation of the standard Serbo-Croat into three separate national languages (Serbian, Croatian and Bosnian) has been more confusing than traumatic to many people, who regard all three languages as their single mother tongue. In the end, speakers of Serbo-Croat did not need to start from scratch and relearn a completely different language as much as consciously repress some words seen as belonging to the languages of the ethnic 'other'. While linguists have been busy with standardising and differentiating the three languages, often at the expense of the local dialects spoken in different regions of the country, displaced Bosnians in diaspora have been less affected than those still in Bosnia by the standardisation and assimilation of the locally spoken dialects into the standard languages (Bosnian, Croatian and Serbian). Once taken for granted back home, for many people in diaspora, speaking their local dialects has become a substitute for the lost home, a basis for intimacy and belonging – i.e., inclusion, as well as for exclusion of fellow Bosnians and non-Bosnians alike. As John Joseph (2004: 37) argues, 'identity as sameness is principally recognised through contact with what is different' – in the case of the displaced Bosnians, contact with Bosnians from other regions speaking different dialects as well as the languages of the host cultures. In line with Alessandro Durnati's (1997: 214–43) argument that speech must be viewed as social action representative of the culture in which it is produced and possibly only having meaning in that culture, local dialects spoken in diaspora reproduce the local cultures of places from where the speakers came. Thus, as Joseph (2004: 136) argues, 'regional and local identities can function as central foci of identity and belonging, complete with linguistic manifestations'. Interestingly, while many older, first generation diaspora Bosnians insist on maintaining the purity of their local dialects far removed from the original locale, what I heard across all sections of the Bosnian diaspora in every country I visited were different versions of distinct migrant languages, a combination of their first language with 'Bosnianised' words from the host countries' languages. As this is not a universal Bosnian diaspora language, each of its versions is only understood by the members of the Bosnian diaspora in a particular country. A meaningful conversation in any of these diaspora slangs with Bosnians from other countries or with their compatriots back in Bosnia could hardly take place. Younger Bosnians have been copying older relatives, adding their own modified vocabulary to the language, combining words from different languages in a variety of ways, and making its spoken version a mixed salad of words. In a bizarre way, the diaspora language, though not a 'real' language and a recognised identity marker, nonetheless separates different groups in the worldwide Bosnian diaspora both from each other and from their compatriots and relatives back in BiH. Even though they may not be aware of it, these different groups are in the process of constructing their separate cultural identities.

The Trans-local within the Transnational

In addition to language (or languages and dialects), as with other diasporic communities, the Bosnian diaspora has to different degrees been consolidated around a shared past – especially the most recent past. Their collective narrative and experiences have been rooted in both social reality and social imaginary. The different aspects of common socio-cultural characteristics and shared values are manifest in a variety of formal and informal social networks that make up a diaspora. Formal networks – often described as 'diaspora' and 'transnational community' (Amit 2002: 46) – are usually constituted around a particular aspect of shared identity such as language, nationality, ethnicity or religion – forms of more abstract or 'imagined' group identities, as Benedict Anderson (1983) famously put it. There are many more informal networks with much stronger social glue representing real relationships based on family background, kinship, friendship, dialect and place of origin – such as a particular region, city, village or neighbourhood. These bonds play a very important cohesive factor in diaspora as they very often link different individuals and groups to a wide global network of like-minded people representing their collective identity and local particularity. I call this phenomenon 'trans-localism', which avoids some of the limitations of the term 'transnationalism', which has increasingly been regarded as a key focus of study in international migration. However, I do not claim to have coined this term, as the adjective 'trans-local' and the noun 'trans-locality' have already been used among scholars researching migration and forced displacement – e.g., Appadurai (1996), Goldring (1998), Guarnizo and Smith (1998), Peleikis (2000), Brun (2001), Čapo Žmegač (2003, 2011), Velayutham and Wise (2005), Wise and Velayutham (2008), Nolin (2006) and Conradson and Mckay (2007) – as well as by many artists and environmentalists.[17]

While some scholars of transnationalism, like Guarnizo and Smith (1998) and Mahler (1998), recognise the presence and reproduction of 'trans-localities' within the transnational process, it is most often the case, as Vered Amit (2002: 21) argues, that transnational process and practices are understood 'to first and foremost involve the production of ethnic [and national] collectivities that straddle state borders'. Glick Schiller et al. (1999) define transnationalism as 'processes by which immigrants build social fields that link together their country of origin and their country of settlement'; while Vertovec (1999) understands transnationalism as 'multiple ties and interactions linking people or institutions across the borders of nation states'. Similarly, Kearney (1995: 548) writes that the 'cultural-political dimension of transnationalism is signalled by its resonance with nationalism as a cultural and political project'. While the concept of transnationalism, as outlined by Glick Schiller et al. (1999), Vertovec (1999) and Kearney (1995: 548), seems to accommodate various immigrants' identities, it still emphasises countries (i.e., states) of origin and settlement, nationality, nationalism, institutions and nation-state borders and underemphasises social factors and identities rooted in a particular locality and specific cultural experiences that often lie beyond – or below – the political supra-identities. Thus, such understanding of transnationalism may be more applicable to broader units of analysis such as institution, organisation, the society, the economy, the polity and the state, explored at a macro level of analysis, while smaller units of analysis like individual, family, group and cultural practices, analysed at meso and micro levels may not be sufficiently understood within a transnationalism paradigm. The concept of transnationalism, as Al-Ali et al. (2001a, 2001b) argue, is especially limited when it comes to interpreting the complexities of refugee identities and experiences involving forced migration from ancestral homes, and often dramatic separation from spatial practices and identities associated with a particular place. In fact, refugees and the forcibly displaced are very often victims of 'nationalism as a cultural and political project' and would not see themselves as part of its larger, transnational form. Moreover, as Amit-Talai (1998: 43) points out, most personal networks and investments maintained by permanent and temporary migrants occur between the migrants' country of origin and country of settlement and as such are 'bi-statal' rather than transnational affiliations. Cano (2005: 12) goes as far as to claim that 'the use of the term "transnationalism" has been transformed to a point in which it is practically impossible to sustain the broader sense of the term beyond its generic roots'. While I would not dismiss transnationalism as an explanatory frame in migration studies, I recognise the limits of this concept when exploring the relationship between place, movement, identity and memory in communities forcefully displaced from BiH.

Over the last two decades an increasing number of anthropologists and social scientists have reinvigorated the debate on the relationship between place, movement and identity in relation to globalisation.[18] While some have radically requestioned place and place making in the era of global mobility, others have re-emphasised the important role that local, place-bound identities continue to play – even if imagined and deterritorialised – in the diasporic construction and enactment of cultural practices and identities. Generally discussed within the framework of transnationalism, such practices most often exist independently of – or in opposition to – institutions of nation states and cannot always be quantified in terms of remittances, dual citizenship, bilateral agreements and other 'transnational criteria' adopted, for instance, by the OECD (2005). Thus, trans-localism may shed more light on those multiple local–local transactions.

Bosnian diasporic communities, as expressions of collective identities and local particularities, have not been created as a spontaneous reaction to enforced displacement, but have involved the active participation of individuals who have made deliberate and informed decisions when choosing destinations for their resettlement. As illustrated in this chapter, in most cases local factors played a decisive role in the migration patterns and social morphology of migrant communities, and trans-local factors and patterns of migration are present in the Bosnian diaspora worldwide. For instance, I discovered that a large number of former residents from the municipality of Zvornik – a regional centre in eastern Bosnia, where residents were forcefully displaced as part of the policy of ethnic cleansing – today live in Austria, mainly in and around Vienna. Upper Austria is home to a sizeable community from Višegrad. On the other side of the globe, Melbourne is home to the largest deterritorialised – and reterritorialised – Brčko community, a community that will be further described in the text below. Prijedor's stronghold is Malmo in Sweden, while St. Louis in the U.S.A, with its 70,000 migrants/refugees mostly from the Podrinje region in eastern Bosnia, is the largest 'eastern Bosnian town' in the world (Hemon 2006; Huremović 2006; Matsuo 2005). While they represent an integral part of the Bosnian diaspora in the cities and countries they settled in, these deterritorialised Bosnian communities maintain strong links with their 'sister' communities spread across the globe in host countries, as well as with their *matica* (the original hometown) or *zavičaj* (the emotional and intimate home where they lived or grew up, usually the neighbourhood or local community). The fact that they migrated in large numbers to specific locations was not a mere coincidence.

Such migration patterns have been created as a result of social networks, usually based on family, friendships and local communities, from the former homeland – a phenomenon known as 'chain migration'. The trans-local identity and chain migration of Bosnian diaspora communities are in no way unique to Bosnians, nor are they new phenomena. As Thomas Sowell (1996: 7) points out, some 90 per cent of immigrants to Australia, over a period of half a century, came via the chain migration process. However, in relation to Bosnia, chain migration has created a vibrant global network of trans-local communities in both real and cyber space.[19]

By referring to these trans-local networks as communities, I do not imply that they are mainly 'imagined communities', as Anderson (1983) and Appadurai (1996) would argue, nor that they are purely 'concrete communities', as Amit (2002) would insist. They are rather both increasingly imagined as well as made up of concrete social relations. As described here and throughout the book, these two aspects of communal identities (imagined and concrete) are encapsulated by memory – shared, embodied and performed – creating a sense of global intimacy among members of such reterritorialised groups.

As I argue in this chapter, trans-local identities supersede and give precise and concrete expression to broader identities, and have many micro ethnic qualities of their own – including a recognisable vernacular dialect, cultural enactments and rituals, shared history, and a common feeling of belonging to a specific region, town or village. To borrow Michael Herzfeld's words, trans-local communities are like '"interior ethnonyms" ... proactive in promoting a sense of local cultural and moral autonomy and dignity' (1997: 16). While emphasising their local distinctiveness and real or imagined autonomy in relation to the state centres of power, many local communities, as Herzfeld argues, also incorporate nationalist state-linked discourses and 'assimilate the bureaucratic structures of statehood into an essentially segmentary view of the world ... thinking of their communities as a kind of small state' (1985: xi–xii).

Similarly, Pierre Bourdieu (1991: 221) has remarked upon how regional and local identities are linked to quasi ethnic identities:

> Struggles over ethnic or regional identity – in other words over properties (stigmata or emblems) linked with the origin through the place of origin and its associated durable marks, such as accent – are a particular case of the different struggles over classifications, struggles over monopoly of the power to make people see and believe, to get them to know and recognise, to impose the legitimate definition of the divisions of the social world and, thereby, to make and unmake groups.

The monopoly on power and the 'right' to speak on behalf of the Bosnian diaspora can be clearly identified in the mostly self-proclaimed 'umbrella organisations' of the Bosnian diaspora such as the Australian Council of Bosnian-Herzegovinian Organisations and the Bosnian-Herzegovinian World Network. In contrast to these monolithic, (mono)ethnic and national(istic) organisations, (trans-)local identities often unmake and challenge broader ethnic, religious and national identities. Therefore these trans-local networks, in many cases, are not linked to the more formalised transnational networks that claim to represent the different, broader (trans)national interests of the wider Bosnian diaspora globally. As Ahmed at al. (2003: 2) argue, 'regroupings – of identity, culture, nation, diaspora – can both resist and reproduce hegemonic forms of home and belonging'. The Bosnian umbrella organisations reproducing the 'hegemonic forms of home and belonging' are quite often hostile to the maintenance of trans-local networks and identities and there is strong pressure on such identities to assimilate into a united national or ethnic diaspora. Many trans-local Bosnians in diaspora perceive that the so-called umbrella organisations to be more concerned with the political and business agendas of their leaders than with the real local issues 'back there at home' or 'over here in exile' of those on whose behalf they claim to be acting. For instance, in Australia the umbrella organisation the Australian Council of Bosnian-Herzegovinian Organisations does not recognise the independent, non-political association of Srebrenica survivors Udruženje Podrinje-Srebrenica and their annual commemoration day on 11 July. Instead, on the same day, the council organises its own commemoration of the Srebrenica genocide – without Srebrenica survivors – and uses it for promotion and legitimisation of its nationalistic, victim-centred political rhetoric. In some ways this replicates the situation in Bosnia.

Brčko in Melbourne

While resisting the double pressure of assimilation – from the monolithic national(istic) diaspora on one side and the mainstream host culture on the other – local identities in diasporic spaces act as factors of cohesion in making a distinct social world in the form of deterritorialised and reterritorialised trans-local communities.[20] Even when they seemingly assimilate into the formal Bosnian diaspora worldwide, a closer look at the social reality of the Bosnian diaspora reveals that it is mostly made up of deterritorialised, locally embedded identities and networks rather than transnational political organisations. In many places where Bosnians settled, instead of grandiose halls and monuments to 'Bosnianness' there are *zavičajni klubovi* (local clubs) with distinctive names from the original home, such as the Brčko-Melbourne (*Klub Brčaka*) in Melbourne or the Podrinje-Srebrenica Association, also based in Melbourne, with sister associations in Sydney and in St. Louis (U.S.A.). The same organisational patterns follow the Prijedor associations in Melbourne, Malmo, Chicago and St. Louis. These and many other similar Bosnian trans-local associations, clubs and networks maintain their own websites, newsletters and mailing lists.[21]

Unlike ethnic diaspora organisations, most of these 'local' clubs and associations are, to various degrees, multi-ethnic or mixed, i.e., include members of all Bosnian ethnic groups who come from a particular locale. Thus, the trans-local networks act as a form of resistance to the ethno-nationalism from above promoted by some of the Bosnian diaspora umbrella organisations. This multi-ethnic aspect is especially true for the Brčko trans-local network, a vibrant trans-local community in Melbourne where I was able to observe and engage with its lived and imagined realities. Brčko-Melbourne is the largest and by far the best organised trans-local community within the Bosnian diaspora in Australia (Halilovich 2011b). According to Agim Dobruna, a Brčko-Melbourne community activist, since 1992 around 250 families from Brčko have settled in Melbourne, with some 150 families settled in other parts of Australia. Melbourne has become an unofficial centre of the wider global Brčko network. Forced displacement, loyalty to locally embedded social networks, and chain migration have all contributed to the formation of the trans-local community of Brčko, 16,000 kilometres from its original location in BiH.

The 'original' town of Brčko is located in north-eastern Bosnia, in the border region close to Serbia to the east and bordering Croatia to the north, making it a crossroad between central Europe and the Balkans. Its geography furnished Brčko with a vibrant social history as a trading centre and a bridge – physically as well as metaphorically – connecting Croatia, Bosnia and Serbia. Brčko has also served as the largest port in Bosnia, with the Sava river – the largest Yugoslav river – flowing through Serbia, Bosnia, Croatia and Slovenia, an important communication route as well as a source of pride and identity for the local population. Dominating the local landscape the river became a symbol, an imagined natural link between the people and the local area, 'representing the memories, meanings and sense of belonging as well as the process of social relations and interactions' (Smith 2003: 72).

Before the war the ethnic composition of the 38,000 residents of Brčko included 45 per cent Bosniaks, 25 per cent Croats, 21 per cent Serbs, 6 per cent Yugoslavs, and 3 per cent 'other'.[22] So-called 'mixed marriages' between members of different ethnic groups were very common among *Brčaci* (Brčko residents). Its strategic location, as a town on the border, sealed its fate: in May 1992 Brčko was one of the first Bosnian towns to come under attack by Serb militias, who committed atrocities:[23] plunder, arbitrary killings and torture of Bosniak and Croat men (Mujkić 2009; Bieber 2005; Jeffrey 2006).

By the end of 1992 most Bosniaks, Croats, the ethnically mixed and the undeclared – more than 70 per cent of the whole town's population – were expelled from Brčko. While many only passed through neighbouring Croatia and Serbia on the way to Austria via Hungary, some decided to stay closer to home in Croatia, Slovenia or Serbia, and wait for the moment when they could return. Many others chose or did not have any other option but to remain in the country as IDPs in Bosnian government-controlled territories. The luckier ones reached the safety of Austria, which became the preferred refugee destination for thousands of expellees from Brčko. The Austrian refugee policy, however, did not take into consideration local identities – neither regional nor ethnic – when distributing Bosnian refugees into refugee centres across the country. This meant that many *Brčaci* were dispersed across different Austrian provinces. Despite the physical separation and inability to travel due to conditions attached to their refugee status, many *Brčaci* as a matter of priority re-established contacts with their home town social networks, to exchange information and follow developments back home. When the war was nearing its end, many realised that they might have lost their home town forever and started contemplating a permanent resettlement in a third country.[24] A few families, the pre-war migrants from Brčko living in Melbourne, assisted the first *Brčaci* from Austria and other European countries to migrate to Australia. Soon after the newcomers arrived in Australia they passed on information about the migration procedure to their fellow *Brčaci* back in Europe and assisted them as 'proposers' and 'guarantors'.[25] Thus a process of chain migration was created, with each family assisting many more families to migrate to Australia. Once reunited with their home-town compatriots in Australia, they were provided with 'on arrival' support and links to government settlement services. In 1996, when they established the Brčko club in Melbourne, there were some 100 families living in Melbourne. In the following years that number almost tripled. But it is not their actual number that makes *Brčaci* such a fascinating trans-local community, so much as how they re-enact, remember and reimagine their collective identity.

While many Bosnian diaspora organisations have been preoccupied with ethnic exclusivity and nationalistic patriotism, the Brčko club defines itself as an exclusively 'local' association of former residents of Brčko. As Nihad Jašarević, the president of the club, put it, Brčko-Melbourne is an apolitical and multi-ethnic association 'reflecting the way of life as it once used to exist in Brčko'. However, like 'all moral communities', as Herzfeld (1985: xii) argues, this community also operates on principles of inclusion and exclusion similar to other larger and smaller entities. In order to 'preserve' and maintain their local values from back home they have positioned themselves as a distinct and exclusive group within the broader Bosnian diaspora in Australia. While *Brčaci* exclude themselves from ethno-nationalist politics, their exclusion also relates to their positioning vis-à-vis those who come from other Bosnian towns or villages, as well as those who come from the villages around Brčko. Thus, trans-local Brčko in Melbourne replicates the exclusion categories from back home where one of the main differentiations has been the division between urban dwellers (*građani*) and village folks (*seljaci*).[26]

The premises of the Brčko-Melbourne club, located in a modern, government-owned building in Prahran, a sought-after location close to Melbourne's central business district, serves as a meeting point for the Brčko community and offers a range of social activities. Over a cup of coffee, or *čevapčići* and a drink, Melbourne *Brčaci* share the news about each other from their everyday Australian life, as well as the news – and gossip – about fellow *Brčaci* in other countries and those who returned to Brčko. Whenever someone from their community returns from a visit to Bosnia and their hometown, there are long presentations and a grilling of the returnee about the place they still imagine as their home. During social gatherings and festivities, which *Brčaci* in Melbourne do not lack, the two home-grown Brčko bands provide entertainment and nurture nostalgia for the old home they left in Bosnia.

The Brčko Portal website,[27] hosted by Hamdija Dobruna, a member of the Brčko community in Melbourne, ensures that information about 'Brčko here and Brčko everywhere' reaches all *Brčaci* wherever they may be. The online portal provides not only up-to-date information from Brčko-Melbourne but also relevant and useful information about back home, such as how to reclaim houses and property confiscated during the war, information about missing *Brčaci*, and news about those who visited or returned to Brčko. Members of the trans-local Brčko community post their photos on the website and create a visual, digital community of people who continue to know each other while living in many different destinations across the globe. Apart from keeping the records of the deterritorialised Brčko community in the present, the Brčko Portal also serves as an online museum for preserving the social history of the town and its people before the war. Pictures of local bands from the 1950s to the 1990s and beyond as well as pictures of the local football club, Borac, represent a part of that history. In addition to the online portal there is a newsletter, *Brčko Bilten*, available both in print and online. Besides its own media outlets and the club's premises, Brčko-Melbourne also utilises the media and infrastructure of the wider Bosnian diaspora such as Bosnian community radio 3ZZZ (one of the radio presenters is a member of the Melbourne Brčko community), the government-owned SBS Radio's *The Bosnian Program, Magazine Bosna*, as well as the facilities of the Australian Bosniak Association, the Bosnian Centre in Springvale, the Australian-Bosnian Islamic Centre in Deer Park, and the stadium facilities of one of the three Melbourne-based Bosnian football clubs. In many of these diaspora organisations *Brčaci* have prominent positions. Also, some of the Bosnian restaurants and coffee shops in Melbourne, such as Hanna Café and the Saraj restaurant in St. Albans, have become places where *Brčaci* regularly meet.

Not only culturally, but also economically, the Australian *Brčaci* have prospered in their newly adopted homeland. Over the last sixteen years many *Brčaci* in Melbourne have established their own businesses, started professional careers and bought houses. They constantly continue to redefine their individual and collective identities: from displaced and dispossessed refugees many have become successful entrepreneurs; from the once hobby fishermen on the river Sava in Brčko some have reinvented themselves as deep-water fishermen in the waters of the Tasman. *Brčaci* – like other Bosnian 'locals' – tend to live in the same neighbourhoods and suburbs. While the original Brčko remains an important symbol, a metaphor and memory, many *Brčaci* have come to accept that they will never return to the place. They are nostalgic for the home lost but do not appear to be concerned about losing their 'local' Brčko identity. Mersa, a woman in her fifties, who spent 'her youth and the happiest days' in Brčko, summed up the *Brčaci* sentiment:

> My Brčko is here with my *Brčaci*. Most of my friends from Brčko live here in Melbourne. I sponsored my best friends to move here from Germany and Austria. That Brčko over there [in Bosnia] used to be my home, but not anymore ... We are much happier as *Brčaci* in Melbourne, in our Brčko club, than we would be in the new Brčko. They erected a monument to the Četnik leader Draža Mihailović on the main square in Brčko. I will never return, and I don't need to – I have my Brčko here.

For Mersa and her fellow *Brčaci* in Melbourne the sense of belonging to a distinct Brčko community is practically enacted through the maintenance of and participation in reconstructed social networks from back home. The old loyalties, friendships and status in the community are reconstructed, re-negotiated and reimagined in Melbourne. Those who were 'someone' back in Brčko enjoy similar status in Brčko-Melbourne. In most cases this status is merely symbolic as the social context has changed. For instance, the titles from back home – such as 'professor', used for anyone who worked as a teacher in a secondary school, or 'director' for managers of state-owned companies, etc. – are still regularly used when addressing the people who once held these titles in Brčko. Those who were once prominent citizens of Brčko, such as sportsmen, politicians, restaurant owners or artists, enjoy the respect of their fellow *Brčaci*. In a way, *Brčaci* need each other not only to socialise in the present but also to remember and be remembered for who they once were and still imagine themselves to be. They exist for each other not only in the diasporic reality of the Brčko-Melbourne club but also in their shared memories. The shared memories of home 'there' in the past are complemented by the present embodied experiences of 'here' in the diaspora.

While the re-enactment of shared memories and sense of common belonging to their Brčko community takes many different forms – from attending weddings, graduations, birthdays and funerals to everyday contacts between members of the Brčko community and speaking a recognisable local dialect – there are also many formal communal events and gatherings. The largest and most important is *Savski cvijet* (Sava's flower), the annual meeting of *Brčaci* in Australia. As its name suggests, *Savski cvijet* evokes memories of the river Sava, Brčko's 'home river' and the most distinct landscape icon. In Melbourne the river transcends its original meaning, to become a mythical river, a natural link between *Brčaci*.[28] As well as 'domestic' Australian *Brčaci*, over the last few years there has been an increasing number of *Brčaci* from Austria, Germany and other sister communities of deterritorialised *Brčaci* attending the *Savski cvijet* event in Melbourne.

An integral part of Brčko and similar trans-local identities revolves around stories, anecdotes, gossip, jokes and funny nicknames – or what Michel Herzfeld (1997) calls 'cultural intimacy' – that require local embodied, or transmitted, knowledge, to tap into (Geertz 1983). These and other forms of local 'intimate self-knowledge', as Herzfeld (1997: 14–16) argues, often 'become a device of social, political and economic exclusion ... and a mark of intimacy as well as security'. Through performances of embodied local knowledge and the creation of imaginary borders of one's own group's distinctiveness, the trans-local communities engage in a complex process of essentialising themselves and others.

Strengthening Unity through Intermarriage

'Overseas *Brčaci*' are also regularly represented as guests at the weddings of fellow *Brčaci* in Melbourne. The prevalent endogamy of this community is only one of its many factors of social cohesion. Over the last few years I have attended numerous weddings, the most recent being that of Adis and Almira, two young people in their mid twenties. Both born in Brčko, in the spring of 1992 they fled their home town with their families. Their parents knew each other well from back home. In fact, as Almira's father Hamdija disclosed in his wedding speech, the two families were neighbours back in Brčko. While Adis and Almira look like any other Australian couple and speak English as their first language, their parents are much more 'traditional *Brčaci*'. Being traditional *Brčaci* does not mean, however, that these two families share all common values: for instance while Adis' father is an observant Muslim who went to *Hajj*, Almira's parents, her Serb mother and Bosniak father, are ethnically mixed atheists. Nonetheless, what unites these two families are their Brčko roots and their loyalty to their memories of the life lived – and remembered – in their *čaršija* (town). Observing their conversations, it is clear that they do not discuss religion, ethnicity and politics, the topics that could set them apart. Rather, their talks revolve round Brčko and *Brčaci*. Thus Adis and Almira's wedding, which would otherwise be regarded as a mixed marriage, was unreservedly blessed by both families and the wider Brčko community. As the various parties present at the wedding stated, they are all happy that these two people have retained their roots. Out of thirty-four marriages of people from Brčko in recent years, twenty-one have been between *Brčaci*, i.e., both partners have been from the Brčko community – either from Melbourne, another Australian city or, as in two cases, from Berlin in Germany and the original Brčko in Bosnia. Four young *Brčaci* found their partners outside the trans-local Brčko, in the displaced communities of Bijeljina, Zvornik and Tuzla, all originally located close to Brčko, in the same region in north-eastern Bosnia. The other four reported marriages included Australian Bosnian partners with origins in different parts of Bosnia, while three marriages were cross-cultural with non-Bosnians, Australians, from an Anglo-Celtic background.

As with the deterritorialised Brčko, the prevalent – or at least highly desired – endogamy trend is present in other Bosnian trans-local communities in Australia and globally; young people are encouraged to marry one of 'their own', from a pool of global trans-local communities. In many instances parents and relatives fund young people of marriageable age to travel back to the original home town or visit other sister trans-local communities in order to meet prospective partners.

The following two stories illustrate this kind of trans-localism in action. Zumra and Samir are a trans-local couple from Srebrenica who welcomed me into their home in St. Louis. They met and fell in love when Zumra, a young woman from the Srebrenica area who settled with her parents in Melbourne in 2000, was visiting her relatives in St. Louis. Samir, a member of the Bosnian community – and more particularly a member of St. Louis' Srebrenica community – had migrated under similar circumstances in 1996. Zumra was nostalgic for her Melbourne and asked me many questions about the people and place she left behind. She said she only realised how much Melbourne had grown on her once she moved to St. Louis. She made jokes about American Bosnians in St. Louis without realising she was gradually becoming one of them. St. Louis was her fourth home, she said. After the ethnic cleansing of Srebrenica, she spent six years in a refugee settlement near Tuzla, in Bosnia, before migrating to Australia. After six years in Melbourne she moved to live with her husband in his adopted hometown in the U.S.A. Samir started a small business in St. Louis and, as he said, would never consider leaving St. Louis for any other place. Most of his surviving relatives live there and *his* Srebrenica was now in St. Louis. He made jokes about Australian Bosnians, calling them the 'Bosnian Kangaroos'. While Zumra and Samir traded jokes about the 'Bosnian Cowboys' in America and the 'Bosnian Kangaroos' in Australia they were conscious of their shared sense of belonging to the trans-local Srebrenica community, the strongest bond they had with each other and other members of the Bosnian diaspora.

I encountered a similar trans-local love story in my 'home town' of Melbourne, where I met Skender and Belma, a young couple in their mid twenties who got married in Bosnia in the summer of 2007. They did not know each other until they met in their original home town of Mostar earlier that year. However, they shared memories of growing up in Mostar where they had lived happily until forced to flee with their parents at the outbreak of the war in the early 1990s. Skender migrated with his parents to Chicago, while Belma and her family ended up in Melbourne. Both families integrated quite well in their host countries and managed to climb the social ladder from dispossessed refugees to relatively affluent middle class by migrants' standards. After they completed their studies, Skender graduating as an electrical engineer and Belma as a biomedical scientist, their parents paid for them to travel to Bosnia, encouraging them to look for prospective partners while revisiting the place they once called home. Their parents secretly hoped that their children would meet 'genuine' local partners who would be both acceptable to them as well as willing to join them in Chicago and Melbourne respectively. In post-war BiH, marriage has become a popular way for young people to migrate to a country where they hope to have better opportunities to find a job and start a family. Thus trans-localism acts as a utility for people to migrate and a source of social and cultural capital for those included in trans-local networks.

Once in Mostar, however, instead of meeting a local boy and girl, Belma, an Aussie girl, and Skender, an American dude, 'coincidentally' met and fell in love. Similar experiences of growing up and being educated in English-speaking countries, Australia and the U.S., was an important cultural bridge for the two young people. They both admitted that they were able to find much more in common with each other than with their local peers who had never left Mostar. Though initially a bit disappointed that they did not marry 'locally', their parents gave their blessing to this trans-local relationship. In August 2007 they followed them to attend their wedding in faraway Mostar. The young couple decided to start their new life together in Chicago. However, they have been quite frequent visitors to Melbourne, and their marriage will further strengthen links between the trans-local Mostar communities in Melbourne and Chicago as well as the links with and the memories of their original home town of Mostar.

Other Forms of Trans-localism in Action

How Mostar has been remembered and memorialised has been discussed in the previous chapter. It is, however, important, in the context of this chapter, to point to the forms of trans-local memory making and resistance to the ethnic division of their city by the former Mostar residents dispersed across many different countries. Many of them represent – or are led by – the pre-war Mostar intelligentsia and cultural elite who turned their initially forced displacement into a self-imposed exile as a protest against the continuation of the ethno-nationalist politics in their home city. In 1995, in collaboration with the Mostar poet Alija Kebo and other like-minded fellow *Mostarci* (citizens of Mostar), a group of exiled Mostar intellectuals – including prominent personalities such as Predrag Matvejević (professor at the Sapienza University of Rome and the University of Paris III: Sorbonne Nouvelle) – relaunched the *Most* (*Bridge*), a journal for education, science and culture.[29] The new series of *Most*, edited and designed in Sweden and managed as a collaborative project between many prominent Mostar intellectuals (Bosniaks, Croats, Serbs and others), has become a trans-local cultural journal and an alternative voice to the nationalist-dominated media back in Mostar. Through various written genres and pictures the contributors call for tolerance and for the rebuilding of the old multi-ethnic Mostar. In the section 'Pisma Mostu' ('Letters to *Most*') the letters of ordinary displaced *Mostarci* are published, in which they express their support for the journal and their longing for the old Mostar. The journal – available online and in print and distributed to sixty destinations on three continents – uses both scripts, Latin and Cyrillic, and has become an unofficial journal of Mostar nostalgia, read and commented on beyond the deterritorialised Mostar community. Apart from this trans-local project there are many other forms of individual creative trans-localism. For instance, Amir Mehičević, a Mostar-born Australian film director, named his Melbourne production company Mostar Vision Motion Pictures, bridging his old home to his new professional identity.

Like *Brčaci*, displaced *Mostarci* claim that they represent the true 'old Mostar' regardless of the fact that they live far from the actual place. In addition to visiting their original home town since they fled, they maintain their local Mostar identity through contacts with friends and families back in Mostar as well as with those living in diaspora. The distinct Herzegovinian dialect is another shared aspect of their identity which crosses ethnic and religious lines. A significant proportion of deterritorialised *Mostarci* are in so-called mixed or multi-ethnic marriages. Vahdet and Marina and their two teenage daughters, living in Melbourne, are such a family. Their suburban home is like an informal Mostar Museum with paintings of Mostar and other memorabilia spread throughout. Their Mostar is the one they remember and the one they maintain with their informal Mostar network, made up of other displaced citizens whose religious and ethnic identity are of secondary or no importance to them.

Trans-local groups like those from Brčko, Srebrenica and Mostar are not simply concerned with nurturing nostalgia for the home lost and with preservation of their distinct local cultures. There are also economic, charitable and even political activities that justify their existence and strengthen trans-local communities. For instance, a number of businesses, predominantly in the building industry, run by members of such communities in

Australia are almost exclusively staffed by fellow trans-locals. During my research in St. Louis (U.S.A.) and in Sweden – as I will discuss in more detail in the final part of the book – I identified the same trends in other businesses run by Bosnians who prefer to employ 'their own people'. This reflects social patterns and moral economies from the original home. It is firstly about communal solidarity and trust; but it is also about the status of the individual within the wider network of his/her trans-local community. For instance, information about the Drina Building Company, based on the Gold Coast, Australia, and its owner Nedžad Izmirlić, originally from Klotjevac near Srebrenica, has been primarily disseminated by those he employs: fellow locals from the Srebrenica region. Within the wider trans-local Klotjevac network it is known that Nedžad has 'made it' and is a successful and generous employer. As with Amir's Mostar Vision Motion Pictures, Nedžad's loyalty to his native region (*zavičaj*) is further exemplified by the name he gave to his company, 'Drina' being the name of the river flowing though his native village. All this helps Nedžad Izmirlić maintain his trans-local status respect as an 'elder' in his deterritorialised community made up of some sixteen trans-local sister communities spread across the globe, as described in Chapter 1. The same could be said for Beriz Nukić, the most successful Bosnian entrepreneur in St. Louis (U.S.A.), the owner of the Berix enterprise, who is respected within the Srebrenica trans-local network for providing support to his native village of Sulice, for employing his fellow Bosnians from the Srebrenica region, and for generous donations to charitable causes.

Charitable and fundraising events for a 'good cause' back home or in diaspora are the most widespread non-profit activities of trans-local groups. For instance, fundraising events are organised for building communal projects, supporting individuals and families affected by illness or hardship, providing scholarships for 'local' students, and similar humanitarian causes. Many of the groups are also politically active, advocating and lobbying for their specific 'local' political cause. Through their formal and informal networks the trans-local communities of Srebrenica and Prijedor have campaigned for the recognition of genocide and the right to memorialise the sufferings in their native towns. As discussed in the previous chapter and as will be discussed in the final part of the book, members of these trans-local networks have organised a number of political events to raise awareness in their host societies about what happened – and continues to happen – in their home towns and villages in Bosnia.

Many charitable actions are intrinsically political and function as performative enactments of identity and memory. In April 2008 I was a participant-observer at a fundraising event (*humanitarno sijelo*) in St. Louis, which was organised by members of the Bukvić family living there. The event was held at the 'Czech Hall', rented for the occasion, while the programme included a Bosnian music band, a folk dance group performing traditional dances, and raffles, as well as speeches by a member of the Bukvić family and the main *imam* from the Bosnian mosque in St. Louis. The Bosnian fast food *ćevapčići* and non-alcoholic beverages were served, and, in the middle of the hall, many participants, especially the women and girls, engaged in dancing *kolo*, a Bosnian folk dance. The funds collected that night from 300 entry tickets, raffles and donations were to support the rebuilding of the mosque destroyed during the war in the Bukvićs' native village of Mahoje, near Zavidovići, in central Bosnia.

This act was more than one of long-distance local patriotism or religious zeal. Through mobilising members of the wider Bosnian diaspora in St. Louis for their cause, the family demonstrated the power of their social capital 'over here' which the village 'back home' was to profit from. Similar use of refugees' social networks in exile employed to advance the interest of the local communities back home has been described by Sergio Diaz-Briquets and Jorge Perez-Lopez (1997), who explored the social networks and remittances among Cuban and Nicaraguan refugees in the U.S. They argue that remittances of labour migrants are qualitatively different from those of refugees because 'labour migration, by definition, involves the voluntary departure from the home country in search of better economic options, whereas refugees ... depart their homelands for a combination of political and economic reasons' (Diaz-Briquets and Perez-Lopez 1997: 411). These differences, as they point out, have a major bearing on how refugees perceive their relationship with their countries of origin and the communities they come from.

The Mahoje villagers used the occasion to remember and commemorate their war-torn community, but also to inspire other members of the Bosnian diaspora in St. Louis to 'remember' Mahoje, though most of these people might never have heard of the village before. Furthermore, the Bukvićs demonstrated an ability to influence social change in 'their' village from far away. On the one hand, rebuilding the destroyed mosque was to send a message of defiance – even from a safe distance – to those who destroyed it: 'We haven't forgotten. We are back! You haven't defeated us!' Indeed these words of defiance were in the speeches delivered at the fundraising event. On the other hand, the action demonstrated practical solidarity with fellow villagers living in Bosnia or dispersed in diaspora. Despite the fact that the Bukvićs have been living far from their original village, they continue to participate in village life much more than in a purely symbolic way. They have restored – or possibly even improved – their standing within the village community by taking their Mahoje and its story to a trans-local level.

Rebuilding mosques in villages like Mahoje is about much more than creating a place for worship for the survivors of ethnic cleansing. Very often those zealously involved in collecting funds and coordinating the building of mosques in post-war Bosnia are not especially observant Muslims. Particularly in ethnically cleansed small village communities, reconstructed mosques serve not only as places of worship but also as monuments to the recent past and shrines to community members who perished. As mentioned previously in the book, mosques – as symbols of the collective cultural identity of Bosnian Muslims – were systematically destroyed by Serb militias during the war. Therefore rebuilding the destroyed mosques as important cultural landmarks is regarded by many survivors as an essential, sometimes final, step in a symbolic return and social reconstruction of war-torn communities.

In June 2008 a fundraising event similar to that held in St. Louis was organised in Melbourne by the members of four families from Klotjevac, the village described in Chapter 1. The setting, the audience and the programme very much resembled the one I had seen in St. Louis a few months previously. The event, held at the Bosniak club, in Melbourne's 'Balkans suburb' of St. Albans, included a video projection, but lacked the religious dimension seen in St. Louis. In fact, the event was very much like any other *zabava* (communal celebration), accompanied by live music, alcohol and food consumption, singing and dancing. Although the village of Klotjevac was an ethnic Bosniak village, the audience at the fundraising event was multi-ethnic, made up of Bosniaks, Croats, Albanians, Australians and even a few Bosnian Serbs. The purpose of the event was to collect funds to build a monument to the victims of war and genocide in the village of Klotjevac. This fundraising activity was supported by other members of the trans-local Klotjevac network and by the returnees to the village as well as a group of Australian students who visited Klotjevac as part of a study tour to Bosnia in July/August 2007. As described in Chapter 1, two years later the monument was erected in Klotjevac's main square, above the village fountain – a highly symbolic location in the life of the village's collective identity, and one where, over many generations, most social activities had taken place.

These two stories, of Mahoje in St. Louis and Klotjevac in Melbourne, are two examples amongst many that demonstrate how the popular memory of ordinary people is performed and turned into action – hence power – in (un)making 'histories from below'. What they demonstrate is how memory-making and -unmaking processes are defined but not limited by place and displacement.

Apart from those described, the trans-local enactments of memory and identity come in a variety of other forms. While trans-local memories and identities derive inspiration from a real and imagined 'over there' home, displaced Bosnians have memories and narratives that often differ from their compatriots who remained 'over there', in the homeland. After ethnic cleansing, for many of the displaced all that is left of the place to which they once belonged are memories of the lost 'ideal home' (Hockey 1999). The memories are regularly nourished by material possessions and memorabilia, such as photo albums, books, diplomas, and household items like manual coffee grinders – a traditional Bosnian 'trademark' – and similar 'precious' objects that were regularly picked up before fleeing. As in Marina's and Vahdet's new home in Australia, in many other Bosnian homes in Austria, Sweden and the U.S.A where I was a guest, these items are visibly displayed in credenzas and on living room walls, making these rooms living museums of the home lost. Far away from Bosnia, items that might have had a utilitarian value back home have assumed highly sentimental and aesthetic functions and significations – prompts to remember, or, as Marilyn Lake (2006: 1) puts it, an 'insurance against failure of collective memory'.

The Formation of Trans-local Diasporic Communities

While trans-localism is a potentiality of all forms of migration, not all diasporic communities, nor all sections of a particular ethnic or national diaspora, create trans-local social networks as a distinct form of deterritorialised identity. For this to happen, certain social conditions need to be met. These relate primarily to a combination of common 'roots and routes', as Gilroy (1995) and Clifford (1997) put it, i.e., shared pre-migration and migration experiences need to be involved in the process. It particularly seems that forced migration from ancestral homes and dramatic separation from spatial practices and identities are decisive factors in the establishment of trans-local networks. Forced migration often involves the temporary and/ or permanent displacement of large (or complete) sections of a local population. In the process, people's roots become their routes as they usually choose (or are forced) to migrate to quite specific locations and their deterritorialisation effectively leads to a new reterritorialisation. The chain-migration process plays an important role in the morphology of the reconstructed groups as trans-local communities do not get formed by some random (mis) fortune, but are rather a result of deliberate decisions and 'local' social networks (Brettell 2003). As described in this chapter, migration often creates a chain reaction with each migrant assisting new fellow locals to reach desired destinations. Medo Čivić, for instance, could rightly be regarded as the founder of the Srebrenica trans-local community in Melbourne. He assisted and was the official migration 'sponsor' (proposer) to hundreds of fellow refugees from the Srebrenica region who settled in Melbourne in the late 1990s. While the 'human magnet' factor is behind all these migration trends, in the age of globalisation the advanced technological means of communication and transportation have greatly influenced and accelerated the formation and maintenance of trans-local networks. Using information technology, for instance, different sister trans-local groups have achieved synchronicity between them in terms of flow of information and coordination of their activities. The means of communication have enabled many individuals to maintain and be part of various such networks across the globe without having to travel. Many members of the trans-local communities regularly 'meet' in cyber space, on one of the many websites dedicated to a particular place in the old homeland – as well as meeting in real space in social clubs like Brčko-Melbourne, Bosna Gold in St. Louis, at a picnic organised by the Prijedor Association in Malmo, or at a commemoration organised by the Srebrenica-Podrinje Association in Sydney. Such direct and indirect forms of interaction imply that connectivity, and not necessarily mobility, has become one of the main features of contemporary diaspora. However, the key in establishing and maintaining the diasporic trans-local social networks remains the desire to keep alive the distinct local culture in the forms of rituals, dialect, social norms, narratives and the maintenance of links with the original home 'over there' (*zavičaj*).

The performance of distinct local identities happens through social gatherings, intermarriage, social clubs, newsletters, websites, mailing lists, commemorations, humanitarian activities, political lobbying and economic activities. While larger towns and cities like Sarajevo and Mostar have their own trans-local networks and identity performances – such as, for instance, the annual *Bal Sarajevske raje* (Sarajevans Ball) in Vienna and Melbourne – villages, neighbourhoods and smaller towns seem to be more inclined to reconstruct, reimagine and hold onto their special practices and local cultures on a day-to-day basis. In the process of trans-local identity (re)construction, the original places – 'mother villages', as Portis-Winner (2002) calls them – if still there, change and gradually position themselves in relation to one or more of the dominant offshoot trans-local communities or replicas of the original place. Thus while attempting to preserve the culture and identity from back home, trans-local communities in reality transform the identity of the original source of a particular culture and identity they imagine they are reviving and preserving.

Conclusion

As we have seen in the case of trans-local communities from Podrinje, Brčko, Prijedor and Mostar described in this chapter, in terms of division, tension and contrast, the relationship between trans-localism and transnationalism, as well as between *zavičaj*-based localism and ethno-nationalism, is more complex than it initially may appear. While, for instance, Melbourne-Brčko trans-localism is zealously anti-nationalist, protecting its pre-war multi-ethnic *zavičaj* reconfigured in Melbourne, other trans-local communities, like those from the mono-ethnic villages of Podrinje and Prijedor, or the village of Mahoje, are more flexible when it comes to tapping into Bosnian/Bosniak nationalism, at times incorporating – or more often being incorporated into – nationalist projects. In fact, there are many instances of Bosnian/Bosniak nationalism appropriating the emotion-laden symbolism of ethnic cleansing and genocide committed against these local communities, elevating them to a nationalist pedestal as crimes against the nation. As in the case of the Srebrenica genocide commemoration described in Chapter 3, the nationalist appropriation of local tragedies and their inclusion in grand narratives of nationhood often leads to tension between local survivors, who have embodied relationships with these tragedies, and nationalists, who claim their connections with the tragedies via their belonging to the Bosnian/Bosniak nation. As Asim, a Srebrenica survivor, put it, 'for them [the nationalists] this is a once-a-year event, while for us Srebrenica is every day'.

Trans-localism, as an explanatory framework for exploring the social realities lived – and imagined – in diasporic local groups, can have an interchangeable relationship with transnationalism, sometimes fitting under the conceptual umbrella of transnationalism and sometimes not – at times complementing and at other times contesting the transnationalist paradigm. Displaced Bosnians are not only members of their broader ethnic or national diasporas, nor simply refugees waiting to return to their original homelands. They have, over time, as Malkki (1992: 38) puts it, formed 'the multiplicity of attachments to places through living in, remembering and imagining them'. Thus these trans-local diasporic communities are not stuck in the past or fixed and stable and localised in time and space in their identities. On the contrary, trans-localism, as performed by war-torn communities from Bosnia, exemplifies how cultural place and embodied local identities transcend geographical space and chronological time – how mobility and attachment to place are not intrinsically contradictory, but can in fact be complementary processes.

As such, trans-localism does not imply complete cultural hybridity nor does it advocate an essentialist, static view of the relationship between people, place, identity and mobility. Rather, it confirms the dynamism and fluidity of the complex relationships in which identity of place as a set of embodied practices transcends its original geographical location and becomes polylocal, or trans-local. Hence, trans-localism encompasses a wide spectrum of practices and relationships as the articulation of distinct (trans-)local identities and reveals how these practices and relationships get reconstructed, readjusted, remembered and reimagined in the world of movement. While trans-local identities represent an important aspect of diversity within the worldwide Bosnian diaspora, there are many other dimensions that need to be unveiled and recognised as part of that diversity – in particular, gender.

Notes

1. I outlined the concept of trans-localism in the article 'Trans-local Communities in the Age of Transnationalism: Bosnians in Diaspora', published in *International Migration*. See Halilovich 2012b.
2. UNHCR (2005), World Bank (2005), Internal Displacement Monitoring Centre/Norwegian Refugee Council (2006) and Bosnia and Herzegovina Ministry for Human Rights and Refugees (2008).
3. Annex 7 of the Dayton Peace Agreement states that people must be 'permitted to return in safety irrespective of ethnic origin, religious belief, or political opinion'.
4. Clifford (1997), R. Cohen (1997), Gilroy (1995), Gonzalez (1992), Hall (1990), Safran (1991), Sheffer (1986) and Vertovec (1999).
5. The stories about 'successful Bosnians' are frequently published in the Bosnian diasporic media as well as in the 'homeland' media in BiH.
6. See also, for instance, Al-Ali (2002), Al-Ali, Black and Koser (2001a), Colic-Peisker and Waxman (2005), Davy (1995), Eastmond (1998, 2005, 2006), Franz (2000, 2005), Hozic (2001), Huttunen (2005), Jansen (2008), Korac (2003), Matsuo (2005) and Valenta (2009).
7. Over the last 150 years Bosnians and Herzegovinians of different ethnic groups have been migrating to different countries within Europe (and Turkey) as well as to faraway destinations in South and North America, South Africa, Australia and New Zealand. In May 2006 Bosnians in the U.S.A. celebrated 100 years of their community.
8. In November 2009, fifteen years after the war ended, the Party for Diaspora (Stranka za dijasporu), was established by members of the Bosnian diaspora in Sweden. The Party for Diaspora plans to open its branches in other countries where Bosnians live as well as to have its permanent office in Sarajevo. The political platform of the Party for Diaspora is based on the idea that Bosnian diaspora should express a united voice exclusively through this party in order to get its representatives in the BiH Parliament (see http://www.strankadijaspore.com/). Taking into consideration that

since 1991 the politics in BiH have been dominated by political parties promoting ethnic agendas of their respective ethnic constituencies, it almost looks like the Bosnian diaspora emerging as a quasi separate ethnic group with its own exclusive political party. As it has been highly unlikely that Bosniaks, Croats or Serbs would vote for the parties of the ethnic 'other', so it is to be expected that people back in Bosnia would not vote for the Party for Diaspora as it would be seen as 'representing the interests of them there', rather than 'us here', as was suggested in the media in BiH.

9. Figures from different sources – such as UNDP, World Bank, IOM and BiH Ministry for Human Rights and Refugees – differ and this is my own rough approximation.
10. The other two official languages of Bosnia-Herzegovina, Croatian and Serbian, had already been introduced into mainstream education in host countries like Australia by the established Croatian and Serbian diaspora communities.
11. Bundesministerium für Unterricht, Kunst und Kultur (2008).
12. In most cases it is possible to recognise the ethnic background in the person's name.
13. The Victorian Certificate of Education (VCE) is a certificate that recognises the successful completion of secondary education in Victoria, Australia.
14. According to the Victorian School of Languages' estimates (http://www.vsl.vic.edu.au/). In addition to this number there are several hundred students of Bosnian origin attending Croatian and Serbian language classes.
15. See Bagshaw (1997), Davy (1995), Dimova (2006, 2007), Graf (1999) and Koser (2001).
16. *Duldung* refers to temporary protection visas.
17. See, for instance, http://www.translocal.org/.
18. See Appadurai (1996), Bhabha (1990), Clifford (1997), Dirlik (2000), Escobar (2001), Feld and Basso (1996), J. Friedman (1998, 2002), Gupta and Ferguson (1992), Hannerz (1996), Kibreab (1999), Malkki (1992, 1995) and Rapport and Dawson (1998).
19. Outstanding ethnographies on the role local factors play in migration patterns have been produced by Anja Peleikes (2000), who researched dislocated Lebanese refugees in the Ivory Coast; Jasna Čapo Žmegač (2003), who completed an ethnographic study on Croatian economic migrants in Germany; Selvaraj Velayutham and Amanda Wise (2005), who wrote about a 'trans-local village' made up of southern Indians living in Singapore; and Irene Portis-Winner (2002), who completed a comparative ethnographic study of Slovene villagers and their ethnic relatives in the U.S.A. These case studies in many respects mirror the migration patterns and trans-local communities of Bosnians.
20. A part of the 'Brčko story' described here was included in the book chapter '(Per)forming "Trans-local" Homes: Bosnian Diaspora in Australia'. See Halilovich (2011b).
21. See, for instance, the Podrinje-Srebrenica Association's website (http://www.srebrenica.org.au/) or the Brčko Portal (http://home.swiftdsl.com.au/~hamdija/stablo.html).

22. Government of Bosnia-Herzegovina (1991); the municipality of Brčko, comprising of fifty-nine 'communities' (the town and surrounding villages) had a population of 87,332.
23. Goran Jelisic and Ranko Cesic, the Serb militiamen, were found guilty of crimes against humanity for the atrocities they committed and ordered in Brčko between 1992 and 1993. An extract from an ICTY report reads: 'In May 1992, Goran Jelisic systematically killed Muslim detainees at the Laser Bus Company, the Brčko police station and Luka camp. He introduced himself as the "Serb Adolf", said that he had come to Brčko to kill Muslims and often informed the Muslim detainees and others of the number of Muslims he had killed' (CC/PIO/285-E The Hague, 22 January 1998). For more information about war crimes committed in Brčko see the ICTY Case Information Sheet (IT-95-10), Jelisic and Cesic, Brčko. See The International Criminal Tribunal for the Former Yugoslavia, 'Case No. It-95-10: The Prosecutor of the Tribunal against Goran Jelisic, a/k/a Adolf and Ranko Cesic': http://www.icty.org/x/cases/jelisic/ind/en/jel-ii950721e.pdf.
24. The 1995 Dayton Peace Agreement defined the status of Brčko as 'the District Brčko', which was left out of the entity structure of post-Dayton Bosnia and Herzegovina. Its status was to be resolved by international arbitration at a later point. In 1999 Brčko was defined as a 'single administrative unit of local self-government existing under the sovereignty of Bosnia and Herzegovina' ('Statute of the Brčko District of Bosnia and Herzegovina', 7 December 1999, see http://www.ohr.int).
25. While most *Brčaci* came as part of the Refugee and Humanitarian Immigration Program, a letter from a 'proposer' in Australia was often a crucial document for the successful outcome of a migration application. Guarantors helped their fellow friends and relatives from Brčko who, after 1995, would not qualify under the refugee programme.
26. Maček (2001, 2007), Stefansson (2004a, 2007), Helms (2007, 2008) and Sorabji (2006) have, among others, described how these and other similar exclusive categories operate in post-war Sarajevo.
27. See http://hamdija.com/stablo.html.
28. The Sava continues to inspire *Brčaci* in many different ways. It is the most common theme of photographs and paintings on the walls of the Brčko-Melbourne club and in the homes of *Brčaci*. Sava and Brčko have also been regular themes in the songs of the renowned rap musician Edo Maajka (Edin Osmić), a Brčko-born artist who as a teenager in 1992 was expelled from his home town and has been living in Zagreb ever since.
29. See http://www.most.ba/.

⊰ Chapter 5 ⊱

Measuring the Pain of Others
Gendered Displacement, Memory and Identity

> Loneliness is a telephone in the asylum seekers' centre, from which you dial the only number you have.
> Melina Kamerić, *Cipele za dodjelu Oskara,*[1] p. 68

This chapter[2] explores how forced displacement has affected Bosnian women and girls and their identities. The 'in-country' case studies described here come from my fieldwork in the wider region of Podrinje, in eastern Bosnia, and the Prijedor region, in western Bosnia, as well as from diasporic places like the Melbourne suburb of St. Albans, where a significant number of women and their surviving family members from these areas settled after the war. While the war has affected almost every single village and town in the country, the regions of Podrinje and Prijedor have become synonymous with ethnic cleansing, concentration camps and genocide. In addition to having suffered the most casualties during the war, the regions have also become infamous for the systematic use of sexual violence against women and girls. Thus it comes as no surprise that the largest number of war criminals processed at the International Criminal Tribunal for the former Yugoslavia (ICTY) have been charged with – and in the majority of cases found guilty of – crimes committed in these two parts of BiH. While the stories described in the chapter come predominantly from Bosniak women, the focus is not on their ethnicity but on their gender.

While the chapter does not focus on sexual violence against women during the war, out of respect for the thousands of women and girls who survived such crimes – including those I met in the course of my research – I do not avoid mentioning these crimes here. As Vesna Kesić concludes, there are multiple layers of suffering for victims of sexual war violence: 'first, the torture of rape, second, the attitudes of a patriarchal community ... and third ... how these rapes are represented and recognised' (2003: 5). These crimes and their long-term effects on individual survivors, their families and their communities deserve much deeper investigation and analysis, which are beyond the scope of this book and limited by the fact that I am a male researcher. Despite dealing empathetically and sensitively with these complex issues, when faced with a woman survivor of sexual violence, there is no way to escape feeling ashamed, even guilty, as well as a sense of it being inappropriate to have a male researcher in such situations. In interview situations, when these episodes were mentioned – or expressed through unambiguous silences and sighs – I was only able to listen silently.

Due to this sensitivity, I initially focused my research on gaining an overall picture of the issue by looking into the official statistics and research findings of organisations and individual researchers who have specialised in the field. The Sarajevo-based Research and Documentation Centre (RDC) has confirmed and documented some 100,000 casualties of the 1992–95 war in BiH. In ethnic terms, 65.88 per cent of those killed were Bosniaks, 25.62 per cent Serbs, 8.01 per cent Croats, and 0.49 per cent others. The region of Podrinje, in eastern Bosnia, suffered most casualties (33.6 per cent). According to the RDC's *Book of the Dead*, 'only' 10 per cent – or 10,000 casualties – were women. However, 96 per cent of the women killed were civilians: 75.5 per cent of them were Bosniaks, 16 per cent Serbs, 8 per cent Croats and 1 per cent others (see Research and Documentation Centre 2007a, 2007b). However, the figure of 10 per cent of overall casualties simply does not capture the depth and continuing significance of women's suffering, and in this chapter I explore how the magnitude of the crimes against women has been officially and unofficially remembered, as well as how it has affected the memories and identities of women survivors, their families and communities. Similarly, in relation to forced migration, 'until recently' – as Catherine Nolin (2006: 32) argues – women were 'statistically invisible in migration data and ignored in policy, research and action', as if they were less affected by migration experiences than men.

The reality I encountered in the field during my research told a different story; women had been severely affected by both forced migration and direct and indirect violence against them, and their suffering seemed to me much greater than any number or graph could possibly express. Based on hard data and raw statistics – expressed in numbers, tables, graphs, categories and reports – the war in BiH looks almost like a conventional armed conflict, with mainly men being killed, while women's casualties could be statistically discounted as 'collateral damage', an aberration of war objectives. In this chapter I argue that the full scale of women's sufferings, during and after the war, has been underrepresented and that a considerable burden of the war and its aftermath was carried by women. As ICTY judgements have confirmed, women were not simply collateral damage of the war but, in most cases, primary targets of organised violence – including sexual violence – by armed men (see International Criminal Tribunal for the Former Yugoslavia 1996). In addition to 10,000 killed, it is estimated that between 20,000 and 50,000 women and girls were raped and systematically abused during the war.[3] But even the most heinous crimes against women committed in the rape camps in Zvornik (Tretter et al. 1994), Višegrad (Irwin and Bećirević 2008), Foča (Hagan 2003)[4] and Prijedor (Blake 2002) – for which a number of war criminals faced trial by the ICTY – remain 'invisible', underreported and un(der)documented. The reason for this can be found in the stigma and the individual and communal shame associated with victims of sexual violence, resulting in a silent collective denial of the war crimes committed against women. These crimes may, therefore, not be remembered and memorialised in the same way as some other crimes. In the collective memory of victimised groups there is a hierarchy of events and suffering that are remembered and memorialised; clearly, in this hierarchy, crimes against women do not feature prominently – if at all. As Xavier Bougarel (2007: 171) points out, '[the] image of a male hero defending his nation and his family is often complemented by that of the passive and powerless female victim (žrtva)'. Many women have not come forward with their testimonies about crimes committed against them; and many of those who did were not adequately supported during the trials (Karup-Druško 2006). As one of the rape victims stated at the trial, 'No-one asked me anything about [what I went through]. I was humiliated enough. There was no need to speak about it ... I'd be ashamed of my child' (FENA 2008). As Olujić (1995) and Hasić (2009) point out, stories of rape have come predominantly from women who were forced by their experience to choose isolation; all have come from divorced women, widows, or unmarried women who do not have to contend with outraged husbands or other family and community members.

The communal and intergenerational aspect of shame and silence surrounding women's sufferings during the war – as well as the hardship of their everyday lives in post-war BiH – are the central themes of the award-winning feature film *Grbavica*.[5] With this film, the Bosnian director Jasmila Žbanić (2006) broke the public silence and raised awareness about the continuing plight of the invisible casualties of war – the women. Thanks to Žbanić's awareness campaign, a number of women have spoken publicly about their ordeals during the war. For instance, in February 2008 many television viewers were shocked when watching an interview with Jasna Fisović on NTV Hayat. Jasna, a survivor from Foča – an eleven-year-old girl in 1992 – spoke openly and graphically about how Serb soldiers killed her father and for many days raped her together with her mother. The communal shame and public disgust, expressed in the media and on online forums like www.sarajevo-x.com[6] after the broadcasting, were not so much about what was done to Jasna by war criminals sixteen years earlier, but rather about how the survivors of such crimes have been completely neglected and ignored by the BiH authorities and society at large. Many invisible women like Jasna Fisović have been living at the margins of society, barely surviving. While generally there has not been adequate compensation for the victims of war – including those who suffered physical injuries – men who participated as soldiers in the war have been able to claim a military pension and compensation, as well as moral recognition and status. In contrast, women's sufferings, especially those involving sexual violence, have not been recognised through regular government payments and other benefits, unless women lost their husbands as soldiers (Hasić 2009). In her interview Jasna Fisović only complained about not being able to find a job due to her isolation and lack of connections. If Jasna had been a married woman who had lost her husband in the war, her status as *šehidska udovica/žena poginuloga borca* (a war widow) would at least be honourable and provide her with certain material privileges. As an unattached young girl – in fact a child when she was abused – she is probably not even included in any of the statistical categories.

The problem with scientific or statistical approaches to war is that they ultimately attempt to quantify human sufferings and by so doing their method often gets reduced to a mere body count. But whatever the final tally of the statistics, it needs to be multiplied many times in order to encompass all those survivors whose lives continue to be affected by the loss of their family and community members. As the RDC, the International Commission on Missing Persons (ICMP), the BiH Missing Persons' Institute and many other sources have confirmed, mostly men perished during the war in BiH: their executions were systematically planned and carried out in Srebrenica, Hegići and other places across the country. Killing male members of these communities was intended to destroy social groups in whole or in part, and in most cases this was partly or completely achieved. While mostly men were killed, it should not be forgotten that they were the husbands, sons, fathers, brothers ... of women. Adam Jones (2004, 2006), the Canadian scholar specialising in researching gender-selective mass killings, calls such killings 'gendercide', a form of genocide. As Raphaël Lemkin (2002: 27) puts it, genocide signifies 'a coordinated plan of different actions aiming at the destruction of essential foundations of the life of national groups, with the aim of annihilating the groups themselves'. Through the physical elimination of men, in the ethnic cleansing campaigns in BiH, it was the essential foundations of communities – namely, families as primary units of communal structure – that were severely affected and in many cases completely destroyed (Gendercide Watch 1996).

In pre-war BiH, roles within a family were, to varying degrees, defined by gender, with the nuclear family being the dominant form, although in many cases families extended to include grandparents. In rural areas, in addition to nuclear and extended family types, the traditional family union called *zadruga* (plural *zadruge*) also existed. As described in Vera Erlich's (1966) anthology, *Family in Transition*, for many centuries before modernisation took hold in the region, *zadruga* had been the fundamental socio-economic organisation among the South Slav peasants. *Zadruga* included many members of an extended family – brothers, uncles, cousins – who worked on common land and shared the income. Many villages in Bosnia, like the village of Hegići described in Chapter 2, had their roots in a *zadruga* – often reflected in the name of the village, which referred to the founding family. Consequently, in these villages, most inhabitants were related to each other. With the war and destruction of the *zadruga* villages and hamlets, the last traces of this traditional family organisation in Bosnia disappeared.

As in Klotjevac and Hegići,[7] many rural communities lost most of their male members and through the killings and expulsions in the course of the war were completely erased as places of habitation. In a series of deliberate violent actions communities were destroyed, through the destruction of families. For this to be accomplished not every member of each family needed to be killed: family heads and community leaders were primary targets for liquidation by the perpetrators or ethnic cleansing, while women were subjected to 'moral destruction' though violence, rape and humiliation. As Boose (2002: 73) points out, '[rape] as a systematically planned Serb instrument of genocide was designed not merely to encourage the evacuation of all non-Serbs but to destroy parent–child and spousal bonds and render a large number of society's child-bearing women contaminated and thus unmarriageable'. Especially in Bosnian rural communities, the concept of collective honour and shame in relation to gender reflected the situation in the rest of the region and the Mediterranean and had not significantly changed over the previous half a century (cf. Peristiany 1966). As Tone Bringa (1995: 85–118) notes, in BiH men might be seen as the breadwinners and the ultimate moral guardians within their families and communities, but women literally embody this morality, being in charge of 'the inner space' and the boundaries of social intimacy, namely the home. That inner space was not only symbolically violated during ethnic cleansing; it was also in many cases physically destroyed through the burning of homes. This ultimately was aimed at the destruction of family and community identities. As Bringa observes, 'when they lose their house, they lose all they have worked for in the past and much of what they would have lived [for] in the future' (1995: 86).

The aim of ethnic cleansing was to create ethnically clean territories – clean of the 'other' – which in mono-ethnic villages often meant clean of any form of human life (Suljagić 2010; Pettigrew and Pettigrew 2009). Thus the war left many previously densely populated rural areas – especially villages along the rivers Drina and Sava – largely or completely depopulated. In many cases the ethnically cleansed autochthonous population has not been replaced by members of the ethnic group in whose name ethnic cleansing was carried out, as the planners of the genocidal policy might have originally hoped. While those who perished have become part of the war statistics – and have been made martyrs by 'their' ethno-nations – the surviving members of the families affected have not only been challenged with their own individual survival but also with the task of reconstituting their shattered families and communities. Many such surviving families and communities today are made up of widows, single mothers and children. Like Edita Hegić's family,[8] there are many other extended families without a single surviving male member. A typical family from pre-war Srebrenica has been reduced to a widowed mother with children born before or during the war. Taking into consideration the strong patriarchal tradition in many regions in BiH and the fact that most men were the family breadwinners, one can begin to realise the social, psychological and economic enormity of the systematic killing of men.

Loss, displacement, psychological issues and the struggle to reconstruct fragmented families and communities have all been a part of the long-term effects of ethnic cleansing on war-torn communities in BiH and in diaspora. In many cases the social fabric of these communities was damaged beyond repair, comprising only fatherless households[9] and detached individuals with no families. In most cases these sole survivors have been women: mothers without sons and wives without husbands. During my fieldwork I was constantly reminded of the absence of fathers, husbands and sons from families – in Tuzla, Sarajevo, Vienna, Norrköping, St. Louis, Melbourne… Their absence was memorialised in the form of photographic images, regularly enshrined on the walls and in cabinets in living rooms – wedding photos, school photos, teenagers in JNA uniforms,[10] holidays on the Adriatic coast, and photos of other moments capturing happier times when families were complete. The photos not only tell stories about who these missing people once were, but also remind the survivors of their own past lives as wives, mothers and family members. The photos are used as photographic memories to complement discursive narratives about that past and, at least in that form and that moment of narration, reconstruct the home lost.

Re-counting the Displaced

While many displaced Bosnians who found refuge in such far places as St. Louis and Melbourne have to different degrees managed to construct and perform a new kind of home, their compatriots whose internal displacement has become a permanent condition often feel homeless and displaced in their own country. Many of those who migrated during the war or in the years afterwards were IDPs themselves and left the country only after they lost hope of ever returning to their original home towns and the way of life they once had. To make a decision to look for a better and safer future somewhere else and to go through a complex migration procedure required both considerable material resources and supporting social networks, usually relatives living overseas. Many of the most vulnerable survivors, such as women with small children who had lost their husbands and other male members of their families, lacked both, and had no other alternative than to accept their fate as IDPs. Thus the IDPs – whether included in the official statistics or not – still remain in limbo years after the end of the war. This is especially true for those who have not been able to find durable solutions for their housing problems. Finding a durable solution in practical terms means buying, exchanging or building a house mostly in places where IDPs initially found temporary refuge. In this way IDPs lose the status of displaced persons and are treated like any other local dweller. However, housing is only one of the issues which IDPs face on a daily basis. Those who are unable to find a durable solution are at the mercy of the local and cantonal governments or foreign humanitarian aid, and include the most vulnerable forcefully displaced persons, such as war widows with children, orphans, survivors of torture, rape and abuse as well as the elderly and the handicapped (Karup-Druško 2006).

Despite the fact that the circumstances in which the displaced live have not changed much over the last decade and a half, based on the official statistics IDPs no longer pose a significant social issue in BiH. While hundreds of thousands of IDPs have remained outside their original home towns and villages – prolonging their stay or settling permanently in regions where they make up an ethnic majority (Bosniaks and Croats in the Federation and Serbs in Republika Srpska) – the statistics show a rapid decline of IDPs in BiH. In 2008 Mirza Pinjo, the Deputy Permanent Representative of BiH to the UN in Geneva, stated that the number of IDPs went from more than half a million in 2000 down to 125,000 in 2008. This reduction, however, has been achieved through bureaucratic revisions rather than the actual return of IDPs to their homes as the Dayton Peace Accords (DPA) originally guaranteed, and ignores how many of those who have lost their IDP status remain psychologically, socially and culturally displaced within their own country.

Displacement and gender are inextricably linked (Salbi 2006). The majority – some 84 per cent – of IDPs within BiH are women and children (Cockburn 1998: 156). Moreover, it is estimated that 20 per cent of all households in Bosnia-Herzegovina are female headed as a direct result of the war (Rehn and Johnson 2000: 2). This in itself is a major social issue, given that many of these women come from a rural background where patriarchal values, in one form or another, continued to define social relationships and gender roles right up to the war. The displaced women – especially those with children who lost their husbands – have been forced not only to cope with all the issues associated with single parenthood, but also to fight for shelter, food and safety. Thousands of them have been waiting for the bodies of their missing husbands, sons and other male relatives to be identified and put to rest. Most of the war widows will never remarry due to a number of socio-cultural and demographic factors, including a lack of marriageable men.

While these are deeply personal issues for individual woman, they have been bureaucratised, monitored and exposed through a complex – and often dehumanising – system of social welfare, invading the most intimate spheres of life in this vulnerable group. The monitoring is related to the fact that many of the surviving women, those who lost husbands and children during the war, claim some sort of pension: a military pension, employment pension, missing person's pension or family pension. These payments are in most cases the sole source of income for the women and their families. All of the pensions have rigid assessment criteria and involve complex bureaucratic procedures. In many instances the same degree of loss is 'measured' differently. For example, a war widow from a Bosnian village whose husband, a farmer, was killed as a civilian, or disappeared after being taken away, may only be able to claim a missing person's pension, and a family pension if she has dependent children. On the other hand, a widow with children whose husband was employed in a company and killed in combat may be able to claim all four different pensions. Therefore, many women declare – or were advised to declare – the civilian losses of their family members as military casualties in order to claim military pensions which provide some additional benefits such as preferential housing treatment, scholarships for students as well as a more honourable status for the family. However, even a combination of different pensions can hardly meet the needs of an average family in post-war BiH. As recent statistics show, an average family of four members needs 509KM[11] per month to meet basic living costs, while an average pensioner's income is 299KM.[12]

Once a pension is approved it does not mean that the issue has been successfully resolved. Every six months the government bureaucracy conducts regular revisions (*revizije*), demanding from the war widows proof that their status has not changed in the meantime. The revisions primarily relate to the women's living arrangements that may include a marriage – or marriage-like relationships. The women are required to provide up-to-date birth certificates proving their unchanged marital status as widows. This is not only an unnecessary humiliation of the women, but takes time, money and a lot of psychological strength to cope with the stress. In order to get the up-to-date birth certificate issued, the claimants need to go personally to their pre-war municipalities and apply for the documents. Sometimes this involves several days' travelling and dealing with the local – and often hostile – administration. For many displaced women from the ethnically cleansed parts of the country that have now become part of Republika Srpska, this eventually means dealing with the administration that caused their sufferings in the first place.

In addition to birth certificates, a number of other up-to-date documents – i.e., not older than six months – such as evidence of school enrolment for dependent children, evidence of unemployment, of residential address and evidence about the missing persons – are required. Thus, in addition to all the issues associated with displacement, missing relatives and single parenthood, many displaced women constantly need to chase all the paperwork to prove their existence in order to sustain it. Moreover, the law regulating employment pensions requires women to be at least forty-five years of age to be eligible to claim their husbands' pensions. Taking into consideration that many war widows were in their early twenties when they lost their husbands, for many this means decades of waiting. But even those without the age problem are required to provide their husbands' death certificates in order to claim their employment pensions. It has been especially painful for many of them to declare their husbands dead, especially when, as in many cases, their bodies have not yet been exhumed, identified and put to rest. Some of them have resisted doing so for years. As Naila Nuhanović[13] confided, 'it felt like giving up the last speck of hope that my husband might be alive somewhere'.

When it comes to reclaiming ownership or selling the family property, the legal procedures involve even more complicated bureaucracy, as ownership titles in BiH are usually in the husband's name. Besides, in rural BiH, it was common for ownership of the land to be in the name of the patriarch of the family (the grandfather) while he was alive, and often even for many years after his death. Thus a lot of land may not have been formally divided between close relatives. They knew de facto who owned what. Having this in mind, one can only imagine all the legal obstacles in the way of a widow trying to get property rights recognised in her name after her husband perished; it regularly involves lengthy and costly court proceedings in which a widow needs to prove that she is the rightful claimant of her husband's property. Many women have given up halfway through as they could not collect all the required documents, statutory declarations and certified witness testimonies about all those who might have had their share of the family's property – many of whom will have either perished or dispersed around the globe.

Many IDPs have reluctantly accepted the official charity categories such as war widows, sole parents, orphans and ethnic cleansing survivors as defined by the BiH government, international organisations and members of host communities. The options for moving on with their lives – provided that they have resources and that these options are really offered to them – include turning their internal displacement into permanent resettlement within BiH, returning to their original places, or emigrating to faraway countries such as the U.S.A. or Australia.[14] None of these options – even if they were all readily available to the IDPs – could ever restore the normal lives they once had. In each of these situations they would need to reinvent themselves and construct new identities. As we have seen in the previous chapters – and as is described later in this chapter – some have been able to do it better than others. The ideal solution promoted by many activists, politicians and the displaced themselves, 'everyone returning to her home' – with 'return' having the symbolic meaning of 'return to normal' – is far from realistic, with 100,000 lives lost, some 800,000 houses destroyed and 1.3 million refugees overseas.

While Annex 7 of the Dayton Peace Accords clearly states that people must be 'permitted to return in safety irrespective of ethnic origin, religious belief, or political opinion', it fails to address the issues confronting displaced women – now often widowed or alone. When counting returnees, the logic of numbers fails again to represent the real lives lived in post-war BiH. For instance, the unquantified truth – not captured by the official statistics – is that within BiH the ethnic homogenisation of Bosnian towns has continued by attrition since the war ended. Hundreds of thousands of people have sold or exchanged their homes and moved into towns dominated by their ethnic group. Thus, as Black (2002: 135) argues, 'ethnic cleansing' has been replaced by 'ethnic engineering'. Statistics about 'the return of refugees and IDPs', even those by the UNHCR,[15] do not really represent reality on the ground, as they refer to the numbers of processed applications for reclaiming property or rebuilding devastated homes rather than the actual number of people returning home permanently. As Kett (2005: 202) correctly notes, '[there] has been a strong focus on property and legislation rather than people'.

After reclaiming their property rights many returnees do not choose to stay in their original home towns and villages. This is especially true for many younger families with children, who stay permanently in their original homes only if no other alternatives are available. There are many political, psychological and social explanations for this. Understandably, after systematic destruction and years of neglect, the places of return hardly resemble the places they left many years ago – especially depopulated villages in the BiH countryside. Those returning – even if they are the ethnic majority in their villages, or in fact the only ethnic group – are officially reduced to the status of an ethnic minority, which practically means a status of second class citizen with lesser rights in all areas of public life. For instance, Bosniak and Croat returnees in RS do not have a choice other than to accept all the clearly exclusive and nationalistic changes introduced by the Serb authorities while they were displaced. The official language in RS is Serbian, written in the Cyrillic alphabet, while the school curriculum treats RS as a Serbian land closely linked to Serbia, with no reference to the state of BiH as a common homeland for all Bosnians. In fact, the adjective 'Bosnian' has almost completely disappeared from public life in RS. As in the case of Prijedor, described in Chapter 3, the trend that started during the war – when everything that did not appear Serbian enough was renamed – continues today. Only recently Milorad Dodik, the current RS president, issued a decree officially removing the prefix 'Bosnian' from all towns in RS – so that towns along the river Sava such as Bosanski Brod, Bosanska Dubica, Bosanska Gradiška, Bosanski Novi, Bosanska Kostajnica and Bosanski Šamac lost the 'Bosnian half' of their names (Katana 2008). The psychological impact on returnees in these towns is as predictable as planned: they feel excluded and unwanted, or, even worse, erased from history like the names of their towns.

'Not in My Front Yard!': The Case of Fata Orlović

The Serbianisation of non-Serbian places in RS affects far more than just the public sphere; it cuts deep into the private and the personal, into homes and even into *avlija* (front yards). The story of the elderly returnee 'Nana' (Grandma) Fata Orlović, as she has become popularly known, is a classic example of how bizarre the usurpation of personal rights and property for ethno-nationalist projects can get (Bećirević 2008).

The village of Konjević Polje was ethnically cleansed in 1992, during which Fata's husband and many of her relatives and neighbours were killed. With her seven children, Fata escaped to Tuzla and for eight years lived as an IDP 'far from home', as it seemed to her at the time. Meanwhile, her children grew up, some got married and all but one daughter migrated to the U.S. Fata did not want to leave Bosnia, and she lived for the day when she could return to her Konjević Polje. The Bosniak village – located at a road junction between the major regional towns of Zvornik, Vlasenica,

Milići and Bratunac – had obvious strategic importance to the creators of the Serb Republic. With the blessing of the RS authorities and the Serb Orthodox bishop Kačavenda, they erected a monumental Orthodox church in the village, as a symbol of Serb victory and the most exclusive sign that Konjević Polje was now a Serb village – even though no Serbs lived in it. In addition to representing an exclusive landmark, the Serb church was intended to send a clear message to the ethnically cleansed Muslims never to come back. However, no one could stop Fata Orlović getting back home. When, in 2001, she finally returned to her village, intending 'to stay, rebuild her life and die' in the only place she could call home, there was no sign of her house. Instead, on the land where her family house once stood, a grandiose white Orthodox church had been erected. Since she returned, Fata Orlović has been fighting many losing legal battles to get the church removed from her private property. Firstly, she needed to prove to the Serb court in Bratunac that her murdered husband Šaćir was indeed her husband, that Hamza Orlović, in whose name the property was still held, was her late father-in-law, and that she was the rightful claimant to the land where her family home once stood (Obradović 2005).

After four years of wrestling with the RS legal system, her property rights were finally recognised and she was allowed to rebuild her house. Once her house was built, the situation was even more bizarre, with a big church in the front yard of a small house. As – legally speaking – the church was on her land, theoretically she was now the owner of the church. Some even started to call it 'Fata's Church'. In reality, however, Fata could not do anything to remove the alien building from her land. Her legal battle to get the church relocated from her front yard continued until 2007, when the court ordered the church to be relocated 'as soon as an alternative location has been found'. However, two years later, at the time of writing this chapter, the Serb Orthodox clergy have continued to stir up tensions in Konjević Polje by using the illegally built place of worship for congregations of radical Serbs, whom they frequently bus to Konjević Polje from neighbouring and distant villages. On many such occasions Fata Orlović has been verbally abused by the priest and his extremist flock, but, as she herself has said, she would expect anything else from those who killed her husband and burned down her house. On one occasion she dared to talk back, cursing Karadžić and Mladić and saying that she did not want any ceremonies on her private property. The priest took legal action against her and subsequently she was charged with 'causing national, ethnic and religious hate, division and intolerance' as well as committing a 'criminal act against the freedom of faith and the performance of religious rituals'. On 16 April 2007 the first instance court declared that Fata Orlović was not guilty (Bećirević 2008). However, the prosecution team lodged an appeal and, on 26 January

2009, Fata Orlović was found guilty as charged and sentenced to a month in prison on a suspended sentence. She was also ordered to pay 150KM in legal costs, an amount that equals her monthly pension.

The war, with all its consequences, not only shattered Fata Orlović's community and family, but it also changed forever the person she once was. Since April 1992 her identity has truly been 'a constant work in progress', often beyond her control and defined by others. From an ordinary, unknown village woman, a hardworking mother of eight and wife to Šaćir Orlović, Fata has metamorphosed into a war widow, a single parent, an IDP, a returnee, a court case. In addition to becoming a persona non grata in her own *avlija* and someone who committed a 'criminal act against the freedom of faith', this simple village woman has become a symbol of defiance for many other women who returned or have been planning to return to their devastated homes in RS. In the process of repossessing her front yard – and symbolically her past – Fata Orlović has gained a public profile for the first time in her life. Her story was picked up by the media, initially as only one of the many tragic stories from Bosnia, but soon as a *cause célèbre* in BiH and beyond. Over the last eight years she has given countless interviews to both local and international media. In August 2007 the BBC ran an extensive interview with her.[16] Based on the votes of the readers of Bosnian daily newspaper *Dnevni Avaz*, she was awarded the Person of the Year for 2007 jointly with the most prominent foreign figure in the country, Mr Miroslav Lajcak, the International Community's High Representative in BiH. As of August 2012 there were 87,000 entries of her name in Google, including more than 22,500 photographs. 'Nana' Fata Orlović is even to be found on Facebook.[17] Despite leading an apparently active public life, as represented on the internet, in reality Fata Orlović continues to live her simple life, with all the problems of a lone war widow and minority returnee. Not only is she a semi-literate woman who does not know how to use modern technology like a computer and the internet, but for most of the time since she returned home she has been living without electricity.

While for Fata Orlović reclaiming her property has meant at least some symbolic moral satisfaction, for many other returnees there has been nothing to sustain them economically, socially and culturally. The returnees to RS have increasingly been single, ageing widows like Fata. Even when families might have stayed together during the flight and the years of displacement, in many instances the long-awaited return home has separated them. The reality of the returnees' life is that many families – if they can afford it – live in two different places simultaneously, with older members of the families spending more time in the old place (now in RS) and younger ones preferring to stay in the new place (in the Federation). As Marita Eastmond (2006: 141) notes, 'while policies have tended to define refugee return as a single and definitive move to the country or place of origin ... return [could] be better conceptualised as a dynamic and open-ended process, one which may extend over long periods of time, involving mobility between places and active links to people and resources'.

Ethnic Engineering

Barriers to education, economic opportunities, troubled memories and the unavoidable feeling of cultural oppression and social isolation have turned many people away from their former homes; they have continued to feel displaced – and misplaced – in their own ancestral places. After fighting hard for the right to return and reclaim what was left of their properties, many returnees have once again abandoned their home towns and villages – this time voluntarily and probably for good. Many have sold their homes to local or displaced Serbs from other parts of BiH or exchanged their homes with them. Some trends in the exchange of domiciles, and hence population, have clear and well known patterns. For instance, the former residents of the towns of Bratunac, in eastern Bosnia (in RS), and Hadžići, near Sarajevo (in the Federation), in most cases exchanged or sold their homes to each other; Bosniaks from Bratunac moved to Hadžići while Serbs from Hadžići moved into Bosniaks' houses in Bratunac. While this population exchange occurred peacefully, the psychological scarring of those who left their home towns where they had lived for generations has been accepted and even promoted as a patriotic act by ethno-nationalist political elites (Black 2002; Halilovich et al. 2006).

But not everyone who had been displaced had a house left to exchange with someone else. As Anders Stefansson (2006: 118) points out, 'to a large extent the conflict in Bosnia ... can be characterised as a "house war", in which hundreds of thousands of homes were destroyed or severely damaged, as a result of both fighting and more or less systematic dynamiting or setting fire to homes', as happened in the villages of Klotjevac, Hegići and across the country.

I found such a displaced and homeless group of people in a camp not far from Fata Orlović's village, located close to the village of Kravica, next to the road connecting Konjević Polje with Bratunac. The camp, comprising some thirty rundown wooden houses, was hastily built in late 1995 as temporary accommodation for some 3,000 Serb IDPs from towns and villages around Sarajevo and central and western Bosnia, which, under the Dayton Peace Accords, had become part of the Bosniak-Croat Federation. Over the years most displaced have found durable solutions for their housing problems and left the camp. Many benefited from the support of the Republika Srpska government, which provided free blocks of land and building material to former Army of Republika Srpska (VRS) soldiers, who settled in neighbouring Bratunac, Zvornik, Bijeljina and other towns in RS. Those who had left houses and apartments in the Federation sold them to or exchanged with Bosniaks who had left property in RS. Some Serb IDPs – especially those from around Sarajevo – returned to their original homes despite the places being regarded as Muslim areas. In the end only the most dispossessed and disconnected from power, politics and social networks remained in the camp fifteen years after finding temporary refuge there. In September 2010 the camp was hosting some eighty Serb refugees, mostly women and the elderly.

The elderly Janja Jović is one of them. In 1995 she was ordered by VRS to leave her village near Glamoč, in south-western Bosnia, as Bosnian and Croatian armies had started an offensive against VRS in that part of the country. She put a few belongings on the tractor and joined the column of thousands of Serb refugees fleeing east. After five days of a rough ride on the tractor driven by her husband, they reached this faraway destination in the eastern corner of the country. Janja had never heard of this place before. She and her husband were hoping to return home as soon as possible, as life in the overcrowded camp was unbearable for the ageing couple used to a daily routine involving hard work on their land. She believes that boredom and longing for home killed her husband, who died in the camp in 2000. Since then Janja has not had any option but to remain indefinitely in the camp. She survives on a government pension of 120KM and the occasional rations the humanitarian organisations deliver to this largely forgotten group of IDPs. Asked about going back to Glamoč, she replied that she would not be able to survive there because, as far as she knew, there have been no returnees to the village. She did not know if her house was still standing, but knew that her three cows and other livestock would not be there. 'I know that we are written off and no-one wants us. It only saddens me that I will die far away from my home like my husband did,' Janja concludes. Her neighbour Milica, originally from 'around Ilijaš', joined the conversation at this point, very bitter about the complete neglect of Serb IDPs by the RS government, and at how the local Serb population from nearby villages looks down on them – 'as if we were lepers and did not have our own homes that were sacrificed for them to feel bigger Serbs than those in Serbia,' she exclaims in anger.

The stories I commonly heard from and about IDPs – who after years of living in limbo have made their homes in host communities – confirm that, despite living with their 'own people', the IDPs might never feel completely at home nor fully accepted by the 'old dwellers'. This is very much in line with Čapo Žmegač's thesis that 'shared ethnicity/nationality, ... [as]

a prerequisite for resettlement, is not sufficient to prevent the local inhabitants from treating the co-ethnic migrants as some (unwanted) foreigners and, vice versa, for the latter not to construct a boundary vis-à-vis the locals' (2005: 199). As the forced movement of people usually went from villages and provincial towns to large urban centres such as Sarajevo and Tuzla, there has also been an urban–rural clash between the newcomers (*došljaci* or *došlje*) and the old dwellers (*domaći* or *starosjedioci*). In fact, the term 'newcomers' has a rather derogatory meaning and could be interpreted as intruders, unwanted guests or nomads,[18] while the term 'old dwellers' is commonly associated with sedentarism and positive values such as stability, dignity and integrity. Portraying the IDPs as rural – with the connotations of primitive, traditional and dirty – has clear discriminatory undertones. A similar observation was described by Bisharat (1997: 216) regarding the process of 'othering' between Palestinian refugees and 'town dwellers'. The common belief held by many Bosnian city dwellers – even by an apparently sympathetic local academic I had an exchange with at a conference in Sarajevo a few years ago – is that the newcomers are not cultured enough and are therefore unsuited to living in the cities. She even claimed that the 'peasants' have ruralised their urban spaces as they inherently lack city culture. Like her, many city dwellers have rediscovered and solidified their urban identities through prejudices and the 'othering' of the IDPs, with whom they are supposed to share the same ethnic, religious and cultural identities. But it's not only the patronising city dwellers who have been positioning themselves in relation to their less fortunate compatriots: local politicians and both local and international government and non-government organisations and staff have used the IDPs to justify their actions and their positions. The IDPs – being dispossessed, victimised, traumatised, manipulated, mythologised, patronised, feared and despised – often do not have a choice other than to adjust to the roles assigned by others.

Uncounted 'Collateral Damage': The Case of Aunt Edina

Even if they do well and integrate into the urban environment, IDPs then risk becoming the subject of envy and prejudice by the 'old dwellers', very often other women. Internally displaced women are regularly depicted as a threat to neighbourhood morality (and husbands!) as there are often clusters of female-headed households living in close proximity. In most cases, these refugee families are related to each other or come from the same place, stereotypically generalised by the city dwellers in a derogatory way as 'coming from a village in eastern Bosnia'. Having widows of all ages in a social environment with a limited number of marriageable men creates rumours about affairs between war widows – as well as other displaced women and girls – and the local, often married men.

Since the war several thousand displaced women and war widows from Srebrenica and the wider region of Podrinje have settled in the Sarajevo suburbs of Dobrinja and Vogošća. This trend has been very much in line with the exchange of territories policy, firstly introduced by Karadžić and his militias through ethnic cleansing and later supported by the Western peace brokers, from Vance-Owen to Holbrook (Kumar 1997). When, in early 1996, the Sarajevo suburbs were 'integrated' with the city through the DPA, Dobrinja and Vogošća were abandoned by most Serb residents, who later reclaimed and then in many cases sold or leased their apartments and houses to Bosniak IDPs from eastern Bosnia.[19]

Edina, her sister Jasmina, their mother Kadira and Jasmina's three children – two daughters and one son – have all been living in a 'Serb' flat in Dobrinja for more than a decade. Initially, in mid 1996, they moved into this abandoned flat as squatters, only to become legal tenants paying rent once the flat was reclaimed by its Serb owner who did not want to return and live in 'Muslim Sarajevo'. Edina's three-storey family house, her sister's house and all they once had was left in their home town of Srebrenica, from where they fled in July 1995. Edina's and Jasmina's brother, who was a medical doctor, was killed in early 1993 in Sarajevo. He was twenty-eight years of age. Their father Avdija, broken by the loss of his only son and realising that for the first time in his life he was not able to protect his family, refused to leave their home and join the tens of thousands of people – in fact, the whole population of the town – who fled when the Serbs overran the UN safe haven of Srebrenica on 11 July 1995. That morning, while the town was pounded by Serb artillery and gunfire, he hugged each member of his family, asking them for forgiveness, before telling them to go to the UN camp in the nearby industrial zone of Potočari. No-one could convince him to join them, nor did he allow his wife Kadira to stay with him, although she kept begging him to be allowed to do so. Avdija was a proud man; his grief and his pride sealed his fate. 'The captain never abandons his ship,' Edina remembers him saying. Edina, her mother, her sister and her sister's children joined tens of thousands of people fleeing the town in panic. They survived the exodus, but their journey from Srebrenica via Tuzla to Sarajevo has scarred their lives forever. They never learned what happened to Avdija, who might have been the only person in town who stayed at his home in Srebrenica on that fatal day in July 1995. Jasmina's husband Nusret fled the town, but he did not survive the 'march of death' in which thousands of Srebrenica men were massacred by the Serb army. Thus, all three primary male relatives from their family perished and became war statistics: Avdija and Nusret have been counted as victims of the Srebrenica genocide, while Edina's and Jasmina's brother Amir has been honoured as a military casualty at a Sarajevo cemetery who died on duty while trying to save the wounded citizens of Sarajevo. 'Our father would have been proud of him,' Edina said.

The story of Edina's family could be told from many different perspectives: from that of Kadira – who lost her son, her husband and her son-in-law and now lives with her daughters, one unmarried and one widowed, and her fatherless grandchildren; from the perspective of Jasmina – who lost her husband, her father and her brother; or from the perspectives of each of Jasmina's two daughters, Anita and Alisa, who were eight and six years of age respectively when they went through what became known as the Srebrenica genocide. The war not only took their innocence and their childhood but also people of great importance to them: their father, grandfather and uncle. Finally, the story could be told from the perspective of the only male survivor in the family, Adi, who was a toddler when all his male relatives perished. In 2008 Adi was seventeen years old, his sisters twenty and twenty-two, their mother Jasmina forty-six and their grandmother Kadira sixty-five. Adi's aunt Edina was forty years of age.

I have chosen to tell the story of this family from Edina's perspective as she is not counted in any category as a casualty or a person significantly affected by the war, although she has been the woman in charge of this family, the breadwinner, the one who could have had her separate life and her own family had she not decided to devote herself completely and selflessly to her surviving relatives. It has been mainly due to her efforts that the family was able to stay together and 'find itself' after severe losses and grief, coupled with dispossession and displacement.

Edina is not the typical Bosnian refugee woman portrayed in the media, or what Elissa Helms calls 'the category of woman defined and affirmed by wartime events ... [in which] victim images have come to stand for all Bosnian womanhood, leaving little space for women to construct identities other than as ethnicised, passive victims of enemy men' (2007: 237). The pictures and stories of these women – especially Bosnian Muslim women – usually portray older village women, dressed in different versions of their traditional dress and ubiquitous headscarfs. Even when well intended, these almost archetypal images of victims and stories of mothers' sufferings 'orientalise' the women survivors, suggesting otherness and implying powerlessness and passivity due to a perceived lack of sophistication on their part (Helms 2008). However, as Fata Orlović's case demonstrates, regardless of their rural background and 'lack of sophistication' these women are not passive victims within structures that are clearly hostile to them; they actively resist oppression and fight not only for their bare survival, but also for the restoration of their rights and their dignity as human beings and women. Edina is neither a war widow nor a 'mother from Srebrenica'[20] – nor could she in any way be perceived as traditional and lacking sophistication.

I might be retelling Edina's story also out of generational solidarity, as the generational aspect of loss often escapes those writing about the war in BiH or analysing the war statistics. Our generation, Edina's and mine, paid a heavy price in the war: it featured prominently among both the victims and perpetrators of the war crimes.[21] Edina's story reflects many aspects of that generational loss as well as disappointment in one's own generation.

Just before the war in BiH broke out, Edina was in what should have been her best years. She was twenty-four and studying law at the University of Sarajevo. Every fortnight she would travel to her home town of Srebrenica to spend the weekend with her family. Edina had many friends in Srebrenica, some of whom studied in Tuzla, some in Sarajevo as she did, a number of others in Novi Sad, Belgrade and Subotica in Serbia. At least once a month the Srebrenica university students would congregate in their home town, to see old friends, attend birthday parties and exchange news about each other. Avdo, Edina's boyfriend of two years, studied agricultural science in Novi Sad. She preferred Sarajevo 'for many different reasons'. Edina and Avdo managed to see each other every second week back in Srebrenica.

Edina's father Avdija, director of a state-owned building company, was a well-respected man in their small town. Those who knew him better also knew that he was a poet and a writer, although he never published any of his writings in his own name. Edina's elder sister Jasmina worked in the local council as an accountant. Their mother was a housewife who helped Jasmina with her three young children while she and her husband Nusret were working and building their house. Edina's and Jasmina's brother Amir was one of the most popular bachelors in the town, a medical doctor, still in his twenties, working in the local hospital and completing his specialisation in surgical procedures. Because of his specialisation, he frequently spent time in Sarajevo, training at the university hospital. Edina adored her brother. She spent time with him in Srebrenica and she would not miss seeing him whenever he was in Sarajevo. Although he was a great source of inspiration to her, Edina did not rely much on her brother's fame; she herself was a confident – some might have said arrogant – young woman, with the sophistication of a law student and the reputation of a girl coming from a good, well-off family. As her old photos show, she was also a stunningly beautiful young woman at the time. No wonder that she felt that all doors were open to her.

In March 1992 she made her regular trip from Sarajevo to Srebrenica, going home to spend a few days with her family and friends and to study for the approaching exams; her brother Amir happened to be in Sarajevo at the time. In the following years Edina would share the fate of some fifty thousand people trapped in her small home town of Srebrenica,[22] while her brother joined those defending Sarajevo by using his medical skills to save lives.

Four years later, when she returned to Sarajevo, neither the city nor Edina was the same. Sarajevo was lying in ruins and its parks and stadiums had become cemeteries for more than ten thousand people who died during the siege. Edina was no longer that young university student whose main concern was how to pass an exam; now she was a displaced person – a genocide survivor – taking care of all her surviving relatives. She described her confrontation with another kind of loss upon returning to Sarajevo:

> All the years I was trapped in Srebrenica, I couldn't wait to get to Sarajevo. I thought I would go back to my studies and life would somehow become normal again. But when I got here, no-one was waiting for me apart from my brother's grave at the Zetra Stadium. The student village where I [once] lived had turned into burned-out shells ... None of my old friends remained in Sarajevo.

While the city was still smouldering and its residents trying to come to terms with what they had lost, with what had happened to them and their city, Edina needed to find ways to feed her relatives and find shelter in the ruins. She initially postponed – and then completely abandoned – her dream of becoming a lawyer. Edina the lawyer became another uncounted 'collateral loss' of the war. But, apart from her academic and professional careers, there were many more personal sacrifices she would be called upon to make in the coming years. As she put it, she needed to 'put her life and her dreams on hold for a while'.

> I had to support my mother, and my sister and her children. My mother and my sister were completely numbed by the loss of their husbands and my brother. My sister had three small children to look after and there was no way she could cope on her own, as there was no one else to provide any kind of support ... Nor could I abandon my mother. My sister and I spent days and days going from one charity to another, trying to get enough food for all of us. We never sent our mother to any of these charities to ask for food; we wanted to spare her this humiliation.

It took many months for Edina to collect all the documents needed for her mother and her sister to claim their husbands' pensions. However, this was hardly enough to meet all the needs of a family starting its life from scratch. She desperately needed a job and thanks to some rediscovered pre-war connections of her father, two years after arriving in Sarajevo she finally got a stable job as a cashier in a supermarket. It was hard work. There were twelve-hour shifts, and often she worked for weeks without a day off. But it was a job and brought in some money to the family. Over time, the supermarket owner built a chain of supermarkets, initially throughout the city and then across the country. Edina was promoted from cashier to store supervisor. By then she had realised that the only empowerment she could gain was through hard work. She worked hard, harder than anyone else at the supermarket. She helped her sister Jasmina and a number of other displaced women from her old home town and her new neighbourhood to get jobs at one of the supermarkets – another example of trans-localism in action. Her work ethic and her business potential did not go unnoticed by her boss. In summer 2011, when I last met her, Edina was a regional manager, managing six supermarkets in different parts of the country and conducting professional training for new staff. Edina the businesswoman – together with her sister – took a home loan and bought the Serb flat in which they'd been living since 1996. The owner took into consideration the improvements they made to the flat and asked a fair price.

Employment improved the lives of Edina and her family. Many other displaced women and their families have been less fortunate when it comes to securing a stable job and breaking the cycle of poverty and marginalisation. Many of the women – especially those from a rural background – have little education and lack professional experience, which further diminishes their employment prospects. With up to 40 per cent unemployment across the country, competition in the labour market has been very tough even for those with professional skills not facing forced displacement and single parenthood.

While the equality of women and their participation in paid employment and public life in post-war BiH has remained below the standards of many other European countries, the displaced women, survivors of ethnic cleansing, are even more affected by this imbalance. When analysing the cost of displacement in terms of labour-market outcomes within BiH, Florence Kondylis (2007) found that displaced men and women are less likely to be in work relative to stayers. She relates this to the informality of the labour market in BiH and destruction of social networks. Hence, displacement for IDPs in BiH – for both women and men – often means that they are also 'out of place' when it comes to securing a job; consequently, prolonged unemployment and underemployment have kept the IDPs at the bottom of the social ladder long after the war has ended. In this way, poverty caused by displacement becomes trans-generational. Despite their social marginalisation, the IDPs are often perceived as an economic burden

– or, alternatively, as a privileged group – because of their meagre pensions and handouts by the communities in which they settled (Black 2002: 136).

Edina once remarked to me that some employees at the supermarket made comments that the company had been 'taken over by the widows from Podrinje'. Some *starosjedioci*[23] in her neighbourhood have accused the displaced women and their families of all sorts of social deviances, from loud noise to stealing and adultery. Many of these accusations – according to Edina – have been baseless, as the newcomers do not create any more trouble than the old dwellers. However, she agrees that young people in the suburbs feel they are outsiders and this sometimes creates tension and even fights between different youth gangs.

These issues have been of particular concern to Edina as her sister's children have now grown into young adults. Anita and Alisa are university students, studying pharmacy and economics respectively, while Adi is still in high school. His sisters seem to be doing better than Adi– not only academically. He has had difficulties coping with some of the challenges associated with being a teenager – or at least this is how his female relatives see it. His marks at school have not been so good, but what make his family worry are the frequent fights at school and on the streets. These incidents have already brought him a police record. Adi does not see himself as the source of these troubles. He expresses his disgust with the politicians and the situation in the country in which no opportunities for young people are provided. He clearly has issues with tolerating any form of authority, including the home-based authorities of his mother, grandmother and aunt Edina.

Edina – like anyone else who knows the history of Adi's family – understands where Adi's anger comes from, but she cannot accept losing him to the street. The family is worried that Adi may turn into one of the young criminals, mostly recruited from the ranks of young men with backgrounds like his. Edina and Jasmina have tried to talk to him, but he does not listen. They just do not know how to approach him anymore. Edina explained:

> It's breaking my heart to see him behave the way he does, showing less and less respect for all of us, even yelling at his grandmother. I know we are all womenfolk at home, but I didn't expect that this may become such a big issue for him ... I know, he has had three mothers and no father, and I guess that this is what bothers him. It might have been our mistake too as we all mothered and protected him more than the girls. Because he has been the only man in our family, we might have spoiled him with too much love.

Edina named many of the issues that any psychologist would have identified and linked to Adi's violent behaviour. However, while the source of

Adi's problems seems to be obvious, there has not been much professional assistance – apart from the police – helping Adi deal with his anger. Some of Adi's friends have already been in jail for repeated offences including violence and robbery. Young people like Adi – with no male role models at home and with the psychosocial issues of anger, shame and guilt associated with loss of fathers and other male relatives – are an additional invisible group uncounted as collateral damage of the war. Often they become visible when it is too late: once they commit a crime and end up in custody, or when they themselves become victims of crime. As has been reported in the media, youth violence is becoming a growing problem in the country, with teenagers being both victims and perpetrators (Rakela 2008; Bećirbašić 2009). So far there has been no comprehensive strategy by the government to address these important social issues.

Another category of uncounted collateral damage comprises the cases of domestic violence Edina has described in their neighbourhood. Sometimes husbands abuse their wives and other family members, but there are also instances where sons are violent towards their mothers. One of her neighbours, a war widow, has been frequently bashed by her lover in front of her children. Everyone in the neighbourhood was afraid of him. 'I don't have such problems,' jokes Edina, 'no husband, no lovers, no worries!' But her humour swiftly vanishes when she is asked directly about her personal relationships:

> Well, there are simply no men from my generation available; they have either been killed, got married or they've gone overseas, and being someone's mistress has been out of the question [for me] ... I really wanted to get married and have my own family, but this wasn't meant to happen. That option was destroyed by the war.

At the age of forty-two – and even before that – Edina was not considered marriageable anymore and had given up all prospects of getting married or living in arrangements that would not include her mother at least. However, she is proud of her choices and, as she said, she 'couldn't have done anything else'. To stick to her mother and her sister's family was the best way 'to honour memories of her brother and her father'. Had any of them been alive her life would have been different.

Asked about her pre-war boyfriend Avdo, Edina said: 'I lost him in the war, although he survived.' Avdo was in Novi Sad, in Serbia, when the war started. He initially fled to Hungary and after spending time in Austria and Germany migrated to the U.S. He married there and has two children. Edina did not blame him for anything.

Asked about the possibility of her sister remarrying, Edina categorically rejected such an option, saying that 'she would never do that; this would be a betrayal of her husband and her children.' She felt even more uncomfortable when asked if that option might have been considered by her mother. For *šehidska majka* (mother of a martyr) and *šehidska udovica* (wife of a martyr) – the double legacy of the loss of husband and son – meant that remarrying could be seen by the community as disrespecting and dishonouring her *šehids*. For women like Edina's mother Kadira, who are both mothers who lost children and war widows who lost husbands, it is expected that, for the rest of their lives, they will continue to perform these roles, adjusting their lives and embodying eternal grief for their loved ones. Across south-eastern Europe and the Balkans this aspect of patriarchal tradition has survived in many communities – among Christians and Muslims alike (cf. Seremetakis 1991). Women are expected to dress more modestly as a sign of their grief; Christian women usually dress completely in black, while Muslim women put on headscarfs. While Christian women, especially Orthodox women at funerals, may be expected to articulate their pain through crying and ritual chanting, Islam requires women to be stoic and not to question God's will, as 'everything comes from God' (Norris 1993). Many women, once they lose their loved ones, spend the rest of their lives in mourning dress. They also tend to become more religious and to perform regular rituals to honour and remember their dead. Even their everyday lives are readjusted so there are constant reminders of those they lost. Their public identities become those of mourning women. Often they remain so for years, sometimes for the rest of their lives. These have been the unwritten rules and expectations of the women's own communities. There are not reciprocal expectations for men. Women are exclusively keepers and performers of the memory of their lost family members. This is seen as a feminine quality, as women are said to have 'softer hearts' and are more sensible than men. While this is understood to be the duty of women, if a man were involved in prolonged mourning it would be considered a weakness, a negative feature, something to worry about.

Community members often judge, gossip and accuse the widows of immoral behaviour if they are not performing their mourning rituals as expected. At times they even manipulate their feelings of guilt and grief. While this moral policing is mostly covert, it often ostracises the women, damaging their reputation and standing within the community. Edina's neighbour Rahima, who lost her only son and her husband at Srebrenica, said that she felt ashamed because she had put weight on. She was worried that her putting on weight might be used by some members of the community to accuse her of not mourning enough for her lost men. She was expected to live an ascetic life and not to enjoy it. Other malicious accusations against war widows go as far as to blame the women for their own misfortune or even to claim that they have been better off with their husbands dead rather than alive, as they have their pensions plus freedom to do whatever they want. Women themselves – both those who lost their male family members and the informal 'community watchdogs' – have thus been replicating patriarchal values despite the absence of men. The de facto matriarchy has often been there to preserve clearly patriarchal values: in Edina's family, through giving preferential treatment to Adi. 'He has always been the most important child,' Edina said. Categorically excluding the possibility for Jasmina and Kadira to remarry in order for them to remain faithful to their dead husbands is another example of reinforcing patriarchal values in a female-dominated household.

Despite being an ordinary woman freed from traditionalism, Edina herself displays many of the deeply held cultural attitudes to war widows, especially those based on honour and shame. Being a war widow is commonly regarded as something highly honourable, even if it means lifelong stoic suffering – and Edina seems to share such views. On the one hand, despite the cultural limitations set by the traditional gender roles and social exclusion imposed on the displaced women, both urban Edina and rural Fata Orlović have found ways to break the cycle of victimisation and restore their pride as women and survivors. At the same time, they continue to experience the pain and hardship associated with their post-war (dis)placement, memory and identity – including the identity ascribed to them by the broader community.

(Mis)using IDPs

As in the case of Fata Orlović, IDPs are in most cases not welcome in the places from where they were expelled by brutal force; they are often hated and discriminated against, and regularly have to endure economic hardship and social isolation as well. This accords with Richard Black's observation that 'many local politicians have had reasons to obstruct the process of return, especially the process of minority return; these include the threat that the return of people from a different ethnic group poses to the power base of nationalist politicians' (Black 2001: 190). While the Serb nationalists have clearly been obstructing the return of IDPs – of Bosniaks and Croats to RS and also of Serbs wanting to return to the Federation – those claiming to be defending the rights of the IDPs, Bosniak and Croat ethnonationalists, have also been using the plight of 'their fellow people' to justify their hardline rhetoric and consolidate their power in their little ethnic fiefdoms (Kumar 1997). In fact, as recent reports from Bosnian independent media such as *BH Dani* and *Slobodna Bosna* have suggested, the ethnonationalist elites in BiH collaborate very well in many areas, from politics to the economy, as long as it is in their own interests.[24] They have turned their ethno-nationalist rhetoric into lucrative personal businesses by selling off publicly owned properties and income-generating infrastructure and services. What they have been selling to their own people is fear of and hatred for the others.

Because of their vulnerability, the IDPs are susceptible to all sorts of manipulation by politicians and other actors. For instance, during the first post-war decade, they overwhelmingly voted for the nationalist parties, who kept promising – but hardly delivered – significant changes in their situation. This support for the nationalist parties alienated them from some progressive – usually city-based – political forces in the country, so the IDPs have sometimes been blamed for the political stalemate in the country and for their own situation. There has not been much understanding for the IDPs' support for the nationalists, while the nationalists have clearly been manipulating them. As an IDP commented, not only do the nationalists 'lie best' and tell the IDPs what they would like to hear, but they are also 'pragmatic' and know best how to 'buy' the votes of IDPs in exchange for necessities such as food or basic home appliances.

Having been not only displaced but also dispossessed, many IDPs, especially war widows with children, have become dependent on such politically motivated favours as well as handouts from various NGOs. Many of these NGOs and charitable organisations are offshoots of larger international religious organisations with a mission not only to help those in need but also to spread the word of God and save lost souls. Even if not always quite transparent, the activities of such organisations are legal in BiH. Through welfare payments, the apparently benevolent donor organisations find easy recruits for their sometimes rigid and, in the Bosnian context, alien religious interpretations and practices. For instance, during my fieldwork with IDPs in Sarajevo and Tuzla I have come across literature referring to 'Islamic practices among Bosnian Muslims that need to be corrected', as well as decorative materials, such as religious stickers on doors and other visible places and religious pictures and calendars on the walls. The benefactors require children and mothers to attend regular religious seminars organised by them. While the Islamic influence on IDPs, particularly the Muslim war widows, and their Islamisation has been written about, the IDPs – non-Muslims and Muslims alike – have also been a fertile ground for various Christian charities with a clear evangelical mission. For instance, Jehovah's Witnesses and numerous born-again Christian sects have been active in 'helping' the IDPs 'in this and eternal life'. Religious indoctrination has affected the identities of many IDPs, war widows and their children, who have had to exchange their local communal identities for membership of exotic religious congregations. By doing this, they have often alienated themselves from close relatives and become a barely tolerated minority among their own people.

However, this trend should not be confused with many widows and single mothers finding God on their own, turning to religion as a spiritual refuge and source of meaning, where they can pray for the souls of their lost loved ones. One such woman is Edina's mother Kadira, who was not particularly religious before the war. She said:

> I pray five times a day but I spend more time praying *fatiha*[25] to my son and my husband than doing actual prescribed prayers. This way I feel I'm with them many times a day. I'm looking forward to seeing them in the afterlife ... Hodža[26] told me that when I pray *fatiha* their souls are smiling.

Kadira has been able to find refuge in her regular rituals and meditations and she needs to believe that this has a purpose, as there is nothing to better soothe her pain.

As Helms (2007: 236) argues, women in post-war BiH are largely excluded from politics, while 'politics itself is often gendered through the common phrase, "politika je kurva" ("politics is a whore"), which is used to emphasise the corrupt, fickle and immoral nature of political deal-making'. However, many Bosnian women have managed to find alternative ways to enter the political arena and raise their voice about women's plight in post-war BiH. Loss of relatives, grief and displacement have often been the basis for organising various women's activities and associations that, to different degrees, substitute for lost forms of communal identity and neighbourliness, but also act as political pressure groups. For instance, women's groups organise regular remembrance days, commemorations and *tehvids*[27] to remember and honour their lost men and children. Most women's associations are local and regional in character, but they increasingly collaborate and meet with similar groups from BiH and the wider region. For instance, an association of women from Prijedor travelled across the country to pay a visit to Fata Orlović, as a gesture of goodwill and to express their moral support and solidarity with her. Most of the women from Podrinje are actively involved in or see their interests represented through The Mothers of Srebrenica Association or other similar women's organisations, such as Women – War Victims, Bosfam, and Women from Podrinje. These associations act as lobbying and self-help groups as well as forms of resistance to further exclusion and marginalisation in a society dominated by masculine nationalism (Nettelfield 2010; Wagner 2008; Helms 2007; Sofos 1996a, 1996b). Some of these forms of resistance, as in the case of Fata Orlović, defy the masculine logic of political organisation and power. Through support from international NGOs, women's cooperatives have also been established, involved in the production of organic food through to interfaith and interethnic dialogue and reconciliation in the region. Similar stories of women sticking together can be found in many Bosnian diasporic communities.

Refugee Women in Diaspora

Once forced to abandon their homes, many of the displaced did not have any option other than to look for safety outside BiH. They hoped this move was of a temporary nature, until normalcy returned to their home towns, villages, hamlets and neighbourhoods. As confirmed in this book, for most of them that was a vain hope: hundreds of thousands of people who might never have contemplated migrating even into a large local town, have become global nomads, refugees, migrants and settlers in many unusual destinations across the globe. People from small Bosnian villages ended up in cities like Melbourne, Chicago and Atlanta. But, as Jansen (2008) argues, it is not only the change of place that has been a major issue for Bosnian refugees; other, no less dramatic changes have included loss of status and misplacement of gender relationships within refugee families. While Jansen develops a convincing argument about 'misplaced masculinities' of Bosnian men in diaspora, other authors, including Barbara Franz and Nadje Al-Ali, have described how Bosnian women have been able to cope with the realities of displacement and migration and readjust their family roles better than men. Al-Ali (2002: 107), who conducted research among displaced Bosnians in the Netherlands and the U.K., found out that 'women proved to be more resourceful and adaptable than their husbands, who appeared to suffer from higher levels of isolation, loneliness and a sense of "living in limbo".' She concludes that 'in the light of the loss of other identifiers traditionally associated with the "male sphere", ethnic, religious, national and political identities have become especially significant to Bosnian men in diaspora' (Al-Ali 2002: 107). On the other hand, as Franz argues, women's new identities in diaspora often include replication of their old Bosnian identities in relation to traditional gender roles – as wives, mothers and housewives – in addition to their new roles as wage earners and sometimes even the sole breadwinners in their families. In practice this has meant that many Bosnian women in diaspora have ended up, as Franz (2005: 110) puts it, 'working in "double shifts" at their job site and at home'.

The migratory process from BiH happened in two phases: during the war – especially in its first year – and then in the years after the war, mainly during the first five years (1995–2000). While the first wave of migration from Bosnia was more of a temporary nature and often involved dramatic flights from violence, the second phase involved more deliberate plans for permanent emigration and settlement in a third country. During the first phase, refugees looked for safety mostly in nearby European countries. In the second most of those leaving post-war BiH were migrating to the U.S.A., Canada, Australia and New Zealand – usually for good. As described in the previous chapter, there were cases of migration within European countries – such as Bosnian refugees leaving Germany and migrating to Sweden – as well as exchanges of temporary refugee status in Europe for permanent residence in North America or Australia.

These migration movements from BiH differ in many significant ways from the temporary labour migration before the war that was dominated by men. One significant difference of the later war and post-war migrations from BiH is that they included complete families – albeit predominantly women and children. This trend bears some similarity with Fortier's observation that Italian women migrants in the U.K. 'are consistently relocated within the family setting, represented as wives and mothers' (Fortier 2000: 50). However, unlike Italian women, a significant number of the Bosnian women did not migrate as wives, but as war widows and mothers who had lost children in the war. Roles within many of those fractured families look quite different from traditional migrant families, with the Bosnian war widows performing the traditional roles as persons in charge of their homes as well as those of sole breadwinners. Fortier (2000: 50) also argues that 'women migrants are integrated as agents of cultural reproduction and stability in the formation of the "community"'. These important roles have definitely been fulfilled by many Bosnian women migrants/refugees in their respective families and trans-local communities. However, the role of war widows 'as agents of cultural reproduction and stability' has not always been so clear, with many of the female-headed families – while integrated into and accepted by their trans-local communities – often feeling merely adjunct to and tolerated by the wider ethnic diaspora. I regularly came across many such shattered families in Austria, Sweden and the U.S.A., and some of their stories have been included in other chapters of this book.[28] However, due to more extensive research and engagement with Bosnian war widows who settled in Australia, in the following pages I focus on their stories and issues they confront, with certain variations described in the final part of the book. Nonetheless, their situation is emblematic of Bosnian women survivors worldwide.

In Australia a significant concentration of Bosnian war widows is to be found in the Melbourne suburb of St. Albans. Apart from the name, St. Albans does not have much in common with its English counterpart, the affluent town in southern Hertfordshire. In terms of infrastructure, property prices, employment rate and other social indicators, St. Albans down under has traditionally been below Melbourne's average. Since the era of post-

Second World War mass migration, Melbourne's west has also been known for having a high concentration of migrant communities. More recently, because of the visible presence of migrant groups from the Balkans, it has been referred to as 'the little Balkans'. Relatively cheap rental prices, the availability of ethnic shops, communal infrastructure – including places of worship – and community networks have been decisive factors as to why many Bosnian refugees have settled there over the last fifteen years.

While it has the largest concentration of Bosnian migrants in Australia, St. Albans also has the largest number of Bosnian female-headed families. In most instances, the female-headed families are the result of war and the loss of husbands, although a number of families were fractured by divorce after migration. Many of the widow-headed families come from Srebrenica, Prijedor and Brčko. The reason so many of the war widows migrated to Australia and settled in St. Albans can be found in Australia's Humanitarian and Refugee Program which gave preference to applicants under the Women at Risk category.[29] Trans-local links and a proposer support scheme – an integral part of the immigration application – also played a decisive role in how the women were accepted for migration and 'sent' specifically to places like St. Albans where their proposers were based.[30] Many women – those from the Podrinje region, Prijedor and Brčko – settled in their own trans-local communities in St. Albans.

In the early 2000s settlement services and local community agencies in Melbourne's western suburbs identified the large number of Bosnian female-headed households in the St. Albans area and attempted to develop a programme to address some of their issues. The Bosnian Women's Group (BWG) was established. It consisted of up to fifty Bosnian women, and was open not only to war widows but also to other Bosnian refugee women. The group meetings and activities were facilitated and organised by social workers, community nurses and counsellors working for one of the settlement services or community health organisations in the area. The BWG was ethnically mixed, but the women rejected being categorised as Bosniaks, Croats or Serbs; they preferred to identify themselves by their common, inclusive and ethnically neutral denominator 'Bosnian'. In fact, they decided to call their group *Ostanimo zajedno* (Let's stay together), referring to their pro-multicultural leanings. The most noticeable diversity in the group was not ethnicity but age difference, as it included women from their mid twenties to late seventies. Some had lost multiple family members across two or three generations. Fata, a woman in her early thirties, had lost two husbands in the war; the first was killed at the beginning of the war. Shortly after she married again, but close to the end of the war her second husband perished. All the women in the BWG have children; some also have grandchildren. Many children do not remember their fathers and some were born after their fathers disappeared. While physically absent, the fathers continue to be important sources of inspiration and moral authority, even if only in the children's and the mothers' memories and imagination. As Mirsada put it, 'as [single] parents we have to be both mothers and fathers to our children. But I know I can only be a good mother and not a good father, regardless of how much I try. My sons only think of their father as a hero and they try to be as good as he would have wanted them to be.'

In addition to providing parenting advice, the purpose of establishing the group was to address some of the common psychosocial and settlement issues, including women's physical and mental health. The programme of the BWG included educational, recreational and social activities. Many meetings turned into grieving sessions, but there were also occasions when all the women laughed until they cried. For many of them it was the only time they were taken to the city, museums, galleries, and even to a women's circus and a beauty salon for make-up sessions. They acknowledged that, in the last two decades, these had been the rare occasions when they were encouraged to have fun together. They rediscovered that, in addition to having a common identity as 'war widows' and 'single mothers', what they also shared with each other was that they were women migrants in a completely new cultural environment. They were very keen to discover this new environment and possibly reinvent themselves as 'migrants'.

It was initially envisaged that over time the group would become independently run by the Bosnian women themselves. However, being a single parent also means sole responsibility for children and all the other family affairs, and after about a year most women were still preoccupied with the issues of raising the children and establishing their lives in the foreign country. So, the BWG *Ostanimo zajedno* gradually died out. However, the women continued socialising individually and in smaller groups, visiting each other privately in their own homes. They continue to share the common legacy of the war that left them widows with all the issues associated with settling in a foreign country as well, having to find their own places and roles in the construction and maintenance of their families, their social networks and the diasporic communities.

While the Australian government has been relatively generous with the Bosnian war widows and similar refugee groups – providing them with social security benefits, healthcare, public housing and options for further training and education – the labour market has been somewhat less accommodating of their needs and skills. This has led to many women being pushed into more informal market niches and finding casual, part-time and seasonal jobs in less regulated industries such as domestic cleaning, hospitality and crop harvesting. These jobs not only involve hard physical labour and less than optimal working conditions, but are also generally the lowest paid jobs available, without basic employees' entitlements and security such as paid overtime, sick leave, annual leave or superannuation. As such jobs rarely turn into ongoing, regulated employment, and the women end up in situations that practically make them welfare cheats and 'dole-bludgers' – continuing to work in these dull jobs while receiving financial support from the government. Knowing that this is not quite legal, many women have been afraid of the authorities and of people who may report them. This leaves them in a vulnerable position, open to exploitation and manipulation by the employers and the middlemen, or 'agents'. The middlemen and women – most often people from the Bosnian and other Balkan communities who act as go-betweens for the refugee women and those looking for cheap unregulated labour – are the biggest profiteers from such arrangements. They take up to 50 per cent of the women's earnings. In exchange, they provide transport to and from the workplaces. Throughout the year, between four and five in the morning, they drive their buses and vans from house to house in the suburbs of St. Albans and nearby Deer Park, collecting women labourers and distributing them across the farms on the outskirts of Melbourne. The women start work at 6 or 7A.M. and finish work around 1P.M. They earn $50 per day. Their wages are paid by the agents, who collect lump-sum payments from the farmers and deduct their own fees as they pay the women. None of the women workers is allowed to negotiate her pay or working conditions directly with the farmers. So many Bosnian refugee women – especially war widows with children – are exploited in very much the same way as illegal migrants get exploited in most developed nations: underpaid and overworked for jobs no one else is willing to do. Thus, it does not come as a surprise that for many Bosnian women in diaspora, employment has not been seen as individual emancipation, economic liberation from husbands and life changing. The experiences of Bosnian women in Australia discussed here mirrors those of Bosnian women in the U.S., as described by Barbara Franz (2003, 2005). As she argues, '[Bosnian refugee women] engaged in wage labour not because they sought independence from their male partners by actively engaging in the public sphere or because they wanted to escape the oppressive patriarchal traditions of their homes, but simply to ensure economic stability and improve their children's living conditions and chances for future advancement' (Franz 2005: 112). While they work, the agents go from field to field to check if the women are working hard enough. If they are not happy with the performance of a particular woman they stop 'employing' her. Sabaheta, a grandmother in her late sixties with fragile health, lost her job because she could not keep up with the younger women's pace. She was later reemployed on lower pay. She said that although it was not easy, she loved the work because she felt useful, was able to contribute to her daughter's family budget, and enjoyed being with other women. 'It reminds me of my youth when I worked on my own fields in Bosnia,' she said. At 1 P.M. the women get collected from the fields and taken back home. As soon as they get home they start preparing meals for their children who return from school around 3.30 P.M. Many of the women have a second job as cleaners or kitchen hands in the evening. Sometimes this involves working from 6 P.M. until midnight, only to be collected at 4 A.M. for another day's work on a farm.

Many members of the Bosnian community – former refugees, who have been lucky and resilient enough to reinvent themselves professionally and to find regular jobs in Australia, or the 'old migrants', who migrated to Australia in the 1970s – tend to look down at the refugee women as welfare cheats and 'dole-bludgers'. From a position of productive and integrated members of society, they moralise about work ethics, accusing the refugee women of exploiting the system and being better off than those who contribute – as the women do not pay tax and have privileges associated with being recipients of social security. In reality, however, these women are much worse off than their accusers, both financially and in terms of their working conditions. Most women would prefer to work in a regulated industry with all the associated employment entitlements rather than work so hard and be involved in something that is not quite legal. However, they recognise that in the absence of 'proper jobs' these alternative employment opportunities help them meet the growing needs of their families.

When visiting the homes of many of the Bosnian war widows involved in such jobs it can be seen that, although they are underpaid, the hard work pays off. Their homes are usually furnished with new furniture and high-tech home appliances such as dishwashers, televisions, DVD players and computers. An increasing number of women have been able to get home loans to buy their own houses. This is seen as a very important step towards integration as it means in practice (re)constructing their lost homes here in Australia. While they still may feel displaced, at least they are no longer homeless. Their new homes – usually the standard Australian suburban one-level brick houses – are conventionally Australian from the outside, but very much Bosnian on the inside. The Bosnian touches start at the doorstep, where visitors entering the house are expected to take off their shoes before stepping in. Covered sofas in living rooms, an abundance of pillows, woollen carpets, pictures with Bosnian motifs, glass cabinets filled with ornamental plates, glasses and cups, hand-crafted nettings and the European-style blinds and curtains welcome any visitor into a typical Bosnian home setting. Traditional Bosnian hospitality – including the unavoidable ritual of drinking Bosnian (Turkish) coffee and eating traditional sweets (*kolači*) and pastry (*pita*) – completes the full Bosnian effect. I have come across almost identical Bosnian homes in the high-rise buildings of Stockholm, colourful weatherboard houses in the suburbs of St. Louis, in the *Altbau* flats of Vienna, and in many other places where Bosnians have settled. In all these places, the majority of Bosnian women have kept their traditional role of being in charge of the inner space – families and homes – while simultaneously adopting the new roles of breadwinner and labourer. The women are particularly proud of the interior of their houses and spend a lot of time keeping the house in order. Most of them would agree that cleanliness is next to godliness and keep their homes clean and ready for inspection at any time by unexpected visitors.

In addition to the 'Bosnian interior', many Bosnian houses in diaspora also include carefully maintained Bosnian-style front and back yards, with plenty of roses and other flowering plants, and benches and tables facing the street. In fact, the space around the houses has often been turned into proper Bosnian *avlija*s, the public–private space designed not only to accommodate the social needs of the inhabitants of the house, but also of the neighbours and the local community. As many Bosnians are not very fond of trimmed lawns they often redesign their own front and back yards. It is not uncommon for green lawns to be replaced by plain concrete for additional car spaces for visiting guests or another utilitarian purpose. A house without a car parked in front does not seem to be a Bosnian house. In late 2008, when I visited former members of the Bosnian Women's Group in St. Albans, each household owned at least one car – in many cases more than one. Sometimes particular attention was given to the type of car the family owned. Though more expensive than other comparable brands, European cars are popular among Bosnians in Australia as well as in the U.S. and in Europe. It is not unusual to recognise Bosnian houses in the suburbs of Melbourne or St. Louis by old (and sometimes newer) Audis, VWs, BMWs and other European brand cars parked in front, as well as by the shoes piled at the doorsteps and on the stairs at the entrance to the house. Often these types of cars were either once owned or aspired to in the old homeland. As Mirsada, a widowed mother of two teenage sons, said, 'we left a brand new [VW] Golf before we fled our hometown. [It] was only six months old and it was the most expensive possession we ever had'. Now her sons own a similar Golf in St. Albans. For Mirsada, the Golf is not about the prestige that may be associated with such cars, but more about the memory of the life she once had. Having attempted to fit as many pieces as possible from her past life into the present, the Golf seems to fit well into her *avlija*.

It would be wrong to suggest that Bosnian women in diaspora have been preoccupied with acquiring material possessions and that this is the main reason they accept work even if it is illegal. Most of the money they earn is spent on the home, on their children and on supporting family members back in Bosnia. They see it as imperative that their children lack nothing, from computers and playstations to cars for teenagers and young adults. As Sabra, a war widow from St. Albans and a mother of two (now also a grandmother) said, '[my] children won't be orphans for as long as I'm alive. They will never feel that I cannot provide for them as other parents, just because I'm on my own.' Sabra's commitment to support her children culminated in lavish weddings for both her son and her daughter a few years ago. Both children completed university degrees and now have professional jobs. However, Sabra's hard physical work has taken its toll on her health. Last year she needed to have a hip replacement and has been physically impaired since. Now she has turned into a full-time grandmother looking after her three young grandchildren.

Many women often send regular monthly payments to their ailing parents left behind in BiH. It is also quite common for women to support the building of houses by their relatives in Bosnia or meet most of their larger financial expenses. In many cases, war widows are so stretched financially between demands 'here' and 'over there' that the only way to meet all their needs and expectations is to work as much as possible. Many of them go for weeks without a single day off. Also, a visit to Bosnia, even if it is once every three to five years, costs a lot. In addition to the expense of airfares, they are expected to bring presents for the many members of their extended families.

Like the IDP women in BiH, the Bosnian women in diaspora are often subject to envy, prejudice and patronising by members of their own diasporic communities. While through migration they might have increased their independence and provided better options for the future of their children, at the same time they have reduced their chances of meeting a prospective partner even further, as there is an even higher scarcity of compatible marriageable men in diaspora. The 'compatibility' relates to many different socio-cultural factors, such as age, ethnicity, religion, regional/local background, as well as acceptance by the children, family members and the community. Among all the war widows in the St. Albans area, only one has started to live in a de facto relationship with a man she met there.

For almost two decades war widows in places like St. Albans have been preoccupied with looking after their children. Now these children have grown into young adults and many have moved out, started their own separate professional and private lives, and got married or moved in with a partner. In many cases these new arrangements almost by default exclude mothers, as the traditional extended families back in Bosnia are only rarely replicated in diaspora. This has led to a situation where an increasing number of war widows from BiH live on their own in their suburban houses and flats. Even in cases when adult children continue caring for their mothers, this separation of households is often interpreted by the community as being 'abandoned by the children', something to be ashamed of. The women have also become older and their roles as mothers have changed; their now grown-up children do not depend on them and do not need them the way they needed them earlier. Despite their trans-local networks, loneliness and social isolation increasingly make the women more aware of their identities as war widows. Flight, years of displacement, the fight to survive and being both parents to their children meant putting themselves, their aspirations and their losses second. There was neither time nor mental energy to confront all the personal issues which accumulated over the years. Now, maybe for the first time, they cannot escape confronting both the past and the present. Reactive depression is often the result, and due to deteriorating mental health, many women have turned to psychiatrists and psychologists. Some have developed severe psychosomatic symptoms and chronic medical conditions (Markovic and Manderson 2002).

Mothers' Children

Mothers cannot be disentangled from their children. Having loving and caring mothers has helped many children[31] who lost their fathers to have a relatively sheltered childhood and develop into confident young adults (Macić 2002; Salihović 2005). Many have done well at school and have since been studying for or have completed university degrees and started professional careers. The refugee experience and living in different countries has benefited many young people, who have not only learned about but also lived in different cultures (Halilovich 2005a, 2006b). It seems, however, that there are some differences in behaviour and level of adaptation between children and young adults who were not directly affected by the war and those who lived in Bosnia throughout the war and left after the war finished. This observation is based on a sample of some one hundred Bosnian youth in Melbourne.[32] Some general patterns in similarities and differences between these two groups of young people can be identified. The girls seem to be generally more resilient and doing better than boys. On average, young people who spent their childhood as refugees in Germany have been doing relatively better academically than those who came to Australia direct from BiH after the war. This may be related to both the level of exposure to violence – described as 'dose effect' by L. Jones (2005) and Jones and Kafetsios (2005: 158) – and lack of proper education during the war in BiH. It is also widely believed that primary education in Germany is one of the finest, 'much more serious than in Australia' as 'Aussie Bosnians from Germany' confirmed. But generalisations can hide profoundly individual differences, as documented in the remainder of this chapter with three of the most extreme and tragic and three of the most successful stories of Bosnian Melbourne youth.

The first example is Amer, who was ten years old when, in 1992, his father was killed in his home town of Bratunac. Together with his mother, his older sister and ailing grandmother, Amer fled to the neighbouring town of Srebrenica. In March 1993 – after eleven months of harsh survival, without adequate food or shelter and under constant artillery attack from the Serb positions around the city – the family had to make an important decision about who would be evacuated in the UN trucks taking women and children from Srebrenica to Tuzla. It was a logical choice for Amer and his grandmother – being the youngest and the oldest – to be chosen for the escape from the place with no shelter, no food and little hope that the situation would improve. With 2,300 other women and children, packed like sardines on nineteen UN trucks, Amer and his grandmother reached Tuzla in late March 1993. Several elderly women and young children suffocated during the transport on open trucks designed to carry freight, not people. As Chuck Sudetic (1993) reported in *The New York Times*, 'Serbian militiamen kept the convoy waiting for several hours on the siege line despite the crowded conditions on the trucks, an order given by the commander of the Serbian forces, General Ratko Mladić'. Sudetic noted at the time that 'the trucks arriving from Srebrenica were coated with filth and stank of sweat and smoke. The sides of some trucks were wet with vomit' (Sudetic 1993). Almost two years later, in January 1995, when conditions in Srebrenica became even less bearable, Amer's mother and sister tried to escape from the besieged enclave. Not far from the town, they were captured by the Serb military and, after surviving almost a year in prisons in Serbia, were registered as 'prisoners of war' by the ICRC; with the help of the UNHCR and IOM they were allowed to resettle in Australia.

Amer continued to live with his grandmother as an IDP in Bosnia for ten more years before he was finally reunited with his mother and sister in Australia in 2002. However, now a young adult, he had difficulties reconnecting with his mother and sister as well as adapting to his new social environment. Shortly after he was reunited with his family, he moved out to live in shared accommodation with three young non-Bosnian men. In what his mother describes as 'caught up in bad company', he developed a drug habit and lost his job as a truck driver. He also committed numerous traffic offences and became a frequent visitor to the local police station and courthouse. Within the Bosnian community in St. Albans he became known as the 'public junky' (*drogeraš*). Some people avoided him and thought him a disgrace to his mother and to the Bosnian community. Others were more sympathetic and loved him for his friendly manners and his never-ending stories in which everything was mixed up and anything was possible. I remember him as a pleasant, somewhat childish, but funny and articulate young man. Knowing his story, I knew that his childhood dreams had been shattered a long time ago and there was not much in place to replace them. He covered his sorrow and his self-destructive tendencies very well with his lucid tales and humour. Once he told me convincingly how he would soon be discovered as the biggest Australian DJ. Instead, one morning, some two years after he arrived in Australia, his body was discovered in the flat he shared with his flatmates, one of whom, in an apparent delusional attack, had stabbed him to death. Amer was twenty-two.

The second example is Ismar, who was a seven-year-old boy when he fled his village near the town of Višegrad in eastern Bosnia. Between 1992 and 2000 he and his family – his mother and two younger brothers – lived as IDPs in Sarajevo. After waiting in vain for years to learn about the fate of Ismar's missing father and uncles, who were taken away by Chetnik militia in 1992, the family decided to look for a brighter future somewhere else. Distant relatives, who had migrated to Australia a few years previously, arranged for them to join them on this distant continent. In Australia the family experienced the issues of settlement and adaptation like many other Bosnian families. Ismar's younger brother has been a good student, studying social work at the local campus. The youngest of the three is still at high school. Ismar, on the other hand, has abandoned school and has frequent run-ins with the law, mostly for his violent behaviour in pubs and clubs. As with Edina's nephew Ado in Sarajevo, Ismar's anger has been directed at anyone representing any form of authority. His own mother has occasionally been on the receiving end. He lost his driver's licence, but this did not stop him driving and he was caught by the police as a repeat offender. In August 2009 he narrowly escaped a jail sentence.[33] Understandably, his mother was devastated by the prospect.

Although I never personally met my third example, in some ways I seem to know more about him than just about any of the participants and research collaborators I have known for years. Like me, not many had heard of 17-year-old Allem Halkić while he was still alive. He only came to our notice on 5 February 2009 when, in the early hours of the morning, he committed suicide by jumping from the notorious Westgate Bridge in Melbourne. The story of his tragic death shook not only his family, but also the Bosnian community in Melbourne and Victoria. His death triggered a public campaign to make the Westgate Bridge less accessible to desperate people seeking to end their lives in this way.[34] The local media were covered with stories about Allem Halkić.[35] His handsome, smiling face can still be viewed on the internet. There are numerous YouTube clips and internet postings honouring his life and mourning his death. At the time of writing this chapter his profile on Facebook was still active.

Although this tragedy might not have a lot to do with Allem's Bosnian past, the Bosnian community has appropriated him in death. The community has been 'trying to learn the lesson' – as a community leader recently said – and to question itself as to why they lost yet another young life. The Bosnian community leader, who claimed he knew the Halkićs, told me that Allem was a toddler when his parents migrated to Australia, after being forced to abandon their home town of Sanski Most in western Bosnia. He grew up as an ordinary Australian suburban boy by all accounts. His parents could be regarded as socially and economically integrated into mainstream Australian society. Some members of the Bosnian community argue that this might have been the problem: Allem was not encouraged by his parents to find his place as a member of the Bosnian community and 'that's why the child got lost'.[36] He did not attend the Bosnian Saturday school or the mosque, nor did he play soccer for any of the three Bosnian soccer clubs in Melbourne, a standard activity for Bosnian youth. Instead, he socialised mainly with Australians and 'played dangerous games on the internet'. His bereaved parents told the media that their son might have been left more to himself than he should have been. 'He spent most of his time on the internet', they said. As a possible reason why their only child took his life, his parents cite the internet and 'cyber bullying'. Some members of the Bosnian community in Melbourne seem to know more. They say that Allem felt split between two worlds, especially after visiting Bosnia for the first time two years prior to his death. They also believe that, regardless of being assimilated into the Australian 'Anglo-mainstream', Allem never lost his Bosnian roots. Allegedly, his last text message sent from the bridge was written in Bosnian. It read: 'Posljednji pozdrav mojim roditeljima' (Last greeting/farewell to my parents). While no one really knows how he felt or what troubled the teenager so much that he decided to take that fatal step, what is relevant here is how a narrative memory of Allem's posthumous Bosnian identity has been constructed by his 'fellow Bosnians'.

Allem's and Amer's tragic deaths, like other tragic events involving Bosnians in Australia, have become part of the collective memory of the Bosnians in Melbourne – part of the gendered pain that this chapter explores. Tragedies seem to unite communities and bring them together, reminding them of – and helping them imagine – their common origins and common destiny in their new homeland. Thus, funerals are performances of common identity, even more so than birthdays and weddings. Unlike birthdays and weddings, which are exclusive events where guests get invited, funerals – at least in the Bosnian tradition – do not require any invitations. They are public rituals and people are simply expected to turn up and bid farewell to members of their community who died, whether they personally knew them or not. Through community networks, mostly word of mouth, but also through community radio, members of the Bosnian community are informed of funerals. Community members and the bereaved family also notice who is (and who is not) present at the funerals. Although most of those attending their funerals might never have met Amer and Allem, their individual life histories have become a part of the collective memory of the diasporic Bosnian community in Melbourne.

The collective memory also celebrates success, and while the majority of the young people who came as refugees to Australia would fit the Australian average when it comes to education and other social indicators – such as youth employment – a significant number of Bosnian youth have been able to rise well above the average. Sara, now a young woman in her mid twenties, could definitely be regarded as an example of success. She gives credit to her mother Jasna and her grandmother Kata, who have supported her throughout her life, especially from the time they fled their home town of Brčko where Sara's father was killed in May 1992. While Sara can remember her father and the happy childhood she once had, her younger brother Dino, who was born in Croatia a few months after their father perished, has been deprived of such memories. As the only male member in the family, he has been looked after well by his grandmother, his mother and his sister. He has been particularly proud of his sister who was a bright student – one of the best – and who now has a successful professional career in Melbourne. She has won many prizes and awards for her academic and professional achievements. Recently she bought her own house in a famed beach suburb of Melbourne.

Adis could also be added to the list of high achievers. At the outbreak of the war, as a young child, he fled his village near Prijedor in northern Bosnia. His father stayed behind and perished. Adis completed primary school in Germany, before migrating to Australia with his mother in 1997. He works as an IT specialist for a large Australian company while completing his Master's degree.

But the success of Bosnian youth in diaspora – particularly in Australia – cannot be measured only by academic and professional achievements. Not every young person has had the same opportunities to study and become a successful professional. Emir, for instance, was not lucky enough to escape to Germany or to another European country and has been deprived not only of a proper education since the age of seven, but also of the guidance and oversight of his parents, both of whom perished in the war. His grandfather looked after him and his younger sister Alma throughout the war. They survived together the exodus from Srebrenica in July 1995. When, in 1998, his Grandpa died, it was only thanks to the intervention of their Aunt Fatima that the siblings did not end up in an institution for war orphans. Aunt Fatima, who lost her own husband in the war, became their de facto foster parent. With their aunt and her ten-year-old son, Emir and Alma migrated to Australia in 2000. They initially landed in Tasmania, but six months later they moved to St. Albans to join the Bosnian community there. Emir was seventeen years old when he started working as a full-time labourer in the building industry in Melbourne. He felt obliged to work to provide for his sister, his aunt and his cousin. He was now the only man in the house. He could not afford to 'waste time' on education, he said, as there was no one else to support 'his' family. Within three years Emir had registered his own business as a renderer, and by 2009 he was employing six other Bosnians, and owned a small truck, a van and all the machinery and tools required for the trade. He has established himself as a reliable partner in the building industry and is getting a larger and larger share of the rendering market. He now lives with his own family, a wife and three young children, in a house he bought recently. He also pays the rent for and financially supports his sister, a full-time university student, his aunt and her mentally impaired son. Emir is also known for his financial contribution to communal projects in St. Albans. Above all, he has remained a very pleasant 'down to earth guy', and is very popular among his Bosnian and non-Bosnian friends and colleagues. Many would say he has realised his Australian dream and is on the way to becoming a rich man. Emir, however, maintains that the only motivation for his hard work – bringing him solid earnings – has been his obligation towards his family. He did not, he maintains, have a choice.

While my research has not been focused on psychological/clinical aspects of 'traumatic' memories, it can be said that different individuals have been affected differently by similar experiences and personal loss (Goldstein et al. 1997). Some have coped with these issues better than others; some have been affected to a level where they need professional assistance, others – like Sara, Adis and Emir – have become even more determined to succeed and not to give in to the challenges. Occasionally their loss and war memories resurface even if only to rationalise their actions. Emir, for instance, once said that he would not do rendering if his father were alive. He would prefer some white-collar job. Ismar has been less able to articulate his feelings about his past and this might be one of the reasons for his anger and his violent behaviour. However, his 'embodied memory' is much easier to read – with a large tattoo of his father's name on his left arm. He had that tattoo inscribed the day he learned that his father's body had been exhumed and positively identified. He has become a walking memorial for his father's death, his own loss and never-ending grief.

That sense of loss and grief can be triggered by more serendipitous events. In late May, 2005, the family Salkić, now living in St. Albans, was shocked by an event that could only be compared with the surrealism of a bad nightmare. It came in the form of a report on the evening news on the Australian public television broadcaster SBS (see R. Adams 2006). What was shown was close-up footage of an execution of six civilians from Srebrenica ten years earlier. Their hands were tied behind their backs, they looked exhausted and one of them, a man wearing a blue shirt, asked the executioners, the Serb soldiers, if he could get some water before they killed him. The request was denied with laughter and abuse by the captors, who continued filming. In that thirsty man in a blue shirt captured on the handheld video, Mido, a 22-year-old university student, and his 17-year-old sister Mubera recognised their father. Their mother, Zifa Salkić, recognised her missing husband, Sidik Salkić. The footage showed how their father and husband was forced to carry the bodies of four men killed seconds earlier and load them onto a truck; then, how he and the remaining captive men were lined up and the gun barrels of the execution squad pointed at their chests before they were gunned down in cold blood. A week after he saw his father's last moments Mido was in Bosnia trying to get any information he could about his father's grave. Nearly two more years passed before Sidik Salkić's remains were positively identified. He was laid to rest at Potočari on 11 July 2007.

Zifa Salkić might be viewed as an exemplar for Bosnian women's continuing pain, for their memorialisation of what they have lost. Her old Bosnian memories are present in her new home in Australia: the photos in her lounge room, the picture of the young smiling Sidik, and the film footage – the family retains a copy of the awful film clip, which now serves a memorialising function like a photograph. Similarly, the homes of mothers who have recently lost their children have become private memorials to their loss. Amer's photos and his music collection function as a shrine for his bereaved mother Fata; newspaper and video clips, including the one broadcast on the national television network ABC,[37] is Dina's way of holding onto memories of her son Allem. Such mementos are testimony to women's continuing sense of loss – simultaneously reflecting and constructing a core component of their continuing identity, which is never fixed.

However, such memorialisation is not only a private matter; it intersects with public commemorations. On 11 July 2010 hundreds of women survivors – with other fellow survivors from Podrinje and across Bosnia – gathered at the Australian-Bosnian Islamic Centre (ABIC), in the Melbourne suburb of St. Albans, to mark yet another commemoration of the Srebrenica genocide. Each of them carried a burden of personal loss and private memories of the tragic event fourteen years earlier. The ABIC provided a context for public mourning and commemoration of these private memories. On the other side of the world, in Bosnia, at the memorial cemetery in Potočari near Srebrenica, with his mother and his two brothers, Ismar was attending the central commemoration and the collective funeral for more than six hundred newly identified victims of the 1995 genocide. Among the victims were Ismar's father Bego and his uncle Hamdija. Like many other survivors who came to bury their relatives on the day, Ismar and his family not only had their private grieving to deal with, but also technical issues with the burial itself: they had two bodies to put in the ground and had to wait for the coffins numbered 189 and 360. The tears ran down their cheeks as they finally carried coffin number 189 containing the bones of their father Bego. After hastily putting the green coffin into the ground, they had to run back through the crowd to collect coffin number 360, that of their uncle Hamdija. Later they returned back to their father's grave, shovelled the remaining earth onto the grave and said their prayers. It was hard to believe that on this day Ismar's mother Zaha, who was burying her husband and her younger brother, was making closure and starting a new chapter in her life. In a few days she would have to cross half the world to get 'back home' to St. Albans.

Notes

1. Translated from Bosnian by Hariz Halilovich.
2. In the title of this chapter I paraphrase Susan Sontag's *Regarding the Pain of Others*.
3. See Beverly (1996), Stiglmayer (1994), Hunt (2005), Drakulić (1999) and Mertus (2000).
4. The Foča rape case was the first time that individuals were convicted for rape as a crime against humanity. See Hagan (2003).
5. For her film *Grbavica*, the Bosnian director Jasmila Žbanić won the Golden Bear for the best film at the Berlin Festival in March 2005.
6. See http://www.sarajevo-x.com/forum/viewtopic.php?f=35andt=47472
7. See Chapters 1 and 2.
8. See Chapter 2.
9. Not just fathers, but other important male members, like grandfathers, uncles, brothers and sons.
10. JNA is a common acronym for the Yugoslav National Army. During 'Yugoslav times' every man was required to serve at least a year of national service in the JNA. For many eighteen-year-olds it was seen as a form of initiation from boyhood into adulthood; it was often the first and sometimes only time they spent a prolonged period of time far from home, usually in other Yugoslav republics. The call to serve in the JNA was seen by many teenagers and their parents as both a civic responsibility and an honour. Tragically, by 1991/2, this same 'people's Army' had been transformed into an occupying force and the killing squads controlled by Milošević and his henchmen Karadžić, Mladić and Martić.

198 *Places of Pain*

11. KM stands for 'Konvertibilna Marka', the Bosnian post-war currency (at the time of writing 1KM was equivalent to approximately €0.5).
12. According to the information by the Federalni zavod za programiranje razvoja (FENA 2008).
13. Sejo's mother – described in Chapter 2.
14. No European country has accepted Bosnian refugees for resettlement since the war ended.
15. While the UNHCR report states that, between 1996 and 2005, there were more than 550,000 registered returns, there are no reliable statistics about the number of people who actually stayed in their homes after they returned. See reports available at http://www.unhcr.ba.
16. See http://news.bbc.co.uk/2/hi/europe/6960579.stm
17. See http://www.facebook.com/pages/Nana-Fata-Orlovic/25446723509
18. In Bosnian/Croatian/Serbian languages (B/H/S) the word *došljaci* also sounds very similar to *divljaci* ('wild people', 'primitives' or 'savages').
19. In early 1992 the JNA units, later VRS, occupied the suburbs of Vogošća, Ilidža, Grbavica and parts of Dobrinja (Dobrinja IV, a part of Dobrinja I and Aerodromsko Naselje), and in the following four years used them as the bases from where they fired at the city and kept it under siege for more than 1,000 days, the longest siege of any European city in modern history. The non-Serbs were ethnically cleansed and Serb militias committed war crimes against the civilian population, including systematic rapes at the 'rape camp' – the guest house *Kod Sonje*. For more details see Olujić (1995). When the suburbs were to become reintegrated into the city, the Serb political and military leadership ordered the Serb population to leave the suburbs. Almost all conformed, some out of fear of revenge by the Bosniaks, others out of fear of the Serb militias – often because of fear from both sides. While some Serb residents reluctantly left their homes, hoping to return soon when the madness ceased, others burned their own homes, dug up the graves of their relatives and took their dead with them. See Donia (2006: 335–49).
20. This term has become a symbol of the Srebrenica genocide.
21. During the war young men in their twenties were conscripted en masse to fight in different military and paramilitary units. Being of military age and able bodied for military service, they were also targeted for killings by those who perceived them as real or potential enemy combatants. Women in their twenties were primary targets for rape and sexual violence. A number of individuals charged with committing war crimes in BiH were in their twenties at the time. See, for instance, the ICTY cases against Drazen Erdemovic, Goran Jelisic, Milan Lukic and Sredoje Lukic.
22. See Chapter 1.
23. 'old dwellers'.
24. See a series of reports on politics, corruption and mismanagement of public funds in *Dani* and *Slobodna Bosna* such as Karup-Druško (2009a); Pećanin and Karup-Druško (2009); and Dedić (2009).

25. Muslim prayers for the souls of those who died, asking God to be merciful to them.
26. A Muslim religious leader, *imam*.
27. Muslim women's religious congregations to pray together for the souls of their lost relatives.
28. See Edita's story in Chapter 2.
29. In March 2007 Teresa Gambaro, Parliamentary Secretary to the Minister for Immigration and Citizenship, stated: 'Australia gives hope to these vulnerable women and children through the Woman at Risk visa category. The visa helps refugee women and their children who are subject to persecution and have no protection from a male relative to rebuild their lives in Australia with dignity and purpose.' See http://www.workpermit.com/news/ 2007_03_09 /australia/ women_at_ risk_visa.htm.
30. 'Proposer' refers to a person or a community organisation nominated in the migration application as a family and/or community link supporting the applicant's endeavour to migrate to Australia. Proposers are obliged to assist the new arrivals with their settlement, often providing them with accommodation at their own place until they are able to find them appropriate housing.
31. According to the Centre for Research and Documentation (2007a), there were 121,856 forcefully displaced children during the war in BiH. 34,394 children suffered physical injury, while around 20,000 children lost one parent and some 2,000 both parents.
32. My initial engagement with the Bosnian youth refugees in Melbourne, particularly in the St. Albans area, started in 2002/03 when I conducted a research project as a part of my Honours thesis at RMIT University. Over the last six years, in addition to my Ph.D. research, my role as a Bosnian high school language teacher in St. Albans has given me a unique opportunity to observe, learn about and be part of various dynamics among Bosnian young people.
33. Instead of a jail sentence, Ismar was ordered by the judge to complete two months of mandatory community service.
34. Throughout 2009 and 2010 numerous reports were published in the Melbourne newspapers: *The Age*, *The Herald Sun*, and *The Leader*.
35. Ibid.
36. This view was held by many Bosnian community members in Melbourne I had informal conversations with in February and March 2009.
37. See ABC's *Four Corners*, 6 April 2009.

⋗ Conclusion ⋖

Concluding the Journey through Bosnian War-torn Communities

> Once upon a time a worthy caller asked:
> Who is that what is that forgive
> Where is that
> Whence is that
> Where to is
> That
> Bosnia
> Tell
>
> And the questioned gave then a prompt reply to him:
> Bosnia forgive there is a land
> Both barren and barefoot forgive
> Both cold and hungry
> And even more
> Forgive
> Defiant
> By
> A dream
>
> Mak Dizdar, 'Inscription of a Land',[1] *Kameni Spavač*, pp. 190–1

This concluding chapter marks the completion of a journey that has been not only a metaphoric and intellectual venture through text, but also literally a journey around the world, from the southern to the northern hemisphere, from Australia to Europe to North America and back again. In this moving fieldwork – which was multi-sited, multidirectional and involved a number of sub-journeys within and between different sites – I encountered many people who became not only research collaborators and informants, but also generous hosts. Many of their stories are 'written' between the lines, this book – like any ethnography dealing with complex fields – being far too limited an artefact to accommodate all the data they have provided. Nonetheless, the methodological approach combining narrative analysis and multi-sited ethnography ensured a degree of interaction and overlapping between different stories, narrators and places.

While recognising the complexity of narrative analysis and multi-sited research, I followed George Marcus's idea that 'any cultural identity or activity is constructed by multiple agents in varying contexts, or places, and that ethnography must be strategically conceived to represent this sort of multiplicity and to specify both intended and unintended consequences in the network of complex connections within a system of places' (Marcus 1989: 25). I have attempted to do this in this study, which, situated in the discipline of social anthropology, explores, draws upon and contributes to the area of Bosnian ethnography, with an emphasis on trans-localism and memory. Drawing from pre-war emic models of social organisation – especially the *zavičaj*[2] model – earlier chapters have described how post-war Bosnian communities within Bosnia and within the diaspora have transformed previously local modes of social organisation into trans-local networks; these continue to provide an enduring Bosnian identity with both the local territory and the local set of social relations that constituted the pre-war Bosnian sense of place and self. While the transformation displays some of the features of transnationalism, the case studies contained in previous chapters suggest that it is 'trans-localism' that constitutes the distinguishing feature of post-war Bosnian identity formation and social organisation. In this concluding chapter I present some final reflections with ethnographic vignettes from Sweden, the U.S., Austria, Bosnia and Australia[3] in a form in keeping with the narrative style of earlier chapters, and focusing on the importance of trans-local networks in the process of deterritorialisation and reterritorialisation of Bosnian war-torn communities. While deterritorialisation and reterritorialisation have transformed previously local, social and cultural patterns that defined what it meant to be Bosnian – the exemplar being the *zavičaj* – similar patterns operate today as trans-local realities for Bosnians worldwide, both within Bosnia and throughout the diaspora.

Almost two decades ago, when Glick Schiller et al. launched the theory of transnationalism, they pointed 'to the need to redefine our terminology and reformulate some of our basic conceptualisations of the current immigrant experience' (1995: 48). Similarly, in this book, I have pointed to the need to redefine terminology and reformulate some of our basic conceptualisations of the current refugee experiences, suggesting that trans-localism may hold at least a part of the answer to understanding the social morphology of forced displacement.

As discussed in detail in Chapter 4, prominent scholars of the transnational paradigm, such as Nina Glick Schiller, Linda Basch and Cristina Szanton-Blanc (1992, 1995, 1999), Steven Vertovec (1999) and Michael Kearney (1995), have discussed movements of people primarily in relation to nation states – or more precisely across different nation-state borders – and how immigrants' 'social fields' are sustained in relation to different nations and their institutions. Outlining anew the concept of transnationalism, 'transmigration' and 'transmigrants', Glick Schiller et al. (1995: 48) argue that, in an era of transnationalism, 'transmigrants are immigrants whose daily lives depend on multiple and constant interconnections across international borders and whose public identities are configured in relationship to more than one nation-state'. They also claim that via transnationalism 'both immigrants and states with dispersed populations … construct a deterritorialised nation-state' (Glick Schiller et al. 1995: 52; Basch et al. 1994). Similarly, the key terms Vertovec (1999) uses in defining transnationalism are 'institutions', 'borders' and 'nation states'.

While the concept of transnationalism, which has become a dominant theoretical framework in migration studies over the last two decades, leaves space for the inclusion of immigrants' different 'social fields' – many of the fields undoubtedly local – there have been oversights of local identities in transnational research, with (trans-)local often being submerged or lost in (trans-)national. A number of other researchers (cf. Al-Ali et al. 2001a, 2000b; Amit-Talai 1998; Cano 2005 Čapo Žmegač 2003; W. Robinson 1998) have recognised the 'nation-state-centrism' of transnationalism, pointing to the need to re-examine the research into transnationalism that 'unfolds within the straightjacket of a nation-state framework' (W. Robinson 1998: 562).

Although the research into transnationalism and transmigration encapsulates many important aspects of, say, economic migration, when it comes to forced migration as a result of violence, ethnic cleansing, genocide and breaking-up of nation states, the transnational structures – i.e., nation states – may not be as solid units of analysis and points of identification as other, more embodied, relationships based on kinship, shared memories and locally embedded cultural identities. Thus, even though such identifications are performatively enacted through multiple and constant interconnections between members of a group, they do not necessarily take place in a strictly 'transnational space', i.e., across international borders. Both 'at home' and in diaspora, many such interactions occur within the borders of a single nation state. Even when such interactions and social transactions involve people dispersed across multiple places and countries they often bypass the institutional frameworks of nation states. Furthermore, the political dimension of transnationalism and 'its resonance with nationalism as a cultural and political project', as Kearney (1995: 548) puts it, is also a problematic aspect of this interpretative framework in relation to forcefully displaced Bosnians. As described in this book, most displaced Bosnians

I engaged with during my fieldwork are not fervent nationalists; on the contrary, they are victims of nationalism who blame nationalist ideologies and nation (para)states for their personal and local tragedies, including forced migration. If anything, they are 'localists'. Thus, rather than being preoccupied with constructing a 'deterritorialised nation-state', displaced Bosnians are much more concerned with (re)constructing their local communities (*zavičaji*). Directly linked to (ethno)nationalism and nation-state (de)formation in the former Yugoslavia is the issue of 'stateless Yugoslavs' and former 'internal migrants' – among them several thousand Bosnians – who happened to live and work outside of their 'home republics' but who, during the 1990s, became transnational migrants without engaging in what is usually regarded as a migration process (cf. Drakulić 1993; Jansen 1998; Ugrešić 1995).

How are we to understand the idea of trans-localism? While trans-localism is not distinctly Bosnian or post-war, and is a potentiality of all forms of migration, its intensity and prevalence seem to be more likely in contexts of forced displacement due to a number of social, political, cultural and psychological factors (as described in Chapter 4), including removal of whole villages and neighbourhoods (domicide), politicisation of local issues, shared embodied memories, and desire for a new, *zavičaj*-like emplacement. Unlike the more abstract national focus of much transnational research, the concrete dimension of memory, instantiated in embodiment and emplacement, lies at the heart of trans-localism – we see and smell villages and know that when we talk about them with someone, we are talking about the same thing.

Hence, as a complementary methodological approach to transnationalism, trans-localism does not equal 'glocalism' or the often-mentioned interdependence between local and global, where local may be a quite specific place while global remains an abstract 'everywhere' (R. Robertson 1995). Rather, trans-localism refers to multiple local–local connections and the performative enactment of embodied identities embedded – or imagined to be embedded – in particular locations. To borrow Appadurai's (1996) term, these communal identities are de facto 'deterritorialised' (or de-localised). Nonetheless, a specific locale (or territory) remains the most powerful motif, a 'symbolic anchor' of displaced communities, for keeping alive their distinct local identities – made up of people sharing a common 'sense of place', memories, rituals, dialect, kinship and social norms (Gupta and Ferguson 1992: 11). In effect, this means that displacement leads to a new placement. Thus, trans-localism is as much about reterritorialisation as it is about deterritorialisation. However, this does not mean that a new territoriality is necessarily – or exclusively – spatially defined, as it includes various forms of identity formation and cultural exchange that take place across and beyond nation state borders, both in real and cyber space. Trans-localism, as practised by the 'deterritorialised–reterritorialised' groups portrayed throughout this book, comes close to the concept of 'transnationalism from below', as outlined by Guarnizo and Smith (1998). However, unlike transnationalism from below, the trans-local groups are not necessarily actively and consciously involved in resisting globalisation as 'transnationalism from above', nor do the members of such groups aspire to become 'transnational subjects of a trans-territorial nation state' (Guarnizo and Smith 1998: 8–10). On the contrary, nation state structures may in fact be quite unaccommodating and even hostile to the existence and preservation of trans-local identities while, on the other hand, actively supporting state-sponsored transnational initiatives involving diaspora. Furthermore, as Lovell (1998: 1) points out, in the context of globalisation 'the interference between localised understanding of belonging, locale and identity often seem to conflict with wider national and international political, economic and social interests'. This is not to say that transnationalism is suddenly an irrelevant and outdated theoretical concept, or that it is going to be replaced by the new paradigm of trans-localism. Rather, I argue that trans-localism complements transnationalism, especially when debating forced displacement and the (re)construction and performance of local identities in refugee and migrant groups as exemplified by Bosnian war-torn and diasporic communities.

The snowballing method used in selecting my participants and research collaborators proved to be very helpful not only in connecting my sites in the search for trans-local within transnational, but also in terms of logistics in the field: wherever I went my Bosnian hosts made sure I was looked after and made me feel at home – very often in their own rented or mortgaged flats and houses. There, in diaspora, as a part of – or in addition to – their hospitality, they would also share their stories of displacement and demonstrate their cultural maintenance, mostly unaware of how much the local, 'foreign' culture and their new 'emplacement' had impacted on their 'Bosnianness'. Moving from site to site confirmed repeatedly that displaced Bosnians did not remain untouched by their experiences and new social surroundings – but neither did their memories of the 'old home' vanish. Though there has been a strong pressure to unite and promote an image of a monolithic worldwide Bosnian diaspora, in reality (like most other diasporas) the Bosnian diaspora displays a high degree of heterogeneity and fragmentation. In exchange for their stories, my informants asked me about 'our' compatriots I visited in other countries, and what life 'over there' was like for 'our people'. Typically, they would ask me about specific trans-local or *zavičaj* communities and people they personally knew: 'How many people from Srebrenica live in Melbourne?' 'Did you meet any people from Prijedor in Austria?' 'Do you know so-and-so?' 'How is the situation back in Klotjevac?'... Thus my multi-sited ethnography generated 'a sense of doing more than just ethnography'. I'd become a 'circumstantial activist' (Marcus 1998: 98–9), a sort of global Ale,[4] often passing on news, greetings, small presents and even remittances from one site to another. While their trans-local identities operated at emotional and embodied levels, the same groups would often tap into other collective identities that may be seen as more transnational or diasporic. In addition to trans-local 'us here' and 'us there', my informants would also regularly look for comparisons and would refer to other, broader diasporic groups of Bosnians as 'them there' (*kod njih tamo*) while making clear that 'us here' (*kod nas ovdje*) was reserved for their own diasporic community in the country and city they settled in. I looked for both similarities and differences between 'them there' and 'us here', constantly shifting the boundaries of the dichotomy. While I did not want to limit my research to concepts of territoriality – imagining at times that I was doing 'research without borders' – the geography of the Bosnians' displacement was an important factor that could not be ignored. And the best way to meaningfully engage with that geography was to get on the move and travel as if on a walkabout[5] in the 'good old days'. In this conclusion I'll begin the journey in Sweden.

Bosnian Vikings

It was a cold morning in mid February 2008 when I finally touched down at the airport Arlanda. This was my first visit to Sweden and, as I had anticipated, everything felt, sounded and looked Swedish – and not just the Scandinavian winter and landscape. At the airport I was greeted by my colleague Nino, once a Bosnian refugee and now a Swedish scholar. A few years earlier I had met Nino at a conference in Sarajevo and a year later I was his 'cultural' host during his two-week stay in Melbourne, where he was attending an international sociological conference.

Unlike many other collegial friendships I have developed over the years with a number of Bosnian and non-Bosnian scholars and researchers from across the globe, Nino's and my friendship goes beyond our academic interests. It was solidly grounded in our generational memory of growing up in Bosnia during the 1970s and 1980s – even though we did not know each other at the time. As 'generational insiders', we could easily identify members of our generation by speech, mannerisms, sense of humour and many other common cultural references that have become integral – and possibly core – parts of our Bosnian identities. Living outside of Bosnia was also something we had in common. While the second half of our lives had been taking place in two very different cultural settings, in two different hemispheres, in Australia and Sweden, the experiences have in both cases resulted in hybridisation – not merely hyphenation – of our identities.[6] As cultural hybrids we could relate to each other's experiences. However, we noticed that this was not the case with our friends who remained in Bosnia, for whom we needed to interpret and often simplify our experiences 'in the West'. With Nino, instead of tapping into our separate trans-local identities, we emphasised our common generational memory – a form of popular memory – and our new hybridised identities. Nonetheless, the trans-local aspects of who we were – and still are – resurfaced in our conversations more often than we might have anticipated.

That February morning Nino came to Arlanda to pick me up in his newly bought BMW. While I was joking about and complimenting his *nova machina* he was apologetic. Only a year before he could not have imagined himself as a BMW driver. Not because he could not afford it, but because he was ideologically against consumerism and luxury. He joked how he was a failure of the Swedish integration policy: after sixteen years of trying to become a Swede he had finally reverted to his true Bosnianness. Nino did indeed 'go Bosnian', in a way that confirms my trans-local thesis of people's attachment to their local place – a place made up of people and memories. While he had maintained a personal, social network involving a number of people from Sarajevo who lived in Sweden, Nino was also a role-model immigrant when it came to integration into Swedish society. However, after fifteen years of living his Swedish life, getting married, becoming a father and then getting divorced from his Swedish wife, Nino started making occasional visits to Sarajevo to visit his ailing parents. Being the only surviving child, he felt responsible for their wellbeing. During these visits he also reconnected with many of his old friends and neighbours back in Sarajevo. Through such networks he also reconnected with his former best friend's sister, Nina, who lived in the old neighbourhood. It was not long before they started a romantic relationship. Within a year they were married. Nina moved to Stockholm and their baby son was born. Now married to a woman from his old neighbourhood and making more frequent visits to Bosnia, Nino felt that he was expected to maintain his status 'back home' by driving a car that matched his position as a university professor in Sweden. For many decades the brand and type of car had been the measure of success of those working in the West, the Bosnian *Gastarbeiter*. For his old friends in Sarajevo, Nino's success in Sweden was seen as one of his adventures, another episode in his Bosnian life. It was easier for Nino to adjust to his old neighbours', friends' and family's perceptions of what it meant to work in the West than to explain that he actually was living in the West permanently, not merely working there temporarily – that his home was now in Sweden. So he reluctantly gave in, and adjusted to the comfort the brand new BMW afforded.

Nino took me to his workplace where he was teaching two days a week: the police academy. There I met some of his academic colleagues, and we had lunch together at the canteen, only a few civilians like me among hundreds of police graduates dressed in their blue uniforms. It was quite a novelty to see a former Bosnian refugee in charge of teaching Swedish police officers. Nino's academic authority was respected and he was in a position of power in relation to the Swedish law-enforcement officers. To my surprise, Nino told me that he also taught several Bosnian students who had graduated from the police academy. Over the coming weeks I was to experience many other situations that illustrated a high degree of integration of Bosnians into Swedish mainstream society: I met and learned about other Bosnian academics, teachers, artists, museum curators, chefs, businessmen, managers, police officers, footballers and politicians. Among the politicians, Amna (Anna) Ibrišagić has been the most prominent, but not the only 'Bosnian' politician in Sweden.[7] Within ten years of arriving in Sweden as a refugee from her ethnically cleansed home town of Sanski Most, Amna had become a Member of the Swedish Parliament, and in 2004 had moved to Brussels as a Member of the European Parliament. Her successful career as a politician is often used as evidence of the integration potential of Bosnians in this Nordic country (Vadchy 2005). Interestingly, Amna's political party, the Moderata Samlingspartiet (Moderate Coalition Party), is a centre-right, liberal conservative political party – the section of the political spectrum not traditionally friendly to immigrants. As Nino and other Bosnians in Sweden that I talked to stated, the party's ideological platform may put off Bosnian voters, who would otherwise vote for Amna, a fellow Bosnian. In the process of becoming a Swedish politician, Amna has, to a great extent, replaced her old *zavičaj* cohort with members of Sweden's political elite.

Asked about her personal sense of belonging, Amna gave a politically correct answer, saying she felt both Swedish and Bosnian. She also had practical – and again politically correct – advice to give to her fellow Bosnians in diaspora, extolling that the key factor for living a normal life in diaspora was to embrace and exercise their rights as both Bosnians and citizens of the country in which they settled. She spoke about Bosnians only in relation to their politically recognised identities, as dual citizens, dismissing the usefulness of their connection to trans-local *zavičaj* communities. 'Those who work only on preserving their Bosnianness,' she maintained, 'usually end up on the margins of society in the new country, while those who completely "abandon" their original background lose a half of themselves without ever gaining a hundred per cent of the "new" selves.'[8]

For high-flyers like Amna there was something outdated and peasant-like in trans-local identification that was of little use to someone wanting to build a career as a mainstream politician. However, while structural differences such as class, urban/rural origins, place of settlement and level of integration/assimilation into the host society are reflected in the level of participation in trans-local networks, in terms that some of those 'at the top' (like Amna) – from an urban background, middle/upper class, well integrated/assimilated – are less likely to identify with the trans-local groups – many other examples (as described in Chapter 4) show that intellectuals, artists and successful businessmen have very often been the key people involved in the formation of trans-local networks.

The Bosnian conquest of mainstream Sweden personified by Amna in the political sphere, continued in 2009: two more Bosnians joined Zlatan Ibrahimović, the famous Swedish footballer of Bosnian descent, as national celebrities; Azra Duliman, a Mostar-born law student, was crowned 'Miss Sweden 2009'; and Mehmed Jakić, a musician from Sarajevo, made it into the finals of the popular television contest *Sweden's Idol 2009*. These and similar success stories have become an important part of the new collective narrative of Bosnians living in Sweden, both at the level of their trans-local communities, as well as at the level of Swedish Bosnians in general. Ordinary 'Bosnian Swedes' fervently identify with their fellow Bosnians' successes, appropriating these successes as their common cultural capital. As Gaca, one of my informants in Sweden, observed, 'The Swedes believe that all Bosnians are good at football, music and politics, and many Bosnians pretend to fit these stereotypes.' The success of the Bosnians at the top is fairly well matched by the high degree of integration of the less visible, ordinary Bosnians in regional Sweden, in smaller towns and cities, like Eskilstuna and Karlskrona, where the impact of trans-localism is even more evident.

An industrial town with some 90,000 inhabitants, located 120 kilometres west of Stockholm, over the last eighteen years Eskilstuna has become home to several hundred Bosnians. According to my informant, Vedad Begović, a former Bosnian refugee from Brčko and since 2004 an integration officer at Eskilstuna's local council, even though Eskilstuna has not become one of the big Bosnian centres, Bosnians who have settled here are representative of the overall integration of Bosnians into Swedish society. In this multicultural town, home to seventy-five different nationalities, in terms of employment, level of education and many other integration indicators, Bosnians are in second place, just after Danes.

Most Bosnians in Eskilstuna come from the Podrinje region. The trans-local networks ensured that *Podrinjci* (people from Podrinje) who became refugees and IDPs continued to migrate to Sweden well after this country closed its borders to Bosnian migrants/refugees. Marriages and other forms of sponsorship proved once again that locally embedded solidarities could bend even rigid immigration policies. In their three-bedroom apartment, furnished and decorated in what could be regarded as a typically Bosnian style – with an abundance of handmade tapestry with Bosnian motifs and meticulously arranged china coffee cups and decorative crystal glasses in the main living room – Mima and Enko shared their trans-local story with me.

At the age of twenty-four and heavily pregnant with her first child, Mima survived the 1995 Srebrenica genocide, where she lost her husband, her only brother and a number of relatives. She gave birth to her daughter Belma in Tuzla a month after her husband perished. In December 1995, with the assistance of a relative who had lived in Sweden since 1992, Mima and her four-month-old baby arrived in Eskilstuna. Soon after, she and her daughter were recognised as genuine refugees, with the right to settle in Sweden. Enko, at the time a 26-year-old man from Podrinje, arrived in Sweden illegally four years after Mima, in a sealed container of a truck, packed with some other forty Bosnian, Kosovar and Middle Eastern would-be refugees. Something went wrong. It took much longer than expected to cross all the borders and the illegal trip to freedom and better opportunities turned into a nightmare in which a 22-year-old fellow Bosnian refugee from Podrinje suffocated. Enko and many other 'passengers' lost consciousness and were saved only at the last moment. For months Enko was recovering from his ordeal in one of Sweden's asylum-seeker centres in Norrköping. During this time Mima and Enko met through Mima's relative and Enko's friend and commenced a romantic liaison. But, a year after arriving illegally in Sweden, Enko was deported back to Bosnia. The relationship continued, with Mima visiting Enko in Tuzla, where they got married. Within a year Enko was back in Sweden, this time legally as Mima's spouse. A year later their son Erik was born. Both feel that the birth of their son was the symbolic start of their new lives in Sweden. Mima and Enko both work in a warehouse in Eskilstuna and live the more or less ordinary lives of the Swedish working class – like the majority of Bosnians in Sweden. Their contacts with fellow Bosnians in Sweden have been mainly, but not exclusively, with other *Podrinjci* living in Eskilstuna, nearby Norrköping, Örebro and other places in Sweden. The first Saturday of each month Eskilstuna *Podrinjci* and those living in this part of Sweden travel to Norrköping to attend the regular monthly *Podrinje zabava*, a social event involving music, food and the company of other *Podrinjci*. Bringing local Podrinje bands and performers from Bosnia to *Podrinje zabava* in Sweden has increasingly become a popular trans-local trend. These bands perform a distinct Podrinje style of folk music, also known as *izvorna muzika*. Podrinje *izvorna muzika* involves instruments like *saz, tambura,* violin and accordion, but it also revolves round very distinct *zavičaj* themes like the river Drina, names of villages in Podrinje, and old local rituals, as well as more recent themes like the Srebrenica genocide and forced migration from Podrinje. In order to bring to Sweden these Podrinje musicians – like the popular *izvorna muzika* bands Sateliti, and Zvorničko Sijelo, that also tour Podrinje communities in Melbourne and St. Louis – *Podrinjci* from Eskilstuna, Norrköping and Örebro collect money and share the costs of travel, accommodation and payment. So far the demand for such bands to perform at these and similar Podrinje events has been bigger than the bands can accommodate.

Some five hundred kilometres to the south of Eskilstuna is Karlskrona, a small, picturesque naval city of some 60,000 inhabitants. It is listed on the UNESCO World Heritage List. As in Stockholm and Eskilstuna, I spent memorable moments with Bosnians who had settled in Karlskrona. They welcomed me not only into their homes, but also into their workplaces, clubs, associations, schools and social events – some of them specially organised to honour my visit and to assist with my research. The trans-local communities that make up the Bosnian diaspora in Karlskrona come mainly from the western Bosnian towns of Banja Luka, Prijedor and Prnjavor, a part of Bosnia also known as Krajina.[9] The fact that all these communities come from the same broader region of western Bosnia has led to the development of a distinct, regional identity of the Bosnian diaspora in Karlskrona. What is also striking about the Bosnian presence in this historical and cultural jewel of southern Sweden is the extent to which, quite disproportionate to their actual numbers in the city, Bosnians feature in Karlskrona's cultural scene.

I was given a tour of the Maritime Museum and a history lesson about the Swedish navy by a group of (western) Bosnian high school students and their Bosnian teacher Gaca, a curator at the Museum. While I could hear, and understand, their distinct Krajina dialect – different from the Bosnian I spoke – during this tour I became even more aware of my outsider role in relation to my hosts, who, through their narrative performance, positioned themselves as insiders, making personal connections with the history of their new country. This was especially obvious when my tour guides used the terms 'we', 'us' and 'our' to refer to Sweden and its history. But, then again, they displayed a degree of pride when, amongst thousands of exhibits – some dating back several hundred years – they showed me a mini submarine made in Sarajevo during the Yugoslav era. This object had a symbolic value to them as a material link between their old and new histories and identities, as if to say: in 'our' Swedish history there is also something from 'our' old country. The history lesson I was given by these teenage Swedish Krajina Bosnians effectively intersected at different local/ regional, national and transnational levels.

Much more than a single piece of history from the 'old' country was to be found in the Museum Leonardo da Vinci Ideale, one of Karlskrona's more recent and unavoidable tourist curiosities.[10] Located in the renovated Water Castle, constructed in 1863 in Karlskrona's main square – the biggest in Scandinavia and the second biggest square in Europe – the museum exhibits a collection of Renaissance to modernist art, including the original version of *The Nativity*, a formerly missing work by Leonardo da Vinci. At least that is the claim of the museum's director and owner of the famed art collection, Rizah Kulenović, a Bosnian painter and aristocrat born in 1947 in Zenica and living in Karlskrona since the early 1970s. Rizah claims that his ancestry goes back to Kulin Ban, the legendary ruler of Bosnia from 1180 to 1204. I was as impressed by Rizah's stories of the history of the Kulenović family's 500-year-old art collection as I was by the tri-dimensional and kinaesthetic effects of *The Nativity*. While he was giving me a private tour through his gallery, I could not escape the feeling that there was something very Bosnian in the whole aristocratic ambience and the way the story was narrated. He proved to be not only an artist who specialised in reverse glass painting and turnings – and in that way able to create something real out of his imagination – he was also skilled at turning parts of reality into a narrative that required his audience's imagination to be fully appreciated. There was a plot – or many plots – to the story about the Bosnian Kulenović family, from medieval Bosnia and Kulin Ban to fifteenth-century Venice and Leonardo da Vinci, through the Ottoman Empire to the more recent history of Bosnia, and the migration of the Kulenovićs and tens of thousands of other Bosnians to Sweden. In the narrative about his family, Rizah connected most of the known history of Bosnia and its people. As he told me, his family's treasure – the art collection comprising several Renaissance and modern paintings and various other artefacts, many of which come from Kulenović's home town of Zenica – was saved over many centuries at different locations only to be entrusted to Rizah before the outbreak of war in Bosnia in 1992. Many different (be)longings and memories intersect in Kulenović's museum and his stories. While there is a clear trans-local element to them (artefacts and carpets from Zenica, the Kulenović family history), Rizah's sense of *zavičaj* goes beyond his embodied memories and social networks from the modern-day city of Zenica to encompass the glorious past of Kulin Ban and the family Kulenović. In the narrative he constructs – and performs – local is elevated to, and beyond, national and transnational levels. In Rizah's narrative, seemingly binary concepts like history and mythology, past and present, fiction and reality, arts and crafts, displacement and emplacement, and homeland and exile all serve important functions in interconnecting people, places and events – placing them in an in-between space at the Museum Leonardo da Vinci Ideale.

The popular Restaurant Montmartre is another Kulenović territory in Karlskrona. Owned and managed by Rizah's younger brother Senad Kulenović, a former Bosnian refugee and another great storyteller with an exceptional sense of humour, the restaurant offers mostly Mediterranean-style food. As Senad told me, it was much easier to sell 'multicultural' south European food to his Swedish guests than to 'educate' them about the local Bosnian cuisine. However, Restaurant Montmartre is also regularly turned into a typical Bosnian pub (*kafana*) for private Bosnian functions, like weddings and birthday parties, and when other *Zeničani* (people from Zenica) living in Scandinavia visit the Kulenović brothers. On such special occasions, Lars, the native Swedish chef at the restaurant, turns into an expert in traditional Bosnian cuisine, skilled even in traditional local Zenica dishes like *zenički čimbur*, adding to the Bosnian and Zenican atmosphere in Karlskrona.

Bosnian Midwesterners

A few weeks later I was discovering a similar Bosnian atmosphere on the other side of the Atlantic, in St. Louis, Missouri – 'the Mecca of the Bosnian diaspora'. Home to many Bosnian restaurants such as Bosna Gold, Berix, Laganini, Grbić Restaurant, and The Lucky Duck, St. Louis has become the main hub of the Bosnian worldwide diaspora, with some 70,000 Bosnian refugees. Most migrated there during the 1990s. While the large-scale migration from BiH to the U.S. ceased in the early 2000s, the number of Bosnians in St. Louis has been steadily increasing due to internal Bosnian migration, as many Bosnians living in other parts of the U.S. decide to move there. Fifty-six-year-old Šukrija Džidžović is one such internal migrant. He arrived in the U.S. in early 1995 and, after living for ten years in New York where he worked as a labourer and doorman in order to be able to finance his Bosnian weekly newspaper *Sabah*, Šukrija moved to St. Louis in 2005 with his wife Mirsada and their daughter Ertana. In St. Louis he had to compete with another two Bosnian newspapers, *Diaspora bošnjačka* and *Peta Strana Svijeta*, but he still felt he had made a good business decision. The much lower costs of housing and running a business as well as the large number of Bosnians living in St. Louis were good enough reasons to justify his move. Being able to greet so many people in his native language while walking down the street was something no amount of money could buy. A cosmopolitan at heart, he nonetheless figured that the chances of his 24-year-old daughter meeting a prospective Bosnian husband would be much higher here than in New York. Ideally, he would prefer his future son-in-law to be someone from Sarajevo, his old home city, but he would accept any Bosnian rather than a non-Bosnian. 'Our home is going to slip away from us,' he told me, 'if we don't preserve it at home.'

Walking down Gravois Avenue in the St. Louis suburb of Bevo, one cannot escape the visual, acoustic and even olfactory signs of the overwhelming Bosnian presence here: many shops like *mesnica* (butcher), *buregdžinica* (pastry shop) and *aščinica* (small restaurant) have names written only in Bosnian, while the aromas of traditional Bosnian fast food like *ćevapčići* (grilled minced-meat sausages), *ražnjići* (shish kebab), *burek* (meat pie) and *zeljanica* (spinach pie), as well as the more demanding Bosnian specialties like *sogan dolma* (stuffed onions), *bosanski lonac* (Bosnian minestrone soup with meat) and *sarma* (cabbage rolls) drift from some of the many restaurants in the main street. Unlike Montmartre in Karlskrona, it seems that the restaurant owners in St. Louis do not worry much about 'educating' their consumers about Bosnian cuisine as most of the guests are Bosnians anyway. In fact, the Bosnian population of St. Louis exceeds that of the whole Karlskrona population, so there is no market pressure to adjust to the tastes of those who might prefer some other cuisine. Background Bosnian tunes – *sevdah*, pop and rock – completed the 'Baščaršija[11] experience' of St. Louis. Just like in Bosnia, people sit in the crowded terraces of the cafes, sipping their espressos, cappuccinos and Bosnian coffee. There seems to be much more laughter than on an average American street. Many parallel conversations go on, even between people sitting in front of different cafes across the street. All this suggests that Bosnians feel truly at home here. However, to go beneath the surface of this Baščaršija experience, sitting at one of the tables and listening to conversations taking place, distinct local Bosnian dialects mixed with American-English slang can be heard. If those speaking different dialects were asked what they thought of each other, one would hear jokes and comments about 'them' speaking improper Bosnian, having weird cultural practices, and other 'othering' observations. The local loyalties and divisions can also be 'head-counted' at these tables, with different cafes and restaurants mostly relying on their *zavičaj* compatriots as clientele. The restaurant Berix, for instance, is unofficially known as the *Podrinje kafana*; a hundred metres away the café-restaurant Laganini is its Prijedor counterpart. It comes as no surprise that the owners of these restaurants come from Podrinje and Prijedor respectively.

After compulsory initiation into the wider Bosnian St. Louis community through attending different community events, interviewing successful Bosnian businessmen and community leaders, and eating too much of all the authentic Bosnian food made in the U.S., in the following weeks I was able to map and engage with different trans-local groups. While there are several such groups in St. Louis I focused on the two largest trans-local groups – Podrinje and Prijedor – and two smaller trans-local village communities – Klotjevac and Mahoje – (described in Chapters 1 and 4). It is estimated that more than half of the Bosnian diaspora in St. Louis comes from the Podrinje region, making St. Louis the largest Podrinje community in the world (Hemon 2006; Huremović 2006; Matsuo 2005). I was especially warmly welcomed by Halćo Mešanović, the older son of Dule Mešanović from the Podrinje village of Klotjevac, described in Chapter 1. Halćo and his family insisted on being my primary hosts, and over the following weeks their home became my research base. Today there are more *Klotivljani* living in St. Louis than in post-war Klotjevac. In addition to the Mešanovićs, there are members of five other families from Klotjevac – Bečić, Sulejmanović, Selimović, Izmirlić and Efendić – living in St. Louis. They all live in the same neighbourhood, mixing with hundreds of other refugees from the Srebrenica region (Podrinje) whom they personally know and with whom they identify. On a number of occasions I organised presentations of the collections of photos from towns and villages in Podrinje I had taken during my fieldwork in Bosnia. It was a moving experience for many who, sometimes for the first time in many years, saw their original places – or what was left of them – and their old neighbours and relatives. During these photographic presentations many people added their own stories to the pictures. 'No way would I be able to recognise the village!' 'This is the place where so-and-so was killed by a shell.' 'This is the front yard of my house, but there is no house.' 'This is where we used to swim,' and so on. Here, in the predominantly Bosnian suburb of Bevo, in Mešanović's freshly renovated weatherboard house, their shared memories of pre-war *zavičaj*, war and displacement intersected with their new realities and emplacement far away from the homes that once were.

The new shared neighbourhood provides *Klotivljani* with the context for nourishing memories of their old shared *zavičaj*. They still refer to each other with the toponyms, nicknames and names of kinship groups from the 'home over there'. While they imagine their *zavičaj* to be over there in Klotjevac, I observed how much of that *zavičaj* they had (re)constructed in St. Louis. They have not only bought and rented their new homes in geographic proximity but have re-enacted many local practices in diaspora. These include regular evening visits, *sijelo*, at least on the weekends when they have more time. During the *sijelo*, which takes place at someone else's home each time, *Klotivljani* update each other with the news from their everyday lives, exchange information about other *Klotivljani* in one of the many destinations in Europe, Australia and Northern America, and engage in the process of remembering and reimagining their *zavičaj* through sharing stories and anecdotes about people and events they remember. They reread emails and go over the photos they receive via the internet from other *Klotivljani*, and sometimes they connect directly through webcams with other *Klotivljani* sitting in their homes in Atlanta, Melbourne, Sarajevo, Vienna, Utrecht, Örebro, Hamburg ... But there are also more embodied, and more traditional performances of *zavičaj* identity taking place at such *sijelo*. One of them is *igranje prstena* (ring game), a social game from Klotjevac which, in the second half of the twentieth century, was almost completely replaced by more modern forms of evening entertainment, namely watching television and listening to the radio. The game has been revived and given new meaning in faraway St. Louis. Based on guessing under which upturned *fildžan* (small coffee cup) a ring – usually a wedding ring – is hidden, the game can be played individually or in pairs. There are no limits to the actual number of players; the availability of coffee cups decides the number of players. In the old days in Klotjevac, those going to *sijelo* would take their own *fildžan* with them to ensure their participation in the game. Then the game was popular among young people who would use it as a cover for romantic liaisons (*ašikovanje*) between unmarried young men and women. Here in St. Louis, in addition to communication via the internet, playing the ring game is yet another enactment of a distinct Klotjevac *zavičaj* identity. However, the trans-local Klotjevac community in St. Louis fulfils not only the sentimental attachment to a place, but also many other practical needs based on reciprocity and mutual support. This includes 'road assistance', as many Podrinje men now in St. Louis, including those from Klotjevac, work as truck drivers and help each other if there are any issues on the road. Knowing that they can rely on each other gives them confidence, and possibly an advantage, in this tough and competitive profession. St. Louis *Klotivljani* maintain a reciprocal relationship in other forms of support and labour exchange, such as repairing each other's cars and renovating houses, two common *moba* (helping out) activities taking place in the trans-local Klotjevac communities.

Halćo has also found his piece of the Drina, his *zavičaj* river, on the banks of the Mississippi river, where he spends any free time he manages to get from work. It was a special, almost ritualistic event when he initiated me into his 'therapy', as he calls it. To me the Mississippi looked huge, nothing even remotely like any river I was so close to before, and definitely not much like the Drina. However, Halćo felt differently about being here: 'When I'm here I get lost and often feel like I am on the Drina in Klotjevac. Sometimes I even wait for my father to call my name and tell me to get home to do some work.'

That day Halćo caught a huge catfish, not the kind of fish he used to catch in Drina; nonetheless, he referred to the fish as *som*, a fish found in the Klotjevac lake. He complained about not being able to come here as often as he would like to. Sometimes it takes him many months before he gets an opportunity to indulge his 'Drina experience'. He told me how he was recently required to work six months without a single day off. Working in one of the largest flour mills in this part of the U.S. means that the demand for flour – and over the last several years this has included an increase in demand from countries like Iraq – dictates the tempo, with not much space to negotiate leisure time. Halćo's American story, if told from his position as a migrant worker, very much fits the common stereotype about Bosnians in the U.S.A. not requiring any civilian clothing as their life circulates between work uniforms and pyjamas – working and sleeping – illustrating the capitalist reality of the migrant working class in this and many other countries. However, Halćo does not identify so much with his job or with any other forms of 'outside' identity. Having coffee, or more often a beer, with his *zavičaj*, relying on his social network for support, catching a catfish á la Drina, provides him with a deep sense of belonging to a familiar home. At the same time, one could argue that it acts as a brake on developing a more relevant and meaningful political consciousness in terms of his life situation as American migrant working class. Thus, while it has many positive aspects, if not balanced well with other competing identities, trans-localism could be seen as a hindering factor in the process of migrants' integration, as implied by the Swedish politician Amna Ibrišagić (Vadchy 2005).

However, what is sometimes seen as successful integration can reflect the dominant – not necessarily progressive – values and prejudices of the host society. So, for instance, rather than developing a strong working class consciousness, as one might expect from people who have spent a large part of their life in socialist Yugoslavia, many Bosnians in St. Louis have 'gone white', rediscovering their Europeanness and commonality with broader American identities beyond the Bosnian community. To many, that European identity is strengthened by the European character of Bevo, the St. Louis suburb established by German immigrants around the 1840s, now the most densely populated Bosnian urban space outside Bosnia. Indeed, thousands of Bosnians who settled in Bevo came to the U.S. via Germany where they had spent up to ten years as temporary refugees, finding safety working and connecting with the German language, culture and people. The German presence in Bevo, mostly reduced to street names like Beethoven Avenue, Schiller Place and Eichelberger Street, gave 'German Bosnians' a feeling of familiarity and helped them imagine they were worthy bearers of European continuity in the area. They also discovered that the U.S. is still a deeply racially segregated society. The segregation is especially visible in the urban spaces with many known black-only and white-only neighbourhoods in areas with a large Bosnian presence like St. Louis, Chicago and Atlanta. A Bosnian businessman and community leader, who gave me a tour of St. Louis, pointed to a Mississippi canal, explaining, 'we are on this side and they are over there … we hardly mix.' It took me a while to figure out that 'us' in this context refers to the whites and 'them' the Afro-Americans.

Apart from attaching pride to their skin colour, a number of Bosnians I spent time with in St. Louis displayed some other stereotypical American values, like being fervent Republicans, supporting the death penalty and believing that the right to carry arms reduces crime in the country. Weapons, they argued, were the best deterrent from violence and had they had arms in Bosnia they would have been able to defend themselves and not become refugees and victims. This sentiment – never raised in my encounters with any other Bosnian diasporic group outside the U.S. – is widely shared within the Bosnian community in St. Louis, for whom becoming the victim would not be an acceptable option ever again. Thus, identifying with and being accepted as part of the dominant (white) section of the population acts almost as an insurance – at least at a psychological level – against possible victimisation in their new homeland. However, while they are eager to live the 'American way of life', and thus 'turn white' if necessary, as Franz (2005: 126) argues, 'America's complex ambivalence towards the newcomers does not allow for swift integration but leaves them, instead, in a mental state of displacement often for decades'.

American flags displayed on verandas of many Bosnian homes in St. Louis are clear signs that they do not want to stand out as a minority. This trend has especially increased since 9/11 and President Bush's rhetoric of 'either with us or against us'. For many Bosnians, repressing the unpopular Muslim aspects of their identities and becoming 'invisible Muslims' serves to make them more visible as white Europeans and Americans (Coughlan 2005, 2011; Coughlan and Owens-Manley 2006). In addition to Franz's study of Bosnians in the U.S., Val Colic-Peisker (2005) and Nadje Al-Ali (2002) have described how Bosnian refugees, especially Bosnian Muslims, emphasise their whiteness and Europeanness, as opposed to their Muslim and refugee identities, in Australia and in Western Europe respectively. In her article '"At least you're the right colour": Identity and social inclusion of Bosnian refugees in Australia', Colic-Peisker (2005) argues that the Australian resettlement of Bosnian refugees – who constitute the largest recent refugee group in Australia – was influenced by them being favourably assessed by immigration officials as having 'settlement potential' because of their white European background. However, while being white – and thus invisible in the predominantly white Australia – gave Bosnians an 'entry advantage', it did not translate into comparative advantage in the labour market; coming come from a non-English-speaking background, most of them have ended up in jobs for which they are overqualified. Nonetheless, as she argues, 'the mainstream perception of Bosnians as white Europeans and their own self-perception as "whites in a white country" [did] impact on their early identity reconstruction' (Colic-Peisker 2005: 621). Similarly, Al-Ali describes how Bosnian Muslim refugees she interviewed in the U.K. and the Netherlands insist on their Europeanness, claiming that 'Bosnian Islam was different from Islam in other parts of the world' and remarking, 'We are European as much as we are Muslim' (Al-Ali 2002: 256).

The 'Americanisation' of Bosnian refugees in St. Louis has been a two-way process, with Bosnians adopting and displaying the dominant American values and cultural norms but also directly influencing the dominant, adopted community. As in many other places where they settled over the years, Bosnians in St. Louis share their stories and their memories with those from outside their *zavičaj* network and Bosnian diaspora – with the mainstream host community. Bosnian stories have become a part of St. Louis' new narrative, and regularly feature in the local St. Louis newspaper, the *STL Today*, under the section 'Bringing Bosnia Home: A continuing look at Bosnian immigrants in St. Louis'.[12] The stories have also been explored by mainstream artists. Playwright Cristina Pippa, for instance, combined a number of oral histories with her own observations to tell a Bosnian story in her play, *Little Bosnia*, based on the lives of St. Louis Bosnians, generally perceived as 'one of the largest cultural groups in the city' (Truckey 2008). The play, about identity and home, includes Bosnian and non-Bosnian actors, and goes beyond the usual pathos of refugee life in exile and includes a good dose of Bosnian-style humour as well as local particularities of St. Louis Bosnians from Podrinje and Prijedor. So popular was the play among the members of the Bosnian community that it quickly sold out for the whole of the 2008 season.

Other forms of storytelling have also reached out to the wider St. Louis public. In 2007 the exhibition *Prijedor: Lives from the Bosnian Genocide* was opened at the Holocaust Museum and Learning Center in St. Louis. The exhibition provides a chronology of atrocities in Prijedor beginning in 1992, focusing on the experience of concentration-camp survivors who now live in St. Louis, and including 'narrative accounts of life before, during and after the war, the concentration camp sites in and around the city, and the search for the missing' (McCarthy 2007). The exhibition also includes a number of material objects and personal belongings of survivors and those who perished – like a pair of worn-out boots, a brown jumper and family photos that once belonged to microbiologist Kemal Cerić, who was among Prijedor's more than 200 intelligentsia killed in the summer of 1992. The author Rezak Hukanović, a prominent Prijedor survivor and returnee to

Prijedor, came to visit his fellow *Prijedorčani* (citizens of Prijedor) in St. Louis to express his support and contribute to the memorialisation of the Prijedor tragedy both in diaspora and back in Bosnia. Like Rezak, many St. Louis *Prijedorčani* attending the exhibition were both visitors and hosts, and even 'walking exhibits' as survivors who contextualised what was on display with their own stories. The exhibition provided the survivors with a context in which they could share their stories and have the hardship they went through recognised. In fact, many of the stories told here were told publicly for the first time. The exhibition also provided the Prijedor survivors with a public space to affirm their identity as *Prijedorčani*. Beyond this, the exhibition brought acknowledgement of and respect for the Prijedor trans-local community by other Bosnian communities in St. Louis, including from Podrinje – who not only acknowledged *Prijedorčani* as survivors but also respected them for being able to organise such an important mainstream event to tell the story of their shattered *zavičaj*.

Similarly, members of the trans-local community of Podrinje have been commemorating their lost *zavičaj*. Like Halćo Mešanović, who lost three uncles and his grandfather, almost all St. Louis' *Podrinjci* were directly or indirectly affected by the 1995 Srebrenica genocide; and their shared tragedy has become a strong point for their collective identification with Srebrenica. The Association of Survivors of the Srebrenica Genocide in St. Louis, their formal organisation through which they have been commemorating their personal and communal tragedy, has institutionalised Srebrenica Remembrance Day on 11 July. In July 2005, at the tenth anniversary commemoration of the Srebrenica genocide, the Missouri House of Representatives issued official *House Resolution No. 3934*,[13] recognising the Srebrenica genocide, followed by a proclamation issued by Francis G. Slay, Mayor of the City of St. Louis, declaring 11 July 'Srebrenica Remembrance Day in Saint Louis'.[14] Since then Srebrenica Remembrance Day has been commemorated each year as an official public event in St. Louis.

Through these recognitions and public acknowledgements the stories of Prijedor and Srebrenica survivors in St. Louis have moved from the realm of 'popular memories' to official, public memories, in the process gaining new meanings, new audiences and new interpretations. The fact that local Bosnian collective memory has become part of the local American collective consciousness is seen as a significant symbolic achievement by survivors – and the Bosnian diaspora in St. Louis – as well as a clear indicator of Bosnian integration into St. Louis' mainstream society. However, this official, once-a-year event could also be seen as a form of instrumental multiculturalism from above, used by local mainstream politicians to appeal to migrants' marginal – or not so marginal – constituencies. While there is a public acknowledgement of and an expression of solidarity with the survivors of genocide on this one day in a year, on the other 364 days the survivors can remain invisible white European migrants/newly emerging Americans, swallowed by the detached capitalist system as a readily available labour force, often working prolonged shifts under conditions that an average mainstream American would not tolerate. However, in terms of the argument of this book, this interpretation does not detract from the organisational and experiential significance of trans-localism among the Bosnian diaspora of St. Louis – or from the continuing pull of *zavičaj* identification.

Leaving St. Louis, I carried with me not only amazing stories, fond memories and data to process, but also dozens of photographs and U.S.$800 which Halćo asked me to pass on to his relatives. U.S.$300 and half of the photos were destined for Halćo's three cousins living in Adelaide, Australia, whom he last saw as toddlers in 1992 when they left the village with their mother. The other photos and U.S.$500 were for Halćo's father Dule back in Klotjevac, whom I would meet again some six months after I left St. Louis. While there were many other, faster ways to transfer money to his relatives, for Halćo the human dimension of handing over the gifts could not be matched by any instant electronic transaction. Money handed over by me to the intended recipients had more than just monetary value: its function was to supplement my stories about Halćo and his life in the U.S. and to act as proof of his generosity and emotional attachment to his relatives. Another function was undoubtedly to impress me, a non-family 'insider', who would meet face-to-face many other *Klotivljani* in the following months. Halćo's implicit message to other *Klotivljani* was that he is still a loyal 'insider'. Later on, Halćo and other *Klotivljani* living in St. Louis confirmed their attachment to their village by donating money for building the monument (described in the introduction and Chapter 1) to their perished fellow *Klotivljani*, which was officially unveiled in July 2009.

Vienna Blues

Over the years Vienna has been an important place on my personal map, a research site at the crossroads of all my other research sites. During my many short and long stays here I have witnessed changes, adjustments, personal crises and successes, as well as just time passing by with no significant changes in my informants' lives. The closeness of BiH made the life of Bosnian refugees in Austria different from those who settled in other, more remote countries. As Barbara Franz (2002, 2005: 9–10) has described, Bosnian refugees in Austria have followed the guest-worker pattern, suggesting a temporary approach to their settlement in Austria; while the Austrian government sees this pattern as successful economic integration of former de facto refugees. However, economic integration has not only been insufficient for effecting overall social integration but has also been changing and temporary in itself. Nonetheless, while full integration of Bosnian refugees into wider Austrian society remains fairly limited, there are clear trans-local settlement patterns to be found here too, some of which have been described in Chapter 4. In this chapter I will reflect on the *zavičaj* community of Zvornik, the largest deterritorialised Bosnian trans-local group in Vienna (also described in Chapter 2).

Zvornik is another Podrinje town that was ethnically cleansed of its dominant ethnic group, Bosniaks, who made up 60 per cent – compared to 38 per cent ethnic Serbs – of Zvornik's 81,000-strong population. By the end of June 1992 Zvornik was close to 100 per cent Serbian (Tretter et al. 1994). One of the first and most efficiently executed ethnic cleansing campaigns in the Bosnian war, it impressed even Samuel Huntington (1996: 272), who used it as a point of reference for his highly controversial thesis on the clash of cultures (Halilovich 2004). The Bosniak civilians who were not killed, and who did not manage to escape to one of the nearby Bosnian government-controlled areas, were put on cargo trains and buses to Subotica, a town in Vojvodina, on the border between Serbia and Hungary. Via Hungary, some 20,000 Zvornik survivors of this ethnic cleansing reached Austria in summer 1992. Most of them settled – i.e., were accommodated in refugee hostels – in and around Vienna, where many of them remain to this day. The strong presence of the Zvornik pre-war *Gastarbeiter* (guest worker) community was an important factor as to why so many Zvornik refugees chose Austria – and Vienna in particular – as their preferred destination.

While over the last seventeen years their status has legally changed from de facto refugees to *Gastarbeiter* to, more recently, Austrian citizens, in reality many of the displaced *Zvorničani* (those from Zvornik) are still where they were when they first arrived in Austria: working in underpaid jobs for which they are usually overqualified, living in almost ghettoised *Ausländer* (foreigner) parts of the city, building and/or exchanging houses and flats in their old homeland – in which they do not live for most of the year – for alternative locations dominated by their own ethnic group. Thus, many Viennese *Zvorničani* are effectively living multiple temporary lives: firstly, as Austrian and EU citizens because of the Austrian passports they obtained through the naturalisation process; secondly, as *Ausländer* (foreigners) and *Gastarbeiter* (guest workers) in Vienna, as that's really how their host community perceives them and how in most cases they experience their life in Austria; thirdly, as 'newcomers' (*došljaci* or *došlje*), not unlike IDPs in Bosnia, who have never returned to their original ethnically cleansed places but have settled in the towns in the Federation closest to Zvornik, in places like Živinice, Tuzla and Srebrenik; fourthly, and, in the eyes of home(land)-

based Bosnian nationalists, as *dijasporci* (a pejorative term for those living outside of BiH) – those who have exchanged the poverty of their homeland for the prestigious West. But it's not only the nationalists who ostracise those who fled and are now temporarily or permanently returning to Bosnia. Even the ordinary stayee population, as Stefansson (2004a: 58) argues, 'at best regards them as innocent victims who had been violently expelled from their homes, at worst the traitors who had voluntarily fled instead of engaging in the defence'.

To paraphrase Jasna Čapo Žmegač (1999, 2007), they remain 'strangers either way'. For many of them, like the Nuhanovićs described below and in Chapter 2, the intimate spaces of home and *zavičaj* as well as their lived reality have for a long time been taking place in these different, temporary in-between spaces as they remember and wait for missing relatives.

In August 2009, for the second time that year, the 55-year-old uncle of Sejo Nuhanović – whose story features in Chapter 2 – was unemployed; Huso Nuhanović was again on *štemplovanje* (unemployment benefit). Huso blamed Polish workers for losing his job as they 'overflowed Austria' and worked for much lower wages than the local Austrian workers. He was not amused when Sejo made a joke about how Huso, 'as an Austrian', felt about those *Ausländer*. Since escaping from Belgrade in 1992, where he had been employed as a supervisor in a building company for some twenty years, Huso had worked as a labourer in dozens of different construction companies in Austria. Many of his colleagues in these firms had been his fellow *Zvorničani*. They helped each other find and keep jobs, as many, like Huso, did not speak sufficient German to get the best deals for themselves. Huso's work required flexibility as the construction sites were spread all over Austria. The presence of other *Zvorničani* made such situations more bearable. After a long, hard, working day, he would most often sleep in the barracks at the site and come 'home' to Vienna only at weekends. There, in Vienna's Tenth *Bezirk*, in an old, neglected building packed with other *Ausländer*, he had been living with his wife Fata, a part-time cleaner, and their surviving younger son Senahid, a truck driver. The building in which they have been living for most of the previous seventeen years looked as if it had not undergone any significant upgrade since it was built about a hundred years ago: tenants still shared communal bathrooms, while in winter the whole building smelled of diesel as each flat used old-fashioned diesel heaters.

In 2006 Senahid, then in his early twenties, married Amela, a Bosnian girl he met through family connections. Amela, displaced in 1992 from her village in Podrinje where Senahid's mother Fata came from, had grown up as an IDP near Tuzla. Senahid brought Amela from Bosnia to live with him in Vienna. There were two weddings, the first big and expensive – with

400 guests packed under two large tents, entertained by two music bands and served an abundance of food and drinks – in Bosnia, in the town of Živinice, where many Zvornik IDPs had turned their temporary refuge into a 'durable solution' and where the Nuhanovićs, like many other diaspora *Zvorničani*, had built a house after the war. A few days later a smaller wedding celebration for the Zvornik *zavičaj* community was held at a Bosnian restaurant in Vienna. Enlarged by a new family member, changed from a nuclear into an extended family, the Nuhanovićs managed to rent another one-bedroom flat on the same floor in the building. It was important to them to remain close. A year later Huso and Fata became grandparents to a baby boy Senad, named after their older son, who had been taken away from their home in June 1992, together with Huso's brother Džemal, Sejo's father, and more than 600 other people from the Zvornik villages of Kaludrani, Klisa, Đulići and surrounding hamlets. Senad was a seventeen-year-old high school student at the time. As Dženana Karup-Druško (2009b) notes, the massacre in Zvornik was a 'little Srebrenica', alluding to the 1995 genocide. While some 350 bodies have been recovered from two mass graves near Zvornik, both Senad and his uncle Džemal remain missing.

In October 2009, for the first time since 1992, Huso, now an (unemployed) Austrian citizen, travelled to Belgrade, once the capital city of the country he was proud to have helped build. He was not there to look at the many reminders of his two-decade-long working presence, materialised by the numerous skyscrapers, but, with a handful of other survivors from his village who came from Austria and Bosnia, to attend the court proceeding against the so-called 'Zvornik group', a number of former members of Serb militias facing charges at the state court in Belgrade for their involvement in the killing of 668 people that summer in Zvornik. Among these 668 people were Huso's son Senad and brother Džemal. Huso was less concerned with justice than with finding out the truth about what happened to his son, his brother and his neighbours. As in many other similar cases, 'the lack of evidence' would result in either acquittal or reduced sentences for those who committed war crimes, he believed. As he had expected, there was not much in the way of the truth that day, just a bitter realisation that the war crime that took the lives of so many of his family and his *zavičaj* was turned into a complicated bureaucratic and legal theatre. Having possibly seen the faces of those who killed his son, he returned to Vienna the same afternoon.

Huso, Sejo, Fata and Senad represent members of only one Viennese Zvornik family affected by forced displacement and the issue of missing relatives. Hundreds of other survivors from the area who settled in Vienna have very similar tales to tell and their 'Austrian' lives have, more or less, run along the same lines as the Nuhanovićs'. Their stories and their missing relatives, as much as the old kinship relations and memories of lost *zavičaj*, make the trans-local Zvornik community a distinct group within the Bosnian diaspora in Austria. Over the years they have almost become an 'interest group' as they write petitions, help various human rights organisations draft reports about the Zvornik tragedy, and try to act as a pressure group to influence those who could help them in getting at least some answers about and some justice for their missing relatives.

Unearthing the Missing in Bosnia

Over the years Omer Sulejmanović – like Sejo – has been one of my key informants, friends and research collaborators. We were childhood friends and went to the same primary school in Podrinje. I have shared Omer's stories and friendship with other researchers interested in displacement, ethnic cleansing and genocide. In this way Omer – who continues to live in Bosnia – has met and made lasting friendships with researchers like Ron Adams from Australia and David Pettigrew from the U.S.[15] Through such contacts Omer has been able to reach the expanded, foreign worlds of other *Klotivljani*, with whom all three of us (Ron, David and myself) have met in different places far from the actual village of Klotjevac. On 11 July 2009, at the fourteenth commemoration of the Srebrenica genocide and the collective funeral for more than 500 identified genocide victims, Omer, together with his two nephews Ado and Edo, buried his brother-in-law Sadik. Ron, David and I were there, not for fieldwork-related reasons, but as Omer's friends.

Two years later, in the weeks before and after 11 July 2011, I made a final visit to all my research sites in Bosnia and met with many of my long-term informants and research collaborators. They asked me about the progress of my 'book about them' and thanked me for writing about their pain and their missing relatives. Hida and Salih Sulejmanović, Omer's ageing parents, now living in an exchanged house in the town of Hadžići, near Sarajevo, wanted, once again, to tell me more about Senad, their older son who went missing at Srebrenica in July 1995. They wanted Senad to find his place in my book, being worried that the true memory of their Senad would perish when they, his parents, were gone. A more pressing worry for them was that they might not live long enough to bury the complete body of their lost son. Recently they were notified by the Missing Persons' Institute that a femur and a piece of cranium were identified as Senad's remains. They had a choice whether to bury these two bones 'as Senad' or wait for more remains to be found and positively identified. No one could tell if and when that might be. Hida and Salih made the decision to wait. Based on the piece of information about two pieces of forensic evidence representing the earthly remains of her son, Hida told me her reconstructed story of Senad's last moments:

> They found him in a paddock, not far from Srebrenica ... He must have got lost as he didn't know the area. His body was not in a mass grave ... He didn't get into their [Serb] hands alive. No, he didn't. He was hit while trying to escape. Maybe it was shrapnel? Fifteen years of rain and snow moved away his bones.

Hida was not trying to tell a tale of a heroic death of her son. She never calls him a martyr (*šehid*) although she is a deeply religious woman. She always refers to him as '*moj* (my) Senad' and through narrating how she imagined his death, she is protecting him, giving herself hope that Senad's death came fast and painlessly; that he was not captured, tortured and then gunned down in a summary execution – as if believing that the more people who know this version of the story, the more true it would become. Hida accepted long ago that her Senad was killed, but for years she has been wrestling with her fears that he was afraid, his hands tied with wire, his eyes blindfolded, that he was thirsty and suffering before his body was spread with hot bullets – as survivors of the massacres have described. While she was retelling me her story about Senad's death, Omer's father kept smoking cigarette after cigarette, occasionally nodding and completing a sentence his wife started, while Omer himself would venture in and out of the house. He had heard this same story far too many times. Senad has been the main topic of any conversation his parents would have with each other or with the increasingly rare visitor. For the last fourteen years Omer has been living in the shadow of his missing brother, numbed by his parents' grief, not having the space, time or mental energy to deal with his own grief for his only brother. It has been hard for Omer to provide much comfort to his parents, to soothe their pain by living *his* life the way Senad would have lived. As Imre Kertész (2003: 121) has written, 'Anyone who stays alive is always guilty' – and too often that guilt has been hard for Omer to bear. He not only feels that he might not be worthy of living the life of his older brother, but also that he could not in any way compensate for his parents' loss. Senad was not married and did not leave any offspring, while, at the age of forty, Omer is still single and only recently in a stable job. There have been no births in Omer's family since the war and no grandson to be named after Senad. Omer knows that his parents have been hoping for this and he believes that this could alleviate some of their pain – pain for the lost son redirected into love for a grandson. But for Omer this would be a form of denial, and he is not ready to deny the long absence of his brother from his life. If he ever were to have a son he would not want him to 'compensate' for his lost brother.

Listening to Hida's retelling of her son's last moments was more than research. It was one of the obligations of an insider, someone who went to school with her Omer. I was here to listen, to empathise, to understand. Not to encourage her to move on, or attempt closure like an outsider might have done. But to listen, and in listening, and in nodding in assent like Salih, allow her to inscribe some meaning on an otherwise meaningless landscape. The telling of a story is in part directed at setting the record straight – the irony being in this case that it is in fact a highly fictionalised account, but is nonetheless a 'true' story in the ends it serves, i.e., to imaginatively spare Senad pain and suffering and humiliation. But a story is also directed at maintaining the deep bonds, the intimacy, the love if you like, between the storyteller and the audience. It is cementing old ties – it is not letting me (or them) forget that there are still others who understand: *zavičaj*, kin, *Klotivljani*. This is trans-localism in action: reaching out across the globe to reconnect with other 'insiders' – with those who understand. This is at the heart of the *zavičaj*: finding an audience that does not judge from an outsider perspective, but engages in a mutual enactment – whether that be witnessing a court case, listening to music, drinking and eating, presenting photographs, attending a genocide exhibition, or simply nodding in assent – where the rules of engagement are implicitly understood.

From St. Louis to St. Albans: All Roads Lead to Hanna's Cafe

Back in Melbourne, my research into displacement, memory and identity in Bosnian war-torn communities has been gradually turning into more than a life-long project – it has become a lifestyle. On most Saturdays I still drive some twenty-five kilometres to have a few hours for coffee, talk and reflection in the 'Bosnian' suburb of St. Albans. My primary research base in St. Albans is Hanna's Cafe, located on the busy intersection of Main Road and St. Albans Avenue. Hanna's Cafe also sits at the intersection of transnationalism and trans-localism, which, as I have argued in this book, in terms of lived experience cannot be neatly separated. Azra and her husband Dženo, once refugees from western Bosnia, now owners of a growing coffee business in Melbourne, have transformed their small cafe into a piece of reterritorialised Bosnia. The smell of freshly roasted, ground and brewed coffee wafts across the street to the train station, often attracting many casual, non-Bosnian passers-by. For Bosnian customers, on the other hand, although many would say, 'I was around and just thought I'd pop in for a coffee', Hanna's Cafe – with its coffee, a wide range of Bosnian groceries, magazines and, recently, books – is the destination. Every Saturday, as on most other days, the cafe is packed with local Bosnians living in the area as well as those (like me) coming from afar, who come to meet people, have a chat, exchange information, and discuss politics, or culture, or literature – or just listen to conversations in their mother tongue.

On one of these Saturdays Hanna's Cafe became a recruiting site for Amir Mehičević, a film director, in search of volunteers for acting roles and extras in his latest film *One More Tonight*. The film, based on a real event that took place a few years ago when a Somali taxi driver was stabbed to death in Melbourne, addresses the life of migrants and racism in mainstream Australia. Some of the key white characters in the movie – including both 'good' and 'bad guys' – were played by Bosnians from Hanna's Cafe. As a regular at Hanna's, I also became involved in Amir's film, getting to play an Australian policeman. I justified my involvement in terms of my reciprocal relationship with Amir, a friend and one of my informants, and in being able to engage in another form of participant observation. In the following weeks, dressed in a police uniform, fully armed and looking very real as Senior Constable Dan Candle, I attended a number of rehearsal and filming sessions. The *One More Tonight* crew was ethnically mixed: in addition to five Bosnians, other crew members came from an Anglo-Australian background, from Northern Africa, Sweden, the Ukraine and Croatia. Thus, Amir's film is not necessarily 'a Bosnian movie about African taxi drivers in Australia', as someone at Hanna's summarised it. It is, rather, a mainstream Australian film in which a Bosnian-Australian director and his cast address pertinent social issues of intolerance, violence and racism. While the author's personal experiences and his Bosnian sensitivity – or possibly more accurately his Mostar sensitivity – might have influenced how the theme has been approached, the film in itself is not based on a Bosnian issue of 'home over there' but confronts a social issue of 'home over here'. Like Bosnians in the U.S. and many other countries, 'Aussie Bosnians' are aware that their skin colour has made them privileged over other, non-white refugees and migrants. Amir's film raises awareness of this fact and of racism, sparking on that Saturday an interesting discussion among the patrons at Hanna's. Many made comments about the importance of tolerance, and how 'unfair' it was to judge someone by the colour of their skin. Even though it took place in a relatively small group, this discussion demonstrates that the issue of race is socially constructed and also context-dependent, reflecting the dominant values (and prejudices) of the adopted society (Jackson 1987). While for the Bosnians in St. Louis race is seen as a source of their newly discovered white identity, an embodied asset – a form of 'cultural capital' if you like – Bosnians in Melbourne are much less attached to the colour of their skin and are more ready to engage critically in deconstructing racial identities and prejudices against which they have not been completely immune. For instance, many of them continue to refer to migrants from Asian backgrounds as 'the yellow ones' (*žuti*), an issue that was raised in the discussion at Hanna's.

So, you never know what awaits you at Hanna's: you may end up playing a role in a film, having a good laugh listening to the jokes and anecdotes, or engaging in serious discussions about sports, politics and racism. Or you can just play safe and stick to your own trans-local table at the cafe and talk *zavičaj*, a topic only a few 'chosen ones' are experts in.

Some regulars at Hanna's remain quiet observers of such discussions, just listening to the different conversations, occasionally greeting the newcomers with a friendly grin or nod, at other times looking somewhat absent from what's happening around them. Hamed, a man whose age could be anywhere between fifty and seventy, is one such quiet regular. For him, Hanna's Cafe has become a second home where he spends some time every day, mostly sitting silently or keeping his conversations to a polite minimum. This does not prevent other guests, mostly those from Podrinje, from sending coffees and Cockta[16] over to Hamed's table. Hamed's story is well known at Hanna's and drinks ordered for him are a sign of respect – *čašćavanje* (buying someone a drink) in Bosnian literally means honouring someone – not pity. And there are many people at Hanna's who want to honour him. For many of them Hamed is the embodiment of their lost Podrinje *zavičaj*, even a living symbol of Bosnian stoicism. Hamed has become even quieter since losing his wife to cancer in early 2009. Living on a disability support pension in a rented house with his university-student daughter Nerka, Hamed has plenty of time and more solitude than he can bear. Since his wife died there has not been much talk at his place; Nerka leaves in the morning and comes home late at night. Sometimes they do not see each other for days.

A migrant in Australia since 2001, Hamed has been through multiple hardships and displacements. In May 1992 his family was expelled from their home town of Bijeljina; Hamed was detained in the concentration camp Batković and then sent to dig trenches on the front lines and do all sorts of forced labour for more than two years. He was tortured and used as a human shield, but somehow he survived. Close to the end of the war, with a handful of other survivors, he was released and went to Tuzla to look for his family. I learned a part of Hamed's story from his daughter Nerka. A few years ago, while she was still at high school, I was her language teacher. Nerka was my best student and very popular among her friends. During one of the class activities, as an example of imaginative writing, I asked the students to write a text on the prescribed theme 'A day I will never forget'. It was anticipated by those who set the topic that students would write about a happy event – like a memorable birthday party, a concert, the first kiss ... This is what Nerka wrote:

> When I had lost every hope that he would ever join us in this strange city where we were living as refugees while waiting to return home, on one autumn day like this, he came. He had been 'only' absent for two years, imprisoned somewhere, but it felt like a hundred years since I last saw him. I did not recognise him at all. Mum said, 'Nerka, come-on, give your father a hug!', but I only saw an old, broken man, dressed in ragged clothes, sitting on the couch in front of me. My father wouldn't be that old and he always wore nice clothes, I thought. Then, in a trembling voice, the old man called my name, the tears running down his old face. And only then did I recognise his eyes and his voice – it was my Dad! I will never forget that day.[17]

Like in Hida Sulejmanović's case, Nerka saw me as a *zavičaj* insider, someone who shared a similar connection with Podrinje, even though I met her and her family for the first time here in Australia, and had never visited the Podrinje town of Bijeljina. Her memories of the 'original' local place, *zavičaj*, might have been very vague, but – after spending a substantial part of her childhood as a homeless IDP and refugee, an expellee from her *zavičaj* – she developed a strong sense of belonging to her Podrinje *zavičaj* community, reterritorialised here in St. Albans. Nerka's *zavičaj* became the Podrinje people she met and their stories. Having her teacher as someone from her imagined *zavičaj* made her proud, wanting to do her best in my class – which she did. Through sharing this very intimate story of her dad with someone who would understand she included me in her *zavičaj*. She was also making a relationship on behalf of her father, whom she wanted to represent to me in a particular way, not as a social welfare dependant who will never integrate into the broader Australian – or even Bosnian – community in Melbourne, but as someone from *our zavičaj*, someone deserving respect for what he had gone through. Perhaps, she hoped that I would, in a parent–teacher interview or in a less formal setting, find ways to convey to Hamed his daughter's affection for him. At a range of levels, Nerka's written story became a piece of our shared *zavičaj*.

The storytelling will continue at Hanna's, in Bosnian-language classrooms in St. Albans, Montmartre in Karlskrona, in various shops along St. Louis' Gravois Avenue, among grieving fathers returning from Belgrade war crimes trials, in Hida Sulejmanović's sitting room in Hadžići – for as long as Bosnians continue to define themselves in relation to their *zavičaji*. But for a book the storytelling needs to end somewhere – and this is, after all, the last paragraph. Looking back at the stories collected from – or more accurately performatively enacted with – displaced Bosnians over three continents, what emerges from the heterogeneity and diversity of the performative enactments of memories and identities is a distinct pattern, a common point of reference. I refer here to the influence of trans-localism, which finds its most powerful expression in the concept of *zavičaj*. The heterogeneity and diversity I have observed and documented in the preceding pages reflect not only a range of transported local cultural practices, dialects and narratives from the old home 'over there', but also many imported local cultural, linguistic and political influences from the new home 'over here', often resulting in innovative and unique expressions of trans-local identities. This cross-fertilisation of cultures involves an ongoing cultural reflexivity, synthesising different cultural elements at hand into an experientially meaningful form of cultural identity. Thus, while we may, and should, talk about a worldwide Bosnian diaspora – as well as about Bosnian Australians, Bosnian Americans, Bosnian Swedes and Bosnian Austrians – in reality these categories, celebrated by (trans)nationalists, may not be as experientially meaningful to displaced Bosnians as their various trans-local social networks. The reality of trans-local life defies dichotomising home and exile, and displacement and emplacement, by redefining the concept of *zavičaj* and taking it from a fixed, local level to a more fluid, global level. I hope that this book will contribute to a deeper understanding and appreciation of Bosnia's war-torn *zavičaji*, the places of pain – transformed, but not destroyed through violence and forced displacement. What my journey through the book has shown is that popular memory and performative enactments of local identities continue to produce and reproduce the idea and experience of *zavičaj* as an intimate and ultimate home, and in so doing defy the ethnic cleansing that sought to destroy it.

Notes

1. Translated by Francis R. Jones. I would like to thank Gorčin Dizdar and The Mak Dizdar Foundation for giving me permission to reprint this great poem in my book.
2. As described earlier in the book (see Chapter 4), the term and concept of *zavičaj* refers to one's 'intimate and ultimate home', a place where one grew up, lived and developed a sense of local belonging. For the displaced, *zavičaj* evokes a feeling of nostalgia for the lost home and community that is no more where it used to be.
3. With more attention given to Sweden and the U.S., which features less prominently in the previous chapters.
4. Edita's father, described in Chapter 2.
5. A 'walkabout' is more than just a journey or an adventure; it is believed that when Australian Aborigines go on walkabout, they undertake a spiritual jour-

ney to a *belonging place* to reaffirm their relationship with their dreaming and the landscape. However, during the colonial oppression of Aborigines, walkabout was also a form of everyday resistance as movement meant freedom from oppressors. See Peterson (2004).
6. By 'hybridisation' I understand fusion of different cultural identities (and experiences), while 'hyphenation' refers to maintenance of dual or bicultural identities that are context dependent – like public identity (e.g., Swedish) and private (e.g., Bosnian), or Swedish-Bosnian.
7. See http://www.europarl.europa.eu/meps/en/28125/Anna_IBRISAGIC.html and http://ibrisagic.blogspot.com/.
8. Translated from Bosnian by the author.
9. *Krajina*, in Bosnian/Croatian/Serbian, usually refers to a border region. Within Bosanska Krajina there are three distinct sub-Krajine, the one around Prijedor, Banja Luka and Sanski Most, the one around Bihać, and the third one, also known as *Ljuta Krajina* (Krajina proper), around the old city of Cazin, on the border with Croatia.
10. See the museum's official website: http://www.museumldv.com/ and O'Mahony (2007).
11. The old part of Sarajevo, once the trading centre of the city, now a popular café and restaurant precinct.
12. http://www.stltoday.com/stltoday/news/special/bosnia.nsf/front?openviewandcount=2000.
13. http://www.house.mo.gov/billtracking/bills051/hlrbillspdf/5903C.01.pdf.
14. http://srebrenica-genocide.blogspot.com.au/2009/10/saint-louis-srebrenica-genocide.html.
15. Omer's story features in the documentary *Geography of Genocide: Redeeming the Earth*, directed by David Pettigrew and his son Jonah (2009).
16. Invented in 1950 in Slovenia, Cockta was the Yugoslav answer to Coca-Cola. Once popular across Yugoslavia, Cockta has become the favourite non-alcoholic beverage among the members of the Bosnian diaspora. Other Yugoslav food and drink products are also regularly imported and consumed in diaspora as a way to nourish sensory nostalgia for the times and homelands (Yugoslavia and Bosnia) now gone.
17. Original text translated and edited by the author.

BIBLIOGRAPHY

Adams, N. 1993. 'Architecture as the Target', *Journal of the Society of Architectural Historians* 52: 389–90.
Adams, R. 2006. 'Srebrenica: Learning from Australian-Bosnian Students', *Local Global Journal: Identity, Security, Community* 2(1): 142–53.
———. 2008. 'Capacity-building in Bosnia-Herzegovina: The Challenge for Universities', *Cesaa Review* 35: 45–56.
Adams, R. and H. Halilovich. 2010. 'Zavičaj in Klotjevac: Recontextualising Local Tradition as Modalities for Reconciliation', *International Conference: Political Mythologies, Reconciliations and the Uncertain Future in the Former Yugoslavia, Edmonton 1–3 October 2010*. Edmonton: University of Alberta.
Ahmed, S., C. Castaneda, A-M. Fortier and M. Sheller. 2003. 'Introduction: Uprootings/Regroundings: Questions of Home and Migration', in S. Ahmed, C. Castaneda, A-M. Fortier and M. Sheller (eds), *Uprootings/Regroundings: Questions of Home and Migration*. Oxford and New York: Berg, pp. 1–22.
Ajduković, D. 2004. 'Social Contexts of Trauma and Healing', *Medicine, Conflict and Survival* 20(2): 120–35.
Al-Ali, N. 2002. 'Trans- or a -national: Bosnian Refugees in the UK and The Netherlands', in N. Al-Ali and K. Koser (eds), *New Approaches to Migration: Transnational Communities and the Transformation of Home*. London and New York: Routledge, pp. 96–117.
———. 2003. 'Loss of Status or New Opportunities? Gender Relations and Transnational Ties among Bosnian Refugees', in D.F. Bryceson and U. Vuorela (eds), *The Transnational Family: New European Frontiers and Global Networks*. Oxford: Berg, pp. 83–102.
Al-Ali, N., R. Black and K. Koser. 2001a. 'Refugees and Transnationalism: The Experience of Bosnians and Eritreans in Europe', *Journal of Ethnic and Migration Studies* 27(4): 615–35.
———. 2001b. 'The Limits to "Trans-nationalism": Bosnian and Eritrean Refugees in Europe as Emerging Trans-National Communities', *Ethnic and Racial Studies* 24(4): 578–600.
Amit, V. 2002. 'An Anthropology without Community?', in V. Amit and N.J. Rapport, *The Trouble with Community: Anthropological Reflections on Movement, Identity and Collectivity*. London: Pluto Press, pp. 13–66.
Amit, V. and N.J. Rapport. 2002. *The Trouble with Community: Anthropological Reflections on Movement, Identity and Collectivity*. London: Pluto Press.
Amit-Talai, V. 1998. 'Risky Hiatuses and the Limits of Social Imagination: Expatriacy in the Cayman Islands', in N. Rapport and A. Dawson (eds), *Migrants*

of Identity: Perceptions of Home in a World of Movement. Oxford: Berg, pp. 39–61.
Anderson, B. 1983. *Imagined Communities: Reflections on the Origin and Spread of Nationalism*. London: Verso.
Andrews, M. 2000. 'Narrative and Life History: Introduction', in M. Andrews, S. Day Sclater, C. Squire and A. Treacher (eds), *Lines of Narrative: Psychosocial Perspectives*. London: Routledge, pp. 77–80.
Andrić, I. 2003. *Na Drini Ćuprija (The Bridge over Drina)*. Beograd: Prosveta.
Antze, P. and M. Lambek. 1996. 'Introduction: Forecasting Memory', in P. Antze and M. Lambek (eds), *Tense Past: Cultural Essays in Trauma and Memory*. London: Routledge, pp. xi–xxxviii.
Anzulović, B. 1999. *Heavenly Serbia: From Myth to Genocide*. New York: New York University Press.
Appadurai, A. 1996. *Modernity at Large: Cultural Dimensions of Globalization*. Minneapolis: University of Minnesota Press.
Arendt, H. 1963. *Eichmann in Jerusalem: A Report on the Banality of Evil*. New York: Viking.
Assmann, A. 2006. *Der Lange Schatten der Vergangenheit: Erinnerungskultur und Geschichtspolitik*. München: C.H. Beck.
Augé, M. 1995. *Non-Places: Introduction to an Anthropology of Supermodernity*. London and New York: Verso.
Bagshaw, S. 1997. 'Benchmarks or Deutschmarks? Determining the Criteria for the Repatriation of Refugees to Bosnia and Herzegovina', *International Journal of Refugee Law* 9(4): 566–92.
Bajina Bašta Portal. 2007. 'Drina River – The Green Beauty'. Retrieved 2 April 2007 from www.bajinaBašta.com/bbportal/main/river/facts/river_facts_e.html
Bakaršić, K. 1994. 'The Libraries of Sarajevo and the Book that Saved our Lives', *New Combat: A Journal of Reason and Resistance*. Autumn: 13–15.
Bakic-Hayden, M. 1995. 'Nesting Orientalisms: The Case of Former Yugoslavia', *Slavic Review* 54(4): 917–31.
Banac, I. 2002. 'The Weight of False History', *Forum Bosnae* 15: 201–06.
Barbir-Mladinović, A. 2009. 'Hrvati i treći entitet', *Radio Slobodna Evropa*. Retrieved 21 November 2009 from http://www.slobodnaevropa.org
Barkan, E. and M. Shelton. 1998. *Borders, Exiles, Diasporas*. Stanford: Stanford University Press.
Barrington, L.W., E.S. Herron and B.D. Silver. 2003. 'The Motherland is Calling: Views of Homeland among Russians in the Near Abroad Source', *World Politics* 55(2): 290–313.
Basch, L., N. Glick Schiller and C. Szanton-Blanc. 1994. *Nations Unbound: Transnational Projects and the Deterritorialised Nation-state*. New York: Gordon and Breach.
Baudrillard, J. 1996. 'The West's Serbianization: When the West Stands in for the Dead', in T. Cushman and S. Meštrović (eds), *This Time We Knew: Western Reponses to Genocide in Bosnia*. New York: New York University Press, pp. 79–89.

Bax, M. 1997a. 'Civilization and Decivilization in Bosnia: A Case-study from a Mountain Community in Herzegovina', *Ethnologia Europaea* 7(2): 163–76.
———. 1997b. 'Mass Graves, Stagnating Identification and Violence: A Case Study in the Local Sources of the War in Bosnia-Herzegovina', *Anthropological Quarterly* 70(1): 11–19.
———. 2000a. 'Warlords, Priests and the Politics of Ethnic Cleansing: A Case-study from Rural Bosnia-Herzegovina, *Ethnic and Racial Studies* 23(1): 16–36.
———. 2000b. 'Holy Mary and Medjugorje's Rocketeers: The Local Logic of an Ethnic Cleansing Process in Bosnia', *Ethnologia Europaea* 30(1): 45–58.
———. 2000c. 'Planned Policy or Primitive Balkanism? A Local Contribution to the Ethnography of the War in Bosnia-Herzegovina', *Ethnos* 65(3): 317–40.
Bećirbašić, B. 2009. 'Istraživanja: Srednjoškolci i nasilje – Elektrošok je moja škola', *BH Dani* 653, 18 December. Retrieved 20 December 2009 from http://www.bhdani.com/
Bećirević, E. 2009. *Na Drini Genocid*. Sarajevo: Buybook.
———. 2008. 'The Bosnian Approach to the Fight against Terrorism', in I. Prezelj (ed.), *The Fight Against Terrorism and Crisis Management in the Western Balkans*. Amsterdam: IOS Press, pp. 77–94.
Behloul, S.M. 2007. 'From "Problematic" Foreigners to "Unproblematic" Muslims: Bosnians in the Swiss Islam-discourse', *Refugee Survey Quarterly* 26(2): 22–35.
Berger, P. and T. Luckmann. 1967. *The Social Construction of Reality*. New York: Doubleday.
Bešlagić, Š. 2004. *Leksikon Stećaka*. Sarajevo: Svjetlost.
Bevan, R. 2004. *The Destruction of Memory: Architectural and Cultural Warfare*. London: Reaktion Books.
Beverly, A. 1996. *Rape Warfare: The Hidden Genocide in Bosnia-Herzegovina and Croatia*. University of Minneapolis: Minnesota Press.
Bhabha, H. 1990. 'The Third Space: Interview with Homi Bhabha', in J. Rutherford (ed.) *Identity, Community, Culture, Difference*. London: Lawrence and Wishart, pp. 207–21.
———. 1994. *The Location of Culture*. London and New York: Routledge.
Bibanović, Z. 2012. 'Šta je ta Srebrenica?', *Depo.ba*, 4 January. Retrieved 5 January 2012 from http://depo.ba/nedjeljni-magazin/danas-grad-genocida-juce-raskrsce-rimske-kulture-ljekovitih-voda-stecaka-i-starih-hamama
Bieber, F. 2005. 'Local Institutional Engineering: A Tale of Two Cities, Mostar and Brčko', *International Peacekeeping* 12(3): 420–33.
Bisharat, G.E. 1997. 'Exile to Compatriot: Transformations in the Social Identity of Palestinian Refugees in the West Bank', in A. Gupta and J. Ferguson (eds), *Culture Power, Place: Explorations in Critical Anthropology*. Durham and London: Duke University Press, pp. 203–33.
Black, R. 2001. 'Return and Reconstruction in Bosnia-Herzegovina: Missing Link, or Mistaken Priority?', *SAIS Review* 21(2): 177–99.
———. 2002. 'Conceptions of "Home" and the Political Geography of Refugee Repatriation: Between Assumption and Contested Reality in Bosnia-Herzegovina', *Applied Geography* 22(2): 123–38.

Blake, F. 2002. 'Nusreta survived the rape camp, but her torture is unending', *The Independent*, 23 November. Retrieved 20 April 2008 from http://www.independent.co.uk/news/world/europe/nusreta-survived-the-rape-camp-but-her-torture-is-unending-605058.html

Bojanovski, I. 1964. 'Rimska Stela iz Klotijevca na Drini', *Naše Starine*, IX(2): 189–92.

Boose, L.E. 2002. 'Crossing the River Drina: Bosnian Rape Camps, Turkish Impalement, and Serb Cultural Memory', *Signs* 8(1): 71–96.

Bose, S. 2002. *Bosnia after Dayton: Nationalist Partition and International Intervention*. London: Hurst and Co Publishers.

Bosnia and Herzegovina, Ministry for Human Rights and Refugees. 2008. 'Pregled stanja bosanskohercegovačkog stanovništva'. Sarajevo: Sektor za Iseljeništvo – Ministarstvo za ljudska prava i izbjeglice Bosne i Hercegovine.

Bosnian Institute. 2008. 'Cultural Heritage and Traditions: The Stecci'. Retrieved 21 November 2008 from http://www.bosnia.org.uk/bosnia/viewitem.cfm?itemID=428

Bougarel, X. 2007. 'Death and the Nationalist: Martyrdom, War Memory and Veterans' Identity among Bosnian Muslims', in X. Bougarel, G. Duijzings and E. Helms (eds), *The New Bosnian Mosaic: Social Identities, Collective Memories and Moral Claims in a Post-war Society*. Aldershot: Ashgate, pp. 167–92.

Bourdieu, P. 1991. *Language and Symbolic Power*. Cambridge: Harvard University Press.

Božić-Vrbančić, S. 2008. *Tarara: Croats and Maori in New Zealand – Memory, Belonging, Identity*. Dunedin: Otago University Press.

Brah, A. 1996. *Cartographies of Diaspora: Contesting Identities*. London: Routledge.

Brennen, T., R. Dybdahl and A. Kapidžić. 2007. 'Trauma-related and Neutral False Memories in War-induced Posttraumatic Stress Disorder', *Consciousness and Cognition* 16(4): 877–85.

Brettell, C. 2003. *Anthropology and Migration: Essays on Transnationalism, Ethnicity and Identity*. Walnut Creek: AltaMira Press.

Bringa, T. 1995. *Being Muslim the Bosnian Way: Identity and Community in a Central Bosnian Village*. Princeton: Princeton University Press.

Brochmann, G. 1997. 'Bosnian Refugees in Scandinavian Countries: A Comparative Perspective on Immigration Control in the 1990s', *New Community* 23(4): 495–509.

Brockett, L.P. 1879. *Bogomils of Bulgaria and Bosnia – The Early Protestants of the East: An Attempt to Restore Some Lost Leaves of Protestant History*. Philadelphia: American Baptist Publication Society.

Brooks, G. 2008. *The People of the Book*. Sydney: Harper Collins.

Broz, S. 2005. *Good People in an Evil Time: Portraits of Complicity and Resistance in the Bosnian War*. New York: Other Press.

Brubaker, R. 1996. *Nationalism Reframed: Nationhood and the National Question in the New Europe*. Cambridge: Cambridge University Press.

Brun, C. 2001. 'Reterritorializing the Relationship between People and Place in Refugee Studies', *Geografiska Annaler, Series B, Human Geography* 83(1): 15–25.

Bryman, A. 2001. *Social Research Methods*. Oxford: Oxford University Press.
Brzezinski, Z. 1993. 'Never Again – Except for Bosnia', *The New York Times*, 22 April, A1.
Bundesministerium für Unterricht, Kunst und Kultur. 2008. 'Auszug aus der Schulbuchliste für das Schuljahr 2008/09'. Vienna: Referat für Migration und Schule.
Cain, K., H. Postlewait and A. Thomson. 2004. *Emergency Sex (And Other Desperate Measures): True Stories from a War Zone*. London: Ebury Press.
Campbell, D. 1998. *National Deconstruction: Violence, Identity and Justice in Bosnia*. Minneapolis: University of Minnesota Press.
———. 1999. 'Apartheid Cartography: The Political Anthropology and Spatial Effects of International Diplomacy in Bosnia', *Political Geography* 18(4): 395–435.
———. 2002. 'Atrocity, Memory, Photography: Imaging the Concentration Camps of Bosnia – the Case of ITN versus Living Marxism, (Part 2)', *Journal of Human Rights* 1(2): 143–72.
Cano, G. 2005. 'The Mexico-North Report on Transnationalism', *63rd Annual Conference of the Midwest Political Science Association, Chicago, 7–9 April 2005*. Chicago: Palmer House Hilton.
Čapo, J. 2011. 'Dvadeset godina poslije: Stvaranje doma u kontekstu prisilno raseljenih osoba', in J. Čapo and V. Gulin Zrnić (eds), *Mjesto, nemjesto: Interdisciplinarna promišljanja prostora i kulture*. Zagreb: Institut za etnologiju i folkloristiku, pp. 335–52.
Čapo Žmegač, J. 1999. '"We are Croats. It is not Our Goal to be Set Apart from Our Own People": A Failed Attempt at Firmer Incorporation of Croatian Migrants', *Ethnologia Balkanica, Journal for Southeast European Anthropology* 3: 121–39.
———. 2003. 'Two Localities, Two Nation-states, Two Homes: Transmigration of Croatian Labour Migrants in Munich', *Narodna Umjetnost Croatian Journal of Ethnology and Folklore Research* 40(2): 117–31.
———. 2005. 'Ethnically Privileged Migrants in Their New Homeland', *Journal of Refugee Studies* 18(2): 199–215.
———. 2007. *Strangers Either Way: The Lives of Croatian Refugees in Their New Home*. Oxford and New York: Berghahn Books.
Čapo Žmegač, J., V. Gulin Zrnić and G.P. Šantek. 2006. 'Ethnology of the Proximate: The Poetics and Politics of Contemporary Fieldwork', in J. Čapo Žmegač, V. Gulin Zrnić and G.P Šantek (eds), *Etnologija Bliskoga. Poetika i politika suvremenih terenskih istraživanja*. Zagreb: Institut za etnologiju i folkloristiku (Biblioteka Nova etnografija)-Naklada Jesenski i Turk (Biblioteka antropologije i etnologije), pp. 261–310.
Carrier, P. 2000. 'Places, Politics and the Archiving of Contemporary Memory in Perre Nora's *Les Lieux de memoire*', in S. Radstone (ed.), *Memory and Methodology*. Oxford and New York: Berg, pp. 37–58.
Castles, S. 2002. 'Migration and Community Formation under Conditions of Globalization', *International Migration Review* 36(4): 1143–68.
Castles, S. and J.M. Miller. 2003. *The Age of Migration: International Population Movements in the Modern World*. New York: Guilford Press.

Cavarero, A. 2000. *Relating Narratives: Storytelling and Selfhood*. London: Routledge.
Čečo, A. 2008. 'O destrukciji, András J. Riedlmayer, ekspert za kulturno naslijeđe: "Džamije su nestajale kao staljinovi komesari"', *Slobodna Bosna* 604: 58–61.
Čekić, S. 2005. *The Aggression against the Republic of Bosnia and Herzegovina, Books I and II*. Sarajevo: Institute for the Research of Crimes against Humanity and International Law.
Christou, A. 2003. '(Re)collecting Memories, (Re)Constructing Identities and (Re)Creating National Landscapes: Spatial Belongingness, Cultural (Dis)Location and the Search for Home in Narratives of Diasporic Journeys', *International Journal of the Humanities* 1: 1456–64.
Cigar, N. 1995. *Genocide in Bosnia: The Policy of 'Ethnic Cleansing' in Eastern Europe*. College Station: Texas A&M University Press.
Clifford, J. 1994. 'Diasporas', *Cultural Anthropology* 9: 302–38.
———. 1997. *Routes: Travel and Translation in the Late Twentieth Century*. Cambridge: Harvard University Press.
Cockburn, C. 1998. *The Space between Us: Negotiating Gender and National Identities in Conflict*. London: Zed Books.
Cohen, A.P. 1985. *The Symbolic Construction of Community*. London and New York: Tavistock Publications.
Cohen, R. 1995. 'CIA Report on Bosnia Blames Serbs for 90% of the War Crimes', *New York Times*, 9 March 1995. Retrieved 13 November 2010 from http://www.nytimes.com/1995/03/09/world/cia-report-on-bosnia-blames-serbs-for-90-of-the-war-crimes.html?pagewanted=all&src=pm
———. 1997. *Global Diasporas: An Introduction*. Seattle: University of Washington Press.
Colic-Peisker, V. 2003. 'Muslims, Refugees, White Europeans, New Australians: Displacement and Re-identification of Bosnians', *Cultures in Collision Colloquium*, 9 May 2003. Sydney: University of Technology. Retrieved 22 November 2010 from www.transforming.cultures.uts.edu.au/pdfs/muslims_refugees_colic-peisker.pdf
———. 2005. '"At Least You're the Right Colour": Identity and Social Inclusion of Bosnian Refugees in Australia', *Journal of Ethnic and Migration Studies* 31(4): 615–38.
Colic-Peisker, V. and P. Waxman, 2005. 'Human and Social Capital in the Process of Economic Adjustment of Refugees: Bosnians in Australia', in P. Waxman and V. Colic-Peisker (eds), *Homeland Wanted: Interdisciplinary Perspectives on Refugee Resettlement in the West*. New York: Nova Science Publishers, pp. 43–69.
Čolović, I. 1999. *The Politics of Symbol in Serbia*. London: Hurst and Company.
Conradson, D. and D. Mckay. 2007. 'Translocal Subjectivities: Mobility, Connection, Emotion', *Mobilities* 2(2): 167–74.
Coughlan, R. 2005. 'Surviving War, Starting Over: Adaptation of Bosnian Refugees in Upstate New York', in P. Waxman and V. Colic-Peisker (eds), *Homeland Wanted: Interdisciplinary Perspectives on Refugee Resettlement in the West*. New York: Nova Science Publishers, pp. 127–47.

———. 2011. 'Transnationalism in the Bosnian Diaspora in America', in M. Valenta and S.P. Ramet (eds), *The Bosnian Diaspora: Integration of Transnational Communities*. Farnham: Ashgate, pp. 105–22.
Coughlan, R. and J. Owens-Manley. 2006. *Bosnian Refugees in America: New Communities, New Cultures*. New York: Springer.
Coward, M. 2002. 'Community as Heterogeneous Ensemble: Mostar and Multiculturalism', *Alternatives: Global, Local, Political* 27(1): 29–66.
———. 2009. *Urbicide: The Politics of Urban Destruction*. London: Routledge.
Cushman, T. 1999. 'On Bosnia: Response to Hayden, *Current Anthropology* 40(3): 365–66.
———. 2004. 'Anthropology and Genocide in the Balkans', *Anthropological Theory* 4(1): 5–28.
Cushman, T. and S. Meštrović. 1996. 'Introduction', in T. Cushman and S. Meštrović (eds), *This Time We Knew: Western Reponses to Genocide in Bosnia*. New York: New York University Press, pp. 1–38.
Dahlman, C.T. 2004. 'Geographies of Genocide and Ethnic Cleansing: The Lessons of Bosnia-Herzegovina', in C. Flint (ed.), *The Geography of War and Peace: From Death Camps to Diplomats*. Oxford: Oxford University Press, pp. 174–97.
Dahlman, C.T. and G.Ó Tuathail, 2005a. 'Broken Bosnia: The Localized Geopolitics of Displacement and Return in Two Bosnian Places', *Annals of the Association of American Geographers* 95(3): 644–73.
———. 2005b. 'The Legacy of Ethnic Cleansing: The International Community and the Returns Process in Post-Dayton Bosnia-Herzegovina', *Political Geography* 24(5): 569–99.
———. 2006. 'Bosnia's Third Space? Nationalist Separatism and International Supervision in Bosnia's Brčko District', *Geopolitics* 11(4): 651–75.
Davies, C.A. 2008. *Reflexive Ethnography: A Guide to Researching Selves and Others*. London: Routledge.
Davy, U. 1995. 'Refugees from Bosnia and Herzegovina: Are They Genuine?', *Suffolk Transnational Law Review* 18: 53–129.
Dedić, M. 2009. 'Debakl Dodikovih strateških partnera', *Slobodna Bosna*, 12 February, 639.
Dedijer, V. and A. Miletić. 1990. *Genocid nad Muslimanima, 1941–1945: Zbornik dokumenta i svjedočenja*. Sarajevo: Svjetlost.
Deleuze, G. and F. Guattari. 1980. *Mille Plateaux: Capitalisme et Schizophrénie*, Paris: Minuit.
Denich, B. 1993. 'Unmaking of Multi-ethnicity in Yugoslavia: Metamorphosis Observed', *Anthropology of East Europe Review, Special Issue: War among the Yugoslavs* 11(1–2): 43–54.
Dening, G. 1996. *Performances*. Chicago: University of Chicago Press.
Deroko, D.J. 1939. *Drina: Geografsko-turistička Monografija*. Novi Sad: Izdanje društva Fruška Gora.
Diaz-Briquets, S. and J. Perez-Lopez. 1997. 'Refugee Remittances: Conceptual Issues and the Cuban and Nicaraguan Experiences', *International Migration Review* 31(2): 411–37.

Ðilas, M. 1996. *The Bosniak – Adil Zulfikarpašić in Dialogue with Milovan Djilas and Nadežda Gaće*. London: Hurst and Company.
Dimova, R. 2006. 'From Protection to Ordeal: Status of Bosnian Refugees in Berlin', *Max Planck Institute Working Paper Series 83*. Retrieved 10 November 2009 from http://www.eth.mpg.de/cms/de/publications/working_papers/index.html_774326879.html
———. 2007. 'From Strategic Remembrance to Politics of Tolerance: Memories of the Srebrenica Massacre among the Bosnians in Berlin', *Berliner Debatte – Initial* 4/5: 96–104.
Dirlik, A. 2000. 'Place-based Imagination: Globalism and the Politics of Place', in R. Prazniak and A. Dirlik (eds), *Places and Politics in the Age of Globalization*. New York: Rowman and Littlefield, pp. 15–52.
Dizdar, M. 1997. 'Zapis o Zemlji' ('Inscription of a Land'), in M. Dizdar, *Kameni Spavač*. Sarajevo: Ljiljan, pp. 190–1.
Dmitruk, D., S. Hadzic and R. Sherman. 2005. 'The Barriers Can be Overcome: The Integration Experience of Bosnian Refugees in Denmark', *Humanity in Action Copenhagen*. Retrieved 29 May 2009 from http://www.humanityinaction.org/
Donia, R. 2006. *Sarajevo: A Biography*. Ann Arbor: University of Michigan Press.
Donia, R. and J. Fine. 1994. *Bosnia and Herzegovina: A Tradition Betrayed*. New York: Columbia University Press.
Drakulić, S. 1993. *Balkan Express*, trans. M. Soljan. London: Hutchinson.
———. 1999. *As if I am Not There*. London: Abacus.
———. 2004. *They Would Never Hurt a Fly: War Criminals on Trial in The Hague*. London: Abacus.
Duijzings, G. 2007. 'Commemorating Srebrenica: Histories of Violence and the Politics of Memory in Eastern Bosnia', in X. Bougarel, G. Duijzings and E. Helms (eds), *The New Bosnian Mosaic: Social Identities, Collective Memories and Moral Claims in a Post-war Society*. Aldershot: Ashgate, pp. 141–66.
Duraković, E. 2006. 'The State of Soul of Bosnian Intellectuals', *Oslobođenje*, 16 December. Retrieved 7 January 2012 from http://www.islamicpluralism.org/422/the-state-of-soul-of-the-bosnian-intellectuals
Duraković, F. 1998. 'A War Letter', in F. Duraković, *Heart of Darkness*. New York: White Pine Press, p. 92.
Durnati, A. 1997. *Linguistic Anthropology*. Cambridge: Cambridge University Press.
Džaja, M.S. 2002. *Die politische Realität des Jugoslawismus (1918–1991): Mit besonderen Berücksichtigung Bosnien-Herzegowinas*. München: Südost-Institut.
Eastmond, M. 1998. 'Discourses and the Construction of Difference: Bosnian Muslim Refugees in Sweden', *Journal of Refugee Studies* 11(2): 161–81.
———. 2005. 'Beyond Exile: Refugee Strategies in Transnational Contexts', in M. Collyer, F. Crepeau and D. Nakache (eds), *Forced Migration and Global Processes: A View from Forced Migration Studies*. Lanham: Rowman and Littlefield Publishing Group, pp. 217–37.
———. 2006. 'Transnational Returns and Reconstruction in Post War Bosnia and Herzegovina', *International Migration* 44(3): 141–66.

Erlich, V. 1966. *Family in Transition: A Study of 300 Yugoslav Villages*. Princeton: Princeton University Press.
Escobar, A. 2001. 'Culture Sits in Places: Reflections on Globalism and Subaltern Strategies of Globalization', *Political Geography* 20: 139–74.
Esterhuizen, L. 2006. 'Us, Them and Reconciliation: A Critical Discussion of the Workings of Bosnian Blame and its Consequences', *Local Global Journal: Identity, Security, Community* 2(1): 46–59.
Federal Commission for Missing Persons/Federalna komisija za nestale osobe. 2005. 'Preliminarni spisak žrtava genocida u Srebrenici 1995'. Sarajevo.
Feld, S. and K.H. Basso. 1996. 'Introduction', in S. Feld and K.H. Basso (eds), *Senses of Place*. Seattle: University of Washington Press, pp. 3–12.
FENA. 2008. 'Zaštićena svjedokinja ispričala da ju je Nikačević silovao', *FENA*, 13 May. Retrieved 22 May 2008 from http://www.sarajevo-x.com/clanak/080513082
Ferrándiz, F. 2006. 'The Return of Civil War Ghosts: The Ethnography of Exhumations in Contemporary Spain', *Anthropology Today* 22(3): 7–12.
Feuchtwang, S. 2000. 'Reinscriptions: Commemoration, Restoration and the Interpersonal Transition of Histories and Memories under Modern States in Asia and Europe', in S. Radstone (ed.), *Memory and Methodology*. Oxford and New York: Berg, pp. 59–78.
Filandra, Š. 2012. *Bošnjaci nakon socijalizma: O bošnjačkom identitetu u postjugoslavenskom dobu*. Sarajevo and Zagreb: Preporod and Synopsis.
Filipović, M. 2007. 'Fenomen dijaspore', *Nezavisne novine*, 25 July. Retrieved 28 July 2007 from http://www.nezavisne.com/komentari/kolumne/Fenomen-dijaspore-12368.html
Fine, J.V.A. 1994. *The Late Medieval Balkans: A Critical Survey from the Late Twelfth Century to the Ottoman Conquest*. Ann Arbor: University of Michigan Press.
Fortier, A.M. 2000. *Migrant Belongings: Memory, Space, Identity*. Oxford and New York: Berg.
Foucault, M. 1975. 'Film and Popular Memory: An Interview with Michel Foucault', *Radical Philosophy* 11: 24–9.
———. 1977. 'Counter-memory: the Philosophy of the Difference', in F. Donald and D.F. Bouchard (eds), *Language, Counter-memory, Practice: Selected Essays and Interviews by Michel Foucault*. Ithaca, New York: Cornell University Press, pp. 113–65.
Franz, B. 2000. 'Ethnic Identity and Gender Roles in Flux: The Adaptation of Bosnian Refugees to Austrian Programs of Humanitarian Relief and Economic Integration: 1992–1999', *e-merge A Graduate Journal of International Affairs* 1: 6–19.
———. 2003. 'Bosnian Refugees and Socio-economic Realities: Changes in Refugee and Settlement Policies in Austria and the United States', *Journal of Ethnic and Migration Studies* 29(1): 5–25.
———. 2005. *Uprooted and Unwanted: Bosnian Refugees in Austria and the United States*. College Station: Texas A&M University Press.

———. 2011. 'The Bosnian Community in Austria: Linking Integration to Transnationalism – Some Comparative Observations', in M. Valenta and S.P. Ramet (eds), *The Bosnian Diaspora: Integration of Transnational Communities*. Farnham: Ashgate, pp. 143–60.
Friedman, F. 1996. *The Bosnian Muslims: Denial of a Nation*. Boulder and Oxford: Westview Press.
Friedman, J. 1998. 'Transnationalization, Socio-political Disorder and Ethnification as Expressions of Declining Global Hegemony', *International Political Science Review* 19(3): 233–50.
———. 2002. 'From Roots to Routes: Tropes for Trippers', *Anthropological Theory* 2(21): 21–36.
Galić, M. 1990. *Politika u Emigraciji: Demokratska Alternativa*. Zagreb: Globus.
Geertz, C. 1973. *The Interpretations of Cultures*. New York: Basic Books.
———. 1983. *Local Knowledge: Further Essays in Interpretative Anthropology*. New York: Basic Books.
Gendercide Watch. 1996. 'Case Study: The Srebrenica Massacre, July 1995'. Retrieved 10 February 2007 from http://www.gendercide.org/case_srebrenica.html
George, U. and A. Tsang. 2000. 'Newcomers to Canada from Former Yugoslavia: Settlement Issues', *International Social Work* 43(3): 381–93.
Giddens, A. 1991. *Modernity and Self-identity: Self and Society in the Late Modern Age*. Cambridge: Polity Press.
Gilroy, P. 1995. 'Roots and Routes: Black Identity as an Outernational Project', in H.W. Harris, H.C. Blue and E.H. Griffith (eds), *Racial and Ethnic Identity: Psychological Development and Creative Expression*. London and New York: Routledge, pp. 15–30.
Glas Srpske. 2007. 'Glas Srpske na prvoj klapi za film "Sveti Georgije ubiva aždahu" u Omarskoj kod Prijedora', *Glas Srpske*, 4 October. Retrieved 7 January 2012 from http://www.glassrpske.com/plus/teme/Srdjan-Dragojevic-Najveca-pobjeda-srpskog-naroda-njegov-najveci-poraz/lat/19099.html
Glenny, M. 1996. *The Fall of Yugoslavia*. London: Penguin Books.
———. 1999. *The Balkans 1804–1999, Nationalism, War and the Great Powers*. London: Granta Books.
Glick Schiller N., L. Basch and C. Szanton-Blanc. 1992. *Toward a Transnational Perspective on Migration*. New York: The New York Academy of Sciences.
———. 1995. 'From Immigrant to Transmigrant: Theorizing Transnational Migration', *Anthropological Quarterly* 68(1): 48–63.
———. 1999. 'Trans-nationalism: A New Analytic Framework for Understanding Migration', in S. Vertovec and R. Cohen (eds), *Migration, Diasporas and Transnationalism*. Cheltenham: Edward Elgar Publishing, pp. 26–50.
Goldring, L. 1998. 'The Power of Status in Transnational Social Spaces', *Comparative Urban and Community Research* 6: 165–95.
Goldstein, R., N.S. Wampler and P.H. Wise. 1997. 'War Experiences and Distress Symptoms of Bosnian Children', *Pediatrics* 100(5): 873–78.
Gonzalez, N.L. 1992. *Dollar, Dove and Eagle: One Hundred Years of Palestinian Migration and the Expression of Ethnicity*. Boulder: Westview Press.

Government of Bosnia-Herzegovina. 1991. 'The 1991 Census of Population of the Republic of Bosnia and Herzegovina'. Sarajevo.
Government of Republika Srpska,1994–2002. *Službeni glasnik Republike Srpske, volumes: 13/94, 10/97, 23/98, 43/02*. Banja Luka: Government of Republika Srpska.
Gow, G. 2002. *The Oromo in Exile: From the Horn of Africa to the Suburbs of Australia*. Melbourne: Melbourne University Press.
Graf, J.C. 1999. 'Has El Dorado Crumbled so Soon After its Cornerstone was Laid: The State of International Refugee Law and the Repatriation of Bosnians in Germany', *Indiana International and Comparative Law Review* 10(115): 121–24.
Grodach, C. 2002. 'Reconstituting Identity and History in Post-war Mostar, Bosnia-Herzegovina', *City Analysis of Urban Trends, Culture, Theory, Policy, Action* 6(1): 61–82.
Guarnizo, L.E. and M.P. Smith. 1998. 'The Locations of Transnationalism', in M.P. Smith and L.E. Guarnizo (eds), *Transnationalism from Below*. London: Transaction Publisher, pp. 3–34.
Gunzburger Makaš, E. 2005, 'Interpreting Multivalent Sites: New Meanings of Mostar's Old Bridge', *Centropa* 5(1): 59–69.
———. 2007. 'Representing Competing Identities in Postwar Mostar', Ph.D. dissertation. New York: Cornell University.
Gupta, A. and J. Ferguson. 1992. 'Beyond Culture: Space, Identity and the Politics of Difference', *Cultural Anthropology* 7: 6–23.
———. 1997. 'Culture, Power, Place: Ethnography at the End of an Era', in A. Gupta and J. Ferguson (eds), *Culture, Power, Place*. Durham: Duke University Press, pp. 1–29.
Gutman, R. 1993. *Witness to Genocide*. New York: Macmillan.
Hadžić, H. 2003. 'Crni Vrh: Najmasovnija masovna grobnica', *BH Dani*, 15 August, 322.
Hadžijahić, M. 1975. 'O nestajanju crkve bosanske', *Pregled* LXV: II–12.
Hadžović, E. 2007. 'Mittal macht frei', *BH Dani*, 10 August, 530.
Hafizović, R. 2006. 'Oni dolaze po našu djecu', *Oslobođenje*, 25 November. Retrieved 4 January 2011 from http://www.bosnjaci.net/prilog.php?pid=19910
Hagan, J. 2003. *Justice in the Balkans: Persecuting War Crimes in The Hague Tribunal*. Chicago: University of Chicago Press.
Hage, G. 1997. 'At Home in the Entrails of the West: Multiculturalism, "Ethnic Food" and Migrant Home-building', in H. Grace, G. Hage, L. Johnson, J. Langsworth and M. Symonds (eds), *Community and Marginality in Sydney's West*. Annandale: Pluto Press, pp. 99–153.
Halbwachs, M. 1992. *On Collective Memory*. Chicago: University of Chicago Press.
Halilovich, H. 2004. 'Reconciliation and Difference in Bosnia and Herzegovina', *The First International Sources of Insecurity Conference, Melbourne, 17–19 November 2004*. Melbourne: RMIT University.
———. 2005a. 'A Unique Identity', *Refugee Transitions* 16: 28–34.

———. 2005b. 'The Outsider: A Story of Refugeedom', in V. Colic-Peisker and P. Waxman (eds), *Homeland Wanted: Interdisciplinary Perspectives on Refugee Resettlement in the West*. New York: Nova Science Publishers, pp. 209–39.

———. 2006a. 'Bosnian-Herzegovinian Diaspora in the Flow of Global Migrations: Challenges and Opportunities for Bosnia-Herzegovina', *Pregled Journal for Social Issues* 3(LXXXVI): 193–221.

———. 2006b. 'Aussie Bosnians from Germany: Reconstructing Identity', *Local Global Journal: Identity, Security, Community* 2(1): 59–72.

———. 2007. 'Polemike: Boomerang – odgovor Paulu B. Milleru', *BH Dani*, 6 July, 525.

———. 2008. 'Ethics, Human Rights and Action Research: Doing and Teaching Ethnography in Post-genocide Communities in Bosnia-Herzegovina', *Narodna Umjetnost – Croatian Journal of Ethnology and Folklore Research* 45(2): 165–90.

———. 2009. 'Patriarch Pavle – High Priest of Hypocrisy', *Henry Jackson Society Project for Democratic Geopolitics*, 23 July. Retrieved 6 January 2012 from http://www.henryjacksonsociety.org/stories.asp?id=1337

———. 2010a. 'Letter from Australia', *Peščanik.net*, 19 January. Retrieved 6 January 2012 from http://pescanik.net/2010/01/pismo-iz-australije/

———. 2010b. 'Meine Verwandten, Bekannten, Freunde, Schulkameraden und die Mehrheit meiner Nachbarn wurden ermordet', *Pogrom: bedrohte Völker* 41(5–6): 48–51.

———. 2011a. 'Beyond the Sadness: Memories and Homecomings among Survivors of "Ethnic Cleansing" in a Bosnian Village', *Memory Studies* 4(1): 42–52.

———. 2011b. '(Per)forming "Trans-local" Homes: Bosnian Diaspora in Australia', in M. Valenta and S.P. Ramet (eds), *Bosnian Diaspora: Integration in Transnational Communities*. Farnham: Ashgate, pp. 63–81.

———. 2011c. 'Memories of a Better Future in the Aftermath of the Srebrenica Genocide', *Open Democracy*, 13 June 2011. Retrieved 6 January 2012 from http://www.opendemocracy.net/hariz-halilovich/memories-of-better-future-in-aftermath-of-srebrenica-genocide

———. 2011d. 'A Dream to End the Nightmare of Srebrenica', *Transitions Online* 7(4): 1–3.

———. 2012a. 'Tako se kalio Reich Šumski', *Peščanik.net*, 11 January. Retrieved 12 January 2012 from http://pescanik.net/2012/01/tako-se-kalio-reich-sumski/

———. 2012b. 'Trans-local Communities in the Age of Transnationalism: Bosnians in Diaspora', *International Migration* 50(1): 162–78.

Halilovich, H. and R. Adams. 2011. 'Life and Death on the Border: Local Genocide in a Global Context', in M. Kreso (ed.), *Genocide in Bosnia and Herzegovina: Consequences of the International Court of Justice*. Sarajevo: Institute for Research of Crimes against Humanity and International Law, pp. 596–626.

Halilovich, H., P. Phipps, R. Adams, S. Bakalis and P. James. 2006. 'Editorial: Pathways to Reconciliation', *Local Global Journal: Identity, Security, Community* 2(1): 4–8.

Hall, S. 1990. 'Cultural Identity and Diaspora', in J. Rutherford (ed.), *Identity: Community, Culture, Difference*. London: Lawrence and Wishart, pp. 222–37.

---. 1996. *Questions of Cultural Identity*. London: Sage.
---. 2006. 'Black Diaspora Artists in Britain: Three "Moments" in Post-war History', *History Workshop Journal* 61(Spring): 1–24.
Halpern, J.M. and D.A. Kideckel. 2000. 'Introduction: The End of Yugoslavia Observed', in J.M. Halpern and D.A. Kideckel (eds), *Neighbors at War: Anthropological Perspectives on Yugoslav Ethnicity, Culture, and History*. Pennsylvania: Penn State University Press, pp. 3–19.
Hamidović, M. 2000. *Gramatika toposa Bosne: Antropološko teorijska studija o spoznaji bitka mjesta*. Zenica: Muzej Grada Zenice.
Hannerz, U. 1996. *Transnational Connections: Culture, People, Places*. New York: Routledge.
Hansen, D. 2003. 'Bosnian Refugees: Adjustments to Resettlement in Grand Forks, North Dakota', *Great Plains Research* 13: 271–90.
Hasić, N. 2009. 'Otac kao zabranjena tema: Djeca silovanih bosanskih žena', *Slobodna Bosna*, 19 March, 644.
Haverić, D. 2009. 'History of the Bosnian Muslim Community in Australia: Settlement Experience in Victoria', Ph.D. dissertation. Melbourne: Victoria University.
Hayden, R.M. 1996. 'Imagined Communities and Real Victims: Self-Determination and Ethnic Cleansing in Yugoslavia', *American Ethnologist* 23(4): 783–801.
---. 2000. *Blueprints for a House Divided: The Constitutional Logic of the Yugoslav Conflicts*. Ann Arbor: University of Michigan Press.
Hećimović, E. 2009. 'Ratni zločini: Potvrđena optužnica za masakr na Korićanskim stijenama – Zločini po planu', *BH Dani*, 16 January, 605.
Heller, A. 2001. 'Cultural Memory, Identity and Civil Society', *Internationale Politik und Gesellschaft Online – International Politics and Society* 2: 139–43.
Helms, E. 2007. '"Politics is a Whore": Women, Morality and Victimhood in Post-war Bosnia-Herzegovina', in X. Bougarel, G. Duijzings and E. Helms (eds), *The New Bosnian Mosaic: Social Identities, Collective Memories and Moral Claims in a Post-war Society*. Aldershot: Ashgate, pp. 235–54.
---. 2008. 'East and West Kiss: Gender, Orientalism, and Balkanism in Muslim-Majority Bosnia-Herzegovina', *Slavic Review* 67(1): 88–119.
Helsinki Committee for Human Rights. 2005. 'Bosnia Report on the Status of Human Rights in Bosnia and Herzegovina (Analysis for the period January–December 2004)'. Sarajevo.
---. 2006. 'Bosnia Report on the Status of Human Rights in Bosnia and Herzegovina (Analysis for the period January–December 2005)'. Sarajevo.
Hemon, A. 2006. 'Hemonwood: Na kapiji Zapada', *BH Dani*, 10 January, 452.
---. 2008. *The Lazarus Project*. New York: Riverhead Books.
Herman, E. 2005. 'The Politics of Srebrenica Massacre', *Z-Net*, 7 July. Retrieved 4 January 2012 from http://www.zcommunications.org/the-politics-of-the-srebrenica-massacre-by-edward-herman
Herman, J. 1992. *Trauma and Recovery*. Boston: Harvard University Press.
Hermann, T. 2001. 'The Impermeable Identity Wall: The Study of Violent Conflicts by "Insiders" and "Outsiders"', in M. Smyth and G. Robinson (eds), *Researching*

Violently Divided Societies: Ethical and Methodological Issues. Tokyo: United Nations University Press, pp. 77–91.

Hervik, P. 2006. 'The Emergence of Neonationalism in Denmark 1992–2002', in A. Gingrich and M. Banks (eds), *Neo-nationalism in Europe and Beyond: Perspectives from Social Anthropology*. Oxford and New York: Berghahn Books, pp. 92–107.

Herzfeld, M. 1985. *The Poetics of Manhood: Contest of Identity in a Cretan Mountain Village*. Oxford: Princeton University Press.

———. 1997. *Cultural Intimacy: Social Poetics in the Nation-State*. London and New York: Routledge.

Hirsch, H. 1995. *Genocide and the Politics of Memory: Studying Death to Preserve Life*. Chapel Hill and London: University of North CarolinaPress.

Hitchcock, W.I. 2003. *The Struggle for Europe: The Turbulent History of a Divided Continent 1945–2002*. Ontario: Doubleday.

Hoare, M.A. 2003. 'Genocide in the Former Yugoslavia: A Critique of Left Revisionism's Denial', *Journal of Genocide Research* 5(4): 543–63.

———. 2004. *How Bosnia Armed*. London: Saqi.

———. 2005. 'Srebrenica and the London Bombings: The "Anti-war" Link', *The Henry Jackson Society Project for Democratic Geopolitics*, 23 July. Retrieved 5 January 2012 from http://www.henryjacksonsociety.org/stories.asp?id=300

———. 2007. *The History of Bosnia: From the Middle Ages to the Present Day*. London: Saqi.

Hockey, J. 1999. 'The Ideal of *Home*: Domesticating the Institutional Space of Old Age and Death', in T. Chapman and J. Hockey (eds), *Ideal Homes? Social Change and Domestic Life*. London: Routledge, pp. 108–18.

Hoepken, W. 1999. 'War, Memory and Education in a Fragmented Society: The Case of Yugoslavia', *East European Politics and Societies* 13(A): 190–227.

Honig, J. and N. Both. 1997. *Srebrenica: Record of a War Crime*. London: Penguin Books.

Hozic, A. 2001. 'Hello. My Name is …: Articulating Loneliness in a Digital Diaspora', *Afterimage* 28(4): 21–2.

Hromadžić, A. 2008. 'Discourses of Integration and Practices of Reunification at the Mostar Gymnasium, Bosnia and Herzegovina', *Comparative Education Review* 52(4): 541–63.

Hukanović, R. 1996. *The Tenth Circle of Hell: A Memoir of Life in the Death Camps of Bosnia*. London: Little, Brown and Co.

Human Rights Watch, 1992/1993. 'Trnopolje Detention Camp: Helsinki Watch Report'. Helsinki.

———. 1996. 'Northwestern Bosnia: Human Rights Abuses During a Cease-Fire and Peace Negotiations 8(1D)'. Helsinki.

———. 1997. 'Helsinki Watch on Prijedor's War Criminals 9(1)'. Helsinki.

Humphrey, M. 2000. 'From Terror to Trauma: Commissioning Truth for National Reconciliation', *Social Identities* 6(1): 7–27.

Hunt, S. 2005. *This Was Not Our War: Bosnian Women Reclaiming the Peace*. Durham: Duke University Press.

Huntington, S. 1996. *The Clash of Civilizations and the Remaking of World Order*. New York: Simon and Schuster.
Huremović, E. 2006. 'Demografija: Deset godina od okončanja agresije na BiH', *Dnevni Avaz*, 3 December. Retrieved 5 December 2006 from http://www.avaz.ba/
Huttunen, L. 2005. 'Home and Ethnicity in the Context of War-hesitant Diasporas of Bosnian Refugees', *European Journal of Cultural Studies* 8(2): 177–95.
Huyssen, A. 2003. *Present Past: Urban Palimpsests and the Politics of Memory*. Stanford: Stanford University Press.
Ibrahimagić, O. 2003. *Bosnian Statehood and Nationality*. Sarajevo: Vijeće Kongresa bošnjačkih intelektualaca.
Imamović, M. 1996. *Bošnjaci u Emigraciji: Monografija 'Bosanskih pogleda'*. Sarajevo: Bošnjački institut Zuerich-odjel Sarajevo.
———. 1997. *Historija Bošnjaka*. Sarajevo: Preporod.
Internal Displacement Monitoring Centre/Norwegian Refugee Council. 2006. 'Internal Displacement: Global Overview of Trends and Developments in 2005'. Geneva.
International Commission on Missing Persons. 2007. 'Tracking Chart for the former Yugoslavia'. Sarajevo. Retrieved 5 February 2007 from http://www.ic-mp.org/downloads/press/EN_TChart.pdf
International Criminal Tribunal for the Former Yugoslavia. 1996. 'Gang Rape, Torture and Enslavement of Muslim Women Charged in ICTY's First Indictment Dealing Specifically with Sexual Offences', media release CC/PIO/093-E, 27 June. The Hague.
Irwin, R. and E. Bećirević. 2008. 'Special Report: Visegrad in Denial Over Grisly Past', *Institute for War and Peace Reporting*, 582. Retrieved 8 October 2008 from http://iwpr.net/report-news/visegrad-denial-over-grisly-past
Isaković, Z. 2008. *Stećak – the Last Bosnian Mystery*. Sarajevo: TVSA.
Ito, A. 2001. 'Politicisation of Minority Return in Bosnia and Herzegovina: The First Five Years Examined', *International Journal of Refugee Law* 13(1/2): 98–122.
Ives, N.G. 2005. 'Understanding Bosnian Refugee Integration and How it Differs by Country of Resettlement: Denmark and the United States of America', Ph.D. dissertation. Philadelphia: University of Pennsylvania.
Jackson, P. 1987. 'The Ideas of "Race" and the Geography of Racism', in P. Jackson (ed.), *Race and Racism: Essays in Social Geography*. Boston: Allen and Unwin, pp. 3–21.
Jansen, S. 1998. 'Homeless at Home: Narrations of Post-Yugoslav identities', in N. Rapport and A. Dawson (eds), *Migrants of Identity: Perceptions of Home in a World in Movement*. Oxford: Berg, pp. 85–110.
———. 2002. 'The Violence of Memories: Local Narratives of the Past After Ethnic Cleansing in Croatia', *Rethinking History* 6(1): 77–93.
———. 2008. 'Misplaced Masculinities: Status Loss and the Location of Gendered Subjectivities amongst "Non-transnational" Bosnian Refugees', *Anthropological Theory* 8(2): 181–200.

Jansen, S. and S. Löfving. 2009. 'Introduction: Towards an Anthropology of Violence, Hope and Movement of People', in S. Jansen and S. Löfving (eds), *Struggles for Home: Violence, Hope and the Movement of People*. Oxford and New York: Berghahn Books, pp. 1–24.

Jeffrey, A. 2006. 'Building State Capacity in Post-conflict Bosnia and Herzegovina: The Case of Brčko District', *Political Geography* 25(2): 203–27.

Jezernik, B. 2004. *Wild Europe: The Balkans in the Gaze of Western Travellers*. London: Saqi.

Johnstone, D. 2003. *Fools' Crusade: Yugoslavia, NATO and Western Delusions*. New York: Monthly Review Press.

Jones, A. 2004. 'Gendercide and Genocide', in A. Jones (ed.), *Gendercide and Genocide*. Nashville: Vanderbilt University Press, pp. 1–38.

———. 2006. *Genocide: A Comprehensive Introduction*. New York: Routledge/Taylor and Francis Publishers.

Jones, L. 2005. *Then They Started Shooting: Growing Up in Wartime Bosnia*. Cambridge: Harvard University Press.

Jones, L. and K. Kafetsios. 2005. 'Exposure to Political Violence and Psychological Well-Being in Bosnian Adolescents: A Mixed Method Approach', *Clinical Child Psychology and Psychiatry* 10(2): 157–76.

Joseph, J.E. 2004. *Language and Identity: National, Ethnic and Religious*. New York: Palgrave Macmillan.

Jukić, I.F. 1953. *Putopisi i istorijsko-etnografski radovi*. Sarajevo: Svjetlost.

Kaiser, C. 2000. 'Crimes against Culture', *The UNESCO Courier*. Retrieved 6 April 2008 from http://unesdoc.unesco.org/images/0012/001203/120395e.pdf

Kalčić, Š. and J. Gombač. 2011. 'The Bosnian Diaspora in Slovenia', in M. Valenta and S.P. Ramet (eds), *The Bosnian Diaspora: Integration of Transnational Communities*. Farnham: Ashgate, pp. 207–21.

Kamber, A. 2006. *Constructing Kamber*. Sarajevo: Omnibus.

Kamerić, M. 2010. *Cipele za dodjelu Oskara*. Sarajevo: Buybook.

Kaplan, R. 1996. *Balkan Ghosts: A Journey Through History*. New York: Vintage Books.

Karon, T. 2001. 'Lessons of the Srebrenica Genocide', *Time*, 2 August. Retrieved 15 January 2007 from http://www.time.com/time/world/article/0,8599,169877,00.html

Karup-Druško, D. 2006. 'Istrgli su mi dijete iz naručja, mučili, silovali i prodali', *BH Dani*, 3 March, 455.

———. 2009a. 'I Dodik i Tihić podržavaju Čauševiće', *BH Dani*, 13 February, 609.

———. 2009b. 'Procesi: Suđenje "Zvorničkoj grupi" u Beogradu zbog zločina nad bošnjačkim stanovništvom – Nikad nije bilo takvog rata', *BH Dani*, 16 October, 644.

Katana, E. 2008. 'Kostajnica i Brod više neće biti Bosanski', *Radio Slobodna Evropa*, 5 December. Retrieved 10 January 2009 from http://www.slobodnaevropa.org/content/article/1356766.html

Kearney, M. 1995. 'The Local and the Global: The Anthropology of Globalisation and Transnationalism', *Annual Reviews Anthropology* 25: 547–65.

Kelly, L. 2003. 'Bosnian Refugees in Britain: Questioning Community', *Sociology* 37(1): 35–49.
Kenny, M. 1996. 'Trauma, Time, Illness and Culture: An Anthropological Approach to Traumatic Memory', in P. Antze and M. Lambek (eds), *Tense Past: Cultural Essays in Trauma and Memory*. London: Routledge, pp. 151–73.
Kent, G. 2008. 'Bosnian Refugees in America: New Communities, New Cultures', *Journal of Refugee Studies* 21(3): 403–7.
Kertész, I. 2003. *Liquidation*. London: Vintage Books.
Kesić, V. 2003. 'Muslim Women, Croatian Women, Serbian Women, Albanian Women', *Eurozine/Belgrade Circle Journal* 1–4: 1–9.
Kett, M.E. 2005. 'Internally Displaced Peoples in Bosnia-Herzegovina: Impacts of Long-term Displacement on Health and Well-being', *Medicine, Conflict and Survival* 21(3): 199–215.
Kibreab, G. 1999. 'Revisiting the Debate on People, Place, Identity and Displacement', *Journal of Refugee Studies* 12(4): 384–428.
Kirmayer, L. 1996. 'Landscape of Memory: Trauma, Narrative and Dissociation', in P. Antze and M. Lambek (eds), *Tense Past: Cultural Essays in Trauma and Memory*. London: Routledge, pp. 173–99.
Koff, C. 2004. *The Bone Women: Among the Dead in Rwanda, Bosnia, Croatia and Kosovo*. Sydney: Hodder Headline Australia Pty Limited.
Kokanovic, R. and M. Stone. 2010. 'Doctors and Other Dangers: Narratives of Distress and Exile in Bosnian Refugees in Australia', *Social Theory and Health* 8(4): 350–69.
Kondylis, F. 2007. *Conflict-induced Displacement and Labour Market Outcomes: Evidence from Post-war Bosnia and Herzegovina, Centre for Economic Performance Discussion Paper No 777*. London: London School of Economics and Political Science. Retrieved 20 February 2008 from http://cep.lse.ac.uk/pubs/download/dp0777.pdf
Koopmans, R. and P. Statham. 2001. 'How National Citizenship Shapes Transnationalism: A Comparative Analysis of Migrant Claims-making in Germany, Great Britain and The Netherlands', *Revue Européenne des Migrations Internationales* 17(2): 63–100.
Korac, M. 2003. 'Integration and How We Facilitate It: A Comparative Study of the Settlement Experiences of Refugees in Italy and The Netherlands', *Sociology* 37(1): 51–68.
Koser, K. 2001. 'Europe in Change: The New Germany and Migration in Europe', *Journal of Refugee Studies* 14(3): 337–338.
Koso, M. and S. Hansen. 2006. 'Executive Function and Memory in Posttraumatic Stress Disorder: A Study of Bosnian War Veterans', *European Psychiatry* 21(3): 167–73.
Kovras, I. 2008. 'Unearthing the Truth: The Politics of Exhumations in Cyprus and Spain', *History and Anthropology* 19(4): 371–90.
Kulenović, S. and A. Suljić. 2006. 'Demografske posljedice genocida nad Bošnjacima sigurnosne zone UN Srebrenica, jula 1995', *Zbornik radova PMF Svezak Geografija* III(3): 7–14.

Kumar, R. 1997. *Divide and Fall?: Bosnia in the Annals of Partition*. London: Verso.
Kurspahić, K. 2003. *Prime Time Crime: Balkan Media in War and Peace*. Washington: United States Institute of Peace Press.
Kurtić, M.M. 2006. *Žepa – Ratni Dnevnik*. Tuzla: BMG.
Lake, M. 2006. 'Introduction: The Past in the Present', in M. Lake (ed.), *Memory, Monuments and Museums: The Past in the Present*. Melbourne: Melbourne University Press, pp. 15–32.
Lambert, M., C. Haasen and H. Halilovic. 1998. 'Differential Diagnosis of Psychotic Disorders in Immigrants', *Psychiatrische Praxis* 25(4): 198–9.
Lampe, J.R. 2000. *Yugoslavia as History: Twice There was a Country*. Cambridge: Cambridge University Press.
Lanzmann, C. 1985. *Shoah*. Paris: Les Films Aleph-Why Not Productions.
Lemkin, R. 2002. 'Genocide', in A. Hinton (ed.), *Genocide: An Anthropological Reader*. Oxford: Blackwell, pp. 27–42.
Levitt, P. and N. Glick Schiller. 2007. 'Conceptualizing Simultaneity: A Transnational Social Field Perspective on Society', in A. Portes and J. DeWind (eds), *Rethinking Migration: New Theoretical and Empirical Perspectives*. Oxford and New York: Berghahn Books, pp. 181–218.
Leys, R. 1996. 'Traumatic Cures: Shell Shock, Janet and the Question of Memory', in P. Antze and M. Lambek (eds), *Tense Past: Cultural Essays in Trauma and Memory*. London: Routledge, pp. 103–51.
Lippman, P. 2006. 'Srebrenica's Search for Justice', *Open Democracy*, 23 August. Retrieved 2 April 2007 from http://www.opendemocracy.net/conflict-yugoslavia/srebrenica_3851.jsp
Lorey, D.E. and W.H. Beezley. 2002. 'Introduction', in D.E. Lorey and W.H. Beezley (eds), *Genocide, Collective Violence and Popular Memory: The Politics of Remembrance in the Twentieth Century*. Wilmington: Scholarly Resources Inc., pp. xi–xxxiii.
Lovell, N. 1998. 'Introduction: Belonging in Need of Emplacement', in N. Lovell (ed.), *Locality and Belonging*. London and New York: Routledge, pp. 1–25.
Lovrenović, D. 2010. *Stećci: bosansko i humsko mramorje srednjeg vijeka*. Sarajevo: Rabic.
Lovrenović, I. 1994. 'Hatred of Memory: In Sarajevo, Burned Books and Murdered Pictures', *The New York Times*, 28 May, 143: 15–19.
———. 2001. *Bosnia: A Cultural History*. New York: New York University Press.
Luebben, S. 2003. 'Testimony Work with Bosnian Refugees: Living in Legal Limbo', *British Journal of Guidance and Counselling* 31(4): 393–402.
Maass, P. 1996. *Love thy Neighbor: A Story of War*. New York: Random House.
Macdonald, B.D. 2003. *Balkan Holocausts?: Serbian and Croatian Victim Centred Propaganda and the War in Yugoslavia*. Manchester: Manchester University Press.
Maček, I. 2001. 'Predicament of War: Sarajevo Experiences and Ethic of War', in I. W. Schröder and B.E. Schmidt (eds), *Anthropology of Violence and Conflict*. London and New York: Routledge, pp. 197–224.
———. 2007. 'Imitation of Life: Negotiating Normality in Sarajevo Under Siege', in X. Bougarel, G. Duijzings and E. Helms (eds), *The New Bosnian Mosaic: Social*

Identities, Collective Memories and Moral Claims in a Post-war Society. Aldershot: Ashgate, pp. 39–58.
Mach, Z. 1993. 'The Symbolic Construction of Identity: Identity, Symbols and Social Order', in Z. Mach (ed.), *Symbols, Conflict and Identity: Essays in Political Anthropology*. Albany: State University of New York Press, pp. 22–94.
Macić, B. 2002. 'Crimes Against Children in Bosnian War Cataclysm', in M. Tokača (ed.), *Pokidani Pupoljci/ (The Plucked Buds)*. Sarajevo: Commission for Gathering Facts on War Crimes in Bosnia and Herzegovina, pp. 353–65.
Madjar, V. and L. Humpage. 2000. *Refugees in New Zealand: The Experiences of Bosnian and Somali Refugees*. Auckland: Massey University.
Mahler, S. 1998. 'Theoretical and Empirical Contributions towards a Research Agenda for Transnationalism', in M.P. Smith and L.E. Guarnizo (eds), *Transnationalism From Below*. New Brunswick and London: Transaction Publishers, pp. 64–100.
Mahmutćehajić, R. 2000. *Bosnia the Good: Tolerance and Tradition*. Budapest: Central European University Press.
———. 2003. *Sarajevo Essays*. Albany: State University of New York Press.
Malcolm, N. 1994. *Bosnia: A Short History*. New York: New York University Press.
Malkki, L. 1992. 'National Geographic: The Rooting of Peoples and the Territorialization of National Identity among Scholars and Refugees', *Cultural Anthropology* 7(1): 24–44.
———. 1995. *Purity and Exile: Violence, Memory, and National Cosmology among Hutu Refugees in Tanzania*. Chicago: University of Chicago Press.
Marcus, G.E. 1989. 'Imagining the Whole: Ethnography's Contemporary Efforts to Situate Itself', *Critique of Anthropology* 9(3): 7–30.
———. 1995. 'Ethnography in/of the World System: The Emergence of Multisited Ethnography', *Annual Review of Anthropology* 24: 95–117.
———. 1998. *Ethnography through Thick and Thin*. New Jersey: Princeton University Press.
Markovic, M. and L. Manderson. 2002. 'Crossing National Boundaries: Social Identity Formation among Recent Immigrant Women in Australia from Former Yugoslavia', *Identity: An International Journal of Theory and Research* 2(4): 303–16.
Markowitz, F. 1996. 'Living in Limbo: Bosnian Muslim Refugees in Israel', *Human Organization* 55(2): 127–32.
Mašić, N. 1999. *Srebrenica: Agresija, Otpor, Izdaja, Genocid*. Sarajevo: DES.
Matsuo, H. 2005. 'Bosnian Refugee Resettlement in St Louis, Missouri', in P. Waxman and V. Colic-Peisker (eds), *Homeland Wanted: Interdisciplinary Perspectives on Refugee Resettlement in the West*. New York: Nova Science Publishers, pp. 109–27.
Mazowiecki, T. 1994. *Human Rights Questions: Human Rights Situations and Reports of Special Rapporteurs and Representatives A/49/641, S/1994/1252*. New York: United Nations.
McCarthy, P. 2000. *After the Fall: Srebrenica Survivors in St Louis*. St Louis: Missouri Historical Society Press.

———. 2007. 'Prijedor: Lives from the Bosnian Genocide', *Missouri Passages*, 4(12). Retrieved 20 November 2009 from http://mohumanities.org/E-News/Dec07/prijedor.htm

Mertus, J. 2000. *War's Offensive on Women: The Humanitarian Challenge in Bosnia, Kosovo and Afghanistan.* Bloomfield: Kumarian Press.

Miletić, N. 1982. *Stećci – Umjetnost na tlu Jugoslavije.* Beograd, Zagreb and Mostar: Izdavački zavod Jugoslavija, Spektar and Prva književna komuna.

Milivojević, S. 2002. 'Priznanja radnicima GP Radnik: Srebreničke Novine', in S. Salimović, *Knjiga o Srebrenici.* Tuzla: Skupština općine Srebrenica, pp. 145–6.

Mišković, M. 2011. 'Of Home(s) and (Be)Longing: Bosnians in the United States', in M. Valenta and S.P. Ramet (eds), *The Bosnian Diaspora: Integration of Transnational Communities.* Farnham: Ashgate, pp. 223–40.

Mujkić, S.M. 2009. *Brčko: Sedam krugova pakla.* Brčko: Gama X/The Author.

Mulahalilović, E. 1989. *Vjerski Običaji Muslimana u Bosni i Hercegovini.* Sarajevo: Starješinstvo Islamske zajednice.

Nettelfield, L.J. 2010. *Courting Democracy in Bosnia and Herzegovina: The Hague Tribunal's Impact in a Postwar State.* New York: Cambridge University Press.

Neuffer, E. 2001. *The Key to my Neighbor's House: Seeking Justice in Bosnia and Rwanda.* New York: Picador.

Nietzsche, F. 1994. *Human, All Too Human.* London: Penguin Group.

Nolin, C. 2006. *Transnational Raptures: Gender and Forced Displacement.* Aldershot: Ashgate.

Norris, H.T. 1993. *Islam in the Balkans: Religion and Society between Europe and the Arab World.* Columbia: University of South Carolina Press.

Nuhanović, H. 2005. *Pod zastavom UN-a: Međunarodna zajednica i zločin u Srebrenici.* Sarajevo: Preporod.

———. 2007. *Under the UN Flag: The International Community and the Srebrenica Genocide.* Sarajevo: DES.

———. 2008. 'Ne miješajte priču o mudžahedinima s genocidom u Srebrenici', *BH Dani*, 25 January, 554.

Nussbaum, M.C. 2001. *Upheavals of Thought.* Cambridge: Cambridge University Press.

Oakes, M.G. 2002. 'Loss and Recovery in War Refugees: A Qualitative Study of Bosnian Refugees in Las Vegas, Nevada', *Journal of Immigrant and Refugee Services* 1(2): 59–76.

Oberschall, A. 2000. 'The Manipulation of Ethnicity: From Ethnic Cooperation to Violence and War in Yugoslavia', *Ethnic and Racial Studies* 23(6): 982–1001.

Obradović, A. 2005. 'Ten Years after Dayton, Divisions Remain', *SETimes.com*, 14 December. Retrieved 17 August 2008 from http://www.setimes.com/cocoon/setimes/xhtml/en_GB/dayton/setimes/special/dayton/life/feature-07

Obradović, G. 2009. 'Iz sudnice: Počinje suđenje za Korićanske stijene', *Glas Srpske*, 20 September. Retrieved 11 December 2009 from http://www.glassrpske.com/vijest/6/hronika/28163/lat/Iz-sudnice-Pocinje-sudjenje-za-Koricanske-stijene.html

OECD. 2005. 'Migration, Remittances and Development'. Paris: OECD Publishing.

Olujić, M. 1995. 'Women, Rape, and War: The Continued Trauma of Refugees and Displaced Persons in Croatia', *Anthropology of East Europe Review Special Issue: Refugee Women of the Balkans* 13(1): 62–7.

Olwig, K.F. 1998. 'Contesting Homes: Home-Making and the Making of Anthropology', in N. Rapport and A. Dawson (eds), *Migrants of Identity: Perceptions of Home in a World in Movement*. Oxford: Berg, pp. 225–36.

———. 2003. '"Transnational" Socio-cultural Systems and Ethnographic Research: Views from an Extended Field Site', *International Migration Review* 37(3): 787–811.

O'Mahony, P. 2007. 'The Mystery of Karlskrona's da Vinci', *The Local – Sweden's News in English*, 22 May. Retrieved 2 February 2008 from http://www.thelocal.se/7381/20070522/

Ong, A. 1999. *Flexible Citizenship: The Cultural Logics of Transnationality*. Durham: Duke University Press.

Palavestra, V. 2004. *Historijska usmena predanja iz Bosne i Hercegovine*. Sarajevo and Zemun: Buybook and Mostart.

Pećanin, S. and D. Karup-Druško. 2009. 'Povratak u predvečerje rata', *BH Dani*, 27 February, 611.

Peleikis, A. 2000. 'The Emergence of a Translocal Community: The Case of a South Lebanese Village and its Migrant Connections to Ivory Coast', *Cahiers d'Études sur la Méditerranée Orientale et le Monde Turco-Iranienn* 30: 297–317.

Pelz, P. and D. Reeves. 2008. *The White House: From Fear to a Handshake*. Hants: O Books.

Peristiany, J.G. 1966. *Honour and Shame: The Values of Mediterranean Society*. Chicago: University of Chicago Press.

Pervanić, K. 1999. *The Killing Days: My Journey Through the Bosnian War*. London: Blake Publishing.

Peterson, N. 2004. 'Myth of the "Walkabout": Movement in Aboriginal Domain', in M. Bell and J. Taylor (eds), *Population Mobility and Indigenous Peoples in Australasia and North America*. London: Routledge, pp. 224–38.

Pettigrew, J.Q. and D. Pettigrew. 2009. *Geography of Genocide: Redeeming the Earth* (DVD). New York: Throwback Pictures.

Pijetlović, N. 2007. 'Filmska Cerska Bitka', *Novosti Online*, 11 October. Retrieved 20 August 2009 from http://www.novosti.rs/vesti/kultura.71.html:203960-Filmska-Cerska-bitka

Pinjo, M. 2008. 'Report by the Deputy Permanent Representative of BiH to the UN in Geneva', *United Nations Conference on Trade and Development Geneva, 4–5 February 2008*. Geneva: UN Trade and Development Board. Retrieved 16 June 2009 from http://www.unhcr.ba/updatesept08/Bosnia%20and%20Herzegovina

Portes, A., L.E. Guarnizo and P. Landolt. 1999. 'The Study of Transnationalism: Pitfalls and Promise of an Emergent Research Field', *Ethnic and Racial Studies* 22(2): 217–37.

Portis-Winner, I. 2002. *Semiotics of Peasants in Transition: Slovene Villagers and Their Ethnic Relatives in America*. Durham: Duke University Press.

Povrzanovic Frykman, M. 2002. 'Violence and the Re-discovery of Place', *Ethnologia Europaea* 32(2): 69–88.
———. 2004. '"Experimental" Ethnicity: Meetings in the Diaspora', *Narodna umjetnost. Croatian Journal of Ethnology and Folklore Research* 41(1): 83–102.
———. 2009. 'Views from Within: Bosnian Refugees' Experiences Related to their Employment in Sweden', in Malmö Institute for Studies of Migration Diversity and Welfare (ed.), *Resettled and Included? The Employment Integration of Resettled Refugees in Sweden*. Malmö: Malmö University, pp. 81–128.
———. 2011. 'Connecting Three Homelands: Transnational Practices of Bosnian Croats Living in Sweden', in M. Valenta and S.P. Ramet (eds), *The Bosnian Diaspora: Integration of Transnational Communities*. Farnham: Ashgate, pp. 241–59.
Power, S. 2002. *A Problem from Hell: America and the Age of Genocide*. New York: Basic Books.
Praštalo, T. 1997. 'Death of a Library', *Logos* 8(2): 96–9.
Prcić, I. 2011. *Shards*. New York: Black Cat.
Rakela, M. 2008. 'Nasilje kao životni stil', *Radio Slobodna Evropa*, 2 June. Retrieved 8 June 2008 from http://www.slobodnaevropa.org/content/article/1119799.html
Ramet, P.S. 2002. *Balkan Babel: The Disintegration of Yugoslavia from the Death of Tito to the Fall of Milosevic*, 4th ed. Cambridge: Westview Press.
———. 2005. *Thinking about Yugoslavia: Scholarly Debates about the Yugoslav Breakup and the Wars in Bosnia and Kosovo*. Cambridge: Cambridge University Press.
Ramet, P.S. and M. Valenta. 2011. 'Changing Places, Changing Identities: A Conclusion', in M. Valenta and S.P. Ramet (eds), *The Bosnian Diaspora: Integration of Transnational Communities*. Farnham: Ashgate, pp. 319–30.
Rapport, N. 1993. *Diverse World-views in an English Village*. Edinburgh: Edinburgh University Press.
Rapport, N. and A. Dawson. 1998. 'Home and Movement: A Polemic', in N. Rapport and A. Dawson (eds), *Migrants of Identity: Perceptions of Home in a World of Movement*. New York: Berg, pp. 19–38.
Redžić, E. 1998. *Bosna i Hercegovina u Drugom svjetskom ratu*. Sarajevo: Oko.
Rehn, E. and S.E. Johnson. 2000. *Women, War and Peace: The Independent Experts: Assessment on the Impact of Armed Conflict on Women and Women's Role in Peace-building*. New York: UNIFEM.
Research and Documentation Centre. 2007a. 'Human Losses in Bosnia and Herzegovina 1991–1995' (DVD). Sarajevo.
———. 2007b. 'Population Losses in Bosnia-Herzegovina: The Status of Database by the Centres, April 2004–January 2007', *Podrinje*. Sarajevo.
Ricoeur, P. 1990. *Time and Narrative (Vol. 1)*, trans. K. McLaughlin and D. Pellauer. Chicago and London: University of Chicago Press.
———. 2006. *Memory, History, Forgetting*, trans. K. Blamey and D. Pellauer. Chicago and London: University of Chicago Press.

Riedlmayer, A.J. 2002a. *Destruction of Cultural Heritage in Bosnia-Herzegovina: A Post-war Survey of Selected Municipalities*. Cambridge, MA.
———. 2002b. 'From the Ashes: The Past and Future of Bosnia's Cultural Heritage', in M. Shatzmiller (ed.), *Islam and Bosnia: Conflict Resolution and Foreign Policy in Multi-Ethnic States*. Montreal: McGill-Queens University Press, pp. 98–135.
———. 2007. 'Crimes of War, Crimes of Peace: Destruction of Libraries During and after the Balkan Wars of the 1990s', *Library Trends* 56(1): 107–32.
Rieff, D. 1995. *Slaughterhouse – Bosnia and the Failure of the West*. Sydney: Simon and Schuster.
Riessman, C.K. 2008. *Narrative Methods for the Human Sciences*. London: Sage.
Robertson, G. 1999. *Crimes against Humanity: The Struggle for Global Justice*. London: Allen Lane.
Robertson, R. 1995. 'Glocalisation: Time–space and Homogeneity Heterogeneity', in M. Featherstone, S. Lash and R. Robertson (eds), *Global Modernities*. London: Sage, pp. 25–44.
Robinson, G. and A. Pobric. 2006. 'Nationalism and Identity in Post-Dayton Accords Bosnia-Herzegovina', *Tijdschrift voor Economische en Sociale Geografie* 97(3): 237–52.
Robinson, V. 2000. 'Lessons Learned?: A Critical Review of the Government Program to Resettle Bosnian Quota Refugees in the United Kingdom', *The International Migration Review* 34(4): 1217–244.
Robinson, W. 1998. 'Beyond Nation-state Paradigms: Globalization, Sociology, and the Challenge of Transnational Studies', *Sociological Forum* 13(4): 561–94.
———. 2001. 'Social Theory and Globalization: The Rise of a Transnational State', *Theory and Society* 30: 157–200.
Rodman, M.C. 1992. 'Empowering Place: Multilocality and Multivocality', *American Anthropologist* 94: 640–56.
Rohde, D. 1997. *A Safe Area: Srebrenica: Europe's Worst Massacre Since the Holocaust*. New York: Farrar, Straus and Giroux.
———. 1998. *Endgame: The Betrayal and Fall of Srebrenica, Europe's Worst Massacre since World War II*. New York: Westview Press.
Sack, R.D. 1997. *Homo Geographicus: A Framework for Action, Awareness, and Moral Concern*. Baltimore and London: Johns Hopkins University Press.
Safran, W. 1991. 'Diasporas in Modern Societies: Myths of Homeland and Return', *Diaspora: A Journal of Transnational Studies* 1(1): 83–99.
Salbi, Z. 2006. *The Other Side of War: Women's Stories of Survival and Hope*. Washington: National Geographic.
Salihović, M. 2005. *Pokidani pupoljci Podrinja*. Sarajevo: IDC.
Salimović, S. 2002. *Knjiga o Srebrenici: Spomenar jednog grada*. Tuzla: Skupština općine Srebrenica.
Samarah, T. 2005. *Srebrenica*. Sarajevo and Zagreb: Synopsis.
Šaponjić, Z. 2001. 'HE Perućac još bez istražitelja', *Glas Javnosti Internet izdanje*, 18 July. Retrieved 16 March 2008 from http://arhiva.glas-javnosti.rs/arhiva/2001/07/18/srpski/H01071704.shtml

Schwartz, S. 2005. *Sarajevo Rose: A Balkan Jewish Notebook*. London: Saqi.
Šehić, F. 2009. 'Kako je Bruce Lee umro u Širokom Brijegu', *Žurnal Online Magazin*, 12 October. Retrieved 13 October 2009 from http://www.zurnal.info/home/
———. 2011. 'Omarska, toponim genocida', *BH Dani*, 13 May, 726.
Selimbegović, V. 2006. 'Kazani sarajevskog srama', *BH Dani*, 26 May, 467.
Sells, M. 1996. *The Bridge Betrayed: Religion and Genocide in Bosnia*. Berkeley: University of California Press.
Seremetakis, N.C. 1991. *The Last Word: Women, Death, and Divination in Inner Mani*. Chicago: University of Chicago Press.
Shaw, R. and C. Stewart. 1994. 'Introduction: Problematizing Syncretism', in C. Stewart and R. Shaw (eds), *Syncretism/Anti-Syncretism: The Politics of Religious Synthesis*. London: Routledge, pp. 1–24.
Sheffer, G. 1986. 'A New Field of Study: Modern Diasporas in International Politics', in G. Sheffer (ed.), *Modern Diasporas in International Politics*. London and Sydney: Croom Helm, pp. 1–15.
Sidran, A. 1998. *Partisan Cemetery*, in C. Agee (ed.), *Scar on the Stone: Contemporary Poetry from Bosnia*. Newcastle upon Tyne: Bloodaxe Books, p. 62.
Silber, L. and A. Little. 1996. *Yugoslavia: Death of a Nation*. London: Penguin Books.
Sivric, I. 1982. *The Peasant Culture of Bosnia and Herzegovina*. Chicago: Franciscan Herald Press.
Skrbiš, Z. 1999. *Long-distance Nationalism: Diasporas, Homelands and Identities*. Sydney: Ashgate.
Slavnić, Z. 2011. 'Conflicts and Inter-ethnic Solidarity: Bosnian Refugees in Malmö', in M. Valenta and S.P. Ramet (eds), *The Bosnian Diaspora: Integration of Transnational Communities*. Farnham: Ashgate, pp. 263–79.
Smith, A. 2003. 'Landscape Representations: Place and Identity in Nineteen-Century Ordnance Survey Maps of Ireland', in P.J. Steward and A. Strathern (eds), *Landscape, Memory and History: Anthropological Perspective*. London: Pluto Press, pp. 71–89.
Sofos, S. 1996a. 'Inter-ethnic Violence and Gendered Constructions of Ethnicity in Former Yugoslavia', *Social Identities* 2(1): 73–92.
———. 1996b. 'Culture, Politics and Identity in Former Yugoslavia', in B. Jenkins and S. Sofos (eds), *Nation and Identity in Contemporary Europe*. London: Routledge, pp. 235–66.
Sontag, S. 2002. *Regarding the Pain of Others*. New York: Farrar, Straus and Giroux.
Sorabji, C. 2006. 'Managing Memories in Postwar Sarajevo: Individuals, Bad Memories, and New Wars', *Journal of the Royal Anthropological Institute* 12: 1–18.
Sowell, T. 1996. *Migrations and Cultures: A World View*. New York: Basic Books.
Squire, C., M. Andrews and M. Tamboukou. 2008. 'Introduction: What is Narrative Research', in M. Andrews, C. Squire and M. Tamboukou (eds), *Doing Narrative Research*. London: Sage, pp. 1–21.
Srebrenica Commission of Republika Srpska. 2004. 'The Report on the Events in and around Srebrenica between 10th and 19th July 1995'. Banja Luka.

SRNA, 2008. 'Kuzmanović podržao izgradnju spomen-obilježja na Zlatištu', *SRNA*, 22 May. Retrieved 21 May 2010 from http://www.youtube.com/watch?v=Zq_5uy-AOR4.

Stefansson, A. 2004a. 'Homecomings to the Future: From Diasporic Mythographies to Social Projects of Return', in F. Markowitz and A. Stefansson (eds), *Homecomings: Unsettling Paths of Return*. Lanham: Lexington Books, pp. 2–20.

———. 2004b. 'The House War: The Politics, Practice and Meaning of Home in Bosnia and Herzegovina', Working Paper No. 10. Göteborg: Department of Social Anthropology, Göteborg University.

———. 2006. 'Homes in the Making: Property Restitution, Refugee Return and Senses of Belonging in a Post-war Bosnian Town', *International Migration* 44(3): 115–39.

———. 2007. 'Urban Exile: Locals, Newcomers and the Cultural Transformation of Sarajevo', in X. Bougarel, G. Duijzings and E. Helms (eds), *The New Bosnian Mosaic: Social Identities, Collective Memories and Moral Claims in a Post-war Society*. Aldershot: Ashgate, pp. 59–78.

Stiglmayer, A. 1994. 'The Rapes in Bosnia-Herzegovina', in A. Stiglmayer (ed.), *Mass Rape: The War against Women in Bosnia-Herzegovina*. Lincoln: University of Nebraska Press, pp. 82–169.

Stover, E. and G. Peress. 1998. *The Graves: Srebrenica and Vukovar*. New York: Scalo.

Sturken, M. 1997. *Tangled Memories*. London: University of California Press.

Sudetic, C. 1998. *Blood and Vengeance: One Family's Story of the War in Bosnia*. New York: W.W. Norton and Company.

———. 1993. 'Thousands Jam U.N. Trucks to Flee Bosnian Town', *The New York Times*, 30 March. Retrieved 10 September 2008 from http://www.nytimes.com/1993/03/30/world/thousands-jam-un-trucks-to-flee-bosnian-town.html

Suljagić, E. 2005. *Postcards From the Grave*. London: Saqi.

———. 2008. 'Kako sam izgubio poštovanje prema Islamskoj zajednici', *Start* 242: 32–5.

———. 2010. *Ethnic Cleansing: Politics, Policy, Violence: Serb Ethnic Cleansing Campaign in Former Yugoslavia*. Baden-Baden: Nomos Verlagsgesellschaft.

Summerfield, D. 2004. 'Cross Cultural Perspectives on the Medicalisation of Human Suffering', in G. Rosen (ed.), *Posttraumatic Stress Disorder: Issues and Controversies*. Chichester: John Wiley, pp. 233–46.

Tamboukou, M. 2008. 'A Foucauldian Approach to Narratives', in M. Andrews, C. Squire and M. Tamboukou (eds), *Doing Narrative Research*. London: Sage, pp. 102–20.

Toal, G. and C.T. Dahlman. 2006. 'Has Ethnic Cleansing Succeeded? Geographies of Minority Return and its Meaning in Bosnia and Herzegovina', in M. Bufon, A. Gosar, S. Nurković and A.L. Sanguin (eds), *The Western Balkans – A European Challenge: On the Decennial of the Dayton Peace Agreement*. Koper: Založba Annales, pp. 349–66.

———. 2011. *Bosnia Remade: Ethnic Cleansing and Its Reversal*. Oxford and New York: Oxford University Press.

Tochman, W. 2008. *Like Eating a Stone: Surviving the Past in Bosnia*, trans. A. Lloyd–Jones. New York: Atlas and Co.

Tönnies, F. 2001. *Community and Civil Society*, ed. J. Harris. Cambridge: Cambridge University Press.

Tretter, H., S. Müller, R. Schwanke, P. Angeli and A. Richter. 1994. *Ethnic Cleansing Operations in the Northeast-Bosnian City of Zvornik from April through June 1992*. Vienna: Ludwig Boltzmann Institute of Human Rights.

Truckey, S. 2008. 'Little Bosnia', *St Louis Magazine*, April 2008. Retrieved 20 May 2008 from http://www.stlmag.com/St-Louis-Magazine/April-2008/Little-Bosnia/#

Tsagarousianou, R. 2004. 'Rethinking the Concept of Diaspora', *Westminster Papers in Communication and Culture* 1(1): 52–66.

Tuan, Y.F. 1977. *Space and Place: The Perspective of Experience*. Minneapolis: University of Minnesota Press.

Tumarkin, M. 2005. *Traumascapes: The Power and Fate of Places Transformed by Tragedy*. Melbourne: Melbourne University Press.

Ugrešić, D. 1995. *The Culture of Lies: Antipolitical Essays*, trans. C. Hawkesworth. London: Phoenix House.

UNHCR. 2005. 'Update on Conditions for Return to Bosnia-Herzegovina'. Sarajevo. Retrieved 16 June 2006 from http://www.unhcr.ba/publications/BandHRET0105.pdf

United Nations. 1999. 'Report of the Secretary-General Pursuant to General Assembly Resolution 53/35: The Fall of Srebrenica'. New York. Retrieved 6 January 2012 from http://www.unhcr.org/refworld/docid/3ae6afb34.html

United Nations Commission of Experts. 1994. 'The Prijedor Report'. New York. Retrieved 6 January 2012 from http://www.ess.uwe.ac.uk/comexpert/anx/V.htm

U.S. Department of State. 1995. 'Annex 7: Agreement on Refugees and Displaced Persons', *The Dayton Peace Accords*. Washington: Bureau of Public Affairs.

Vadchy, A. 2005. 'Bosanska u Evropskom parlamentu', *Start* 166: 52–4.

Valenta, M. 2009. 'Selective Networking as Identity Project: The Social Integration of First Generation Immigrants in Norway', *Journal of International Migration and Integration* 10(2): 177–95.

Valenta, M. and Z. Strabac. 2011. 'Bosnians in Norway: How do They Adjust Compared with Other Refugee Groups?', in M. Valenta and S.P. Ramet (eds), *The Bosnian Diaspora: Integration of Transnational Communities*. Farnham: Ashgate, pp. 83–104.

Van Gelder, L. 2008. *Weaving a Way Home: A Personal Journey Exploring Place and Story*. Ann Arbor: University of Michigan Press.

Velayutham, S. and A. Wise. 2005. 'Moral Economies of a Translocal Village: Obligation and Shame among South Indian Transnational Migrants', *Global Networks* 5(1): 27–47.

Verdery, K. 1999. *The Political Lives of Dead Bodies*. New York: Columbia University Press.

Vertovec, S. 1999. 'Conceiving and Researching Transnationalism', *Ethnic and Racial Studies* 22(2): 447–62.

———. 2001. 'Transnationalism and Identity', *Journal of Ethnic and Migration Studies* 27(4): 573–82.
———. 2004. 'Cheap Calls: Social Glue of Migrant Transnationalism', *Global Networks* 4(2): 219–24.
———. 2007. 'Migrant Transnationalism and Modes of Transformation', in A. Portes and J. DeWind (eds), *Rethinking Migration: New Theoretical and Empirical Perspectives*. Oxford and New York: Berghahn Books, pp. 149–80.
Vetters, L. 2007. 'The Power of Administrative Categories: Emerging Notions of Citizenship in the Divided City of Mostar', *Ethnopolitics* 6(2): 187–209.
Voloder, L. 2008. 'Autoethnographic Challenges: Confronting Self, Field and Home', *Australian Journal of Anthropology* 19(1): 27–40.
Vujcich, D. 2007. 'Faith, Flight and Foreign Policy: Effects of War and Migration on Western Australian Bosnian Muslims', *The Australian Journal of Social Issues* 42(1): 71–86.
Vulliamy, E. 1994. *Seasons in Hell: Understanding Bosnia's War*. New York and London: Simon and Schuster.
———. 2004. 'We Can't Forget', *The Guardian*, 1 September. Retrieved 25 February 2007 from http://www.guardian.co.uk/world/2004/sep/01/warcrimes.balkans
———. 2005. 'Srebrenica: Ten Years On', *Open Democracy*, 6 July. Retrieved 28 February 2007 from http://www.opendemocracy.net/conflict-yugoslavia/srebrenica_2651.jsp
Wagner, S.E. 2008. *To Know Where He Lies: DNA Technology and the Search for Srebrenica's Missing*. Berkeley and Los Angeles: University of California Press.
Waxman, P. 1999. 'The Residential Location of Recently Arrived Bosnian, Afghan and Iraqi Refugees and Humanitarian Entrants in Sydney, Australia', *Urban Policy and Research* 17(4): 287–99.
———. 2001. 'The Economic Adjustment of Recently Arrived Bosnian, Afghan and Iraqi Refugees in Sydney, Australia', *International Migration Review* 35(2): 472–505.
Weine, S. 1999. *When History is a Nightmare: Lives and Memories of Ethnic Cleansing in Bosnia-Herzegovina*. New Brunswick: Rutgers University Press.
Weinstein, H. and E. Stover. 2004. 'Introduction: Conflict, Justice and Reclamation', in E. Stover and H. Weinstein (eds), *My Neighbour, my Enemy: Justice and Community in the Aftermath of Mass Atrocity*. Cambridge: Cambridge University Press, pp. 1–26.
Wesselingh, I. and A. Vaulerin. 2005. *Raw Memory: Prijedor, Laboratory of Ethnic Cleansing*. London: Saqi.
Wilkes, J.J. 1992. *The Illyrians*. Oxford: Blackwell.
———. 2003. 'Cultural Identities in the Illyrian Provinces (2nd century BC to 3rd century AD): Old Problems Re-examined', *Dall'adriatico Al Danubio. L'illirico Nell'età Greca e Romana* Cividale Del Friuli, 25–27 September. Convegno: Fondazione Niccolò Canussio.
Wise, A. and S. Velayutham. 2008. 'Second-generation Tamils and Cross-cultural Marriage: Managing the Translocal Village in a Moment of Cultural Rupture', *Journal of Ethnic and Migration Studies* 34(1): 113–31.

World Bank. 2005. 'Bosnia and Herzegovina', *Migration and Remittances Factbook*. Washington: World Bank Development Prospects Group.
Young, A. 1996. 'Bodily Memory and Traumatic Memory', in P. Antze and M. Lambek (eds), *Tense Past: Cultural Essays in Trauma and Memory*. London: Routledge, pp. 89–102.
Zaitchik, A. 2006. 'Mostar's Little Dragon', *reason.com*, April 2006. Retrieved 6 January 2012 from http://reason.com/archives/2006/04/01/mostars-little-dragon
Žanić, I. 2007. *Flag on the Mountain: A Political Anthropology of War in Croatia and Bosnia*. London: Saqi.
Žbanić, J. 2006. *Grbavica: Esma's Secret*. Sarajevo and London: Deblokada and Dogwoof Pictures.
Žižek, S. 1994. 'Caught in Another's Dream in Bosnia', in R. Ali and L. Lifschultz (eds), *Why Bosnia?: Writings on the Balkan War*. Stony Creak: Pamphleteer's Press, pp. 233–40.
———. 1999. 'NATO, the Left Hand of God', *Nettime*, 29 June. Retrieved 6 January 2012 from http://www.lacan.com/zizek-nato.htm
Zulfikarpašić, A. 2005. *Osvrti*. Sarajevo: Bošnjački institut.

INDEX

A
Abdić, Fikret, 18n2
Adams, Ron, x, 225
America, 143, 213–14
    Northern, 5, 119, 125, 183, 201, 215
    see also the U.S.A
American
    Bosnians, 126, 143, 231
    identities, 217
    migrant working class, 217
    values, 218–19
    see also Bosnian Americans
'Americanisation', 219
Americans, 123, 218, 221
Andrić, Ivo, 21, 34
ARBiH – Army of the Republic of Bosnia and Herzegovina, 18n2, 38, 99
Atlanta, 23, 182, 216, 218
Australia, 5–8, 13–17, 22, 25, 44, 48, 87, 107, 118–19, 123–25, 128–29, 131, 135, 138–39, 143–44, 146, 149, 164, 183–84, 187, 190–96, 200, 202, 207, 215, 218, 221, 225, 228–30
    Aussie Bosnians, 130–31, 144, 190, 228
    Australia's Humanitarian and Refugee Program, 184
Australian
    Bosniak Association (ABA), 140
    Bosnians, 126, 129, 143
    Brčaci, 141–42

    Council of Bosnian–Herzegovinian Organisations, 136–37
    Government, 185
    passports, 131
    resettlement policy, 218
    society, 193
    students, 17, 129, 148
Australians, 143, 148, 193
Austria, 6–8, 23, 28, 34, 48, 53, 58–59, 60, 72, 74–77, 84, 91, 113, 118, 125, 127–28, 135, 138–39, 141–42, 149, 177, 183, 202, 206, 221–25
Austrians, 19, 123

B
Bajina Bašta, 28, 33, 37, 51n19
Bakaršić, Kemal, 103–4, 109
Balić, Smail, 124
Balkans, 121, 138, 148, 178, 184, 186
Banja Luka, 211
Belgrade, 28, 38, 44, 58, 64, 98, 173, 223, 230
    University, 34, 58
belonging, 7, 9, 18n3, 41, 46, 48, 62, 118, 127, 131–32, 136, 151, 205
    sense of, 11, 13, 54, 58, 138, 141, 143, 208, 217, 230, 231n2, 232n7
Bihać, 82, 92, 232
Bijeljina, 18, 21, 142, 169, 229–30
Bišćani, 62, 69
Bosanska Dubica, 165
Bosanska Gradiška, 165

Bosanska Kostajnica, 165
Bosanski Brod, 165
Bosanski Novi, 165
Bosanski Šamac, 3, 165
Bosna (the river), 2
Bosnia (Bosnia-Herzegovina, 'Bosnia and Herzegovina' and BiH), x, 2–3, 7–8, 11, 15–17, 23, 28, 32, 39–40, 45, 47–48, 54, 65, 67, 69–70, 76–77, 82, 120, 140, 190, 201, 224–25
   central, 72, 91, 147, 168
   eastern, 7, 21, 26–27, 36, 55–58, 135, 157, 171, 192
   ethnic cleansing and genocide in, 14, 59, 76, 84, 90
   north-eastern, 138, 143
   north-western, 62
   post-war, 84, 90, 148
   south-western, 169
   western, 8, 58, 72, 92, 168, 193, 227
Bosniak
   civilian victims, 23, 36, 222
   nationalism, 34, 66, 97, 124, 151
   nationalists, 97
   villages around Prijedor, 70, 75, 92
Bosniaks (Bosnian Muslims), 2–3, 18, 21, 28, 36, 40–41, 44–45, 65–66, 68, 70, 82, 89, 91, 93, 99–102, 106, 112, 114, 119, 138, 145, 148, 153, 156, 161, 168–69, 184, 222
Bosnian
   Croats, 3–4, 18n2, 65, 91, 128, 138, 148
   deterritorialised communities, 89, 135, 151, 202, 205, 227
   diaspora, 6–9, 89, 120–28, 133–37, 139–40, 143, 147, 153, 182, 202–3, 205, 211, 213, 215, 225, 231
   ethnic groups, 54, 65, 67, 119
      see also Bosniaks; Croats; Serbs
   government, 36, 66, 72, 125, 138
   language, 117, 128–31, 208, 230
   nationalism, 34, 151, 223
   refugee women, 156, 186, 172, 181, 183–84, 186, 188–89
   refugees, 6, 13, 47, 53–56, 60, 74, 122, 138, 182–84, 213, 218, 219
   Serbs, 3, 21, 65, 128, 148
   side of the Drina, 27, 34, 35, 37
   war (1992–95), 1, 2, 10, 56, 58, 79, 80, 119, 222
   war widows, 183–85, 187, 196
Bosnians, 2–3, 5, 7–8, 10, 23, 25, 33, 55, 57, 74, 106, 117–18, 120, 123, 126, 135, 143, 146, 149, 151, 161, 165, 168, 193, 195, 203
   in Australia, 6, 118, 140, 188, 193, 218, 228
   in Austria, 6, 53, 221–22, 225
   displacement of, 6, 55, 119, 121, 125, 206
   in St Louis, 143, 213–15, 217, 219–21, 228
   in Sweden, 6, 130, 208, 210–11
Bratunac, 21, 24, 28, 34, 40, 166, 168–69, 191
Brčko, 18, 114, 118, 135, 137–43, 151, 184, 194, 209
Brčaci, 138–43, 145, 154
Brčko-Melbourne (*Klub Brčaka*), 137, 139–41
Savski cvijet (Sava's flower), 141, 142
Brdo (village near Prijedor), 62–63, 69–70, 73–75

C
Čačak, 37
Canada, 6, 85, 183
Canadian
   soldiers in Srebrenica, 38
   UN battalion, 38

Chetniks (Četniks), 24, 36–37, 44,
    49n5, 51n20, 51n22, 114, 141,
    192
Chicago, 125, 137, 144, 182, 218
citizenship, 3, 19n10, 59, 123, 134
Colombia, 126
community, 1, 4, 7–11, 14, 16, 22,
    27–32, 35, 41, 45–46, 48, 54,
    57, 62–64, 75, 82, 86, 93–94,
    99, 101, 119–20, 123–28, 131,
    139, 157–59, 164, 167, 170, 176,
    178–79, 183–84, 189, 193, 202,
    206, 214, 227
    international, 5, 100
    see also Bosnian; trans-local;
    transnational
Croatia, 3, 6, 26, 48, 64–67, 72, 74,
    91–92, 98, 100, 127–28, 138,
    194
Croatian
    army, 169
    HDZ based in Zagreb, 65
    language, 100, 127, 132

D
Dayton Peace Accords (DPA), 18n4,
    120, 152n3, 154n24, 161, 164,
    168
Delibašić, Mirza, 107
Denmark, 6, 48
Dobrak, 37
displacement, x, 1, 2, 5–15, 21, 41,
    45–46, 53–56, 94, 99, 118–21,
    125, 133–34, 138, 144, 148–49,
    155, 160–64, 167, 171, 175, 179,
    181–82, 190, 202, 204–6, 212,
    215, 218, 224, 227, 229, 231
Divić, 26, 28
Dobrinja, 171, 198
Dodik, Milorad, 165
Drina river, 2, 8, 21–22, 25–28, 32,
    34–37, 40, 45, 48, 112, 146, 160,
    211, 216–17
    canyon, 21, 33–34, 51–52
    valley, 26–27, 42

Đulići, 224
Duliman, Azra, 209
Đurđevac, 26, 37
Dutch troops, 24, 38, 52

E
emplacement, x, 10, 112–13, 212
Erdemović, Dražen, 25, 50nn6–7,
    108n17, 198n21
Eskilstuna, 8, 209–11
ethnic cleansing, 1, 3–5, 10–11,
    14–15, 39, 54, 120, 124, 151,
    155, 158, 160, 171, 203, 222,
    225, 231
    in eastern Bosnia, 21, 37, 40, 135,
    143
    effects of, 16, 43, 82, 159–60
    in Prijedor, 68, 75, 82, 85, 87–90
    survivors of, 13, 82, 143, 148–49,
    164, 175
EU – European Union, 5, 43, 84
Europe, 14, 27, 39, 53, 107, 118, 123,
    125, 139, 183, 188, 201, 212,
    215
    Central, 138
    refugee crisis in, 5
    South-eastern, 178
    Western, 85, 124
Europeanness, 217, 219
Europeans, 218–19

F
Federation of BiH/Bosniak-Croat
    Federation/Federation, 3, 18,
    40–41, 45, 82, 161, 167–69,
    179, 222
Ferhatović, Asim, 107
Filipović, Muhamed, 120–21
Finland, 6, 120
First World War, 86
Fisović, Jasna, 157–58
Foča, 21, 26, 36, 51, 156–57

G

genocide, 1, 5, 8–9, 14, 16, 76, 95, 111, 148, 151, 158, 172, 203, 225, 227
    convicted of, 39
    definition of, 39
    effects of, 16, 40, 221
    in Prijedor, 9, 68, 84, 93, 114, 146, 155
    in Srebrenica, 9, 94, 146
    See also the Srebrenica genocide
    in Zvornik, 224
German
    Bosnians, 130–31, 217
    government, 130
    immigrants in Bevo, 217
    language, 58, 127, 131, 217, 223
Germans, 28, 123, 217
Germany, 6, 13–14, 23, 28, 34, 43–44, 48, 92, 104, 125, 127, 130–31, 141–43, 177, 183, 190, 194, 217
Glamoč, 169
Goražde, 21, 26, 36, 40
Gutman, Roy, 68, 85

H

Hadžići, 40, 48, 112, 168, 225, 230
Hambarine, 69, 84
Hamburg, 14, 44, 48, 216
HDZ – Croat Democratic Union, 18n2, 65, 66
Hegić, Edita, 53, 57–58, 60–63, 70–77, 81–82, 113, 118, 160
Hegići, 8, 62–63, 70–76, 80–84, 93, 97–98, 113, 158–59, 168
Herzegovina (region), 2
    Hercegovci, 2
Holocaust, 13, 39, 85
HOS – Croatian Armed Forces, 18n2
Hukanović, Rezak, 9, 86, 88–89, 219–20
Hum (Mount), 99–102
Hungary, 138, 177, 222
HVO – Croatian Defence Council, 18n2, 99

I

Ibrahimović, Zlatan, 209
Ibrišagić, Amna (Anna), 217, 208
Iceland, 126
ICMP – International Commission on Missing Persons, 88, 158
ICRC – International Committee of Red Cross, 85, 191
ICTY – International Criminal Tribunal for the Former Yugoslavia, 39, 49n2, 50n7, 54nn26–27, 86–87, 90, 94, 108n7, 107n11, 107n13, 107nn15, 107n17, 154n23, 155, 157, 198n21
identity, 1–11, 18n3, 45–49n1, 51n21, 53–54, 59–60, 76, 95, 104, 107, 119, 121, 131–32, 134, 137, 145–46, 149, 152, 167, 179, 196, 204, 228, 231
    collective, 14, 32, 46, 56, 82, 93, 96, 100–2, 123, 133, 139, 148, 185, 193, 202
    local 31, 84, 118, 126, 138, 141, 181, 205, 216–20
    See also trans-local; transnational; *zavičaj*
IDPs – Internally Displaced Persons, 5–6, 8–9, 27, 40, 43, 56, 94, 119, 138, 161–62, 164, 168–71, 175, 179–81, 192, 209, 222, 224
Ilijaš, 169
IOM – International Organisation for Migration, 85, 153n9, 191
Israel, 6, 125
Izetbegović, Alija, 66–67, 105

J

Jakić, Mehmed, 209
Jakina Kosa, 72

K

Kaludrani, 58, 70, 224
Karačići, 38

Karadžić, Radovan, 21, 49n2, 52n24, 65–66, 85, 108n21, 166, 171, 197n10
Karlovac, 74
Karlskrona, 9, 209, 211–14, 230
    Maritime Museum in, 211
    Montmartre restaurant in, 230
    Museum Leonardo da Vinci Ideale in, 212–13
Kebo, Alija, 145
Keraterm, 9, 68–69, 90–91
Klisa, 224
Ključ, 82
Klotjevac, 7–8, 16–17, 21–22, 25–38, 40–49, 54–55, 84, 111–12, 115, 146–48, 159, 168, 206, 215–17, 221, 225
    Jerina, 27–28
    Klotivljani, 28, 30, 32, 45, 47–49, 116, 215–16, 221, 225, 227
    Klotjevačka klisura, 34
    Stari Grad, 28, 35
Konjević Polje, 116, 165–66, 168
Korićanske stijene, 91
Kosovo, 64, 108
Kozarac, 69, 92
Krajina
    Bosnian (Bosanska Krajina), 2, 211–12, 232
    in Croatia, 21
    Krajišnici, 2
Krstić, Radislav, 39, 52n27, 108n17
Kulenović, Rizah, 212–13
Kuwait, 105

L
Lee, Bruce, 103–4, 107
Lemkin, Raphaël
    on genocide, 39, 158
Ljeskovik, 32, 38
Ljubija, 72

M
Mahoje, 147–48, 151, 215
Malaysia, 44, 126, 105

Malmo, 41, 84, 135, 137, 218, 150
Marković, Ante, 65
Mašović, Amor, 94
Matvejević, Predrag, 145
Mazowiecki, Tadeusz, 68
Mehičević, Amir, 145, 228
Melbourne, 8–9, 23, 25, 41, 48, 101, 116–17, 125, 131, 135, 137, 139–45, 148–49, 150–51, 155, 160–61, 182, 183–84, 186, 188, 190–96, 205–6, 211, 216, 227–30
    Hanna Café in, 117, 140, 227–30
    Saraj restaurant in, 140
    St Albans, a suburb in, 48, 117, 140, 148, 156, 183–84, 188–89, 191, 195–97, 228, 230
    Westgate Bridge in, 192
memory, 1, 7, 14, 18n3, 53, 55–59, 75, 77, 79–81, 85–87, 89–90, 93, 95–97, 102, 105–7, 111, 121, 123, 134–35, 141, 144, 146, 179, 188, 193, 202, 204, 206, 225, 227
    collective, 84, 100–1, 103–4, 149, 157, 193–94, 220
    cultural, 56, 99, 104, 119
    embodied, 48, 195
    official, 81, 93
    performance of, 56, 148, 178
    popular, 1, 8, 12, 81–82, 97, 148, 207, 232
    sites of, 9, 87, 90, 97, 114
Mešanović, Dule, 42–43, 45–46, 215, 221
migration 7, 9, 19n10, 121, 124, 135, 139, 149, 161, 182–84, 189, 203, 212–13
    chain, 135, 138–39, 149
    forced, 122, 134, 149, 156, 203–4, 211
    labour, 147, 183
    patterns, 135, 153n19
    post-war, 183

trends, 150
voluntary, 122
Mihailović, Draža, 36, 51n19, 114, 141
Milići, 166
Milošević, Slobodan, 39, 64–65, 85, 197n10
Mississippi river, 216–18
Mittal Steel, 85, 87–89
Mladić, Ratko, 38, 49n2, 52n24, 108n21, 166, 191, 197n10
Montenegro, 21, 26, 34, 64, 68
Mostar, 8–9, 18, 81, 98–107, 118, 143–45, 151, 228
Mostarci, 145
Old Bridge, 99, 100, 109n23
Murselović, Muharem, 9, 89–90

N
NATO, 38
Neretva (the river), 99
Netherlands, the, 6, 43, 48, 182, 219
New Zealand, 6, 183
Norrköping, 161, 210–11
Norway, 6, 89
Novi Sad, 37, 173, 178
Nuhanović, Hasan, 9, 51–52, 96
Nuhanović, Sejo, 53, 57–60, 74, 76–77, 119, 223–25

O
Omarska, 9, 68–69, 84–91, 97
Örebro, 210–11, 216
Orlović, Fata, 9, 116, 165–68, 172, 179, 181
Osat, 42

P
Paljevine, 37
Peći, 37
Perućac lake, 26, 33, 36–37, 49
Pervanić, Kemal, 9, 88–89
Pettigrew, David, 223n15, 225
Podrinje, 2, 8, 21, 23, 26–27, 31–38, 40, 46, 48, 51, 97, 111–12, 116, 135, 151, 155–56, 171, 176, 181, 184, 196, 209–20, 222–23, 225, 229–30
Podrinjci, 2, 209–11, 220
Poljak, 37
Popović, Davorin, 107
Posavina, 2
Posavci, 2
Potočari, 9, 23–25, 38, 41, 93, 94–98, 171, 196
Prijedor, 8–9, 53, 62–63, 68–70, 72, 74–75, 77, 80–93, 97, 104, 114, 118, 135, 137, 146, 151, 155, 157, 165, 181, 184, 194, 206, 211, 214–15, 219–20
Prijedorčani, 220
Prnjavor, 211
Prohići, 28, 32, 35, 37–38, 111

R
racism, 228–29
Republika Srpska (RS), 3–4, 18, 37, 39–41, 45, 68, 81, 83–84, 86, 90–91, 93, 102, 114, 161, 163, 165, 168
authorities, 45, 84, 87–90, 166
the government of, 17, 81–82, 86, 114, 168–89
the legacy of, 93
returnees, 9, 17, 37, 42, 44, 46–48, 55–56, 75, 83–84, 89, 113, 116, 148, 164–65, 167–69, 198n15, 219
Rogatica, 36

S
Salkić family, 195–96
Sana river, 74
Sanski Most, 82, 193, 208, 232
Šantić, Aleksa, 101
Sarajevo, 2, 5, 8–9, 22, 28, 31, 34, 40–41, 48, 65, 81, 95, 99, 103–7, 120, 150, 160, 168–75, 180, 192, 207, 211, 214, 216
Koševo stadium, 107
Sarajevans, 98, 104–7, 151

'Sarajevo Roses', 106, 115
  the siege of, 98
  Tito Street, 107
  University of, 14, 107
Saudi Arabia, 105
Sava river, 2, 138, 140–41, 154, 160, 165
SDA – Party of Democratic Action, 65–66, 70–71
SDS – Serb Democratic Party, 17–18n2, 21, 65–66, 68
Second World War, 23, 26, 35–36, 51, 64, 85, 107
Sejdinovići, 28, 32, 35, 111
Serbia, 4, 6, 21, 26–27, 33–37, 43, 58, 64–67, 86, 100, 128, 138, 165, 169, 177, 222
  Greater, 21, 67
Serb/Serbian
  Academy of Arts and Sciences (SANU), 64, 78
  aggression of 1992–95, 27, 34, 36, 38, 44, 97
  authorities in Prijedor, 89, 165
  language, 100, 127–28, 132, 165
  militants, 36–37
  military, 35, 37–39, 91–92, 191
  militias, 18, 58, 69, 72, 82, 99, 148, 191, 224
  nationalists, 36, 39, 49, 82, 96, 97, 101, 106, 179
  Orthodox bishop Kačavenda, 166
  Orthodox church, 166
  Republic, 37, 40, 42, 92, 166
    see also Republika Srpska
    -run concentration camps, 85, 114
    see also Keraterm; Omarska; Trnopolje
  soldiers, 73, 86, 90–93, 157, 196
  troops, 38, 42, 45, 73, 191
Serbo–Croat language, 128, 131

Serbs, 34, 37–38, 40, 64–70, 81, 87, 94, 101, 112, 119, 138, 145, 161, 166, 168–69, 179, 184, 222
SFOR – Stabilisation Forces, 42, 45
Sjedaće, 11, 111
Skelani, 36–37
Slovenia, 4, 6, 14, 138
Srebrenica, xi, 5, 7, 9, 14, 16, 218, 34, 36–42, 94, 104, 118, 143, 145, 149, 150, 171–74, 178, 184, 191, 216
  commemoration, 24, 81, 93–94, 96–97, 116
  enclave, 38, 39, 191
  genocide, 14–15, 21, 40–42, 44, 50, 93–95, 97, 111, 137, 151, 158, 160, 171–72, 194, 196, 210–11, 220, 225–26
  The Mothers of Srebrenica Association, 181
  UN Safe area (UN safe haven), 23–24, 37, 38, 52, 172
St Louis, 41, 43, 48, 89, 112, 117, 125, 135, 137, 143, 146–48, 150, 160–61, 188, 211–21, 227, 229, 231
  Berix restaurant, 146, 213–14
  Bevo suburb, 112, 214–15, 217
  Bosna Gold restaurant, 150, 213
  Gravois Avenue, 214–15, 217, 231
  Grbić Restaurant, 213
  Laganini restaurant, 213–14
  The Lucky Duck restaurant, 213
Stockholm, 23, 118, 206–7, 209, 211
Studenac, 33, 37, 111
Styer, 8, 48, 74
Subašić, Munira, 9
Subotica, 173, 222
Sulejmanović, Omer, 22–23, 25, 27, 37, 40, 43, 47, 112, 225–27
Suljagić, Emir, 51–52, 96
Sušić, Ibro, 53, 63, 64, 66–68, 73–75, 77

Sweden, 6–8, 23, 44, 47–48, 75, 84, 92, 117–18, 125, 128–31, 135, 145–46, 149, 183, 202, 206–12
Swedes, 123, 209
Swedish
    Bosnians, 126, 129, 131, 209, 211–12
    see also Bosnian Swedes
    government, 128
    Parliament, 208
    policy of active integration, 131
    police, 208
    society, 130, 207–9

T
Tara (Mount), 27–28, 35
Tara (river), 34
Tito – Josip, Broz, 33, 51
trans-local
    communities, 47, 119, 133, 135–59, 142–46, 149–51, 183–84, 216, 220, 225
    identities, 14, 84, 135–36, 142, 148, 152, 205–6
    networks, 7, 10, 136–37, 144, 148–49, 150, 190, 202, 209–10
trans-localism, 118, 133, 143–45, 151, 175, 202, 205, 209, 217, 221
    definition of, 135, 149, 151–52, 204
transnational
    community, 133
    networks, 136
transnationalism, 10, 118, 122, 133, 151, 203, 205
    definition of, 133–34, 203
Travnik, 72
Trnopolje, 9, 68–69, 73–75, 90–93, 97, 114
Tudjman, Franjo, 65
Tuzla, xi, 38, 40–42, 94, 143, 165, 170–73, 191, 210, 222, 229

U
Udruženje Podrinje–Srebrenica, 136–37, 150
U.K. – United Kingdom, 6, 48, 88, 120, 182–83, 219
UN – United Nations, 5, 24, 38, 52n23, 84, 191
    safe haven, 23, 171
UNESCO – UN Educational, Scientific and Cultural Organisation, 99, 101, 211
UNHCR – UN High Commissioner for Refugees, 19n10, 85, 125, 164, 191
UNPROFOR – United Nations Protection Force, 51–52n23
Urisići, 28, 32, 35, 38
U.S./U.S.A – United States of America, 6–8, 23, 34, 44, 48, 75, 84–85, 89, 107, 118, 123, 127, 135, 137, 143–44, 146–47, 149, 164–65, 177, 183, 186, 188, 202, 213–14, 217–18, 221, 225, 228
    The U.S. President Bill Clinton, 24
    see also America
Ustaše, 69
Utrecht, 44, 48, 216
Užice, 28, 37, 51

V
Velež (Mount), 99
Vienna, 8, 9, 58, 60–62, 72, 76–77, 125, 135, 150, 160, 188, 216, 221–24
    Bachinger's salon, 60–62, 76
Vijećnica, 103–4, 106
violence, 9, 13, 53–55, 59, 72, 80, 91, 101, 156, 177, 182, 190, 198n19, 198n21, 203, 218, 228, 231
    collective, 84
    domestic, 177
    ethnic, 4, 10
    memories of, 53, 59
    sexual, 69, 155–58

see also ethnic cleansing; genocide
Višegrad, 21, 26–28, 34, 36, 51, 135, 157, 192
  bridge, 21
  the victims from, 36, 49
Vlasenica, 165
Vlašić (Mount), 72, 78, 91
Vogošća, 171, 198
Vojvodina, 64, 222
VRS – Army of Republika Srpska, 18, 169, 198
Vulliamy, Ed, 50n6, 68, 85–86

Y
Yugoslav
  Communist League, 31, 36, 65
  diaspora, 124
  National Army (JNA), 18, 21, 67–68, 99, 160, 197n10, 198n19
  peoples, 64
  successor states, 11, 36
Yugoslavia, 5, 15, 26–27, 33–34, 62–63, 65–67, 107, 124, 204
Yugoslavs, 2, 68, 125, 138, 204, 217
YUTEL, 64, 67

Z
Zagreb, 48, 65
zavičaj, 7, 11, 43, 46, 116, 118, 135, 146, 150–51, 202, 204–5, 208, 211–12, 214–17, 219–20, 222–25, 227–31
  associations, 12, 137
  concept of, 10–11
Zavidovići, 147
Žbanić, Jasmila, 157, 197
Žepa, 26, 34, 36, 51
  enclave, 51
Živinice, 57–58, 222, 224
Zulfikarpašić, Adil, 124
Zvornik, 18, 21, 24, 26, 57–58, 135, 143, 157, 165, 169, 222, 224–45
Zvorničani, 222–24

www.ingramcontent.com/pod-product-compliance
Lightning Source LLC
Chambersburg PA
CBHW072147100526
44589CB00015B/2125